CAMBRIDGE ENGLISH CLASSICS

English Works
of
Roger Ascham

ROGER ASCHAM

Born 1515
Died 1568

ROGER ASCHAM

ENGLISH WORKS

TOXOPHILUS
REPORT OF THE AFFAIRES AND STATE OF GERMANY
THE SCHOLEMASTER

EDITED BY

WILLIAM ALDIS WRIGHT, M.A.,

VICE-MASTER OF TRINITY COLLEGE, CAMBRIDGE

CAMBRIDGE:
at the University Press
1904
reprinted
1970

Published by the Syndics of the Cambridge University Press
Bentley House, 200 Euston Road, London, N.W.1
American Branch: 32 East 57th Street, New York, N.Y. 10022

PUBLISHER'S NOTE

Cambridge University Press Library Editions are re-issues of out-of
print standard works from the Cambridge catalogue. The texts are
unrevised and, apart from minor corrections, reproduce the latest
published edition.

Standard Book Number: 521 07768 0

First published 1904
Reprinted 1970

First printed in Great Britain at the University Press, Cambridge
Reprinted in Great Britain by John Dickens & Co. Ltd, Northampton

PREFACE.

OF the three English Works by Ascham printed in this volume, the Toxophilus is probably the only one which appeared in his lifetime. It was first published in 1545 by Edward Whitchurch. A second edition printed by Thomas Marshe appeared in 1571, and a third in 1589 printed by Abell Ieffes. As copies of the first edition vary slightly, it is as well to state that I have followed one in the Library of Jesus College, Cambridge, for which I have been indebted to the kindness of Mr Arthur Gray, with occasional reference to the Capell copy in Trinity Library. There are some readings in one of the copies in the British Museum (C. 31. c. 27) which I have found nowhere else. Mr Arber in his reprint appears to have followed this.

The Report and Discourse of the affairs and state of Germany was written in 1553, about the time of the death of Edward the Sixth (see p. 138), but it was apparently not printed till after Ascham's death by John Daye, without date but probably about 1570. In Bohn's edition of Lowndes's Bibliographer's Manual it is said that 'there are two other editions, one 1570, the other without date,' but I can find no other record of them. In the Dictionary of National Biography it is said to have been republished in 1572, but I do not know on what authority.

The Scholemaster first appeared in 1570, two years after Ascham's death, and was printed by John Daye. A second edition, also printed by Daye, was issued in 1571, and a third in 1589, printed by Abell Ieffes. Other editions in 1572, 1573, 1579, and 1583, 'according to the bibliographers,' are mentioned in the Dictionary of National Biography. I have not been able to discover any trace of them, except that in the edition of 1571, although 1571 is on the title-page, we find 1573 in the colophon.

In giving the list of Errata in the early copies, I have not thought it necessary to record any but those which are misleading, nor have I mentioned the many printer's errors in Greek which have been silently corrected. On pages 72 and

168 I have substituted 'leste' for 'lesse,' supposing it to be a misprint, but not feeling certain that it might not be a provincialism if not an archaism, I have allowed 'lesse' to stand on pages 215 and 258, though it is altered in the edition of 1571. In the curious Italian Pasquinade in the Report (p. 136) I have been assisted by the kindness of Count della Rocchetta, Mr Arthur Tilley, and Mr E. G. W. Braunholtz, to whom are due the corrections which have brought it to its present form. It originally stood as follows :

Interlocutori Pasquillo et Romano.

Pasq. H*Anno vn bel gioco il Re, et l'Imperatore*
per terzo el Papá, e giocano à Primera.
Rom. *che v' e d' in vito?* Pasq. *Italia tutta intera.*
Rom. *Chi vi l' ha messa?* Pasq. *il coglion del pastore.*
Rom. *Che tien in mano il Re?* Pasq. *Ponto magiere*
el Papa hacinquant' vno, e se despera.
Rom. *Cæsar che Ponto sa?* Pasq. *lui sta a Primera*
Rom. *che gli manca?* Pasq. *danari a far sauore*
Il Papa dice à vol, e voll Partito:
Cæsar Pensoso sta Sopra di questo,
teme à Scropir di trouar moneta
Il Re dico, no, no, Scoprite Presto,
che io tengo Ponto, a guadagnar l' in vito
l' ho li danari, et Cæsar se gli aspeta.

¶ *Tutti stanno a vedetta.*

Chi di tor dui guadagni. Rom. *il Papa?* Pas. *e fuora*
vinca chi vol, lui Perda, in sua mal' hora.

¶ *Le Jmperatore anchora.*

Teme, étien stretto, è Scope Piau le carte,
e qui, la sorte gioca, pin che l' Arte.

¶ *Metra questi indisparte.*

Stabilito e nel Ciel quelle, che esserdé,
ne giona al nostro dic, questo Sara questo è.

W. A. W.

20 *October* 1904.

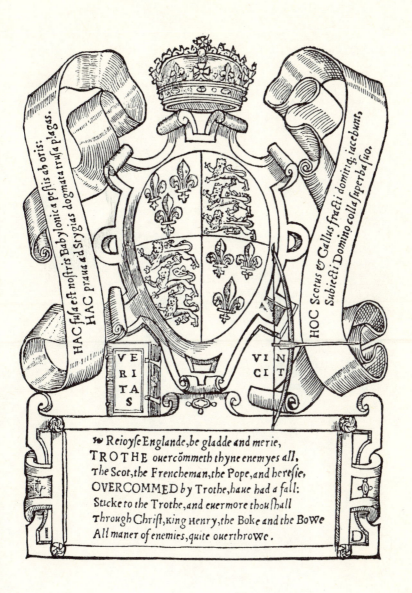

HAC fusa est nostris Babylonica pestis ab oris:
HAC prauæd Stygias dogmata trusa plagas.

HOC Scotus & Gallus fracti domitúq; iacebunt,
Subiecti Domino colla superba suo.

VE
RI
TA
S

VIN
CI
T

Reioyſe Englande, be gladde and merie,
TROTHE ouercommeth thyne enemyes all,
The Scot, the Frencheman, the Pope, and hereſie,
OVERCOMMED by Trothe, haue had a fall:
Sticke to the Trothe, and euermore thou ſhall
Through Chriſt, King Henry, the Boke and the Bowe
All maner of enemies, quite ouerthrowe.

Gualterus Haddonus
Cantabrigien.

Mittere qui celeres summa uelit arte sagittas,
  Ars erit ex isto summa profecta libro.
Quicquid habent arcus rigidi, neruiq̓ rotundi,
  Sumere si libet, hoc sumere fonte licet.
Aschamus est author, magnū quē fecit Apollo
  Arte sua, magnum Pallas & arte sua.
Docta manꝰ dedit hūc, dedit hūc mēs docta libellū :
  Quæ uidet Ars Vsus uisa, parata facit.
Optimus hæc author quia tradidit optima scripta,
  Conuenit hec uobis optima uelle sequi.

To the moste graciouse, and our most drad Soueraigne lord,
Kyng Henrie the .viii, by the grace of God, kyng
of Englande, Fraunce and Irelande, Defen
der of the faythe, and of the churche
of Englande & also of Irelande
in earth supreme head, next vn
der Christ, be al health
victorie, and fe-
licitie.

WHAT tyme as, moste gracious Prince, your highnes this last year past, tooke that your moost honorable and victorious iourney into Fraunce, accompanied vvith such a porte of the Nobilitie and yeomanrie of Englande, as neyther hath bene lyke knovven by experience, nor yet red of in Historie : accompanied also vvith the daylie prayers, good hartes, and vvilles of all and euery one your graces subiectes, lefte behinde you here at home in Englande : the same tyme, I beinge at my booke in Cambrige, sorie that my litle habilitie could stretche out no better, to helpe forvvard so noble an enterprice, yet with my good vvylle, prayer, and harte, nothinge behynde hym that vvas formoste of all, conceyued a vvonderful desire, bi the praier, vvishing, talking, & communicatiō that vvas in euery mās mouth, for your Graces moost victoriouse retourne, to offer vp sumthinge, at your home cumming to your Highnesse, vvhich shuld both be a token of mi loue and deutie tovvard your

Maiestie, & also a signe of my good minde and zeale tovvarde mi countrie.

This occasion geuen to me at that time, caused me to take in hand againe, this litle purpose of shoting, begon of me before, yet not ended thā, for other studies more mete for that trade of liuinge, vvhiche God and mi frendes had set me vnto. But vvhen your Graces moste ioifull & happie victorie preuēted mi dailie and spedie diligencie to performe this matter, I vvas compelled to vvaite an other time to prepare & offer vp this litle boke vnto your Maiestie. And vvhan it hath pleased youre Highenesse of your infinit goodnesse, & also your most honorable Counsel to knovv and pervse ouer the contentes, & some parte of this boke, and so to alovv it, that other mē might rede it, throughe the furderaunce and setting forthe of the right worshipfull and mi Singuler good Master sir Vvilliam Pagette Knight, moost vvorthie Secretarie to your highnes, & most open & redie succoure to al poore honest learned mēs sutes, I moost humblie beseche your Grace to take in good vvorthe this litle treatise purposed, begō, and ended of me onelie for this intent, that Labour, Honest pastime & Vertu, might recouer againe that place and right, that Idlenesse, Vnthriftie gamning and Vice hath put them fro.

And althoughe to haue vvritten this boke either in latin or Greke (vvhich thing I vvold be verie glad yet to do, if I might surelie knovv your Graces pleasure there in) had bene more easier & fit for mi trade in study, yet neuerthelesse, I supposinge it no point of honestie, that mi commodite should stop & hinder ani parte either of the pleasure or profite of manie, haue vvritten this Englishe matter in the Englishe tongue, for Englishe men : vvhere in this I trust that your Grace (if it shall please your Highnesse to rede it) shal perceaue it to be a thinge Honeste for me to vvrite, pleasaunt for some to rede, and profitable for manie to folovv, contening a pastime, honest for the minde, holsome for the body, fit for eueri man, vile for no man, vsing the day & opē place for Honestie to rule it, not lurking in corners for misorder to abuse it. Therfore I trust it shal apere, to be bothe a sure token of my zeele to set forvvarde shootinge, and some signe of my minde, tovvardes honestie and learninge.

Thus I vvil trouble your Grace no longer, but
vvith my daylie praier, I vvil beseche God to
preserue your Grace, in al health and felicitie : to the feare and ouerthrovve
of all your ennemies : to the
pleasure, ioyfulnesse and
succour of al your sub-
iectes : to the vtter
destruction
of papi-
strie and heresie : to the continuall setting forth of
Goddes vvorde
and his glo
rye.

Your Graces most
bounden Scholer,

Roger Ascham.

TO ALL GENTLE MEN AND YOMEN OF ENGLANDE.

Bias the wyse man came to Cresus the ryche kyng, on a tyme, when he was makynge newe shyppes, purposyng to haue subdued by water the out yles lying betwixt Grece and Asia minor: What newes now in Grece, saith the king to Bias? None other newes, but these, sayeth Bias: that the yles of Grece haue prepared a wonderful companye of horsemen, to ouerrun Lydia withall. There is nothyng vnder heauen, sayth the kynge, that I woulde so soone wisshe, as that they durst be so bolde, to mete vs on the lande with horse. And thinke you sayeth Bias, that there is anye thyng which they wolde sooner wysshe, then that you shulde be so fonde, to mete them on the water with shyppes? And so Cresus hearyng not the true newes, but perceyuyng the wise mannes mynde and counsell, both gaue then ouer makyng of his shyppes, and left also behynde him a wonderful example for all commune wealthes to folowe: that is euermore to regarde and set most by that thing whervnto nature hath made them moost apt, and vse hath made them moost fitte.

By this matter I meane the shotyng in the long bowe, for English men: which thyng with all my hert I do wysh, and if I were of authoritie, I wolde counsel all the gentlemen and yomen of Englande, not to chaunge it with any other thyng, how good soeuer it seme to be: but that styll, accordyng to the oulde wont of England, youth shulde vse it for the moost honest pastyme in peace, that men myght handle it as a mooste sure weapon in warre. Other stronge weapons whiche bothe experience doth proue to be good, and the wysdom of the kinges Maiestie & his counsel prouydes to be had, are not ordeyned to take away shotyng : but y^t both, not compared togither, whether shuld be better then the other, but so ioyned togither that the one shoulde be alwayes an ayde and helpe for the other, myght so strengthen the Realme on all sydes, that no kynde of enemy in any kynde of weapon, myght passe and go beyonde vs.

For this purpose I, partelye prouoked by the counsell of some gentlemen, partly moued by the loue whiche I haue alwayes borne towarde shotyng, haue wrytten this lytle treatise, wherin if I haue not satisfyed any man, I trust he wyll the rather be content w^t my doyng, bycause I am (I suppose) the firste, whiche hath sayde any thynge in this matter (and fewe begynnynges be perfect, sayth wyse men) And also bycause yf I haue sayed a misse, I am content that any man amende it, or yf I haue sayd to lytle, any man that wyl to adde what hym pleaseth to it.

My minde is, in profitynge and pleasynge euery man, to hurte or displease no man, intendyng none other purpose, but that youthe myght be styrred to labour, honest pastyme, and vertue, and as much as laye in me, plucked from ydlenes, vnthriftie games, and vice : whyche thing I haue laboured onlye in this booke, shewynge howe fit shootyng is for all kyndes of men, howe honest a pastyme for the mynde, howe holsome an excercise for the bodye, not vile for great men to vse, not costlye for poore men to susteyne, not lurking in holes and corners for ill men at theyr pleasure, to misvse it, but abiding in the open sight & face of the worlde, for good men if it fault by theyr wisdome to correct it.

And here I woulde desire all gentlemen and yomen, to vse this pastime in suche a mean, that the outragiousnes of great gamyng, shuld not hurte the honestie of shotyng, which of his owne nature is always ioyned with honestie : yet for mennes faultes oftentymes blamed vnworthely, as all good thynges haue ben, and euermore shall be.

If any man woulde blame me, eyther for takynge such a matter in hande, or els for writing it in the Englyshe tongue, this answere I maye make hym, that whan the beste of the

realme thinke it honest for them to vse, I one of the meanest
sorte, ought not to suppose it vile for me to write : And though
to haue written it in an other tonge, had bene bothe more
profitable for my study, and also more honest for my name, yet
I can thinke my labour wel bestowed, yf w^t a little hynder-
aunce of my profyt and name, maye come any fourther-
aunce, to the pleasure or commoditie, of the gentlemen and
yeomen of Englande, for whose sake I tooke this matter in
hande. And as for ye Latin or greke tonge, euery thyng is so
excellently done in them, that none can do better : In the
Englysh tonge contrary, euery thinge in a maner so meanly,
bothe for the matter and handelynge, that no man can do
worse. For therin the least learned for the moste parte, haue
ben alwayes moost redye to wryte. And they whiche had
leaste hope in latin, haue bene moste boulde in englyshe : when
surelye euery man that is moste ready to taulke, is not moost
able to wryte. He that wyll wryte well in any tongue, muste
folowe thys councel of Aristotle, to speake as the cōmon people
do, to thinke as wise men do : and so shoulde euery man vnder-
stande hym, and the iudgement of wyse men alowe hym.
Many English writers haue not done so, but vsinge straunge
wordes as latin, french and· Italian, do make all thinges darke
and harde. Ones I communed with a man whiche reasoned
the englyshe tongue to be enryched and encreased therby,
sayinge : Who wyll not prayse that feaste, where a man shall
drinke at a diner, bothe wyne, ale and beere ? Truely quod I,
they be all good, euery one taken by hym selfe alone, but if you
putte Maluesye and sacke, read wyne and white, ale and beere,
and al in one pot, you shall make a drynke, neyther easie to be
knowen, nor yet holsom for the bodye. Cicero in folowyng
Isocrates, Plato and Demosthenes, increased the latine tounge
after an other sorte. This waye, bycause dyuers men y^t write,
do not know, they can neyther folowe it, bycause of theyr
ignorauncie, nor yet will prayse it, for verye arrogauncie, ii.
faultes, seldome the one out of the others companye.

Englysh writers by diuersitie of tyme, haue taken diuerse
matters in hande. In our fathers tyme nothing was red, but
bookes of fayned cheualrie, wherin a man by redinge, shuld be
led to none other ende, but onely to manslaughter and baudrye.

Yf any man suppose they were good ynough to passe the time with al, he is deceyued. For surelye vayne woordes doo woorke no smal thinge in vayne, ignoraunt, and younge mindes, specially yf they be gyuen any thynge thervnto of theyr owne nature. These bokes (as I haue heard say) were made the moste parte in Abbayes, and Monasteries, a very lickely and fit fruite of suche an ydle and blynde kinde of lyuynge.

In our tyme nowe, whan euery manne is gyuen to knowe muche rather than to liue wel, very many do write, but after suche a fashion, as very many do shoote. Some shooters take in hande stronger bowes, than they be able to mayntayne. This thyng maketh them sūmtyme, to outshoote the marke, sūmtyme to shote far wyde, and perchaunce hurte sūme that looke on. Other that neuer learned to shote, nor yet knoweth good shafte nor bowe, wyll be as busie as the best, but suche one cōmonly plucketh doune a syde, and crafty archers which be agaynst him, will be bothe glad of hym, and also euer ready to laye and bet with him: it were better for suche one to sit doune than shote. Other there be, whiche haue verye good bowe and shaftes, and good knowlege in shootinge, but they haue bene brought vp in suche euyl fauoured shootynge, that they can neyther shoote fayre, nor yet nere. Yf any man wyll applye these thynges togyther, [he] shal not se the one farre differ from the other.

And I also amonges all other, in writinge this lytle treatise, haue folowed sūme yonge shooters, whiche bothe wyll begyn to shoote, for a lytle moneye, and also wyll vse to shote ones or twise about the marke for nought, afore they beginne a good. And therfore did I take this little matter in hande, to assaye my selfe, and hereafter by the grace of God, if the iudgement of wyse men, that looke on, thinke that I can do any good, I maye perchaunce caste my shafte amonge other, for better game.

Yet in writing this booke, some man wyll maruayle per-chaunce, why that I beyng an vnperfyte shoter, shoulde take in hande to write of makyng a perfyte archer: the same man peraduenture wyll maruayle, howe a whettestone whiche is blunte, can make the edge of a knife sharpe: I woulde ye same man shulde consider also, that in goyng about anye matter, there be .iiii. thinges to be considered, doyng, saying, thinking and perfectnesse : Firste there is no man that doth so wel, but he can saye better, or elles summe men, whiche be now starke nought, shuld be to good : Agayne no man can vtter wyth his tong, so wel as he is able to imagin with his minde, & yet perfectnesse it selfe is farre aboue all thinking. Than seing that saying is one steppe nerer perfectenesse than doyng, let euery man leue maruaylyng why my woorde shall rather expresse, than my dede shall perfourme perfecte shootinge.

I truste no man will be offended with this litle booke excepte it be sūme fletchers and bowiers, thinking hereby that manye that loue shootynge shall be taughte to refuse suche noughtie wares as they woulde vtter. Honest fletchers and bowyers do not so, and they that be vnhonest, oughte rather to amende them selues for doinge ill, than be angrie with me for sayinge wel. A fletcher hath euen as good a quarell to be angry w^t an archer that refuseth an ill shaft, as a bladesmith hath to a fletcher y^t forsaketh to bye of him a noughtie knyfe : For as an archer must be content that a fletcher know a good shafte in euery poynte for the perfecter makynge of it, So an honeste fletcher will also be content that a shooter knowe a good shafte in euery poynt for the perfiter vsing of it : bicause the one knoweth like a fletcher how to make it, the other knoweth lyke an archer howe to vse it. And seyng the knowlege is one in them bothe, yet the ende diuerse, surely that fletcher is an enemye to archers and artillery, whiche can not be content that an archer knowe a shafte as well for his vse in shotynge, as he hym selfe shoulde knowe a shafte, for hys aduauntage in sellynge. And the rather bycause shaftes be not made so muche to be solde, but chefely to be vsed. And seynge that vse and occupiyng is the ende why a shafte is made, the making as it were a meane for occupying, surely the knowelege in euery poynte of a good shafte, is more to be required in a shooter than a fletcher.

Yet as I sayde before no honest fletcher wil be angry with me, seinge I do not teache howe to make a shafte whiche belongeth onelye to a good fletcher, but to knowe and handle a shafte, which belongeth to an archer. And this lytle booke I truste, shall please and profite both partes : For good bowes and shaftes shall be better knowen to the cōmoditie of al shoters,

and good shotyng may perchaunce be the more occupied to
the profite of all bowyers and fletchers. And thus I praye
God that all fletchers getting theyr lyuynge truly, and al
archers vsynge shootynge honestly, and all maner of men
that fauour artillery, maye lyue continuallye in
healthe and merinesse, obeying theyr
prince as they shulde, and louing
God as they ought, to whom
for al thinges be al ho-
nour and glorye for
euer. Amen

TOXOPHILVS,

The schole of shootinge conteyned in tvvo bookes.

To all Gentlemen and yomen of Englande,
pleasaunte for theyr pastyme to rede,
and profitable for theyr use
to folow, both in war
and peace.

The contentes of the first booke.

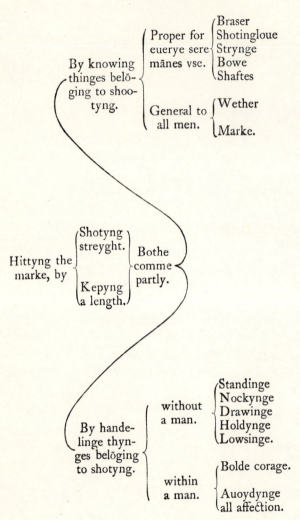

A Table conteyning
the seconde booke.

By knowing thinges belō-ging to shoo-tyng.

Proper for euerye sere-mānes vse.
- Braser
- Shotingloue
- Strynge
- Bowe
- Shaftes

General to all men.
- Wether
- Marke.

Hittyng the marke, by
- Shotyng streyght.
- Kepyng a length.

Bothe comme partly.

By handelinge thynges belōging to shotyng.

without a man.
- Standinge
- Nockynge
- Drawinge
- Holdynge
- Lowsinge.

within a man.
- Bolde corage.
- Auoydynge all affection.

TOXOPHILVS,

A,

𝕿𝖍𝖊 𝖋𝖎𝖗𝖘𝖙 𝖇𝖔𝖐𝖊 𝖔𝖋 𝖙𝖍𝖊 𝖘𝖈𝖍𝖔𝖑𝖊 𝖔𝖋 𝖘𝖍𝖔𝖙𝖎𝖓𝖌.

Philologus.   *Toxophilus.*

PHILOLOGUS. You studie to sore Toxophile. TOX. I
wil not hurt my self ouermoche I warraūt you. PHI. A
Take hede you do not, for we Physicions saye, that it is
nether good for the eyes in so cleare a Sunne, nor yet holsome
for yᵉ bodie, so soone after meate, to looke vpon a mans
boke. TOX. In eatinge and studyinge I will neuer folowe anye
Physike, for yf I dyd, I am sure I shoulde haue small pleasure in
the one, and lesse courage in the other. But what newes draue
you hyther I praye you? PHI. Small newes trulie, but that as
I came on walkynge, I fortuned to come wᵗ thre or foure that
went to shote at the pryckes : And when I sawe not you amonges
them, but at the last espyed you lokynge on your booke here
so sadlye, I thought to come and holde you with some com
munication, lest your boke shoulde runne awaye with you.
For me thought by your waueryng pace & earnest lokying,
your boke led you, not you it. TOX. In dede as it chaunced,
my mynde went faster then my feete, for I happened here to
reade in *Phedro Platonis*, a place that entretes wonderfullie of
the nature of soules, which place (whether it were   *In Phedro.*
for the passynge eloquence of Plato, and the
Greke tongue, or for the hyghe and godlie description of
the matter, kept my mynde so occupied, that it had no leisure
to loke to my feete. For I was reding howe some soules being
well fethered, flewe alwayes about heauē and heauenlie matters,
other some hauinge their fethers mowted awaye, and droupinge,
sanke downe into earthlie thinges. PHI. I remēbre the place
verie wel, and it is wonderfullie sayd of Plato, & now I se it

was no maruell though your fete fayled you, seing your minde
flewe so fast. TOX. I am gladde now that you letted me,
for my head akes w^t loking on it, and bycause you tell me so,
I am verye sorie y^t I was not with those good feloes you spake
vpon, for it is a verie faire day for a mā to shote in. PHI. And
me thinke you were a great dele better occupied & in better
cōpanie, for it is a very faire daye for a mā to go to his boke
in. TOX. Al dayes and wethers wil serue for that purpose,
and surelie this occasiō was ill lost. PHI. Yea but clere
wether maketh clere mindes, and it is best as I suppose, to
spend ye best time vpon the best thinges : And me thought you
shot verie wel, and at that marke, at which euery good scoler
shoulde moste busilie shote at. And I suppose it be a great
dele more pleasure also, to se a soule flye in Plato, then a shafte
flye at the prickes. I graunte you, shoting is not the worst
thing in the world, yet if we shote, and time shote, we ar not
like to be great winners at the length. And you know also we
scholers haue more ernest & weightie matters in hand, nor
we be not borne to pastime & pley, as you know wel ynough

M. Cic. ī off.   who sayth. TOX. Yet the same man in the
same place *Philologe*, by your leue, doth admitte
holsome, honest and manerlie pastimes to be as necessarie
to be mīgled with sad matters of the minde, as eating
& sleping is for the health of the body, and yet we be borne
for neither of bothe. And Aristotle him selfe

Arist. de mo-   sayth, y^t although it were a fonde & a chyldish
ribus. 10. 6.   thing to be to ernest in pastime & play, yet doth
he affirme by the authoritie of the oulde Poet Epicharmus,
that a man may vse play for ernest matter sake.

Arist. Pol.   And in an other place, y^t as rest is for labour, &
8. 3.   medicines for helth, so is pastime at tymes for
sad & weightie studie. PHI. How moche in this matter is to
be giuen to ye auctoritie either of Aristotle or Tullie, I cā not
tel, seing sad mē may wel ynough speke merily for a merie
matter, this I am sure, whiche thing this faire wheat (god saue
it) maketh me remēbre, y^t those husbādmen which rise erliest,
and come latest home, and are content to haue their diner and
other drinckinges, broughte into the fielde to them, for feare of
losing of time, haue fatter barnes in haruest, than they whiche
will either slepe at none time of the daye, or els make merie

w^t their neighbours at the ale. And so a scholer y^t purposeth
to be a good husband, and desireth to repe and enioy much
fruite, of learninge, muste tylle and sowe thereafter. Our
beste seede tyme, whiche be scholers, as it is verie tymelye, and
whan we be yonge : so it endureth not ouerlonge, and therfore
it maye not be let slippe one houre, oure grounde is verye
harde, and full of wedes, our horse wherw^t we be drawen very
wylde as Plato sayth. And infinite other mo
lettes whiche wil make a thriftie scholer take *In Phedro.*
hede how he spēdeth his tyme in sporte and pleye. TOX. That
Aristotle and Tullie spake ernestlie, and as they thought, the
ernest matter which they entreate vpon, doth plainlye proue.
And as for your husbandrie, it was more probablie tolde with
apt wordes propre to ye thing, then throughly proued with
reasons belongynge to our matter. For contrariwise I herd my
selfe a good husbande at his boke ones saye, that to omit studie
somtime of the daye, and sometime of the yere, made asmoche
for the encrease of learning, as to let the lād lye sometime
falloe, maketh for the better encrease of corne. This we se,
yf the lande be plowed euerye yere, the corne commeth thinne
vp : the eare is short, the grayne is small, and when it is brought
into the barne and threshed, gyueth very euill faul. So those
which neuer leaue poring on their bokes, haue oftētimes as
thinne inuention, as other poore mē haue, and as smal wit and
weight in it as in other mens. And thus youre husbandrie me
thinke, is more like the life of a couetouse snudge that oft very
euill preues, then the labour of a good husbād that knoweth
wel what he doth. And surelie the best wittes to lerning must
nedes haue moche recreation and ceasing from their boke, or
els they marre them selues, whē base and dompysshe wittes
can neuer be hurte with continuall studie, as ye se in luting,
that a treble minikin string must alwayes be let down, but at
suche time as when a man must nedes playe : when ye base
and dull stryng nedeth neuer to be moued out of his place.
The same reason I finde true in two bowes that I haue, wherof
the one is quicke of cast, tricke, and trīme both for pleasure
and profyte : the other is a lugge slowe of cast, folowing the
string, more sure for to last, then pleasaunt for to vse. Now
sir it chaūced this other night, one in my chābre wolde nedes
bende them to proue their strength, but I can not tel how,

they were both left bente tyll the nexte daye at after dyner:
and when I came to them, purposing to haue gone on shoting,
I found my good bowe clene cast on the one side, and as
weake as water, that surelie (if I were a riche man) I had
rather haue spent a crowne: and as for my lugge, it was not
one whyt the worse: but shotte by and by as wel and as farre
as euer it dyd. And euen so I am sure that good wittes,
except they be let downe like a treble string, and vnbent like
a good casting bowe, they wil neuer last and be able to cōtinue
in studie. And I know where I speake this *Philologe*, for I
wolde not sayé thus moche afore yong men, for they wil take
soone occasion to studie litle ynough. But I saye it therfore
bicause I knowe, as litle studie getteth litle learninge or none
at all, so the moost studie getteth not yᵉ moost learning of all.
For a mans witte sore occupied in ernest studie, must be as wel
recreated with some honest pastime, as the body sore laboured,
must be refreshed with slepe and quietnesse, or els it can not
endure very longe, as the noble poete sayeth.

Ouid. *What thig wātſ quiet & meri rest endures but a smal while.*

And I promise you shoting by my iudgement, is yᵉ moost
B honest pastime of al, & suche one I am sure, of all other, that
hindreth learning litle or nothing at all, whatsoeuer you &
some other saye, whiche are a gret dele sorer against it
alwaies thā you nede to be. PHI. Hindereth learninge litle or
nothinge at all? that were a meruayle to me truelie, and I am
sure seing you saye so, you haue some reason wherewith you
can defende shooting wᵗall, and as for wyl (for the loue that
you beare towarde shotinge) I thinke there shall lacke none in
you. Therfore seinge we haue so good leysure bothe, and no
bodie by to trouble vs: and you so willinge & able to defende
it, and I so redy and glad to heare what may be sayde of it
I suppose we canne not passe the tyme better ouer, neyther
you for yᵉ honestie of your shoting, nor I for myne owne
mindsake, than to se what can be sayed with it, or agaynste it,
and speciallie in these dayes, whan so many doeth vse it, and
euerie man in a maner doeth common of it. TOX. To speake
of shootinge Philologe, trulye I woulde I were so able, either
as I my selfe am willing or yet as the matter deserueth, but
seing with wisshing we can not haue one nowe worthie, whiche

so worthie a thinge can worthilie praise, and although I had
rather haue anie other to do it than my selfe, yet my selfe
rather then no other. I wil not fail to saye in it what I can
wherin if I saye litle, laye that of my litle habilitie, not of the
matter it selfe whiche deserueth no lyttle thinge to be sayde
of it. PHI. If it deserue no little thinge to be sayde of it
Toxophile, I maruell howe it chaunceth than, that no man
hitherto, hath written any thinge of it : wherin you must
graunte me, that eyther the matter is noughte, vnworthye, and
barren to be written vppon, or els some men are to blame,
whiche both loue it and vse it, and yet could neuer finde in
theyr heart, to saye one good woorde of it, seinge that very
triflinge matters hath not lacked great learned men to sette
them out, as gnattes and nuttes, & many other mo like thinges,
wherfore eyther you may honestlie laye verie great faut vpō
men bycause they neuer yet praysed it, or els I may iustlie take
awaye no litle thinge from shooting, bycause it neuer yet
deserued it. TOX. Trulye herein Philologe, you take not so
muche from it, as you giue to it. For great and commodious
thynges are neuer greatlie praysed, not bycause they be not
worthie, but bicause their excellencie nedeth no man hys prayse,
hauinge all theyr cōmendation of them selfe not borowed of
other men his lippes, which rather prayse them selfe, in
spekynge much of a litle thynge than that matter whiche they
entreat vpon. Great & good thinges be not praysed. For who
euer praysed Hercules (sayeth the Greke prouerbe) And that
no man hitherto hath written any booke of shoting the fault is
not to be layed in the thyng whiche was worthie to be written
vpon, but of men which were negligent in doyng it, and this
was the cause therof as I suppose. Menne that vsed shootyng
moste and knewe it best, were not learned : men that were
lerned, vsed litle shooting, and were ignorant in the nature
of the thynge, and so fewe menne hath bene that hitherto were
able to wryte vpon it. Yet howe longe shotying hath con-
tinued, what common wealthes hath moste vsed it, howe honeste
a thynge it is for all men, what kynde of liuing so euer they
folow, what pleasure and profit cōmeth of it, both in peace and
warre, all maner of tongues & writers, Hebrue, Greke and
Latine, hath so plentifullie spoken of it, as of fewe other thinges
like. So what shooting is howe many kindes there is of it,

what goodnesse is ioyned with it, is tolde : onelye howe it is to be learned and brought to a perfectnesse amonges men, is not toulde. PHI. Than *Toxophile*, if it be so as you do saye, let vs go forwarde and examin howe plentifullie this is done that you speke, and firste of the inuention of it, than what honestie & profit is in the vse of it, bothe for warre & peace, more than in other pastimes, laste of all howe it ought to be learned amonges men for the encrease of it, whiche thinge if you do, not onelye I nowe for youre cōmunication but many other mo, when they shall knowe of it, for your labour, & shotying it selfe also (if it coulde speke) for your kyndnesse, wyll can you very moche thanke. TOXOPH. What good thynges mē speake of shoting & what good thinges shooting bringes to men as my wit & knowlege will serue me, gladly shall I say my mind. But how the thing is to be learned I will surely leue to some other which bothe for greater experience in it, & also for their lerninge, can set it out better than I. PHI. Well as for that I knowe both what you can do in shooting by experience, & yᵗ you cā also speke well ynough of shooting, for youre learning, but go on with the first part. And I do not doubt, but what my desyre, what your loue toward it, the honestie of shoting, the profite that may come therby to many other, shall get the seconde parte out of you at the last.

C   TOXOPH. Of the first finders out of shoting, diuers men diuerslye doo wryte. Claudiane the poete

Claudianus in histri. sayth that nature gaue example of shotyng first, by the Porpentine, whiche doth shote his prickes, and will hitte any thinge that fightes with it : whereby

Plin. 7. 56. men learned afterwarde to immitate the same in findyng out both bowe and shaftes. Plinie referreth it to Schythes the sonne of Iupiter. Better and more noble wryters bringe shoting from a more noble inuentour : as

In sympo. Plato, Calimachus, and Galene from Apollo.
In hym. Yet longe afore those dayes do we reade in the
Apoll'. bible of shotinge expreslye. And also if we shall
Gen. 21. beleue Nicholas de Lyra, Lamech killed Cain
Nic. de lyra. with a shafte. So this great continuaunce of shoting doth not a lytle praise shotinge : nor that neither doth not a litle set it oute, that it is referred to thinuention of Apollo, for the which poynt shoting is highlye praised of

Galene : where he sayth, y^t mean craftes be first foũd out by men or beastes, as weauing by a spider, and suche other : but high and cōmendable sciences by goddes, as shotinge and musicke by Apollo. And *Galen in exhor. ad bonas artes.* thus shotynge for the necessitie of it vsed in Adams dayes, for the noblenesse of it referred to Apollo, hath not ben onelie cōmended in all tunges and writers, but also had in greate price, both in the best cōmune wealthes in warre tyme for the defēce of their countrie, and of all degrees of men in peace tyme, bothe for the honestie that is ioyned with it, and the profyte that foloweth of it. PHILOL. Well, as concerning the fyndinge oute of it, litle prayse is gotten to shotinge therby, seinge good wittes maye mooste easelye of all fynde oute a trifelynge matter. But where as you saye that mooste commune wealthes haue vsed it in warre tyme, and all degrees of men maye verye honestlye vse it in peace tyme : I thynke you can neither shewe by authoritie, nor yet proue by reason. TOXOPHI. The vse of it in warre tyme, I wyll declare hereafter. And firste howe all kindes and sortes of men (what degree soeuer they be) hath at all tymes afore, and nowe maye honestlye vse it : the example of mooste noble men verye well doeth proue.

Cyaxares the kynge of the Medees, and greate graundefather to Cyrus, kepte a sorte of Sythians with him onely for this purpose, to teache his sonne Astyages to shote. Cyr⁹ being a childe was brought vp in shoting, which thinge Xenophon wolde neuer haue made mention on, except it had ben fitte for all princes to haue vsed : seing that Xenophō wrote Cyrus lyfe (as Tullie sayth) not to shewe what Cyrus did, but what all maner of princes both in pastimes and ernest matters ought to do. *Herod. ī clio.* *Xen. in insti. Cyri. 1.* *Ad. Quint. Fra. 1. 1.*

Darius the first of that name, and king of Persie shewed plainly howe fit it is for a kinge to loue and vse shotynge, whiche commaunded this sentence to be grauen in his tombe, for a Princelie memorie and prayse.

> *Darius the King lieth buried here* *Strabo. 15.*
> *That in shoting and riding had neuer pere.*

Agayne, Domitian the Emperour was so cũning in shoting that he coulde shote betwixte a mans *Tranq. suet.*

fingers standing afarre of, and neuer hurt him. Comodus also
was so excellent, and had so sure a hande in it,
that there was nothing within his retche & shote,
but he wolde hit it in what place he wolde: as beastes runninge,
either in the heed, or in the herte, and neuer mysse, as Herodiane sayeth he sawe him selfe, or els he coulde neuer haue
beleued it. PHI. In dede you praise shoting very wel, in y^t
you shewe that Domitian and Commodus loue shotinge, suche
an vngracious couple I am sure as a man shall not fynde agayne,
if he raked all hell for them. TOXOPH. Wel euen as I
wyll not commende their ilnesse, so ought not you to dispraise
their goodnesse, and in dede, the iudgement of Herodian vpon
Commodus is true of them bothe, and that was this: that
beside strength of bodie and good shotinge, they hadde no
princelie thing in them, which saying me thinke commendes
shoting wonderfullie, callinge it a princelie thinge.

Herodia. 1.

Furthermore howe commendable shotinge is for princes:
Themistius the noble philosopher sheweth in a
certayne oration made to Theodosius themperoure,
wherein he doeth commende him for .iii. thinges,
that he vsed of a childe. For shotinge, for rydinge of an horse
well, and for feates of armes.

Themist.
in ora. 6.

Moreouer, not onelye kinges and emperours haue ben brought
vp in shoting, but also the best cōmune wealthes that euer were,
haue made goodlie actes & lawes for it, as the Persians which
vnder Cyrus cōquered in a maner all the worlde,
had a lawe that their children shulde learne thre
thinges onelie, from v. yeare oulde vnto .xx. to ryde an horse
well, to shote well, to speake truthe alwayes &
neuer lye. The Romaines (as Leo themperour
in his boke of sleightes of warre telleth) had a lawe
that euery man shoulde vse shoting in peace tyme, while he
was .xl. yere olde and that euerye house shoulde haue a bowe,
and .xl. shaftes ready for all nedes, the omittinge of whiche lawe
(sayth Leo) amonges the youthe, hath ben the onely occasion
why the Romaynes lost a great dele of their empire. But more
of this I wil speake whē I come to the profite of shoting in
warre. If I shuld rehearse the statutes made of noble princes
of Englande in parliamentes for the settyng forwarde of shoting,
through this realme, and specially that acte made for shoting

Herod. ī clio.

Leo de stra-
tag. 20.

the thyrde yere of the reygne of our moost drad soueraygne lorde
king Henry the .viii. I could be very long. But these fewe
exāples specially of so great men & noble cōmon wealthes,
shall stand in stede of many. PHI. That suche princes and
suche cōmune welthes haue moche regarded shoting, you haue
well declared. But why shotinge ought so of it selfe to be
regarded, you haue scarcelye yet proued. TOX. Examples
I graunt out of histories do shew a thing to be so, not proue
a thing why it shuld be so. Yet this I suppose, yᵗ neither
great mens qualities being cōmēdable be without great
authoritie, for other men honestly to folow them : nor yet
those great learned men that wrote suche thinges, lacke good
reasō iustly at al tymes for any other to approue thē. Princes
beinge children oughte to be brought vp in shoting : both bycause it is an exercise moost holsom, and also a pastyme moost
honest : wherin labour prepareth the body to hardnesse, the
minde to couragiousnesse, sufferyng neither the one to be marde
with tendernesse, nor yet the other to be hurte with ydlenesse :
as we reade how Sardanapalus and suche other were, bycause
they were not brought vp wᵗ outwarde honest payneful pastymes
to be men : but cockerde vp with inwarde noughtie ydle
wantonnesse to be women. For how fit labour is for al
youth, Iupiter or else Minos amonges them of Grece, and
Lycurgus amonges the Lacedemonians, do shewe
by their lawes, which neuer ordeyned any thing   *Cic. 2. Tus.*
for yᵉ bringyng vp of youth that was not ioyned   *Qu.*
with labour. And the labour which is in shoting of al other
is best, both bycause it encreaseth strength, and preserueth
health moost, beinge not vehement, but moderate, not ouerlay-
ing any one part with werysomnesse, but softly exercisynge
euery parte with equalnesse, as the armes and breastes with
drawinge, the other parties with going, being not so paynfull
for the labour as pleasaunt for the pastyme, which exercise by
the iudgement of the best physicions, is most alowable. By
shoting also is the mynde honestly exercised where
a mā alwaies desireth to be best (which is a worde   *Gal. 2. de*
of honestie) and that by the same waye, that   *san. tuend.*
vertue it selfe doeth, couetinge to come nighest a moost perfite
ende or meane standing betwixte .ii. extremes, eschewinge
shorte, or gone, or eithersyde wide, for the which causes

Aristotle him selfe sayth that shoting and vertue be very like.
Moreouer that shoting of all other is the moost
honest pastyme, and hath leest occasion to
noughtinesse ioyned with it .ii. thinges very
playnelye do proue, which be as a man wolde saye, the tutours
and ouerseers to shotinge : Daye light and open place where
euerye man doeth come, the maynteyners and kepers of shoting,
from all vnhonest doing. If shotinge faulte at any tyme, it
hydes it not, it lurkes not in corners and huddermother : but
openly accuseth & bewrayeth it selfe, which is the nexte waye
to amendement, as wyse men do saye. And these thinges
I suppose be signes, not of noughtinesse, for any man to
disalowe it : but rather verye playne tokens of honestie, for
euerye man to prayse it.

Arist. 1. *de morib.*

The vse of shotinge also in greate mennes chyldren shall
greatlye encrease the loue and vse of shotinge in all the residue
of youth. For meane mennes myndes loue to be lyke greate
menne, as Plato and Isocrates do saye. And that
euerye bodye shoulde learne to shote when they be
yonge, defence of the cōmune wealth, doth require whē they
be olde, which thing can not be done mightelye when they be
men, excepte they learne it perfitelye when they be boyes.
And therfore shotinge of all pastymes is moost fitte to be vsed
in childhode : bycause it is an imitation of moost ernest
thinges to be done in manhode.

Iso. in nic.

Wherfore, shoting is fitte for great mens children, both
bycause it strengthneth the body with holsome labour, and
pleaseth the mynde with honest pastime and also encourageth
all other youth ernestlye to folowe the same. And these
reasons (as I suppose) stirred vp both great men to bring vp
their chyldren in shotinge, and also noble commune wealthes so
straytelye to commaunde shoting. Therfore seinge Princes
moued by honest occasions, hath in al commune wealthes vsed
shotynge, I suppose there is none other degree of men, neither
D lowe nor hye, learned nor leude, yonge nor oulde. PHIL. You
shal nede wade no further in this matter *Toxophile*, but if
you can proue me that scholers and men gyuen to learning
maye honestlie vse shoting, I wyll soone graūt you that
all other sortes of men maye not onelye lefullie, but ought of
dutie to vse it. But I thinke you can not proue but that all

these examples of shotinge brought from so longe a tyme, vsed
of so noble princes, confirmed by so wyse mennes lawes and
iudgementes, are sette afore temporall men, onelye to followe
them: whereby they may the better and stroglyer defende the
commune wealth withall. And nothing belongeth to scholers
and learned men, which haue an other parte of the commune
wealth, quiete and peaceable put to their cure and charge, whose
ende as it is diuerse frō the other, so there is no one waye that
leadeth to them both. TOXO. I graunte *Philologe,* that
scholers and lay men haue diuerse offices and charges in the
cōmune wealth, whiche requires diuerse brīging vp in their
youth, if they shal do them as they ought to do in their age.
Yet as temporall men of necessitie are compelled to take somewhat of learning to do their office the better withal: So scholers
maye the boldlyer borowe somewhat of laye mennes pastimes,
to maynteyne their health in studie withall. And surelie of
al other thinges shoting is necessary for both sortes to learne.
Whiche thing, when it hath ben euermore vsed in Englande
how moche good it hath done, both oulde men and Chronicles
doo tell: and also our enemies can beare vs recorde. For if it
be true (as I haue hearde saye) when the kynge of Englande
hath ben in Fraunce, the preestes at home bicause they were
archers, haue ben able to ouerthrowe all Scotlande. Agayne
ther is an other thing which aboue all other doeth moue me,
not onely to loue shotinge, to prayse shoting, to exhorte all other
to shotinge, but also to vse shoting my selfe: and that is our
kyng his moost royall purpose and wyll, whiche in all his
statutes generallye doth commaunde men, and with his owne
mouthe moost gentlie doeth exhorte men, and by his great
gyftes and rewardes, greatly doth encourage men, and with his
moost princelie example very oft doth prouoke all other mē
to the same. But here you wyll come in wᵗ tēporal man and
scholer: I tell you plainlye, scholer or vnscholer, yea if I were
.xx. scholers, I wolde thinke it were my dutie, bothe with
exhortinge men to shote, and also with shoting my selfe to
helpe to set forwarde that thing which the kinge his wisdome,
and his counsell, so greatlye laboureth to go forwarde: whiche
thinge surelye they do, bycause they knowe it to be in warre,
the defence and wal of our countrie, in peace, an exercise
moost holsome for the body, a pastime moost honest for the

mynde, and as I am able to proue my selfe, of al other moste fit and agreable with learninge and learned men.

PHI. If you can proue this thing so playnly, as you speake it ernestly, thē wil I, not only thinke as you do, but become a shooter and do as you do. But yet beware I saye, lest you for the great loue you bear towarde shotinge, blindlie iudge of shootinge. For loue & al other to ernest affections be not for nought paynted blinde. Take hede (I saye) least you prefer shootinge afore other pastimes, as one Balbinus through blinde affection, preferred his louer before all other wemen, although she were deformed with a polypus in her nose. And although shooting maye be mete sometyme for some scholers, and so forthe: yet the fittest always is to be preferred. Therefore if you will nedes graunt scholers pastime and recreation of their mindes, let them vse (as many of thē doth) Musyke, and playing on instrumentes, thinges moste semely for all scholers, and moste regarded alwayes of Apollo & the Muses. TOX. Euen as I can not deny, but some musike is fit for lerning so I trust you can not chose but graunt, that shoting is fit also, as Calimach⁹ doth signifie in this verse.

Cal. hym. 2.   *Both merie songes and good shoting deliteth Appollo.*

But as concerning whether of them is moste fit for learning, E and scholers to vse, you may saye what you will for your pleasure, this I am sure that Plato and Aristotle bothe, in their bookes entreatinge of the cōmon welthe, where they shew howe youthe shoulde be brought vp in .iiii. thinges, in redinge, in writing, in exercise of bodye, and singing, do make mention of Musicke & all kindes of it, wherein they both agre, that Musike vsed amonges the Lydians is verie ill for yong men, which be studentes for vertue and learning, for a certain nice, softe, and smoth swetnesse of it, whiche woulde rather entice thē to noughtines, than stirre them to honestie.

An other kinde of Musicke inuented by the Dorians, they both wonderfully prayse, alowing it to be verie fyt for the studie of vertue & learning, because of a manlye, rough and stoute sounde in it, whyche shulde encourage yong stomakes, to attempte manlye matters. Nowe whether these balades & roundes, these galiardes, pauanes and daunces, so nicelye fingered, so swetely tuned, be lyker the Musike of the Lydians or the

Dorians, you that be learned iudge. And what so euer ye iudge, this I am sure, y^t lutes, harpes, all maner of pypes, barbitons, sambukes, with other instrumentes euery one, whyche standeth by fine and quicke fingeringe, be cōdemned of Aristotle, as not to be brought in & vsed amonge them, whiche studie for learning and vertue.

*Aristot. pol.
8. 6.*

Pallas when she had inuented a pipe, cast it away, not so muche sayeth Aristotle, because it deformed her face, but muche rather bycause suche an Instrumente belonged nothing to learnynge. Howe suche Instrumentes agree with learning, the goodlye agrement betwixt Apollo god of learninge, & Marsyas the Satyr, defender of pipinge, doth well declare, where Marsyas had his skine quite pulled ouer his head for his labour.

Muche musike marreth mennes maners, sayth Galen, although some man wil saye that it doth not so, but rather recreateth and maketh quycke a mannes mynde, yet me thinke by reason it doth as hony doth to a mannes stomacke, whiche at the first receyueth it well, but afterwarde it maketh it vnfit, to abyde any good stronge norishynge meate, orels anye holsome sharpe and quicke drinke. And euen so in a maner these Instrumentes make a mannes wit so softe and smoothe so tender and quaisie, that they be lesse able to brooke, stronge and tough studie. Wittes be not sharpened, but rather dulled, and made blunte, wyth suche sweete softenesse, euen as good edges be blonter, whiche menne whette vpon softe chalke stones.

And these thinges to be true, not onely Plato Aristotle & Galen, proue by authoritie of reason, but also Herodotus and other writers, shewe by playne and euident example, as that of Cyrus, whiche

*Herodotus
in Clio.*

after he had ouercome the Lydians, and taken their kinge Cresus prisoner, yet after by the meane of one Pactyas a verye headie manne amonges the Lydians, they rebelled agaynste Cyrus agayne, then Cyrus had by an by, broughte them to vtter destruction, yf Cresus being in good fauour with Cyrus had not hertelie desyred him, not to reuenge Pactyas faulte, in shedynge theyr blood. But if he would folowe his counsell, he myght brynge to passe, that they shoulde neuer more rebel agaynst hym, And y^t was this, to make them weare lōg kyrtils, to ye foot lyke woomen, and that euerye one of them shoulde haue a harpe or a lute, and learne to playe and sing whyche thinge if you do sayth Cresus (as he dyd in dede) you shall se them quickelye of men, made women. And thus lutinge and singinge take awaye a manlye stomake, whiche shulde enter & pearce depe and harde studye.

Euen suche an other storie doeth Nymphodorus an olde

Nymphod. greke Historiographer write, of one Sesostris kinge of Egypte, whiche storie because it is somewhat longe, and very lyke in al poyntes to the other and also you do

Comment. *in Antig.* well ynoughe remembre it, seynge you read it so late in Sophoclis commentaries, I wyll nowe passe ouer. Therefore eyther Aristotle and Plato knowe not what was good and euyll for learninge and vertue, and the example of wyse histories be vainlie set afore vs or els the minstrelsie of lutes, pipes, harpes, and all other that standeth by suche nice, fine, minikin fingering (suche as the mooste parte of scholers whom I knowe vse, if they vse any) is farre more fitte for the womannishnesse of it to dwell in the courte among ladies, than for any great thing in it, whiche shoulde helpe good and sad studie, to abide in the vniuersitie amonges scholers. But perhaps you knowe some great goodnesse of suche musicke and suche instrumentes, whervnto Plato & Aristotle his brayne coulde neuer attayne, and therfore I will saye no more agaynst it. PHI. Well Toxophile is it not ynoughe for you to rayle vpon Musike, excepte you mocke me to? but to say the truth I neuer thought my selfe these kindes of musicke fit for learninge, but that whyche I sayde was rather to proue you, than to defende the matter. But yet as I woulde haue this sorte of musicke decaye amonge scholers, euen so do I wysshe from the bottome of my heart, that the laudable custome of Englande to teache chyldren their plainesong and priksong, were not so decayed throughout all the realme as it is. Whiche thing howe profitable it was for all sortes of men, those knewe not so wel than whiche had it most, as they do nowe whiche lacke it moste. And therfore it is true that Teucer sayeth in Sophocles.

Sophocles *in Aiace.* *Seldome at all good thinges be Knowen how good to be* *Before a man suche thinges do misse out of his handes.*

That milke is no fitter nor more naturall for the bringing
vp of children than musike is, both Gallen proueth by authoritie,
and dayly vse teacheth by experience. For euen the litle
babes lacking the vse of reason, are scarse so well stilled in
suckyng theyr mothers pap, as in hearynge theyr mother syng.
Agayne how fit youth is made, by learning to sing, for
grammar and other sciences, bothe we dayly do see, and
Plutarch learnedly doth proue, and Plato wiselie did alowe,
whiche receyued no scholer in to his schole, that had not learned
his songe before. The godlie vse of praysing God, by singinge
in the churche, nedeth not my prayse, seing it is so praysed
through al the scripture, therfore nowe I wil speke nothing of
it, rather than I shuld speke to litle of it.

Besyde al these commodities, truly .ii. degrees of mēne, which
haue the highest offices vnder the king in all this realme, shal
greatly lacke the vse of Singinge, preachers and lawiers, bycause
they shal not without this, be able to rule their brestes, for euery
purpose. For where is no distinction in telling glad thinges and
fearfull thinges, gentilnes & cruelnes, softenes and vehementnes,
and suche lyke matters, there can be no great perswasion.

For the hearers, as Tullie sayeth, be muche affectioned, as he
is that speaketh. At his wordes be they drawen, yf he stande still
in one facion, their mindes stande still with hym : If he thundre,
they quake : If he chyde, they feare : If he cōplayne, they sory
with hym : and finally, where a matter is spoken, with an apte
voyce, for euerye affection, the hearers for the moste parte, are
moued as the speaker woulde. But when a man is alwaye in
one tune, lyke an Humble bee, or els nowe vp in the top of the
churche, nowe downe that no manne knoweth where to haue
hym : or piping lyke a reede, or roring lyke a bull, as some
lawyers do, whiche thinke they do best, when they crye
lowdest, these shall neuer greatly mooue, as I haue knowen
many wel learned, haue done, bicause theyr voyce was not
stayed afore, with learnyng to synge. For all voyces, great
and small, base & shril, weke or softe, may be holpen and
brought to a good poynt, by learnyng to synge.

Whether this be true or not, they that stand mooste in nede,
can tell best, whereof some I haue knowen, whiche, because they
learned not to sing, whan they were boyes, were fayne to take
peyne in it, whā they were men. If any man shulde heare me

Toxophile, that woulde thinke I did but fondly, to suppose
that a voice were so necessarie to be loked vpon, I would aske
him if he thought not nature a foole, for makīg such goodly
instrumentes in a man, for wel vttring his woordes, or els if
the .ii. noble orators Demosthenes & Cicero were not fooles,
wherof the one dyd not onelie learne to sing of a man : But
also was not ashamed to learne howe he shoulde vtter his soūdes
aptly of a dogge, the other setteth oute no poynte of rhetorike,
so fullie in all his bookes, as howe a man shoulde order his
voyce for all kynde of matters. Therfore seinge men by
speaking, differ and be better than beastes, by speakyng wel,
better than other men, and that singing is an helpe towarde the
same as dayly experiēce doth teache, example of wysemē doth
alowe, authoritie of learned men doth approue wherwith the
foundacion of youth in all good common wealthes alwayes hath
bene tempered; surelye if I were one of the parliament house,
I woulde not fayle, to put vp a bill for the amendment of this
thynge, but because I am lyke to be none this yeare, I wil
speake no more of it, at this time. TOX. It were pitie truly
Philologe, that the thinge shoulde be neglected, but I trust it is
not as you say. PHI. The thing is to true, for of them that
come daylye to yᵉ vniuersitie, where one hath learned to singe,
vi. hath not. But nowe to oure shotinge Toxophile agayne,
wherin I suppose you can not say so muche for shotyng to be fitte
for learninge, as you haue spoken agaynste Musicke for the same.

Therfore as concerning Musike, I can be content to graunt
you your mynde : But as for shooting, surely I suppose
that you can not perswade me, by no meanes, that a man can
be earnest in it, and earnest at his booke to : but rather I thynke
that a man wᵗ a bowe on his backe, and shaftes vnder hys
girdell, is more fit to wayte vpon Robin Hoode, than vpon
Apollo or the Muses. TOX. Ouer ernest shooting surely I
will not ouer ernestlye defende, for I euer thought shooting
shoulde be a wayter vpon lerning not a mastres ouer learning.
Yet this I maruell not a litle at, that ye thinke a man with a
bowe on hys backe is more like Robin Hoode seruaūt, than
Apollose, seing that Apollo him selfe in Alcestis of Euripides,
whiche tragidie you red openly not long ago, in a maner glorieth
saying this verse.

Euripid. in　　*It is my wont alwaies my bowe with me to beare*
Alcest.

Therfore a learned man ought not to much to be ashamed to
beare that some tyme, whiche Apollo god of lerning him selfe
was not ashamed always to beare. And bycause ye woulde
haue a man wayt vpon the Muses, and not at all medle with
shotyng I maruell that you do not remembre howe that the ix.
muses their selfe as sone as they were borne, wer put to norse
to a lady called Euphemis whiche had a son named Erotus with
whome the nine Muses for his excellent shootinge, kepte euer
more companie w^tall, & vsed dayly to shoote togither in y^e
mount Pernasus : and at last it chaūced this Erotus to dye,
whose death the Muses lamented greatly, and fell all vpon theyr
knees afore Iupiter theyr father, and at theyr request, Erotus
for shooting with the Muses in earth was made a signe, and
called Sagittarius in heauen. Therfore you se, that if Apollo
and the Muses either were examples in dede, or onelye fayned
of wise men to be examples of learninge, honest shoting maye
well ynough be companion with honest studie. PHI. Well
Toxophile, if you haue no stronger defence of shotinge then
Poetes, I feare yf your companions which loue shotinge, hearde
you, they wolde thinke you made it but a triflyng and fabling
matter, rather then any other man that loueth not shotinge
coulde be persuaded by this reason to loue it. TOXO. Euen
as I am not so fonde but I knowe that these be fables, so I am
sure you be not so ignoraunt, but you knowe what suche noble
wittes as the Poetes had, ment by such matters : which often-
tymes vnder the couering of a fable, do hyde & wrappe in goodlie
preceptes of philosophie, with the true iudgement of thinges.
Whiche to be true speciallye in Homer and Euripides, Plato,
Aristotle and Galene playnelye do shewe : when through all
their workes (in a maner) they determine all cōtrouersies, by
these .ii. Poetes and suche lyke authorities.   Therfore if in this
matter I seme to fable, and nothynge proue, I am content you
iudge so on me : seinge the same iudgement shal condemne
with me Plato, Aristotle, and Galene, whom in that errour I
am wel content to folowe. If these oulde examples proue
nothing for shoting, what saye you to this ? that the best learned
and sagest men in this Realme, whiche be nowe alyue, both loue
shoting and vse shoting, as the best learned bisshoppes that be :
amonges whome *Philologe*, you your selfe knowe .iiii. or .v.
which as in all good learning, vertue and sagenesse they gyue

other men example what thing they shoulde do, euen so by
their shoting, they playnely shewe what honest pastime, other
mē giuē to learning, may honestly vse. That ernest studie
must be recreated with honest pastime sufficientlye I haue
proued afore, both by reason and authoritie of the best learned
men that euer wrote. Then seing pastymes be lefull, the
moost fittest for learning, is to be sought for. A pastyme,
Arist. po. 7. saith Aristotle, must be lyke a medicine. Medicines stande by contraries, therfore the nature of
studying considered, the fittest pastyme shal soone appeare. In
studie euery parte of the body is ydle, which thing causeth grosse
and colde humours, to gather togyther & vexe scholers verye
moche, the mynde is altogyther bent and set on worke. A
pastyme then must be had where euery parte of the bodye must
be laboured to separate and lessen suche humours withal : the
mind must be vnbent, to gather & fetche againe his quicknesse
withall. Thus pastymes for the mynde onelye, be nothing fit
for studentes, bycause the body which is moost hurte by studie,
shulde take away no profyte at all thereat. This knewe Erasmus
verye well, when he was here in Cambrige : which when he
had ben sore at his boke (as Garret our bookebynder hath verye
ofte tolde me) for lacke of better exercise, wolde take his horse,
and ryde about the markette hill, and come agayne. If a
scholer shoulde vse bowles or tennies, the laboure is to vehement and vnequall, whiche is cōdempned of Galene : the
example very ill for other men, when by so manye actes they
be made vnlawfull.

Running, leaping, and coyting be to vile for scholers, and
so not fit by Aristotle his iudgement : walking alone into the
Aristot. felde, hath no token of courage in it, a pastyme
pol. 7. 17. lyke a simple man which is neither flesh nor fisshe.
Therfore if a man woulde haue a pastyme hole-
some and equall for euerye parte of the bodye, pleasaunt and full
of courage for the mynde, not vile and vnhoneste to gyue ill
example to laye men, not kepte in gardynes and corners, not
lurkynge on the nyght and in holes, but euermore in the face
of men, either to rebuke it when it doeth ill, or els to testifye
on it when it doth well : let him seke chefelye of all other for
shotynge. PHILOL. Suche commune pastymes as men com-
menlye do vse, I wyll not greatlye allowe to be fit for scholers :

seinge they maye vse suche exercises verye well (I suppose) as Galene him selfe doth allowe. TOXOPH. Those exercises I remember verye well, for I read them within these two dayes, of the whiche, *Gal. de san. tuend. 2.* some be these : to runne vp and downe an hyll, to clyme vp a longe powle, or a rope, and there hange a while, to holde a man by his armes and waue with his heeles, moche lyke the pastyme that boyes vse in the churche whē their master is awaye, to swinge and totter in a belrope: to make a fiste, and stretche out bothe his armes, and so stande lyke a roode. To go on a man his tiptoes, stretching out thone of his armes forwarde, the other backewarde, which if he blered out his tunge also, myght be thought to daunce Anticke verye properlye. To tūble ouer and ouer, to toppe ouer tayle : To set backe to backe, and se who cā heaue an other his heles highest, with other moche like : whiche exercises surelye muste nedes be naturall, bycause they be so childisshe, and they may be also holesome for the body : but surely as for pleasure to the minde or honestie in the doinge of them, they be as lyke shotinge as Yorke is foule Sutton. Therfore to loke on al pastymes and exercises holsome for the bodye, pleasaunt for the mynde, comlye for euery man to do, honest for all other to loke on, profitable to be sette by of euerye man, worthie to be rebuked of no man, fit for al ages persōs and places, onely shoting shal appeare, wherin all these commodities maye be founde.

PHIL. To graunt Toxophile, that studentes may at tymes conuenient vse shoting as moost holsome and honest pastyme : yet to do as some do, to shote hourly daylie, wekelye, and in a maner the hole yere, neither I can prayse, nor any wyse man wyl alowe, nor you your selfe can honestlye defende. TOXOPH. Surely Philologe, I am very glad to se you come to that poynte that moost lieth in your stomake, and greueth you and other so moche. But I truste after I haue sayd my mynde in this matter, you shal cōfesse your selfe that you do rebuke this thing more thā ye nede, rather then you shal fynde that any man may spende by anye possibilittie, more tyme in shotinge then he ought. For first and formoost the hole tyme is deuyded into .ii. partes, the daye and the night : whereof the night maye be both occupyed in many honest businesses, and also spent in moche vnthriftinesse, but in no wise it can be

applyed to shoting. And here you se that halfe oure tyme,
graunted to all other thinges in a maner both good and ill, is at
one swappe quite taken awaye from shoting. Now let vs go
forward, and se how moche of halfe this tyme of ours is spē̃t in
shoting. The hole yere is deuided into .iiii. partes, Spring
tyme, Somer, faule of the leafe, and winter wherof the whole
winter, for the roughnesse of it, is cleane taken away from
shoting : except it be one day amonges .xx. or one yeare
amonges .xl. In Somer, for the feruent heate, a man maye
saye likewyse : except it be somtyme agaynst night. Now
then spring tyme and faule of the leafe be those which we
abuse in shoting. But if we consider how mutable & chaunge-
able the wether is in those seasons, and howe that Aristotle him
selfe sayth, that mooste parte of rayne fauleth in these two
tymes : we shall well perceyue, that where a man wolde shote
one daye, he shall be fayne to leaue of .iiii. Now when tyme
it selfe graū̃teth vs but a litle space to shote in, lette vs se if
shoting be not hindered amonges all kyndes of men as moche
otherwayes. First, yong childrē̃ vse not, yong men for feare of
them whom they be vnder to moche dare not : sage men for
other greater businesses, wyll not : aged men for lacke of
strengthe, can not : Ryche men for couetousnesse sake, care
not : poore men for cost and charge, may not : masters for their
housholde keping, hede not : seruaū̃tes kept in by their maisters
very oft, shall not : craftes men for getting of their lyuing, verye
moche leysure haue not : and many there be that oft beginnes,
but for vnaptnesse proues not : and moost of all, whiche when
they be shoters gyue it ouer and lyste not, so that generallye
men euerye where for one or other consideration moche shoting
vse not. Therfore these two thinges, straytenesse of tyme,
and euery man his trade of liuing, are the causes that so fewe
men shotes : as you maye se in this greate towne, where as
there be a thousande good mens bodies, yet scarse .x. yᵗ vseth
any great shoting. And those whome you se shote the moost,
with how many thinges are the[y] drawen, or rather driuen, frō̃
shoting. For first, as it is many a yere or they begyn to be
greate shoters, euen so the greate heate of shotinge is gone
within a yere or two : as you knowe diuerse Philologe your
selfe, which were sometyme the best shoters, and now they be
the best studentes.

If a man faule sycke, farewell shoting, maye fortune as long as he lyueth. If he haue a wrentche, or haue takē colde in his arme, he may hang vp his bowe (I warraunt you) for one season. A litle blayne, a small cutte, yea a silie poore worme in his finger, may kepe him from shoting wel ynough. Breaking and ill luck in bowes I wyll passe ouer, with an hūdred mo sere thinges, whiche chaunceth euerye daye to them that shote moost, wherof the leest of them may compell a man to leaue shoting. And these thinges be so trewe and euident, that it is impossible either for me craftelye to fayne them, or els for you iustly to deny thē. Thā seing how many hundred thinges are required altogyther to giue a man leaue to shote, and any one of thē denied, a mā can not shote : and seing euery one of them maye chaunce, and doth chaunce euery day, I meruayle anye wyse man wyll thynke it possible, that any greate tyme can be spent in shoting at all.

PHI. If this be true that you saye Toxophile, and F in very dede I can denye nothinge of it, I meruayle greatly how it chaunceth, that those, whiche vse shoting be so moche marked of men, and ofttymes blamed for it, and yᵗ in a maner as moche as those which pleye at cardes and dise. And I shal tell you what I hearde spoken *Cardes and dyse.* of the same matter. A man no shoter, (not longe agoo) wolde defende playing at cardes & dise, if it were honestly vsed, to be as honest a pastime as youre shotinge : For he layed for him, that a man might pleye for a litle at cardes and dyse, and also a man might shote away all that euer he had. He sayd a payre of cardes cost not past .ii.d. and that they neded not so moche reparation as bowe and shaftes, they wolde neuer hurte a man his hande, nor neuer weare his gere. A man shulde neuer slee a man with shoting wyde at the cardes. In wete and drye, hote and coulde, they woulde neuer forsake a man, he shewed what great varietie there is in them for euerye mans capacitie : if one game were harde, he myght easelye learne an other : if a man haue a good game, there is greate pleasure in it : if he haue an ill game, the payne is shorte, for he maye soone gyue it ouer, and hope for a better : with many other mo reasons. But at the last he concluded, that betwixt playinge and shoting, well vsed or ill vsed, there was no difference : but that there was lesse coste and trouble, and a greate deale more pleasure in playing, then in shotynge.

TOX. I can not deny, but shoting (as all other good thinges) may be abused.   And good thinges vngoodlye vsed, are not good, sayeth an honorable bishoppe in an ernester matter then this is : yet we muste beware that we laye not mennes faultes vpō the thing which is not worthie, for so nothing shulde be good.   And as for shoting, it is blamed and marked of men for that thing (as I sayde before) which shoulde be rather a token of honestie to prayse it, then any signe of noughtinesse to disalowe it, and that is bycause it is in euerye man his sight, it seketh no corners, it hydeth it not : if there be neuer so litle fault in it, euerye man seeth it, it accuseth it selfe.   For one houre spente in shoting is more sene and further talked of, then .xx. nightes spent in dysing, euen as a litle white stone is sene amonges .iii. hundred blacke.   Of those that blame shotinge and shoters, I wyll saye nomore at this tyme but this, that beside that they stoppe and hinder shoting, which the kinges grace wolde haue forwarde, they be not moche vnlyke in this poynt to Wyll' Somer the king his foole, which smiteth him that standeth alwayes before his face, be he neuer so worshipfull a man, and neuer greatly lokes for him whiche lurkes behinde an other man his backe, that hurte him in dede.

But to him that compared gamning with shoting somewhat wyll I answere, and bycause he went afore me in a cōparison : and comparisons sayth learned men, make playne matters : I wyl surely folowe him in the same.   Honest thynges (sayeth Plato) be knowen from vnhonest thinges, by this *In phedro.*   difference, vnhonestie hath euer present pleasure in it, hauing neyther good pretence going before, nor yet any profit folowing after; which saying descrybeth generallye, bothe the nature of shooting & gamning whiche is good, and which is euyl, verie well.

Gamninge hath ioyned with it, a vayne presente pleasure, but there foloweth, losse of name, losse of goodes, and winning of an hundred gowtie, dropsy diseases, as euery man can tell. Shoting is a peynfull pastime, wherof foloweth health of body quiknes of witte, habilitie to defende oure countrye, as our enemies can beare recorde.

Loth I am to compare these thinges togyther, & yet I do it not bicause there is any comparison at al betwixte them, but therby a man shal se how good the one is, howe euil the other.

For I thinke ther is scarse so muche contrariousnes, betwixte hotte and colde, vertue & vice, as is betwixte these .ii. thinges: For what so euer is in the one, the cleane contrarye is in the other, as shall playnlye appere, if we consider, bothe theyr beginnynges, theyr encreasynges, theyr fructes, and theyr endes, whiche I wyl soone rydde ouer.

❡ The fyrste brynger in to the worlde of shootynge, was Apollo, whiche for his wisdome, & great com- *Pla. ī symp.* modities, brought amonges men by him, was estemed worthie, to be counted as a God in heauen. Disyng surely is a bastarde borne, because it is said to haue .ii. fathers, and yet bothe noughte: The one was an vngracious God, called *Theuth*, which for his noughtines, came *Plato In Phedro.* neuer in other goddes companyes, and therfore Homer doth despise onse to name him, in all his workes. The other father was a Lydian borne, whiche people for suche gamnes, and other vnthriftines, as *Herodot. in Clio.* boowlyng and hauntyng of tauernes, haue bene euer had in most vile reputation, in all storyes and writers.

The Fosterer vp of shoting is Labour, yᵉ companion of vertue, the maynteyner of honestie, the encreaser of health and welthinesse, whiche admytteth nothinge in a maner in to his companye, that standeth not, with vertue and honestie, and therefore sayeth the oulde poete Epicharmus very pretelye in Xenophon, that God selleth vertue, & all other good thinges to men for labour. The Nource of *Xen. de dict. & fact. Soc.* dise and cardes, is werisom Ydlenesse, enemy of vertue, yᵉ drowner of youthe, that tarieth in it, and as Chauser doth saye verie well in the Parsons tale, the greene path waye to hel, hauinge this thing appropriat vnto it, that where as other vices haue some cloke of honestie, onely ydlenes can neyther do wel, nor yet thinke wel. Agayne, shooting hath two Tutours to looke vpon it, out of whose companie, shooting neuer stirreth, the one called Daye light, yᵉ other Open place, whyche .ii. keepe shooting from euyl companye, and suffers it not to haue to much swinge, but euermore kepes it vnder awe, that it darre do nothyng in the open face of the worlde, but that which is good and honest. Lykewyse, dysinge and cardynge, haue .ii. Tutours, the one named Solitariousenes, whyche lurketh in holes and corners, the other called Night an vngratiouse couer of noughtynesse, whyche two thynges be very Inkepers & receyuers of all noughtynesse and noughtye thinges, and therto they be in a maner, ordeyned by Nature. For on the nighte tyme & in corners, Spirites and theues, rattes and mise, toodes and oules, nyghtecrowes and poulcattes, foxes and foumerdes, with all other vermine, and noysome beastes, vse mooste styrringe, when in the daye lyght, and in open places whiche be ordeyned of God for honeste thynges, they darre not ones come, whiche thinge Euripides noted verye well, sayenge.

Il thinges the night, good thinges the daye doth haunt & vse.
Iphi. ī Tau.

Companions of shoting, be prouidens, good heed giuing, true meatinge, honest comparison, whyche thinges agree with vertue very well. Cardinge and dysinge, haue a sorte of good felowes also, goynge commonly in theyr companye, as blynde Fortune, stumbling chaunce, spittle lucke, false dealyng, crafty conueyaunce, braynlesse brawlynge, false forswerynge, whiche good feloes wyll sone take a man by the sleue, and cause him take his Inne, some wᵗ beggerye, some wyth goute & dropsie, some with thefte and robbery, & seldome they wyl leaue a man before he comme eyther to hangyng or els somme other extreme misery. To make an ende, howe shoting by al mennes lawes hath bene alowed, cardyng and dysing by al mennes iudgementes condemned, I nede not shewe the matter is so playne.

Therfore, whan the Lydians shall inuent better thinges than Apollo, when slothe and ydlenes shall encrease vertue more than labour, whan the nyghte and lurking corners, giueth lesse occasion to vnthriftinesse, than lyght daye and opennes, than shal shotynge and suche gamninge, be in sūme comparison lyke. Yet euen as I do not shewe all the goodnes, whiche is in shotynge, whan I proue it standeth by the same thinges that vertue it selfe standeth by, as brought in by God, or Godlyelyke men, fostered by labour, committed to the sauegarde of lyght and opennes, accompanied with prouision and diligens, loued and allowed by euery good mannes sentence, Euen lykewyse do I not open halfe the noughtines whiche is in cardyng & dising, whan I shewe howe they are borne of a desperate mother, norished in ydlenes, encresed by licence of nyght and corners, accompanied wyth Fortune, chaunce, deceyte, & craftines: condemned and banished, by all lawes & iudgementes.

For if I woulde enter, to descrybe the monstruousenes of it, I shoulde rather wander in it, it is so brode, than haue any readye passage to the ende of the matter: whose horriblenes is so large, that it passed the eloquence of oure Englyshe Homer, to compasse it: yet because I euer thought hys sayinges to haue as muche authoritie, as eyther Sophocles or Euripides in Greke, therfore gladly do I remember these verses of hys.

Hasardry is Very mother of lesinges,
And of deceyte, and cursed sweringes,
Blasphemie of Ch[r]ist, manslaughter, and vvaste also,
Of catel of tyme, of other thynges mo.

¶ *Mother of lesinges*) trulye it maye well be called so, if a man consydre howe manye wayes, and how many thinges, he loseth thereby, for firste he loseth his goodes, he loseth his tyme, he loseth quycknes of wyt, and all good lust to other thinges, he loseth honest companye, he loseth his good name and estimation, and at laste, yf he leaue it not, loseth God, & heauen and all: and in stede of these thinges winneth at length, eyther hangyng or hell.

¶ *And of deceyte*) I trowe if I shoulde not lye, there is not halfe so muche crafte vsed in no one thinge in the worlde, as in this cursed thynge. What false dise vse they? as dise stopped with quicksiluer and heares, dise of a vauntage, flattes, gourdes to chop and chaunge whan they lyste, to lette the trew dise fall vnder the table, & so take vp the false, and if they be true dise, what shyfte wil they make to set ye one of them with slyding, with cogging, with foysting, with coytinge as they call it. Howe wyll they vse these shiftes, whan they get a playne man that can no skyll of them? Howe will they go about, yf they perceyue an honest man haue money, which list not playe, to prouoke him to playe? They wyl seke his company, they wil let hym paye nought, yea and as I hearde a man ones saye that he dyd, they wil send for hym to some house & spend perchaunce, a crown on him, and at last wyll one begin to saye: what my masters, what shall we do? shall euerye man playe his .xii. d. whyles an apple roste in the fyre, and than we wyll drinke & departe: Naye wyl an other saye, as false as he, you

can not leaue whan you begyn, and therfore I wyll not playe:
but yet yf you wyll gage, that euery man as he hath lost his
.xii. d. shall sit downe, I am content, for surely I woulde winne
no mannes money here, but euen as much as wolde paye for
mye supper.   Than speketh the thyrde, to the honest man that
thought not to playe, what wylle you playe your .xii. pence if
he excuse hym, tush man wyll the other saye, sticke not in
honest company for xii. d. I wyll beare your halfe, and here
is my mony.

Nowe al this is to make him to beginne, for they knowe if
he be ones in, and be a looser, y^t he wyl not sticke at his .xii.
d. but hopeth euer to gette it agayne, whiles perhaps, he loose
all.   Than euery one of them setteth his shiftes abroche, some
w^t false dise, some wyth settynge of dyse, some with hauinge
outelandishe syluer coynes guylded, to put away at a tyme for
good gold.   Than yf ther come a thing in controuersie, muste
you be iudged by the table, and than farewell the honest man
hys parte, for he is borne downe on euerye syde.

Nowe sir, besyde all these thinges they haue certayne
termes, as a man woulde saye, appropriate to theyr playing:
wherby they wyl drawe a mannes money, but paye none,
whiche they cal barres, that surely he that knoweth them not,
maye soone be debarred of all that euer he hath, afore he lerne
them.   Yf a playne man lose, as he shall do euer, or els it is a
wonder, than the game is so deuilysh, that he can neuer leaue:
For vayn hope (which hope sayth Euripides, destroyeth many
In suppli.   a man and Citie) dryueth hym on so farre, that
            he can neuer retourne backe, vntyl he be so lyght,
that he nede feare no theues by the waye.   Nowe if a simple
man happen onse in his lyfe, to win of suche players, than will
they eyther entreate him to kepe them company whyles he
hath lost all agayne, or els they will vse the moste dyuellyshe
fashion of all, For one of the players that standeth nexte him,
shall haue a payre of false dise, and cast them out vpon the
bourde, the honest man shall take them & cast them, as he did
the other, the thirde shall espye them to be false dise, and shall
crye oute, haroe, wyth all the othes vnder God, that he hath
falselye wonne theyr moneye, and than there is nothynge but
houlde thy throte from my dagger, than euery man layeth
hande on the simple man, and taketh all theyr moneye from

him, and his owne also, thinking himselfe wel, that he scapeth
with his lyfe.

Cursed swerying, blasphemie of Christe.) These halfe verses
Chaucer in an other place, more at large doth well set out, and
verye liuely expresse, sayinge.

> *Ey by goddes precious hert and his nayles*
> *And by the blood of Christe, that is in Hales,*
> *Seuen is my chaunce, and thine is sinke and treye,*
> *Ey goddes armes, if thou falsly playe,*
> *This dagger shall thorough thine herte go*
> *This frute commeth of the beched boones twoo*
> *Forsweringe, Ire, falsnes and Homicide. &c.*

Thoughe these verses be very ernestlie wrytten, yet they do
not halfe so grisely sette out the horyblenes of blasphemy, which
suche gamners vse, as it is in dede, and as I haue hearde my
selfe.   For no man can wryte a thing so earnestlye, as whan it
is spokē wyth iesture, as learned men you knowe do saye.
Howe will you thinke that suche furiousenes wyth woode
countenaunces, and brenning eyes, with staringe and bragging,
with heart redie to leape out of the belly for swelling, can be
expressed yᵉ tenth part, to the vttermost.   Two men I herd
my selfe, whose sayinges be far more grisely, than Chaucers
verses.   One, whan he had lost his moneye, sware me God,
from top to toe with one breath, that he had lost al his money
for lacke of sweringe : The other, losyng his money, and
heaping othes vpon othes, one in a nothers necke, moost
horrible & not spekeable, was rebuked of an honest man whiche
stode, by for so doynge, he by and by starynge him in the face,
and clappyng his fiste with all his moneye he had, vpon the
boorde, sware me by the flesshe of God, that yf sweryng woulde
helpe him but one ace, he woulde not leue one pece of god
vnsworne, neyther wythin nor without.   The remembraūce of
this blasphemy Philologe, doth make me quake at the hart,
& therefore I wyll speake no more of it.

And so to conclude wyth suche gamnying, I thynke there
is no vngraciousenes in all thys worlde, that carieth so far from
god, as thys faulte doth.   And yf there were anye so desperate
a persone, that woulde begynne his hell here in earth, I trowe
he shoulde not fynde hell more lyke hell it selfe, then the lyfe

of those men is which dayly haunt and vse suche vngracious games. PHIL. You handle this gere in dede : And I suppose if ye had ben a prentice at suche games, you coulde not haue sayd more of them then you haue done, and by lyke you haue had somwhat to do with them. TOX. In dede, you may honestlye gather that I hate them greatly, in that I speake agaynst them : not that I haue vsed them greatlye, in that I speake of them. For thynges be knowen dyuerse wayes, as Socrates (you knowe) doeth proue in Alcibiades. And if euery man shulde be that, that he speaketh or wryteth vpō, then shulde Homer haue bene the best capitayne, moost cowarde, hardye, hasty, wyse and woode, sage and simple : And Terence an ouldeman & a yong, an honest man and a bawde : with suche lyke. Surelye euerye man ought to praye to God dayly, to kepe them frō suche unthriftynesse, and speciallye all the youth of Englande : for what youth doth begynne, a man wyll

Euripides in suppli. folowe cōmonlye, euen to his dyinge daye : whiche thinge Adrastus in Euripides pretelye doth expresse, sayinge.

VVhat thing a man in tender age hath most in vre
That same to death always to kepe he shal be sure
Therfore in age who greatly longes good frute to mowe
In youth he must him selfe aplye good seede to sowe.

For the foundation of youth well sette (as Plato doth saye) the whole bodye of the commune wealth shal floryshe therafter. If the yonge tree growe croked, when it is oulde, a man shal rather breake it thā streyght it. And I thinke there is no one thinge yᵗ crokes youth more then suche vnlefull games. Nor let no mā say, if they be honestly vsed they do no harme. For how can that pastyme whiche neither exerciseth the bodye with any honest labour, nor yet the minde with any honest thinking, haue any honestie ioyned with it. Nor let noman assure hym selfe that he can vse it honestlye : for if he stande therein, he may fortune haue a faule, the thing is more slipperye then he knoweth of. A man maye (I graunt) syt on a brante hyll syde, but if he gyue neuer so lytle forwarde, he can not stoppe though he woulde neuer so fayne, but he must nedes runne heedling, he knoweth not how farre. What honest pretences, vayne pleasure layeth dayly (as it were entisemētes or baytes, to pull men forwarde withall) Homer doeth well shewe, by the Sirenes, and Circes. And amonges all in that shyp there was but one Vlysses, and yet he hadde done to as the other dyd, yf a goddesse had not taught hym : And so lykewyse I thinke, they be easye to numbre, whiche passe by playing honestlye, excepte the grace of God saue and kepe them. Therfore they that wyll not go to farre in playing, let them folowe this coūsell of the Poete.

Stoppe the begynninges.

PHILOLO. Well, or you go any further, I pray you tell me this one thing : Doo ye speake agaynste meane mennes playinge onelye, or agaynste greate mennes playinge to, or put you anye difference betwixte them? TOXOPHI. If I shulde excuse my selfe herein, and saye that I spake of the one, and not of the other, I feare leaste I shoulde as fondlye excuse my selfe, as a certayne preacher dyd, whome I hearde vpon a tyme speake agaynste manye abuses, (as he sayde) and at last he spake agaynst candelles, and then he fearynge, least some men woulde haue bene angrye and offended with him, naye sayeth he, you must take me as I meane: I speake not agaynst greate candelles, but agaynst lytle candels, for they be not all one (φ he) I promyse you: And so euerye man laughed him to scorne.

In dede as for greate men, and greate mennes matters, I lyst not greatlye to meddle. Yet this I woulde wysshe that all great men in Englande had red ouer diligentlye the Pardoners tale in Chaucer, and there they shoulde perceyue and se, howe moche suche games stande with theyr worshyppe, howe great soeuer they be. What great men do, be it good or yll, meane men communelye loue to followe, as many learned men in many places do saye, and daylye experience doth playnelye shewe, in costlye apparell and other lyke matters.

Therfore, seing that Lordes be lanternes to leade the lyfe of meane men, by their example, eyther to goodnesse or badnesse, to whether soeuer they liste : and seinge also they haue libertie to lyste what they will, I pray God they haue will to list that which is good, and as for their playing, I wyll make an ende with this saying of Chaucer.

Lordes might finde them other maner of pleye
Honest ynough to driue the daye away.

But to be shorte, the best medicine for all sortes of men both high and lowe, yonge and oulde, to put awaye suche vnlawfull games is by the contrarye, lykewyse as all physicions do alowe in physike. So let youthe in steade of suche vnlefull games, whiche stande by ydlenesse, by solitarinesse, and corners, by night and darkenesse, by fortune & chaunce, by crafte and subtiltie, vse suche pastimes as stand by labour : vpon the daye light, in open syght of men, hauynge suche an ende as is come to by cōning, rather then by crafte : and so shulde vertue encrease, and vice decaye. For contrarye pastimes, must nedes worke contrary mindes in men, as all other contrary thinges doo.

And thus we se Philologe, that shoting is not onely the moost holesome exercise for the bodye, the moost honest pastime for the mynde, and that for all sortes of men : But also it is a moost redy medicine, to purge the hole realme of suche pestilent gamning, wherw^t many tymes it is sore troubled and ill at ease.

PHI. The more honestie you haue proued by shoting *Toxophile*, and the more you haue perswaded me to loue it, so moche truly the soryer haue you made me with this last sentence of yours, wherby you plainly proue that a man maye not greatly vse it. For if shoting be a medicine (as you saye that it is) it maye not be vsed very oft, lest a man shuld hurt him selfe with all, as medicines moche occupyed doo. For Aristotle him selfe sayeth, that medicines be no meate to lyue withall : and thus shoting by the same reason, maye not be moche occupyed.

TOX. You playe your oulde wontes Philologe, in dalying with other mens wittes, not so moche to proue youre owne matter, as to proue what other mē can say. But where you thinke that I take awaye moche vse of shoting, in lykening it to a medicine : bycause men vse not medicines euery daye, for so shoulde their bodyes be hurt : I rather proue daylye vse of shoting therby. For although Aristotle sayeth that some medicines be no meate to lyue withall, whiche is true : Yet Hippocrates sayth that our daylye meates be medicines, to withstande euyll withall, whiche is as true. For he maketh two kyndes of medicines, one our meate that we vse dailye, whiche purgeth softlye and slowlye, and in this similitude maye shoting be called a medicine,

Hippo. de
med. purg.

wherwith dayly a man maye purge and take away al vnlefull de-
syres to other vnlefull pastymes, as I proued before. The other is
a quicke purging medicine, and seldomer to be occupyed, excepte
the matter be greater, and I coulde describe the nature of a quicke
medicine, which shoulde within a whyle purge and plucke oute all
the vnthriftie games in the Realme, through which the commune
wealth oftentymes is sycke. For not onely good quicke wittes
to learnyng be thereby brought out of frame, and quite marred :
but also manlye wittes, either to attempt matters of high courage
in warre tyme, or els to atcheue matters of weyght and wisdome
in peace tyme, be made therby very quaisie and faynt. For
loke throughoute all histories written in Greke, Latyne, or other
language, and you shal neuer finde that realme prosper in the
whiche suche ydle pastymes are vsed. As concerning the
medicyne, although some wolde be miscontent, if they hearde
me meddle anye thynge with it : Yet betwixte you and me
here alone, I maye the boldlyer saye my fantasie, and the rather
bycause I wyll onelye wysh for it, whiche standeth with
honestie, not determyne of it which belongeth to authoritie.
The medicine is this, that wolde to God and the kynge, all
these vnthriftie ydle pastymes, whiche be very bugges, that the
Psalme meaneth on, walking on the nyght and in
corners, were made felonye, and some of that   *Psalm.* 90.
punyshment ordeyned for them, which is appoynted for the
forgers and falsifyers of the kynges coyne. Which punishment
is not by me now inuented, but longe agoo, by
the mooste noble oratour Demosthenes : which   *Demost. cō-*
meruayleth greatly that deathe is appoynted for   *tra Leptinē.*
falsifyers and forgers of the coyne, and not as great punysh-
mente ordeyned for them, whiche by theyr meanes forges and
falsifyes the commune wealthe. And I suppose that there is
no one thyng that chaungeth sooner the golden and syluer
wyttes of men into copperye & brassye wayes then dising and
suche vnlefull pastymes.

And this quicke medicine I beleue wolde so throwlye pourge
them, that the daylye medicines, as shoting and other pastymes
ioyned with honest labour shoulde easelyer withstande them.
PHIL. The excellent commodityes of shotynge in peace tyme,
Toxophile, you haue very wel and sufficiently declared. Wherby
you haue so persuaded me, that God wyllyng hereafter I wyll

both loue it the better, and also vse it the ofter. For as moche
as I can gather of all this communication of ours, the tunge,
the nose, the handes and the feete be no fytter membres, or
instrumentes for the body of a man, then is shotinge for the
hole bodye of the realme. God hath made the partes of men
which be best and moost neccessarye, to serue, not for one
purpose onelye, but for manye: as the tungue for speaking and
tasting, the nose for smelling, and also for auoyding of all
excremētes, which faule oute of the heed, the handes for
receyuynge of good thinges, and for puttyng of all harmefull
thinges, from the bodye. So shotinge is an exercyse of healthe,
a pastyme of honest pleasure, and suche one also that stoppeth
or auoydeth all noysome games gathered and encreased by ill
rule, as noughtye humours be, whiche hurte and corrupte sore
that parte of the realme, wherin they do remayne.

But now if you can shewe but halfe so moche profyte in
warre of shotynge, as you haue proued pleasure in peace, then
wyll I surelye iudge that there be fewe thinges that haue so
manifolde commodities, and vses ioyned vnto them as it hath.

G   TOX. The vpperhande in warre, nexte the goodnesse of
God (of whome al victorie commeth, as scripture sayth)
standeth chefelye in thre thinges : in the wysedome of the
Prince, in the sleyghtes and pollicies of the
Mach. 1. 3.   capitaynes, and in the strength and cherefull
forwardnesse of the souldyers. A Prince in his herte must
be full of mercy and peace, a vertue moost pleasaunt to Christ,
moost agreable to mans nature, moost profytable for ryche
and poore.

For thā the riche man enioyeth with great pleasure that
which he hath: the poore may obtayne with his labour, that
which he lacketh.   And although there is nothing worse then
war, wherof it taketh his name, through the which great men
be in daunger, meane men without succoure, ryche men in
feare, bycause they haue somwhat : poore men in care, bycause
they haue nothing: And so euery man in thought and miserie :
Yet it is a ciuill medicine, wherewith a prince maye from the
bodye of his commune wealth, put of that daunger whiche maye
faule: or elles recouer agayne, whatsoeuer it hath lost.   And
therfore as Isocrates doth saye, a prince must be
Ad Nico.   a warriour in two thinges, in conninge and know-

ledge of all sleyghtes and feates of warre, and in hauing al
necessarye habilimentes belongyng to the same. Whiche matter
to entreate at large, were ouerlonge at this tyme to declare, &
ouermoche for my learning to perfourme.

After the wisdome of the prince, are valiaunt capitaynes
moost necessary in warre, whose office and dutye is to knowe
all sleightes and pollicies for all kyndes of warre, which they
maye learne .ii. wayes, either in daylye folowing and haunting
the warres or els bicause wisdome bought with strypes, is many
tymes ouercostlye : they maye bestowe some tyme in Vegetius,
which entreateth suche matters in Latin metelye well, or rather
in Polyçnus, and Leo the Emperour, which setteth out al pollicies
and duties of capitaynes in the Greke tunge very excellentlye.
But chefely I wolde wisshe and (if I were of authoritie) I wolde
counsel al the yong gentlemen of this realme, neuer to lay out
of theyr handes .ii. authors Xenophon in Greke, and Cçsar in
Latyn, where in they shulde folowe noble Scipio
Africanus, as Tullie doeth saye: In whiche .ii. *De Sen.*
authours, besydes eloquence a thing moste necessary of all
other, for a captayne, they shulde learne the hole course of
warre, whiche those .ii. noble menne dyd not more wyselye
wryte for other men to learne, than they dyd manfully excercise
in the fyelde, for other men to folowe.

The strengthe of war lyeth in the souldier, whose chyefe
prayse and vertue, is obedience towarde his
captayne, sayth Plato. And Xenophon being a *Obedience.*
gentyle authour, moste christianlye doeth saye, *Plat. leg.* 12.
euen by these woordes, that that souldyer whiche *Xen. Ages.*
firste serueth god, & than obeyeth hys captayne, maye boldelie
with all courage, hope to ouerthrowe his enemy. Agayne, wᵗout
obedience, neither valiant man, stout horse, nor
goodly harnes doth any good at al. Which obedi- *Xen. Hippar.*
ence of yᵉ souldier toward his captane, brought the hole empyre
of yᵉ worlde, into the Romanes hãdes, & whan it was brought,
kepte it lenger, than euer it was kept in any cõmon welth
before or after.

And this to be true, Scipio Africanus, the moste noble
captayne that euer was amonge the Romaynes, *Plutarchus*
shewed very playnly, what tyme as he went in to
Afryke, to destroye Cartage. For he restinge hys hooste by

the waye in Sicilie, a daye or twoo, and at a tyme standing
with a great man of Sicilie, and looking on his souldiers howe
they exercised them selues in kepyng of araye, and other feates,
the gentleman of Sicilie asked Scipio, wherein laye hys chyefe
hope to ouercome Cartage : He answered, in yonder feloes of
myne, whom you se play : And why sayth the other, bycause
sayeth Scipio, that if I cōmaunded them to runne in to the
toppe of this high castel, and cast them selues doune backeward
vpon these rockes, I am sure the[y] woulde do it.

  Salust also doth write, yᵗ there were mo Romanes put to
Sal. in. Cat.   death of theyr captaynes for setting on theyr
      enemyes before they had licence, than were for
running away out of the fyelde, before they had foughten.
These two examples do proue, that amonges the Romaynes,
the obedience of the souldyer was wonderfull great, and the
seueritie of the Captaynes, to se the same kepte wonderfull
strayte.   For they wel perceyued that an hoste full of obedyence,
falleth as seldome into the handes of theyr enemies as that
bodye fawleth into Jeoperdye, the whiche is ruled by reason.
Reason and Rulers beynge lyke in offyce, (for the one ruleth
the body of man, the other ruleth the bodye of the cōmon
wealthe) ought to be lyke of condicions, and oughte to be
obeyed in all maner of matters.   Obedience is nourysshed by
feare and loue, Feare is kepte in by true iustice and equitie,
Loue is gotten by wisdome, ioyned wᵗ liberalitie : For where
a souldyer seeth ryghteousenesse so rule, that a man can neyther
do wronge nor yet take wronge, and that his capitayne for his
wysedome, can mayntayne hym, & for his liberalitie will
mayntayne him, he must nedes both loue him & feare him,
of the whiche procedeth true & vnfayned obedience.   After
this inwarde vertue, the nexte good poynt in a souldier, is to
haue and to handle his weapō wel, whereof the one must be at
the appoyntment of the captayne, the other lyeth in the courage
and exercise of the souldier : yet of al weapōs the best is, as
In Herc. fu.   Euripides doth say, wherwᵗ with leest daūger of
     our self we maye hurt our enemye moost.   And
that is (as I suppose) artillarie.   Artillarie now a dayes is taken
for .ii. thinges : Gunnes & Bowes, which how moch they do in
war, both dayly experience doeth teache, and also Peter Nānius
a learned man of Louayn, in a certayne dialoge doth very well

set out, wherin this is most notable, that when he hath shewed excedyng commodities of both, and some discōmodities of gunnes, as infinite cost and charge, combersome carriage : and yf they be greate, the vncertayne leuelyng, the peryll of them that stand by them, the esyer auoydyng by them that stande far of : & yf they be lytle, the lesse both feare and ieoperdy is in them, besyde all contrary wether and wynde, whiche hyndereth them not a lytle : yet of all shotyng he can not reherse one discommoditie. PHI. That I meruayle greatly at, seing Nannius is so well learned, & so exercised in the authours of both the tūges : for I my selfe do remember that shotying in war is but smally praysed, and that of diuers captaynes in dyuers authors. For first in Euripides (whom you so highly prayse) and very well, for Tullie thynketh euerye verse in him to be an authoritie, what I praye you, doth Lycus that ouercame Thebes, say as concernyng shoting ? whose words as farre as I remember, be these, or not muche vnlyke.

What prayse hath he at al, whiche neuer durst abide,
The dint of a speares poynt thrust against his side
Nor neuer bouldlie buckeler bare yet in his lefte hande
Face to face his enemies bront stiffelie to wythstande,   *Eurip. in*
But alwaye trusteth to a bowe and to a fethered sticke   *Herc. furent.*
Harnes euer most fit for him which to flie is quicke,
Bowe and shafte is Armoure metest for a cowarde
Which dare not ones abide the bronte of battel sharpe & harde.
   But he a man of manhode most is by mine assent
Which with harte and corage boulde, fullie hath him bent,
His enemies looke in euery stoure floutelie to a bide,
Face to face, and fote to fote, tide what maye be tide.

Agayne Teucer the best Archer amonges all the Grecians, in Sophocles is called of Menelaus, a boweman, & a shooter as in villaynie and reproche, to be a   *Soph in* thing of no price in warre. Moreouer Pandar⁹   *Aia. flag.* the best shooter in the worlde, whome Apollo hym selfe taught to shoote, bothe he and his shotynge is   *Iliad.* 5. quyte contemned in Homer, in so much that Homer (which vnder a made fable doth alwayes hyde hys iudgement of thinges) doeth make Pandarus him selfe crye out of shooting, and cast his bowe awaye, and take him to a speare,

makynge a vowe that if euer he came home, he woulde breake
his shaftes, & burne his bowe, lamentyng greatly, that he was
so fonde to leaue at home his horse and charyot wyth other
weapons, for the trust y^t he had in his bowe. Homer signifieng
therby, that men shoulde leue shoting out of warre, and take
them to other wepons more fitte and able for the same, and I
trowe Pandarus woordes be muche what after thys sorte.

> *Ill chaunce ill lucke me hyther broughte*
> *Ill fortune me that daye befell,*
> *Whan first my bowe fro the pynne I roughte*
> *For Hectors sake, the Grekes to quell.*
> *But yf that God so for me shap*
> *That home agayne I maye ones come,*
> *Let me neuer inioye that hap,*
> *Nor euer twyse looke on the sonne,*
> *If bowe and shaftes I do not burne*
> *Whyche nowe so euel doth serue my turne.*

But to let passe al Poetes, what can be sorer said agaynst
any thing, than the iudgement of Cyrus is agaynst shotynge,
Xen. Cyri whiche doth cause his Persians beyng the best
Inst. 6. shooters to laye awaye theyr bowes and take them
to sweardes and buckelers, speares and dartes, and
other lyke hande weapons. The which thing Xenophon so
wyse a philosopher, so experte a captayne in warre hym selfe,
woulde neuer haue written, and specially in that booke wherin
he purposed to shewe, as Tullie sayeth in dede, not the true
Epist. 1. ad historie, but the example of a perfite wise prince
Q. Fra. and cōmon welthe, excepte that iudgement of
chaūgyng Artillerie, in to other wepons, he had
always thought best to be folowed, in all warre. Whose
Plutarch counsell the Parthians dyd folowe, whan they
M. Ant. chased Antonie ouer the moūtaines of Media,
whiche being the best shoters of the worlde, lefte
theyr bowes, and toke them to speares and morispikes.
And these fewe examples I trowe, of the best shooters, do
well proue that the best shotinge is not the best thinge as you
call it in warre. TOX. As concernynge your first example,
taken oute of Euripides, I maruayle you wyl bring it for y^e

disprayse of shotyng, seyng Euripides doth make those verses, not bicause he thinketh thē true, but bicause he thinketh them fit for the person that spake them. For in dede his true iudgement of shoting, he doth expresse by & by after in the oratiō of the noble captaine Amphytrio agaynste Lycus, wherein a man maye doubte, whether he hath more eloquentlye confuted Lycus sayenge, or more worthelye sette oute the prayse of shootynge. And as I am aduised, his woordes be muche hereafter as I shall saye.

Against the wittie gifte of shotinge in a bowe   Eurip. in
Fonde and leude woordes thou leudlie doest out throwe,   Herc. fur.
Whiche, if thou wilte heare of me a woorde or twayne
Quicklie thou mayst learne howe fondlie thou doest blame,
  Firste he that with his harneis him selfe doth wal about,
That scarce is lefte one hole through which he may pepe out,
Such bondmen to their harneis to fight are nothinge mete
But sonest of al other are troden vnder fete.
Yf he be stronge, his felovves faynt, in whome he putteth his trust,
So loded with his harneis must nedes lie in the dust,
Nor yet frō death he can not starte, if ones his weapon breke,
Howe stoute, howe strong, howe great, howe longe,
  so euer be suche a freke.
But who so euer can handle a bowe
  sturdie stiffe and stronge
Wherwith lyke hayle manie shaftes he shootes
  into the thickest thronge :
This profite he takes, that stanaing a far
  his enemie he maye spill
Whan he and his full safe shall stande
  out of all daunger and ill.
And this in War is wisedome moste, which
  workes our enemies woo.
Whan we shal be far from all feare
  and ieoperdie of our foo.

Secondarily euen as I do not greatlye regarde what Menelaus doth say in Sophocles to Teucer, bycause he spake it bothe in anger, and also to hym that he hated, euen so doo I remember very well in Homer, that when Hector and the Troians woulde

haue set fyre on the greke shippes, Teucer with his bowe made
them recule backe agayne, when Menelaus tooke
hym to his feete, and ranne awaye.

Iliad. 8.

Thirdlye as concerning Pandarus, Homer doth not disprayse
the noble gyfte of shotynge, but therby euery man is taught,
that whatsoeuer, and how good soeuer a weapon a man doth
vse in war, yf he be hym selfe a couetouse wretche,
a foole wythoute counsell, a peacebreaker as Pandarus was, at last he shall throughe the punishment of God fall
into his enemyes handes, as Pandarus dydde, whome Diomedes
throughe the helpe of Minerua miserablye slue.

Hom. Ili. 5.

And bycause you make mencion of Homer, & Troye
matters, what can be more prayse for anye thynge, I praye
you, than that is for shootyng, that Troye coulde neuer be
destroyed without the helpe of Hercules shaftes, whiche thinge
doeth signifie, that although al the worlde were gathered in an
army togyther, yet without shotinge they can neuer come to
theyr purpose, as Vlysses in Sophocles very plainlye doth saye
vnto Pyrrhus, as concernyng Hercules shaftes to be caried vnto
Troye.

Soph. phil.   *Nor you without them, nor without you they do ought.*

Fourthlye where as Cyrus dyd chaunge parte of his bowemen, wherof he had plentie, into other mē of
warre, wherof he lacked, I will not greatlye
dispute whether Cyrus did well in that poynt in
those dayes or no, bycause it is not playne in Xenophon howe
strong shooters the Persians were, what bowes they had, what
shaftes and heades they occupyed, what kynde of warre theyr
enemies vsed.

Xen. Cyri.
Instit. 6.

But trulye as for the Parthians, it is playne, in Plutarche,
that in chaungyng theyr bowes in to speares, they
brought theyr selfe into vtter destruction. For
when they had chased the Romaynes many a
myle, through reason of theyr bowes, at the last the Romaynes
ashamed of their fleing, and remembrynge theyr owlde noblenesse and courage, ymagined thys waye, that they woulde
kneele downe on theyr knees, and so couer all theyr body wyth
theyr shyldes and targattes, that the Parthians shaftes might
slyde ouer them, & do them no harme, whiche thing when the

Plu. ī M.
Anton.

Partiãs perceyued, thinking that yᵉ Romaynes were forweryed with laboure, watche, and hũgre: they layed downe their bowes, and toke speres in their handes, and so ranne vpon them: but the Romaynes perceyuinge them without their bowes, rose vp manfully, and slewe them euery mother son, saue a fewe that saued them selues with runnyng awaye. And herein our archers of Englande far passe the Parthians, which for suche a purpose, whẽ they shall come to hande strokes, hath euer redy, eyther at his backe hangyng, or els in his next felowes hande a leadẽ maule, or suche lyke weapon, to beate downe his enemyes withall. PHI. Well *Toxophile*, seinge that those examples whiche I had thought to haue ben cleane agaynst shoting, you haue thus turned to the hygh prayse of shotinge: and all this prayse that you haue now sayd on it, is rather come in by me thã sought for of you: let me heare I praye you nowe, those examples whiche you haue marked of shotyng your selfe: whereby you are, and thinke to persuade other, yᵗ shoting is so good in warre. TOX. Exãples surely I haue marked very many: frõ the begynning of tyme had in memorie of wrytyng, throughout all cõmune wealthes, & Empires of the worlde: wherof the mooste part I wyll passe ouer, lest I shoulde be tediouse: yet some I wyll touche, bycause they be notable, bothe for me to tell and you to heare.

And bycause the storye of the Iewes is for the tyme moost auncient, for the truthe mooste credible, it shalbe moost fitte to begynne with them. And although I knowe that God is the onely gyuer of victorie, and not the weapons, for all strength and victorie (sayth Iudas Machabeus) cõmeth from heauen: Yet surely strong weapons be the instru- *Mach.* 1. 3. H
mentes wherwith god doth ouercome yᵗ parte, which he wil haue ouerthrowen. For God is well pleased wyth wyse and wittie feates of warre: As in metinge of enemies, for truse takyng, to haue priuilye in a bushment harnest men layd for feare of treason, as Iudas Machabeus dyd wyth *Mach.* 2. 14. Nicanor Demetrius capitayne: And to haue engines of warre to beat downe cities with all: and to haue scoutwatche amõges our enemyes to knowe their counsayles, as the noble captaine Ionathas brother to Iudas *Mach.* 1. 12. Machabeus did in the countrie of Amathie against the mighty hoste of Demetrius. And besyde al this, god

is pleased to haue goodly tombes for them which do noble feates in warre, and to haue their ymages made, and also their cote Armours to be set aboue theyr tombes, to their perpetual laude and memorie: as the valiaunt capitayne Symon, dyd cause to be made for his brethren Iudas Machabeus and Ionathas, whē they were slayne of the Gētiles. And thus of what authoritie feates of warre, and strong weapons be, shortly and playnelye we maye learne: But amonges the Iewes as I began to tell, I am sure there was nothing so occupyed, or dydde so moche good as bowes dyd: insomoche that when the Iewes had any great vpperhande ouer the Gentiles, the fyrste thinge alwayes that the captayne dyd, was to exhort the people to gyue all the thankes to God for the victorye, & not to theyr bowes, wherwith they had slayne their enemyes: as it is playne that the noble Iosue dyd after so many kynges thrust downe by hym.

Mach. 1. 13.

Iosue. 23.

God, when he promyseth helpe to the Iewes, he vseth no kynde of speakyng so moche as this, that he wyll bende his bowe, and die his shaftes in the Gentiles blood: whereby it is manifest, that eyther God wyll make the Iewes shoote stronge shotes to ouerthrowe their enemies: or at leeste that shotinge is a wōderful mightie thing in warre, whervnto ye hygh power of God is lykened. Dauid in the Psalmes calleth bowes the vessels of death, a bytter thinge, & in an other place a myghty power, and other wayes mo, which I wyll let passe, bycause euerye man readeth them daylye: But yet one place of scripture I must nedes remembre, which is more notable for ye prayse of shoting, then any yᵗ euer I red in any other storie, and that is, when Saul was slayne of ye Philistians being mightie bowmen, and Ionathas his sonne with him, that was so good a shoter, as ye scripture sayth, that he neuer shot shafte in vayne, and yᵗ the kyngdome after Saules deathe came vnto Dauid: the first statute & lawe that euer Dauid made after he was king, was this, that al ye children of Israel shulde learne to shote, according to a lawe made many a daye before yᵗ tyme for the setting out of shoting as it is written (sayeth Scripture) *in libro Iustorum*, whiche booke we haue not nowe: And thus we se plainelye what greate vse of shoting, and what prouision euen

Deutero. 32.

Psal. 7. 63. 75.

Regum. 1. 31.

Regum. 2. 1.

from the begynnynge of the worlde for shotyng, was amonge
the Iewes.

The Ethiopians which inhabite the furthest part South in
the worlde, were wonderfull bowmen : in somoche that when
Cambyses king of Persie being in Egipt, sent
certayne ambassadours into Ethiope to the kynge   *Herodot⁹ in*
there, with many great gyftes : the king of   *Thalia.*
Ethiop perceyuinge them to be espyes, toke them vp sharpely,
and blamed Cambyses greatly for such vniust enterprises : but
after that he had princely entertayned them, he sent for a bowe,
and bente it and drewe it, and then vnbent it agayne, and
sayde vnto the ambassadours, you shall cōmende me to Cambyses, and gyue him this bowe fro me, and byd him when any
Persian can shote in this bowe, let him set vpon the Ethiopians :
In the meane whyle let hym gyue thankes vnto God, whiche
doth not put in the Ethiopiās mynde to cōquere any other
mans lande. This bowe, when it came amonge the Persians,
neuer one man in suche an infinite host (as Herodotus doth
saye) could styrre the stryng, saue onely Smerdis the brother of
Cambyses, whiche styrred it two fingers, and no further : for the
which aꝰt Cambyses had suche enuy at him, that he afterward
slewe him : as doth appeare in the storye.

Sesostris the moost mightie king that euer was in Egipt, ouercame a great parte of the worlde, and that by archers : he subdued
the Arabians, the Iues, the Assyrians : he wēt farther into Scythia
then any man els : he ouercame Thracia, euen to the borders of
Germanie. And in token how he ouercame al men he set vp in
many places great ymages to his owne lykenesse, hauynge in the
one hande a bowe, in the other a sharpe heeded   *Herod. in*
shafte : that men myght knowe, what weapon   *Euterpe.*
his hooste vsed, in conqueryng so manye people.   *Diod. Sic.* 2

Cyrus, counted as a god amonges the Gentyles, for his
noblenesse and felicitie in warre : yet at the last   *Herod. ī clio.*
when he set vpon the Massagetanes (which people
neuer went without their bowe nor their quiuer, nether in
warre nor peace) he and all his were slayne, and that by
shotyng, as appeareth in the storye.

Polycrates the prince of Samos (a very little yle) was lorde ouer
all the Greke sees, and withstode the power of the   *Herod. ī that*
Persians, onely by the helpe of a thousande archers.

The people of Scythia, of all other men loued, and vsed moost shotyng, the hole rychesse and householde stuffe of a man in Scythia, was a yocke of oxen, a plough, his nagge and his dogge, his bowe and his quiuer: which quiuer was couered with the skynne of a man, which he toke or slewe fyrste in battayle. The Scythians to be inuincible by reason of their shotyng, the greate voyages of so manye noble conquerours spent in that countrie in vayne, doeth well proue: But specially that of Darius the myghtie kyng of Persie, which when he had taryed there a great space, and done no good, but had forweryed his hoste with trauayle and hunger: At last the men of Scythia sent an ambassadour with .iiii.

Herod. in Melpomen. gyftes: a byrde, a frogge, a mouse, and .v. shaftes. Darius meruaylyng at the straungenesse of the gyftes, asked the messenger what they signifyed: the messenger answered, that he had no further cōmaundement, but onely to delyuer his gyftes, and retourne agayne with all spede: but I am sure (sayeth he) you Persians for your great wysdome, can soone boult out what they meane. When the messenger was gone, euery man began to say his verdite. Darius Iudgement was this, that ye Scythians gaue ouer into the Persians handes, their lyues, theyr hole power, both by lande and see, signifyinge by the mouse the earthe, by the frogge the water, in which they both liue, by ye birde their lyues which lyue in the ayer, by the shaft their hole power and Empire, that was maynteyned alwayes by shotinge. Gobryas a noble and wyse captayne amonges the Persians, was of a cleane cōtrary minde, saying, nay not so, but the Sythiās meane thus by their gyftes, that except we get vs wynges, and flye into the ayer lyke birdes, or run into ye holes of the earth lyke myse, or els lye lurkyng in fennes & marisses lyke frogges, we shall neuer returne home agayne, before we be vtterly vndone with their shaftes: which sentence sanke so sore into their hertes, yᵗ Darius with all spede possible, brake vp his campe, and gat hym

Herod. ī clio. selfe homewarde. Yet howe moche the Persians
Xenoph. in them selues set by shotinge, wherby they en-
cyrop. creased their empire so moche, doth appeare by
Strab. 11. .iii. manifest reasons: firste that they brought vppe theyr youth in the schole of shoting, vnto .xx. yere of age, as dyuerse noble Greke authours do saye.

Agayne, bycause the noble kyng Darius thought hym selfe to be praysed by nothyng so moch, as to be counted a good shoter, as doth appeare by his sepulchre, wherin he caused to be written this sentence :

> *Darius the King lieth buried here*   *Strab.* 15.
> *That in shoting and riding had neuer pere.*

Thirdlye the coyne of the Persians, both golde & siluer had the Armes of Persie vpon it, as is customably vsed in other realmes, and that was bow and arowes :   *Plutarch. in* by the which feate they declared, how moch they   *Agesila.* set by them.

The Grecians also, but specially the noble Athenienses, had all their strength lyinge in Artillarie : and for y^t purpose the citie of Athēs had a м. men which   *Suidas.* were onely archers, in dayly wages, to watche and kepe the citie frō al ieoperdie & sodein daūger : which archers also shuld cary to prisō & warde any misdoer at ye cōmaundemēt of the hygh officers, as playnlye doth appeare in Plato. And surely the bowmen of Athens did wōderful feates in many battels, but specially when Demosthenes   *Plato in pro-* the valiaūt captayne slue and toke prisoners all   *tagora.* the Lacedemonians besyde ye citie of Pylos, where Nestor somtyme was lord : the shaftes went so thicke that daye (sayth Thucydides) that no man could   *Thucydid.* 4. se theyr enemies. A Lacedemonian taken prisoner, was asked of one at Athens, whether they were stoute fellowes that were slayne or no, of the Lacedemonians : he answered nothing els but this : make moche of those shaftes of youres, for they knowe neyther stoute nor vnstoute : meanynge therby, that no man (though he were neuer so stout) came in their walke, that escaped without death.

Herodotus descrybing the mighty hoost of Xerxes especially doth marke out, what bowes and shaftes they vsed, signifying y^t therin lay their chefe strēgth. And   *Herod. in* at the same tyme Attossa, mother of Xerxes, wyfe   *Polym.* to Darius, and doughter of Cyrus, doeth enquire (as Aeschylus sheweth in a Tragedie) of a cer-   *Esch. ī Pers.* tayne messenger that came from Xerxes hoste, what stronge and fearfull bowes the Grecians vsed : wherby it is playne, that

Artillarie was the thing, wherin both Europe and Asia at those dayes trusted moost vppon.

The best parte of Alexanders hoste were archers as playnelye doth appeare by Arianus, and other y[t] wrote his life : and those so stronge archers, that they onely, sundrye tymes ouercame their enemies, afore any other neded to fyght : as was sene in the battayl which Nearchus one of Alexanders capitaynes had besyde the ryuer of Thomeron. And therfore as concerning all these kyngdomes and cōmune wealthes, I maye cōclude with this sentence of Plinie, whose wordes be, as I suppose thus : If any man woulde remēbre the Ethiopians, Egyptians, Arabians, the men of Inde, of Scythia, so many people in y[e] east of the Sarmatianes, and all the kyngdomes of the Parthians, he shall well perceyue halfe the parte of the worlde, to lyue in subieƈtion, ouercome by the myght and power of shotinge.

Arianus. 8.

Plin. lib. 16. Cap. 36.

In the commune wealth of Rome, which exceded all other in vertue, noblenesse, and dominion litle mētion is made of shoting, not bycause it was litle vsed amonges them, but rather bycause it was bothe so necessarye and cōmune, that it was thought a thing not necessarye or requyred of anye man to be spoken vpon, as if a man shoulde describe a greate feaste, he woulde not ones name bread, although it be mooste common and necessarye of all : but surely yf a feaste beynge neuer so great, lacked bread, or had fewsty and noughty bread, all the other daynties shulde be vnsauery, and litle regarded, and than woulde men talke of the commodity of bread, whan they lacke it, that would not ones name it afore, whan they had it : And euen so dyd the Romaynes as concernynge shootyng. Seldome is shootinge named, and yet it dyd the moste good in warre, as didde appere, verye playnlye in that battell, whiche Scipio Aphrican[9] had with the Numantines in Spayne, whome he coulde neuer ouercome, before he sette bowemen amonges his horse men, by whose myght they were clean vanquished.

Agayne, Tiberius fyghtynge with Armenius and Inguiomerus princis of Germanie, had one wing of archers on horsebacke, an other of archers on foot, by whose might the Germanes were slayne downe ryghte, and

Cor. Tac. 2

so scattered and beate oute of the feelde, that the chase lasted
.x. myles, the Germanes clame vp in to trees for feare, but the
Romanes dyd fetche them downe with theyr shaftes as they had
bē birdes, in whyche battell the Romaynes lost fewe or none, as
dothe appeare in the historie.

But as I began to saye, the Romaynes dyd not so muche
prayse the goodnesse of shootinge, whan they had it, as they
dyd lament the lacke of it, whan they wanted it, as Leo the .v.
the noble Emperour doth playnly testifie in sundrie places in
those bokes whiche he wrote in Greke, of the sleyghtes and
pollicies of warre. PHIL. Surelie of that booke I haue not
heard before, and howe came you to the syghte of it. TOX.
The booke is rare trulie, but this laste yeare when master
Cheke translated the sayd booke out of greke in to Latin, to yᵉ
kinges maiestie, he of his gentlenesse, wolde haue me very ofte
in hys chāber, and for the familiaritie that I had wyth hym,
more than manye other, woulde suffer me to reade of it, whan
I woulde, the whiche thinge to do, surelye I was very desirous
and glad, because of the excellent handelynge of all thynges,
that euer he taketh in hande. And verily *Philologe*, as ofte as
I remembre the departynge of that man from the vniuersitie,
(whiche thinge I do not seldome) so ofte do I well perceyue our
moste helpe and furtheraunce to learnynge, to haue gon awaye
with him. For by yᵉ great cōmoditie yᵗ we toke in hearyng
hym reade priuatly in his chambre, all Homer, Sophocles, and
Euripides, Herodotus, Thucydides, Xenophon, Isocrates and
Plato, we feele the great discommoditie in not hearynge of
hym, Aristotle & Demosthenes, whiche ii. authours with all
diligence last of all he thought to haue redde vnto us. And
when I consider howe manye men he succoured with his helpe,
& hys ayde to abyde here for learninge, and howe all men were
prouoked and styrred vp, by his councell and daylye example,
howe they shulde come to learning, surely I perceyue that
sentence of Plato to be true, which sayeth that there is nothyng
better in any common wealthe, than that there shoulde be
alwayes one or other, excellent passyng man, whose lyfe and
vertue, shoulde plucke forwarde the will, diligence, laboure and
hope of all other, that folowyng his footesteppes, they myght
comme to the same ende, wherevnto labour, lerning & vertue,
had cōueied him before. The great hinderance of learning, in

lackinge thys man greatly I shulde lament, if this discōmoditie of oures, were not ioyned with the cōmoditie & welth, of yᵉ hole realme, for which purpose, our noble king full of wysedome hath called vp this excellent man full of learnynge, to teache noble prince Edwarde, an office ful of hope, comforte & solace to al true hertes of England : For whome al England dayly doth praye, yᵗ he passing his Tutour in learnyng & know-ledge, folowynge his father in wisedome & felicitie, accordyng to yᵗ example which is set afore his eyes, may so set out and mayntayne goddes worde to the abolishment of al papistry, the confusion of al heresie, that therby he feared of his en-nemies, loued of al his subiectes, maye bring to his own glory, immortal fame & memorie, to this realme, welthe, honour & felicitie, to true and vnfayned religion perpetuall peace, concorde and vnitie.

But to retourne to shootynge agayne, what Leo sayeth of shootynge amonges the Romaynes, hys woordes, be so muche for the prayse of shootynge, and the booke also so rare to be gotten,

Leo. 6. 5. that I learned the places by harte, whyche be as I suppose, euen thus. Fyrste in his sixte booke, as concerning what harneys is best : Lette all the youth of Rome be compelled to vse shootyng, eyther more or lesse, & alwayes to bear theyr bowe & theyr quiuer aboute with them, untyll they be .xl. yeares oulde.

For sithens shootynge was necglected and decayed among the Romaynes, many a battayle and fyelde hath been loste.

Leo. 11. 50. Agayne in the 11. booke and .50. chapiter, (I call that by bookes and chapiters, whyche the greke booke deuideth by chapiters and paragraphes) Let your soul-dyers haue theyr weapons wel appoynted and trimmed, but aboue all other thynges regarde moste shootinge, and therfore lette men when there is no warre, vse shootynge at home : For the leauynge of, onely of shotynge, hath broughte in ruyne and decaye, the hole Empire of Rome. Afterwarde he commaund-eth agayne, hys capitayne by these wordes : Arme your hoste

Leo. 18. 21. as I haue appoynted you, but specially with bowe and arrowes plentie. For shootynge is a thinge of muche myghte and power in warre, and chyefely agaynst the Sarracenes and Turkes, whiche people hath all their hope of victorie in theyr bowe and shaftes : Besydes all this, in an other

place, he wryteth thus to his Captayne : Artillerie is easie to be
prepared, and in time of great nede, a thing moste profitable,
therfore we straytlye commaunde you to make proclamation to
al men vnder our dominion, which be eyther in war or peace,
to all cities, borowes and townes, and fynally to all
maner of men, that euerye seare persone haue   *Leo. 20. 79.*
bowe and shaftes of his owne, & euerye house besyde this, to
haue a standing bearyng bowe, and xl. shaftes for all nedes, and
that they exercise them selues in holtes, hilles, and dales, playnes
and wodes, for all maner of chaunces in warre.

Howe muche shooting was vsed among the olde Romanes
and what meanes noble captaynes and Emperou[r]s made, to
haue it encrease amonge them, and what hurte came by the
decaye of it, these wordes, of Leo the emperour, which in a
maner I haue rehersed woorde for woorde, playnly doth declare.
And yet shotynge, although they set neuer so muche by it,
was neuer so good than, as it is nowe in Englande, whiche
thing to be true, is very probable, in that Leo doth saye, that
he woulde haue his souldiers take of theyr arrowe
heads, and one shote at an other, for theyr   *Leo. 7. 18.*
exercise, whiche playe yf Englyshe archers vsed, I thinke they
shoulde fynde smal play and lesse pleasure in it at all.

The great vpperhande maynteyned alwayes in warre by
artillery, doeth appeare verye playnlye by this reason also,
that whan the spanyardes, franchmen, and germanes, grekes,
macedonians, and egyptians, eche contry vsing one singuler
weapon, for whyche they were greatelye feared in warre, as the
Spanyarde *Lancea*, the Francheman *Gesa*, the German *Framea*,
the Grecian *Machera*, the Macedonian *Sarissa*, yet coulde they
not escape, but be subiectes to the Empire of Rome, whan the
Parthians hauyng all theyr hope in artillerie, gaue no place to
thē, but ouercame the Romanes, ofter than the Romaynes
them, and kepte battel with them, many an hundred yeare,
and slue the ryche Crassus and hys son wyth   *Plutarch. ī*
many a stoute Romayne more, with their bowes.   *M. Crass. &*
They draue Marcus Antonius ouer the hylles of   *ī M. Anto.*
Media & Armenia, to his great shame and reproch.   *Ael. Spart.*
They slue Iulianus Apostata, and Antoninus Caracalla, they
helde in perpetual pryson, yͤ most noble emperour Valerian in
despite of all the Romaynes and many other princes, whiche

wrote for his delyueraunce, as Bel solis called kynge of kynges,
Valerius kynge of Cadusia, Arthabesdes kyng of Armenia, and
many other princes more, whom ye Parthians by reason of
theyr artillerie, regarded neuer one whitte, and thus with the
Romaynes, I maye conclude, that the borders of theyr empyre
were not at the sunne rysinge and sunne settynge, as Tullye
sayeth : but so farre they went, as artillarie woulde gyue them
leaue. For I thinke all the grounde that they had, eyther
northewarde, farther than the borders of Scythia, or Easte-
warde, farther than the borders of Parthia, a man myght haue
boughte w^t a small deale of money, of whiche thynge surely
shotyng was the cause.

From the same contrie of Scythia the Gothians Hunnes,
Paul. Diac. and Wandalians came wyth the same wepons of
artillarie, as Paulus Diaconus doth saye, & so
berafte Rome of her empyre wyth fyre, spoyle, & waste, so y^t
in suche a learned citie was lefte scarce one man behynde, that
had learnynge or leysoure to leue in writinge to them whiche
shoulde come after howe so noble an Empyre, in so shorte a
whyle, by a rable of banyshed bondemen, wythoute all order
and pollicie, saue onelye theyr naturalle and daylye excercise in
artillarye, was broughte to suche thraldome and ruine.

After them the Turkes hauing an other name, but yet the
P. Mela. 1. same people, borne in Scythia, brought vp onely
in artillarie, by the same weapon haue subdued
and beraft from the Christen men all Asia and Aphrike (to
speake vpon,) and the moost noble countries of Europe, to the
greate diminishing of Christe his religion, to the great reproche
of cowardyse of al christianitie, a manifest token of gods high
wrath & displeasure ouer the synne of the worlde, but
speciallye amonges Christen men, which be on slepe made
drunke with the frutes of the flesh, as infidelitie, disobedience
to Goddes worde, and heresie, grudge, euelwyll, stryfe, contention, and priuie enuye, coueytousnesse, oppression, vn-
mercifulnesse, with innumerable sortes of vnspeakeable daylye
bawdrye : which thinges surely, yf God holde not his holy
hande ouer vs, and plucke vs from them, wyl bryng vs to a
more Turkishnesse and more beastlye blynde barbarousnesse :
as callyng ill thinges good, and good thynges ill, contemnyng
of knowledge & learnynge, settynge at nought, and hauyng for

a fable, God and his high prouidence, wyll bring vs (I say) to a more vngracious Turkishnesse (if more Turkishnesse can be then this) thā if the Turkes had sworne, to bring al Turkye agaynst vs. For these frutes surelye must neades sprynge of suche seede, and suche effect nedes folowe of suche a cause : if reason, truthe, and God, be not altered, but as they are wont to be. For surely no Turkyshe power can ouerthrowe vs, if Turkysshe lyfe do not cast vs downe before.

If god were wyth vs, it buted not the turke to be agaynst vs, but our vnfaythful sinfull lyuyng, which is the Turkes moder, and hath brought hym vp hitherto, muste nedes turne god from vs, because syn and he hath no felowshyp togither. If we banished ill liuyng out of christendome, I am sure the Turke shulde not onelye, not ouercome vs, but scarce haue an hole to runne in to, in his own countrye.

But Christendome nowe I may tell you Philologe is muche lyke a man that hath an ytche on him, and lyeth drōke also in his bed, and though a thefe come to the dore, and heaueth at it, to come in, and sleye hym, yet he lyeth in his bed, hauinge more pleasure to lye in a slumber and scratche him selfe wher it ytcheth euen to the harde bone, than he hath redynes to ryse up lustelye, & dryue him awaye that woulde robbe hym and sleye hym. But I truste Christe wyl so lyghten and lyfte vp Christen mennes eyes, that they shall not slepe to death, nor that the turke Christes open enemy, shall euer boste that he hath quyte ouerthrowen vs. But as I began to tell you, shootynge is the chefe thinge, wherewith God suffereth the turke to punysh our noughtie liuinge wyth all: The youthe there is brought vp in shotyng, his priuie garde for his own person, is bowmen, the *Cusp. de rebus Turc.* might of theyr shootynge is wel knowen of the Spanyardes, whiche at the towne called Newecastell in Illirica, were quyte slayne vp, of the turkes arrowes : whan the Spanyardes had no vse of theyr gunnes, by reason of the rayne. And nowe last of all, the emperour his maiestie him selfe, at the Citie of Argier in Aphricke had his hooste sore handeled wyth the Turkes arrowes, when his gonnes were quite dispatched and stode him in no seruice, bycause of the raine that fell, where as in suche a chaunce of raine, yf he had had bowmen, surelye there shoote myghte peraduenture haue bene a litle

hindred, but quite dispatched and marde, it coulde neuer haue
bene.

But as for the Turkes I am werie to talke of them partlye
because I hate them, and partlye bycause I am now affectioned
euen as it were a man that had bene longe wanderyng in
straūge contries & would fayne be at home to se howe well his
owne frendes prosper and leade theyr lyfe, and surely me
thincke I am verie merye at my harte to remember how I shal
finde at home in Englande amonges Englysh men, partlye
by hystories, of them that haue gone afore vs, agayne by
experience of thē whych we knowe, & lyue with vs as
greate noble feates of warre doone by Artillarye, as euer was
done at any tyme in any other common welthe.　And here I
Textor.　　　must nedes remēber a certaine Frēchman called
Textor, that writeth a boke whiche he nameth
Officina, wherin he weueth vp many brokenended matters
and settes out much rifraffe, pelfery, trumpery, baggage &
beggerie ware clamparde vp of one that would seme to be fitter
for a shop in dede than to write any boke.　And amonges all
other yll packed vp matters, he thrustes vp in a hepe togyther
all the good shoters that euer hathe bene in the worlde as he
saythe hymselfe, and yet I trow Philologe that of all the
examples whiche I now by chaūce haue rehersed out of the
best Authors both in greke and latin, Textor hath but .ii. of
them, which .ii. surely yf they were to rekē agayne, I wold not
ones name thē, partly bycause they were noughtie persons, and
shoting somoche the worse, bycause they loued it, as Domitian
and Commodus the emperours : partelye bycause Textor hath
them in his boke, on whom I loked on bychaunce in the
bookebynders shope, thynkynge of no suche matter.　And one
thing I wyl say to you *Philologe*, that if I were disposed to do
it, and you hadde leysure to heare it, I coulde soone do as
Textor doth, and reken vp suche a rable of shoters that be
named here and there in poetes, as wolde holde vs talkyng
whyles tomorowe : but my purpose was not to make mention
of those which were feyned of Poetes for theyr pleasure, but of
suche as were proued in histories for a truthe : but why I
bringe in Textor was this : At laste when he hath rekened all
P. Crin. 3. 10.　　shoters that he can, he sayeth thus, Petrus
Crinitus wryteth, that the Scottes whiche dwell

beyonde Englande be verye excellent shoters, and the best
bowmen in warre. This sentence whether Crinitus wrote it
more leudly of ignoraunce, or Textor confirmeth it more
piuyshlye of enuye, may be called in question and doubte : but
this surelye do I knowe very well that Textor hath both red in
Gaguinus the Frenche hystorie, and also hath hearde his father
or graundfather taulke (except perchaūce he was borne and
bred in a Cloyster) after that sort of the shotynge of Englisshe
men, that Textor neded not to haue gone so piuishlye beyonde
Englande for shoting, but myght very soone, euē in the first
towne of Kent, haue founde suche plentie of shotinge, as is not
in al the realme of Scotland agayne. The Scottes surely be
good men of warre in theyr owne feate as can be : but as for
shotinge, they neyther can vse it for any profyte, nor yet wil
chalēge it for any prayse, although master Textor of his
gētlenesse wold gyue it them. Textor neaded not to haue
fylled vppe his booke with suche lyes, if he hadde read the
storye of Scotlande, whiche Ioannes Maior doeth
wryte : wherein he myghte haue learned, that *Ioan. Ma. 6.*
when Iames Stewart fyrst kyng of that name, at the Parliamēt
holden at Saynt Iohnnes towne or Perthie, commaunded vnder
payne of a greate forfyte, that euerye Scotte shoulde learne to
shote : yet neyther the loue of theyr coūtrie, the feare of their
enemies, the auoydying of punishment, nor the receyuinge of
anye profyte that myght come by it, coulde make them to be
good Archers : whiche be vnapte and vnfytte therunto by Gods
prouidence and nature.

Therfore the Scottes them selues proue Textor a lyer,
bothe with authoritie and also daily experience, and by a
certayne Prouerbe that they haue amonges them in theyr
cōmunication, wherby they gyue the whole prayse of shotynge
honestlye to Englysshe men, saying thus : that euery Englysshe
Archer beareth vnder hys gyrdle .xxiiii. Scottes.

But to lette Textor and the Scottes go : yet one thynge
woulde I wysshe for the Scottes, and that is this, that seinge
one God, one faythe, one compasse of the see, one lande and
countrie, one tungue in speakynge, one maner and trade in
lyuynge, lyke courage and stomake in war, lyke quicknesse of
witte to learning, hath made Englande and Scotlande bothe
one, they wolde suffre them no longer to be two : but cleane

gyue ouer the Pope, which seketh none other thinge (as many a noble and wyse Scottish man doth knowe) but to fede vp dissention & parties betwixt them & vs, procuryng that thynge to be two, which God, nature, and reason, wold haue one.

Howe profytable suche an attonement were for Scotlande, both Iohannes Maior, and Ector Boetius which *Iohn. Ma-* wrote the Scottes Chronicles do tell, & also all *ior. 6. hist.* the gentlemen of Scotlande with the poore *Scot.* cōmunaltie, do wel knowe : So that there is nothing that stoppeth this matter, saue onelye a fewe freers, and suche lyke, whiche with the dregges of our Englysh Papistrie lurkyng now amonges them, study nothing els but to brewe battell and stryfe betwixte both the people : Wherby onely they hope to maynetayne theyr Papisticall kyngdome, to the destruction of the noble blood of Scotlande, that then they maye with authoritie do that, whiche neither noble man nor poore man in Scotlande yet doeth knowe. And as for Scottishe men and Englishe men be not enemyes by nature, but by custome : not by our good wyll, but by theyr owne follye : whiche shoulde take more honour in being coupled to Englande, then we shulde take profite in being ioyned to Scotlande.

Wales being headye, and rebelling many yeares agaynst vs, laye wylde, vntylled, vnhabited, without lawe, iustice, ciuilitie and ordre : and then was amōges them more stealing thā true dealing, more suretie for them that studyed to be noughte, then quyetnesse for them that laboured to be good : when nowe thanked be God, and noble Englande, there is no countrie better inhabited, more ciuile, more diligent in honest craftes, to get bothe true and plentifull lyuynge withall. And this felicitie (my mynde gyueth me) within these few dayes shal chaūce also to Scotlande, by the godly wysedome of oure mooste noble Prince kynge Henrye the .viii. by whome God hath wrought more wonderfull thynges then euer by any prince before : as banishing the byshop of Rome and herisie, bringyng to light god his worde and veritie, establishing suche iustice and equitie, through euery parte of this his realme, as neuer was sene afore.

To suche a Prince of suche a wysdome, God hath reserued this mooste noble attonement : wherby neither we shalbe any more troubled, nor the Scottes with their best

countries any more destroyed, nor yᵉ see, whiche God or-
deyneth profytable for both, shall from eyther be any more
stopped : to the great quietnesse, wealth & felicitie of all the
people dwellynge in this Ile, to the high renoume & prayse of
our moost noble kyng, to the feare of all maner of nacions that
owe ill wyll to either countrie, to the hygh pleasure of God,
which as he is one, and hateth al diuision, so is he best of all
pleased, to se thinges which be wyde and amysse, brought to
peace and attonement. But Textor (I beshrowe him) hath
almooste broughte vs from our cōmunicatiō of shoting. Now
sir by my iudgement, the Artillarie of England farre excedeth
all other realmes : but yet one thing I doubt & longe haue
surely in that point doubted, whē, or by whom, shotyng was
first brought in to Englande, & for the same purpose as I was
ones in companye wyth syr Thomas Eliot knight, which
surelie for his lerning in all kynde of knowlege bringeth much
worshyp to all the nobilite of Englande, I was so bould to aske
hym, yf he at any tyme, had marked any thing, as cōcernynge
the bryngynge in of shootynge in to Englande : he aunswered
me gentlye agayne, that he had a worcke in hand which he
nameth, *De rebus memorabilibus Anglię*, which I trust we shal
se in print shortlye, and for the accomplyshmente of that boke,
he had read & perused ouer many olde monumētes of Englande,
and in seking for that purpose, he marked this of shootynge in
an excedyng olde cronicle, the which had no name, that what
tyme as the Saxons came first into this realme in kyng
Vortigers dayes, whē they had bene here a whyle and at last
began to faull out with the Brittons, they troubled and
subdewed the Brittons wyth nothynge so much, as with theyr
bowe and shaftes, whiche wepon beynge straunge & not sene
here before, was wonderfull terrible vnto them, and this
beginninge I can thynke verie well to be true. But now as
concerning many exāples for the prayse of English archers in
warre, surely I wil not be long in a matter yᵗ no mā doubteth
in, & those few yᵗ I wil name, shal either be proued by yᵉ
histories of our enemies, or els done by men that now liue.

Kynge Edward the thirde at the battel of Cressie ageinst
Philip yᵉ Frēche king as Gaguinus the frēch Historiographer
plainlye doeth tell, slewe that daye all the nobilite of Fraunce
onlye wyth hys archers.

Such lyke battel also fought yᵉ noble black prince Edward beside Poeters, where Iohn yᵉ french king wᵗ hys sonne & in a maner al yᵉ peres of Fraūce were taken beside .xxx. м. which that daye were slayne, & verie few Englyshe men, by reason of theyr bowes.

Kynge Henrie the fifte a prince pereles and moste vyctori- ouse conqueroure of all that euer dyed yet in this parte of the world, at the battel of Dagin court with .vii. м. fyghtynge men, and yet many of them sycke, beynge suche Archers as the Cronycle sayeth that mooste parte of them drewe a yarde, slewe all the Cheualrie of Fraunce to the nomber of .XL. м. and moo, and lost not paste .xxvi. Englysshe men.

The bloudye Ciuil warre of England betwixt the house of Yorke and Lancaster, where shaftes slewe of both sydes to the destruction of mannye a yoman of Englande, whome foreine battell coulde neuer haue subdewed bothe I wyll passe ouer for the pyttyefulnesse of it, and yet maye we hyghelye prayse GOD in the remembraunce of it, seynge he of hys prouydence hath so knytte to gether those .ii. noble houses, with so noble and pleasunte a flowre.

The excellent prince Thomas Hawarde nowe Duke of Northfolk, for whose good prosperite wᵗ al his noble familie al English hertes dayly doth pray wᵗ bowmē of England slew kyng Iamie wᵗ many a noble Scot euē brāt agēst Flodō hil, in which battel yᵉ stoute archers of Cheshire & Lanchasshire for one day bestowed to yᵉ death for their prīce & coūtry sake, hath gotten immortall name and prayse for euer.

The feare onely of Englysh Archers hathe done more wonderfull thinges than euer I redde in anye historye greke or latin, and moost wonderfull of all now of late beside Carlile betwixt Eske and Leuen at Sandy sikes, where the hoole nobilite of Scotlande for fere of the Archers of Englonde (next the stroke of God) as both Englysh men and Scotyshe men that were present hath toulde me were drowened and taken prisoners.

Nor that noble acte also, whyche althoughe it be almost lost by tyme, commeth not behynd in worthinesse, whyche my synguler good frende and Master Sir William Walgraue and Sir George Somerset dyd with a few Archers to yᵉ number as it is sayd of .xvi. at the Turne pike besyde Hāmes where they turned with so fewe Archers, so many Frenchemen to flight, and turned so many oute of theyr Iackes, whych turne turned all fraunce to shame & reproche and those .ii. noble Knightes to perpetuall prayse & fame.

And thus you se Philologe, in al contries Asia, Aphrike and Europe, in Inde, Aethiop, Aegypt & Iurie, Parthia, Persia, Grece, and Italie, Schythia, Turky, and Englande, from the begynninge of the world euen to thys daye, that shotynge hath had the cheife stroke in warre. PHI. These examples surelye I apte for the prayse of shotynge, not feyned by poetes, but proued by trewe histories, distinct by tyme and order, hath delyted me excedyng muche, but yet me thynke that all thys prayse belongeth to stronge shootynge and drawynge of myghtye bowes not to prickyng and nere shotinge, for which cause you and many other bothe loue & vse shootyng. TOX. Euer more Philologe you wyl haue some ouertwhart reson to drawe forthe more communication w^{t}all, but neuerthe-lesse you shall perceaue if you wyl, that vse of prickyng, and desyre of nere shootynge at home, are the onelye causes of stronge shootyng in warre, and why? for you se, that the strongest men, do not drawe alwayes the strongest shoote, whiche thyng prouethe that drawinge stronge, liethe not so muche in the strength of man, as in the vse of shotyng. And experience teacheth the same in other thynges, for you shal se a weake smithe, whiche wyl wyth a lipe and turnyng of his arme, take vp a barre of yron, y^t another man thrise as stronge, can not stirre. And a strong man not vsed to shote, hath his armes breste and shoulders, and other partes wherwith he shuld drawe stronglye, one hindering and stoppinge an other, euen as a dosen strong horses not vsed to the carte, lettes & troubles one another. And so the more stronge man not vsed to shote, shootes moost vnhāsumlye, but yet if a strong man with vse of shooting coulde applye all the partes of hys bodye togyther to theyr moost strengthe, than should he both drawe stronger than other, and also shoote better than other. But nowe a stronge man not vsed to shoote, at a girde, can heue vp & plucke in sūder many a good bowe, as wild horses at a brunte doth race & pluck in peces many a stronge carte. And thus strong mē, without vse, can do nothynge in shoting to any purpose, neither in warre nor peace, but if they happen to shoote, yet they haue done within a shoote or two when a weake man that is vsed to shoote, shal serue for all tymes and purposes, and shall shoote .x. shaftes, agaynst the others .iiii. & drawe them vp to the poynte, euerye tyme, and shoote them to the mooste aduauntage, drawyng and withdrawing his shafte when he list, markynge at one man, yet let driuyng at an other man : whiche thynges in a set battayle, although a man, shal not alwayes vse, yet in bickerynges, and at ouerthwarte meatinges, when fewe archers be togyther, they do moste good of all.

Agayne he that is not vsed to shoote, shall euermore with vntowardnesse of houldynge his bowe, & nockynge his shafte, not lookyng to his stryng betyme, put his bowe alwayes in ieoperdy of breakynge, & than he were better to be at home, moreouer he shal shoote very fewe shaftes, and those full vnhandsumlye, some not halfe drawen, some to hygh and some to lowe, nor he can not driue a shoote at a tyme, nor stoppe a shoote at a neede, but oute muste it, and verye ofte to euel profe.   PHI. And that is best I trow in war, to let it go, and not to stoppe it.   TOX. No not so, but somtyme to houlde a shafte at the heade, whyche if they be but few archers, doth more good with the feare of it, than it shoulde do if it were shot, with the stroke of it.   PHI. That is a wonder to me, y^t the feare of a displeasure, shoulde do more harme than the displeasure it selfe.   TOX. Yes, ye knowe that a man whiche fereth to be banyshed, out of hys cuntrye, can neyther be mery, eate, drynke nor sleape for feare, yet when he is banished in dede, he slepeth and eateth, as well as any other.   And many menne doubtyng and fearyng whether they shoulde dye or no, euen for verye feare of deathe, preuenteth them selfe with a more bytter deathe then the other death shoulde haue bene in deade.   And thus feare is euer worse than the thynge feared,

Ciri. ped. 3.   as is pratelye proued, by the communication of Cyrus and Tigranes, the kynges sunne of Armenie, in Xenophon.

PHI. I grante Toxophile, that vse of shotyng maketh a man drawe strong, to shoote at most aduauntage, to kepe his gere, whiche is no small thinge in war, but yet me thinke, that the customable shoting at home, speciallye at buttes and prickes, make nothynge at all for stronge shooting which doth moste good in war.   Therfore I suppose yf men shulde vse to goo into the feyldes, and learne to shote myghty stronge shootes, and neuer care for any marke at al, they shulde do muche better. TOX. The trouthe is, that fashion muche vsed, woulde do muche good, but this is to be feared, least that waye coulde not prouoke men to vse muche shotyng, bycause ther shulde be lytle pleasure in it. And that in shoting is beste, y^t prouoketh a man to vse shotinge moste: For muche vse maketh men shoote, bothe strong & well, whiche two thinges in shootinge, euery man doeth desyre. And the chyefe mayntayner of vse, in any thyng, is comparyson, and honeste contention. For whan a manne stryueth to be better than an other, he wyll gladly vse that thing, though it be neuer so paynful wherein he woulde excell, whiche thynge Aristotle verye pratelye doth note, sayenge.

Where is comparison, there is victorie: where is victorie, there is pleasure: And where is pleasure, no man careth what labour or payne he taketh, bycause of the prayse, and pleasure, that he shal haue, in doynge better than other men.

Aristo. rheto.
ad Theod.

Agayne, you knowe Hesiodus wryteth to hys brother Perses, y^t al craftes men, by contending one honestly w^t an other, do encrease theyr cūnyng w^t theyr substance. And therfore in London, and other great Cities, men of one crafte, moste commonly, dwelle togyther, bycause in honest stryuyng togyther, who shall do best, euery one maye waxe bothe cunninger and rycher, so lykewyse in shootynge, to make matches to assemble archers togyther, to contende who shall shoote best, and winne the game, encreaseth ye vse of shotynge wonderfully amonges men.

Hesio. ī ope.
et die.

PHI. Of Vse you speake very much Toxophile but I am sure in al other matters, Vse can do nothing, wythoute two other thinges be ioyned wyth it, one is a natural Aptnesse to a thinge, the other is a true waye or Knowledge, howe to do the thing, to which ii. yf Vse be ioyned, as thirde felowe, of them thre, procedeth perfectnesse and excellencie: If a manne lacke the first two, Aptnesse and Cunnyng, Vse can do lytle good, at all. For he y^t woulde be an oratour and is nothinge naturallye fitte for it, that is to saye lacketh a good wytte and memorie, lacketh a good voyce, countenaunce and body, and other suche like, ye[t] yf he had all these thinges, and knewe not what, howe, where, when nor to whome he shulde speake, surelye the vse of spekynge, woulde brynge out none other frute but playne follye and bablyng, so y^t Vse is the laste and the least neccessarye, of all thre, yet no thing can be done excellently without them al thre. And therfore Toxophile I my selfe bicause I neuer knewe, whether I was apte for shooting or no, nor neuer knewe waye, howe I shulde learne to shoote I haue not vsed to shoote : and so I thinke fiue hundred more in Englande do besyde me. And surely yf I knewe that I were apte, and y^t you woulde teach me howe to shoote, I woulde become an archer, and the rather, bycause of the good communication, the whiche I haue had with you this daye, of shotyng. TOX. Aptnesse, Knowlege, and Vse, euen as you saye, make all thinges perfecte. Aptnesse is the fyrst and chyefest thinge, without whiche the other two do no good at all. Knowledge doeth encrease al maner of Aptnesse, bothe lesse and more. Vse sayth Cicero, is farre aboue all teachinge. And thus they all three muste be had, to do any thinge very well, and yf anye one be awaye, what so euer is done, is done verye meanly. Aptnesse is ye gyfte of nature, Knowlege, is gotten by ye helpe of other : Vse lyeth in our owne diligence & labour. So that Aptnesse & vse be ours and w^{t}in vs, through nature & labour : Knowledge not ours, but cōmynge by other : and therfore moost dilligently, of all men to be sought for. Howe these three thinges stande with the artillery of Englande, a woorde or twoo I will saye.

All Englishe men generally, be apte for shotyng, and howe? Lyke as that grounde is plentifull and frutefull, whiche withoute anye tyllynge, bryngeth out corne, as for example, yf a man shoulde go to the myll or market with corne, and happen to spyl some in the waye, yet it wolde take roote and growe, bycause ye soyle is so good : so Englād may be thought very frutefull and apt to brynge oute shoters, where children euen from the cradell, loue it : and yong men without any teachyng so diligentlye vse it. Agayne, lykewyse as a good grounde, well tylled, and well husbanded, bringeth out great plentie of byg eared corne, and good to the faule : so if the youthe of Englande being apte of it selfe to shote, were taught and learned how to shote, the Archers of England shuld not be only a great deale rāker, and mo then they be : but also a good deale

bygger and stronger Archers then they be. This cōmoditie
shoulde folowe also yf the youth of Englande were taught to
shote, that euen as plowing of a good grounde for wheate, doth
not onely make it mete for the seede, but also riueth and
plucketh vp by the rootes, all thistles, brambles and weedes,
which growe of theyr owne accorde, to the destruction of
bothe corne and grounde: Euen so shulde the teaching of youth
to shote, not only make them shote well, but also plucke
awaye by the rootes all other desyre to noughtye pastymes, as
disynge, cardyng, and boouling, which without any teaching
are vsed euery where, to the great harme of all youth of this
realme.   And lykewise as burnyng of thistles and diligent
weding them oute of the corne, doth not halfe so moche ryd
them, as whē yᵉ ground is falloed and tilled for good grayne, as
I haue hearde many a good husbandman say: euen so, neither
hote punishment, nor yet diligent searching out of suche
vnthriftinesse by the officers, shal so throwly wede these
vngracious games out of the realme, as occupying and bringyng
vp youth in shotynge, and other honest pastyme.   Thirdly, as
a grounde which is apt for corne and also wel tilled for corne:
yet if a man let it lye stil and do not occupye it .iii. or .iiii. yeare:
but then wyll sow it, if it be wheate (sayth Columella) it wil
turne into rye: so if a man be neuer so apte to shote, nor neuer
so wel taught in his youth to shote, yet if he giue it ouer, and
not vse to shote, truly when he shalbe eÿther cōpelled in war
tyme for his countrye sake, or els prouoked at home for his
pleasure sake, to faule to his bowe: he shal become of a fayre
archer, a stark squyrter and dribber.   Therefore in shotynge,
as in all other thinges, there can neyther be many in number,
nor excellent in dede: excepte these .iii. thynges, Aptnesse,
Knowledge, and Vse goo togyther.

PHIL. Very well sayde *Toxophile*, and I promyse you, I
agree to this iudgement of yours altogyther and therefore I can
not a lytle maruayle, why Englysshe men brynge nomore helpe
to shotynge, then nature it selfe gyueth them.   For you se that
euen children be put to theyr owne shiftes in shotyng, hauing
nothynge taughte them: but that they maye chose, and chaunce
to shoote ill, rather then well, vnaptlye soner then fitlye, vnto-
wardlye, more easely then wel fauouredlye, whiche thynge
causeth manye neuer begynne to shoote: and moo to leaue it

of when they haue begone, and moost of all to shote both worse
& weaker, then they might shote, if they were taught.   But
peraduenture some men wyll saye, that wyth vse of shootynge
a man shall learne to shoote, true it is he shall learne, but what
shal he learne? marye to shoote noughtly.   For all Vse, in all
thynges, yf it be not stayed with Cunnyng, wyll verie easely
brynge a man to do y^t thynge, what so euer he goeth aboute
with muche illfauorednes and deformitie.

Which thinge how much harme it doth in learning both
Crassus excellencie dothe proue in Tullie, and I
De Orat. 1. my selfe haue experiens in my lytle shootyng.
And therfore Toxophile, you must nedes graunt me that ether
Englishe men do il, in not ioynyng Knowlege of shooting to
Vse, or els there is no knowlege or cūninge, which can be
gathered of shooting.   TOX.   Learnyng to shoote is lytle
regarded in England, for this consideration, bycause men be so
apte by nature they haue a greate redy forwardnesse and wil to
vse it, al though no man teache them, al thoughe no man byd
them, & so of theyr owne corage they rūne hedlynge on it, and
shoote they ill, shote they well, greate hede they take not.   And
in verie dede Aptnesse w^t Vse may do sumwhat without Knowlege, but not the tenthe parte, if so be they were ioyned with
knowlege.

Whyche thre thynges be seperate as you se, not of theyr
owne kynde, but through the negligence of mē whyche coupleth
them not to gyther.   And where ye doubte whether there can
be gadered any knowlege or arte in shootyng or no, surely
I thynke that a mā being wel exercised in it and sumwhat
honestly learned with all, myght soone with diligent obseruynge
and markynge the hole nature of shootynge, find out as it were
an Arte of it, as Artes in other matters haue bene founde oute
afore, seynge that shootyng stādeth by those thinges, which
maye both be thorowlye perceued, and perfitly knowen, and
suche that neuer failes, but be euer certayne, belongynge to one
moost perfeĉt ende, as shootyng streight, and keping of a lenght
bring a man to hit the marke, ye chefe end in shootyng: which
two thynges a man may attaine vnto, by diligent vsynge, and
well handlynge those instrumentes, which belong vnto them.
Therfore I can not see, but there lieth hyd in the nature of
Shootynge, an Arte, whiche by notynge, and obseruynge of

him, that is exercised in it, yf he be any thyng learned at al,
maye be taught, to the greate forderaunce of Artillarie through
out al this Realme. And trewlye I meruell gretelye, that
Englysshe men woulde neuer yet, seke for the Arte of shootynge,
seinge they be so apte vnto it, so praysed of there frendes, so
feared of there ennemyes for it. Vegetius woulde
haue maysters appointed, whyche shoulde teache
youthe to shoote faire. Leo the Emperour of Rome, sheweth
the same custome, to haue bene alwayes amongest
ye olde Romaynes: whych custome of teachyng
youth to shoote (saythe he) after it was omitted, and litle hede
taken of, brought the hole Empire of Rome, to grete Ruine.
Schola Persica, that is the Scole of the Persians,
appoynted to brynge vp youthe, whiles they were
.xx. yeres olde in shooting, is as notably knowne in Histories
as the Impire of ye Persians: whych schole, as doth apere in
Cornelius Tacitus, as sone as they gaue ouer and
fell to other idle pastimes, brought bothe them
and ye Parthians vnder ye subiection of the Romaines. Plato
would haue common maisters and stipendes, for
to teache youthe to shoote, & for the same purpose
he would haue a brode feylde nere euery Citie, made common
for men to vse shotyng in, whyche sayeng the more reasonably
it is spoken of Plato, the more vnresonable is theyr dede
whiche woulde ditche vp those feeldes priuatly for ther owne
profyt, whyche lyeth open generallye for the commō vse: men
by suche goodes be made rycher not honester sayeth Tullie.
Yf men can be perswaded to haue shootynge
taughte, this aucthorite whyche foloweth will
perswade them, or els none, and that is as I haue ones sayde
before, of Kynge Dauyd, whose fyrste acte and ordinaunce was
after he was kynge that all Iudea should learne to shoote. Yf
shotyng could speake, she would accuse England of vnkyndnesse
and slouthfulnesse, of vnkyndnesse toward her bycause she
beyng left to a lytle blynd vse, lackes her best maintener which
is cunnynge: of slouthfulnesse towarde theyr owne selfe, bycause
they are content wyth that whych aptnesse and vse doth graunt
them in shootynge, and wyl seke for no knowlege as other
noble cōmon welthes haue done: and the iustlier shootynge
myght make thys complaynt, seynge that of fence and weapons

Vegetius.

Leo. 6. 5.

Strabo. 11.

Cor. Ta. 2.

De leg. 7.

De Offi. 2.

there is made an Arte, a thyng in no wyse to be compared to shootynge.

For of fence all mooste in euerye towne, there is not onely Masters to teache it, wyth his Prouostes Vsshers Scholers and other names of arte & Schole, but there hath not fayled also, whyche hathe diligently and well fauouredly written it and is set out in Printe that euery man maye rede it.

What discommoditie doeth comme by the lacke of knowlege, in shootynge, it were ouer longe to rehearce. For manye that haue bene apte, and loued shootynge, bycause they knewe not whyche way to houlde to comme to shootynge, haue cleane tourned them selues from shootynge.

And I maye telle you Philologe, the lacke of teachynge to shoote in Englande, causeth very manye men, to playe with the kynges Aĉtes, as a man dyd ones eyther with the Mayre of London or Yorke I can not tel whether, whiche dyd commaund by proclamation, euerye man in the Citie, to hange a lanterne wyth a candell, afore his dore : whiche thynge the man dyd, but he dyd not lyght it : And so many bye bowes bicause of the aĉte, but yet they shote not : not of euyll wyll, but bycause they knowe not howe to shoote. But to conclude of this matter, in shoting as in all other thynges, Apte-nesse is the fyrste, and chyefe thynge, whiche if it be awaye, neyther Cunnynge or Vse, doeth anye good at all, as the Scottes and Fraunce men, wyth knowledge and Vse of shootynge, shall become good Archers, whan a cūnynge shypwright shall make a stronge shyppe, of a Salowe tree : or whan a husbandman shall becom ryche, wyth sowyng wheat on Newmarket heath. Cunnynge muste be had, bothe to set out, & amende Nature, and also to ouersee, and correĉte vse : which vse yf it be not led, & gouerned wyth cunnyng, shall sooner go amisse, than strayght.

Aptnesse.

Cunnynge.

Vse maketh perfitnesse, in doinge that thynge, whervnto nature maketh a man apte, and knowlege maketh a man cunninge before. So yᵗ it is not so doubtful, which of them three hath moost stroke in shoting as it is playne & euident, that all thre must be had, in excellent shootynge. PHI. For this communicaciō Toxophile I am very glad, and yᵗ for myn owne sake bicause I trust now, to become a shoter, And in dede I thought a fore, English mē most apte for shoting, and

I sawe them dayelye vse shotyng, but yet I neuer founde none, that woulde talke of anye knowlege whereby a man might come to shotynge. Therfore I trust that you, by the vse you haue had in shoting, haue so thorowly marked and noted the nature of it, that you can teache me as it were by a trade or waye how to come to it. TOX. I graunte, I haue vsed shootinge meetly well, that I might haue marked it wel ynoughe, yf I had bene diligent. But my much shootynge, hath caused me studie litle, so that thereby I lacke learnynge, whych shulde set out the Arte or waye in any thynge. And you knowe that I was neuer so well sene, in the Posteriorums of Aristotle as to inuent and searche out general Demonstrations for the setting forth of any newe Science. Yet by my trothe yf you wyll, I wyll goe with you into the fealdes at any tyme and tel you as much as I can, or els you maye stande some tyme at the prickes and looke on thē which shoote best and so learne. PHI. Howe lytle you haue looked of Aristotle, and how muche learnynge, you haue lost by shotynge I can not tell, but this I woulde saye and yf I loued you neuer so ill, that you haue bene occupied in sumwhat els besyde shotynge. But to our purpose, as I wyll not requyre a trade in shotinge to be taught me after the sutteltye of Aristotle, euen so do I not agre with you in this poynt, that you wold haue me learne to shoote with lokyng on them which shoote best, for so I knowe I should neuer come to shote meanelye. For in shotyng as in all other thynges which be gotten by teachynge, there must be shewed a waye & a path which shal leade a man to yᵉ best and cheiffest point whiche is in shootynge, whiche you do marke youre selfe well ynough, and vttered it also in youre communication, when you sayde there laye hyd in ye nature of shootyng a certayne waye whych wel perceyued and thorowlye knowen, woulde bring a mā wythout any wanderyng to yᵉ beste ende in shotyng whych you called hitting of the pricke. Therfore I would refer all my shootinge to that ende which is best, and so shuld I come the soner to some meane. That whiche is best hath no faulte, nor can not be amended. So shew me beste shootynge, not the beste shoter, which yf he be neuer so good, yet hath he many a faulte easelye of any man to be espyed. And therfore meruell not yf I requyre to folowe that example whych is without faulte, rather than that which hath so manye faultes. And thys waye euery wyse man doth folow in teachynge any maner of thynge. As Aristotle when he teacheth a man to be good he settes not before hym Socrates lyfe whyche was ye best man, but chiefe goodnesse it selfe accordynge to whych he would haue a man direᶜte his lyfe. TOX. This waye which you requyre of me *Philologe*, is to hard for me, and to hye for a shooter to taulke on, & takē as I suppose out of the middes of Philosophie, to serche out the perfite ende of any thyng, ye which perfite ende to fynde out,

Ora. ad Bru.   sayth Tullie, is the hardest thynge in the worlde, the onely occasyon and cause, why so many seᶜtes of Philosophers hathe bene alwayse in learnynge. And althoughe as Cicero saith a man maye ymagine and dreame in his mynde of a perfite ende in any thynge, yet there is no experience nor vse of it, nor was neuer sene yet amonges men, as alwayes to heale the sycke, euer more to leade a shyppe without daunger, at al times to hit the prick : shall no Physicion, no shypmaster, no shoter euer do. And Aristotle saith that in

Arist. pol. 8. 6.   all deades there are two pointes to be marked, possibilitie & excelēcie, but chefely a wise mā must folow & laye hand on possibilitie for feare he lease bothe. Therfore seyng that which is moost perfeᶜt and best in shootyng as alwayes to hit ye pricke, was neuer sene nor hard tel on yet amōges men, but onelye ymagined and thought vpon in a man his mynde, me thinck this is the wisest coūsel & best for vs to folow rather that which a man maye come to, than y^t whyche is vnpossible to be attained to, leste iustely that sayeng of ye wyse mayde Ismene in Sophocles maye be verifyed on vs.

Soph. Anti.   *A foole he is that takes in hande he can not ende.*

PHI. Well yf the perfite ende of other matters, had bene as perfitlye knowne, as the perfite ende of shotynge is, there had neuer bene so manye seᶜtes of Philosophers as there be, for in shoting both man & boye is in one opinion, that alwayes to hit the pryck is mooste perfeᶜte end that can be imagyned, so that we shal not nede gretly contend in this matter. But now sir, whereas you thynke y^t a man in learning to shoote or any thyng els, shuld rather wyselye folow possibilitie, thā vainly seke for perfite excellencie, surelye I wyl proue y^t euery wyse man, y^t wisely wold learne any thyng, shal chiefly go aboute y^t whervnto he knoweth wel he shal neuer come. And you youre selfe I suppose shal confesse ye same to be ye best way in teachyng, yf you wyl answere me to those thinges whych I wyl aske of you. TOX. And y^t I wyl gladlye, both bycause I thynke it is vnpossible for you to proue it, & also bycause I desire to here what you cā saye in it. PHI. The studie of a good Physiciō Toxophile, I trow be to know al diseases & al medicines fit for them. TOX. It is so in dede. PHI. Bicause I suppose he would gladly at al tymes heale al diseases of al men. TOX. Ye truely. PHI. A good purpose surely, but was ther euer physiciō yet among so many whyche hath laboured in thys study, that at al times coulde heale all diseases? TOX. No trewly ; nor I thyncke neuer shalbe. PHI. Than Physicions by lyke, studie for y^t, whiche none of them cōmeth vnto. But in learning of fence I pray you what is y^t which men moost labor for ? TOX. That they may hit a nother I trow & neuer take blow theyr selfe. PHI. You say trothe, & I am sure euery one of thē would faine do so whē so euer he playethe. But was there euer any of thē so conning yet, which at one tyme or other hath not be[n] touched ? TOX. The best of them all is glad somtyme to escape with a blowe. PHIL. Thā in fence also, men are taught to go aboute that thing, whiche the best of them all knowethe he shall neuer attayne vnto. Moreouer you that be shoters, I pray you, what meane you, whan ye take so great heade, to kepe youre stand- ynge, to shoote compasse, to looke on your marke so diligently, to cast vp grasse diuerse tymes and other thinges more, you know better thā I. What would you do thā I pray you ? TOX. Hit ye marke yf we could. PHIL. And doth euery mā go about to hit the marke at euery shoote ? TOX. By my trothe I trow so, and as for my selfe I am sure I do. PHIL. But al men do not hit it at al tymes. TOX. No trewlye for that were a wonder. PHIL. Can any man hit it at all tymes ? TOX. No man verilie. PHIL. Than by likely to hit the pricke alwayes, is vnpossible. For that is called vnpossible whych is in no man his power to do. TOX. Vnpossible in dede. PHIL. But to shoote wyde and far of the marke is a thynge possyble. TOX. No man wyll denie that. PHIL. But yet to hit the marke alwayse were an excellent thyng. TOX. Excellent surelie. PHIL. thā I am sure those be wiser men, which couete to shoote wyde than those whiche couete to hit the prycke. TOX. Why so I pray you.   PHIL. Because to shote wyde is a thynge possyble, and therfore as you saye youre selfe, of euery wyse mā to be folowed.   And as for hittinge yᶜ prick, bycause it is vnpossible, it were a vaine thynge to go aboute it : but in good sadnesse *Toxophile* thus you se that a man might go throghe all craftes and sciences, and proue that anye man in his science coueteth that which he shal neuer gette. TOX. By my trouth (as you saye) I can not denye, but they do so : but why and wherfore they shulde do so, I can not learne. PHILO. I wyll tell you, euerye crafte and science standeth in two thynges : in Knowing of his crafte, & Working of his crafte : For perfyte knowlege bringeth a man to perfyte workyng This knowe Paynters, karuers, Taylours, shomakers, and all other craftes men, to be true. Nowe, in euery crafte, there is a perfite excellencie, which may be better knowen in a mannes mynde, then folowed in a mannes dede : This perfytenesse, bycause it is generally layed as a brode wyde example afore al mē, no one particuler man is able to compasse it : and as it is generall to al men, so it is perpetuall for al time whiche proueth it a thynge for man vnpossible : although not for the capacitie of our thinkyng whiche is heauenly, yet surelye for the habilitie of our workyng whyche is worldlye.

God gyueth not full perfytenesse to one man (sayth Tullie) *De. Inuen. 2* lest if one man had all in any one science, ther shoulde be nothyng lefte for an other. Yet God suffereth vs to haue the perfyt knowledge of it, that such a knowledge dilligently folowed, might bring forth accordyng as a man doth labour, perfyte woorkyng.   And who is he, that in learnynge to wryte, woulde forsake an excellent example, and folowe a worse ?   Therfore seing perfytenesse it selfe is an example for vs, let euerye man studye howe he maye come nye it, which is a poynt of wysdome, not reason with God why he may not attaine vnto it, which is vayne curosite. TOX. Surely this is gaily said Philologe, but yet this one thinge I am afraide of, lest this perfitnesse which you speke on wil discourage men to take any thynge in hande, bycause afore they begin, they know, they shal neuer come to an ende. And thus dispayre shall dispatche, euen at the fyrste entrynge in, many a good man his purpose and intente. And I thinke both you your selfe, & al other men to, woulde counte it mere folie for a man to tell hym whome he teacheth, that he shal neuer optaine that, whyche he would fainest learne. And therfore this same hyghe and perfite waye of teachyng let vs leue it to hygher matters, and as for shootynge it shalbe content with a meaner waye well ynoughe. PHI. Where as you saye y^t this hye perfitnesse will discorage mē, bycause they knowe, they shall neuer attayne vnto it, I am sure cleane contrarie there is nothynge in the world shall incourage men more than it. And whye? For where a man seith, that though a nother man be neuer so excellente, yet it is possible for hym selfe to be better, what payne or labour wyl that man refuse to take? yf the game be onse wonne, no mā wyl set forth hys foote to ronne. And thus perfitnesse beynge so hyghe a thynge that men maye looke at it, not come to it, and beynge so plentifull and indifferent to euerye bodye that the plentifulnesse of it maye prouoke all men to labor, bycause it hath ynoughe for all mē, the indifferencye of it shall encourage euerye one to take more paine than hys fellowe, bycause euerye man is rewarded accordyng to his nye cōmyng, and yet whych is moste meruel of al, ye more men take of it, the more they leue behynd for other, as Socrates dyd in wysdome, and Cicero in eloquens, whereby other hath not lacked, but hathe fared a greate deele ye better. And thus perfitnesse it selfe bycause it is neuer obteyned, euen therfore only doth it cause so many men to be so well sene & perfite in many matters, as they be. But where as you thynke y^t it were fondnesse to teache a man to shoote, in lokyng at the most perfitnesse in it, but rather woulde haue a manne go some other way to worke, I trust no wyse man wyl discomend that way, except he thincke himselfe wyser than Tullye, whiche doeth playnlye saye, that yf he teached any maner of crafte as he dyd Rhetorike he would labor to *De Orat.* 3. bringe a man to the knowlege of the moost perfitnesse of it, whyche knowlege should euer more leade and gyde a manne to do that thynge well whiche he went aboute. Whych waye in al maner of learnyng to be best, Plato dothe also declare in Euthydemus, of whome Tullie learned it as he dyd many other thynges mo. And thus you se Toxophile by what reasons and by whose authorite I do require of you this waye in teachynge me to shoote, which waye I praye you withoute any more delaye shew me as far forth as you haue noted and marked. TOX. You cal me to a thyng Philologe which I am lothe to do. And yet yf I do it not beinge but a smale matter as you thynke, you wyll lacke frendeshyp in me, yf I take it in hande and not bring it to passe as you woulde haue it, you myghte thyncke great wāt of wysdome in me.

But aduyse you, seing ye wyll nedes haue it so, the blame shalbe yours, as well as myne: yours for puttynge vpon me so instauntlye, myne in receyuynge so fondly a greater burthen then I am able to beare. Therfore I, more wyllynge to fulfyll your mynde, than hopyng to accomplysh that which you loke for, shall speake of it, not as a master of shotynge, but as one not altogyther ignoraunt in shotynge. And one thynge I am glad of, the sunne drawinge downe so fast into the west, shall compell me to drawe a pace to the ende of our matter, so that his darkenesse shall
somethyng cloke myne ignoraunce. And bycause
you knowe the orderynge of a matter better
then I: Aske me generallye of it, and I
shall particularly answere to it. PHI.
Very gladly Toxophile: for so
by ordre, those thynges
whiche I woulde
knowe, you shal
tell the bet-
ter: and
those
thynges
whiche you shall tell, I
shall remembre
the better.

TOXOPHI-
LVS. B.

THE SECONDE BOOKE OF
the schole of shotyng.

PHILOL. What is the cheyfe poynte in shootynge, that euerye manne laboureth to come to? TOX. To hyt the marke. PHI. Howe manye thynges are required to make a man euer more hyt the marke? TOX. Twoo. PHI. Whiche twoo? TOX. Shotinge streyght and kepynge of a lengthe. PHIL. Howe shoulde a manne shoote strayght, & howe shulde a man kepe a length? TOX. In knowynge and hauynge thinges, belongynge to shootyng: and whan they be knowen and had, in well handlynge of them: whereof some belong to shotyng strayght, some to keping of a lēgth, some commonly to them bothe, as shall be tolde seuerally of them, in place conuenient. PHI. Thynges belongyng to shotyng, whyche be they? TOX. All thinges be outwarde, and some be instrumentes for euery sere archer to brynge with him, proper for his owne vse: other thynges be generall to euery man, as the place and tyme serueth. PHI. which be instru-mētes? TOX. Bracer, shotynggloue, stryng, bowe & shafte. PHI. Whiche be general to all men? TOX. The wether and the marke, yet the marke is euer vnder the rule of the wether. PHI. wherin standeth well handlynge of thynges? TOX. All togyther wythin a man him selfe, some handlynge is proper to instrumentes, some to the wether, somme to the marke, some is within a man hym selfe. PHI. what handlyng is proper to the Instrumentes. TOX. Standynge, nockyng, drawyng, holdyng, lowsing, wherby cōmeth fayre shotynge, whiche neyther belong· to wynde nor wether, nor yet to the marke, for in a rayne and at no marke, a man may shote a fayre shoote. PHI. well sayde, what handlynge belongeth to the

wether? TOX. Knowyng of his wynde, with hym, agaynst
hym, syde wynd, ful syde wind, syde wynde quarter with him,
syde wynde quarter agaynste hym, and so forthe. PHI. well
than go to, what handlynge belongeth to the marke? TOX. To
marke his standyng, to shote compasse, to draw euermore lyke,
to lowse euermore lyke, to consyder the nature of the pricke,
in hylles & dales, in strayte planes and winding places, & also
to espy his marke. PHI. Very well done. And what is
onely within a man hym selfe? TOX. Good heede gyuynge,
and auoydynge all affections: whiche thynges oftentymes do
marre and make all. And these thynges spoken of me generally
and brefely, yf they be wel knowen, had, and handled, shall
brynge a man to suche shootynge, as fewe or none euer yet
came vnto, but surely yf he misse in any one of thē, he can
neuer hyt the marke, and in the more he doth misse, the farther
he shoteth from his marke. But as in all other matters the
fyrst steppe or stayre to be good, is to know a mannes faulte,
and than to amende it, and he that wyl not knowe his faulte,
shall neuer amende it. PHI. You speake nowe Toxophile,
euen as I wold haue you to speake: But lette vs returne agayne
vnto our matter, and those thynges whyche you haue packed
vp, in so shorte a roume, we wyll lowse thē forthe, and take
euery pyece as it were in our hande and looke more narowlye
vpon it. TOX. I am content, but we wyll rydde them as
fast as we can, bycause the sunne goeth so faste downe, and
yet somewhat muste needes be sayde of euerye one of them.
PHI. well sayde, and I trowe we beganne wyth those thynges
whiche be instrumentes, whereof the fyrste, as I suppose, was
Bracer.   the Braser. TOX. Litle is to be sayd of the
          braser. A bracer serueth for two causes, one to
saue his arme from the strype of the strynge, and his doublet
from wearynge, and the other is, that the strynge glydynge
sharpelye & quicklye of the bracer, maye make the sharper
shoote. For if the strynge shoulde lyght vpon the bare sleue,
the strengthe of the shoote shoulde stoppe and dye there. But
it is best by my iudgemente, to gyue the bowe so muche bent,
that the strynge neede neuer touche a mannes arme, and so
shoulde a man nede no bracer as I knowe manye good Archers,
whiche occupye none. In a bracer a man muste take hede of
.iii. thinges, yᵗ it haue no nayles in it, that it haue no bucles,

that it be fast on with laces wythout agglettes. For the nayles wyll shere in sunder, a mānes string, before he be ware, and so put his bowe in ieoperdy: Buckles and agglettes at vnwares, shall race hys bowe, a thinge bothe euyll to the syghte, & perilous for freatynge. And thus a Bracer, is onely had for this purpose, that the strynge maye haue redye passage. PHI. In my Bracer I am cunnyng ynough, but what saye you of the shootyng gloue.

TOX. A shootynge Gloue is chieflye, for to saue a mannes fyngers from hurtynge, that he maye be able to beare the sharpe stryng to the vttermost of his strengthe. And whan a man shooteth, the might of his shoote lyeth on the formooste fynger, and on the Ringman, for the myddle fynger whiche is the longest, lyke a lubber starteth backe, and beareth no weyght of the strynge in a maner at all, therfore the two other fyngers, muste haue thicker lether, and that muste haue thickest of all, where on a man lowseth moste, and for sure lowsyng, the formoste finger is moste apte, bycause it holdeth best, & for y^t purpose nature hath as a man woulde saye, yocked it w^t the thoumbe. Ledder, if it be nexte a mans skynne, wyl sweat, waxe hard and chafe, therefore scarlet for the softnes of it and thicknesse wyth all, is good to sewe wythin a mānes gloue. If that wylle not serue, but yet youre finger hurteth, you muste take a searynge cloth made of fine virgin waxe, and Deres sewet, & put nexte your fynger, and so on wyth youre gloue. If yet you fele your fynger pinched, leaue shootyng both because than you shall shoote nought, & agayn by litle & lytle, hurtynge your finger, ye shall make it longe and longe to or you shoote agayne. A newe gloue pluckes many shootes bycause the stringe goeth not freelye of, and therefore the fingers muste be cut short, and trimmed with some ointment, that the string maye glyd wel awaye. Some with holdynge in the nocke of theyr shafte too harde, rub the skyn of there fingers. For this there be .ii. remedyes, one to haue a goose quyll splettyd and sewed againste the nockynge, betwixt the lining and the ledder, whyche shall helpe the shoote muche to, the other waye is to haue some roule of ledder sewed betwixt his fingers at the setting on of the fingers, which shall kepe his fingers so in sunder, that they shal not hold the nock so fast as they did. The shootyng gloue hath a purse whych shall serue to put fine linen cloth and wax in, twoo necessary thynges for a shooter, some men vse gloues or other suche lyke thyng on their bow hād for chafyng, bycause they houlde so harde. But that commeth commonlye, when a bowe is not rounde, but somewhat square, fine waxe shall do verye well in such a case to laye where a man holdeth his bow : and thus muche as concernynge your gloue. And these thynges althoughe they be trifles, yet bycause you be but a yonge shoter, I woulde not leue them out. PHI. And so you shal do me moost pleasure : The string I trow be the next. TOX. The next in dede.

Stringe. A thing though it be lytle, yet not a litle to be regarded. But here in you muste be contente to put youre truste in honest stringers. And surely stringers ought more diligently to be looked vpon by the officers thā ether bower or fletcher, bycause they may deceyue a simple man the more easelyer. An ill stringe brekethe many a good bowe, nor no other thynge halfe so many. In warre if a string breke the man is loste and is no man, for his weapon is gone, and althoughe he haue two stringes put one at once, yet he shall haue small leasure & lesse roume to bend his bow, therfore god send vs good stringers both for war and peace. Now what a stringe ought to be made on, whether of good hempe as they do now a dayes, or of flaxe or of silke, I leue that to the *Eustathius.* iugemente of stringers, of whome we muste bye them on. Eustathius apon this verse of homere

Twāg q̄ the bow, & twāg q̄ the string, out quicklie the shaft flue
Iliad. 4.

doeth tel, that in oulde tyme they made theyr bowe strynges of bullox thermes, whiche they twyned togither as they do ropes, & therfore they made a great twange. Bowe strynges also hath bene made of the heare of an horse tayle called for the matter of them Hippias as dothe appeare in manye good authors of the *Fauorinus.* Greke tongue. Great stringes, and lytle strynges be for diuerse purposes : the great string is more surer for the bowe, more stable to pricke wythal, but slower for the cast, the lytle stringe is cleane contrarye, not so sure, therfore to be taken hede of, leste with longe tarienge on, it breake your bowe, more fit to shoote farre, than apte to pricke nere, therfore when you knowe the nature of bothe bigge and

lytle, you must fit your bow, according to the occasion of your
shootinge. In stringinge of your bow (though this place belong
rather to the hādlyng than to the thyng it selfe, yet bycause the
thynge, and the handlynge of the thynge, be so ioyned together,
I must nede some tyme couple the one wyth the other,) you
must mark the fit length of youre bowe. For yf the stringe be
to short, the bending wyll gyue, and at the last slyp and so put
the bowe in ieopardye. Yf it be longe, the bendynge must
nedes be in the smal of the string, which beynge sore twined
muste nedes knap in sunder to yᵉ distruction of manye good
bowes. Moreouer you must looke that youre bowe be well
nocked for fere the sharpnesse of the horne shere a sunder the
strynge And that chaunceth ofte when in bending, the string
hath but one wap to strengthe it wyth all. You must marke
also to set youre stringe streygte on, or elles the one ende shall
wriethe contrary to the other, and so breke your bowe. When
the stringe begynnethe neuer so lytle to were, trust it not, but
a waye with it for it is an yll saued halpeny yᵗ costes a man
a crowne Thus you se howe many ieopardyes hangethe ouer
the selye poore bowe, by reason onlye of the strynge. As when
the stringe is shorte, when it is longe, whē eyther of the nockes
be nought, when it hath but one wap, and when it taryethe
ouer longe on. PHI. I se wel it is no meruell, though so
many bowes be broken. TOX. Bowes be broken twise as
many wayes besyde these. But a gayne in stringynge youre
bowe, you must loke for muche bende or lytle bende for they
be cleane contrarye.

The lytle bende hath but one commoditie, whyche is in
shootyng faster and farther shoote, and yᵉ cause therof is,
bycause the strynge hath so far a passage, or it parte wyth the
shafte. The greate bende hath many commodities: for it
maketh easyer shootynge the bowe beyng halfe drawen afore.
It needeth no bracer, for the strynge stoppeth before it come at
the arme. It wyl not so sone hit a mannes sleue or other
geare, by the same reason: It hurteth not the shaft fedder, as
the lowe bende doeth. It suffereth a man better to espye his
marke. Therfore lette youre bowe haue good byg bend,
a shaftemente and .ii. fyngers at the least, for these which
I haue spoken of. PHI. The braser, gloue, and
strynge, be done, nowe you muste come to the

Bowe.

bowe, the chefe instrument of all. TOX. Dyuers countryes and tymes haue vsed alwayes dyuers bowes, and of dyuers fashions. Horne bowes are vsed in some places nowe, & were vsed also *Iliad.* 4. in Homerus dayes, for Pandarus bowe, the best shooter among al the Troianes, was made of two Goete hornes ioyned togyther, the lengthe wherof sayth Homer, was .xvi. handbredes, not far differing from the lengthe of our bowes.

Scripture maketh mention of brasse bowes. Iron bowes, *Psalm.* 17. and style bowes, haue bene of longe tyme, and also nowe are vsed among the Turkes, but yet they must nedes be vnprofitable. For yf brasse, yron or style, haue theyr owne strength and pith in them, they be farre aboue mānes strength : yf they be made meete for mannes strengthe, theyr pithe is nothyng worth to shoote any shoote wyth all.

The Ethiopians had bowes of palme tre, whiche seemed to *Hero. in pol.* be very stronge, but we haue none experience of them. The lengthe of them was .iiii. cubites The men of Inde had theyr bowes made of a rede, whiche was of a great strengthe. And no maruayle though bowe and shaftes were made therof, for the redes be so great in Inde, as *In Thalia.* Herodotus sayth, that of euery ioynte of a rede, a man may make a fyshers bote. These bowes, sayeth Arrianus in Alexanders lyfe, gaue so great a stroke, that *Arrianus.* 8. no harneys or buckler though it were neuer so strong, could wythstand it. The length of suche a bowe, was euen wyth the length of hym, that vsed it. The *In Polym.* Lycians vsed bowes made of a tree, called in Latyn *Cornus,* (as concernyng the name of it in English, I can soner proue that other men call it false, than I can tell the right name of it my selfe) this wood is as harde as horne and very fit for shaftes, as shall be toulde after.

Ouid sheweth that Syringa the Nymphe, and one of the *Metamor.* 1. maydens of Diana, had a bowe of this wood wherby the poete meaneth, that it was verye excellent to make bowes of

As for brasell, Elme, Wych, and Asshe, experience doth proue them to be but meane for bowes, and so to conclude Ewe of all other thynges, is that, wherof perfite shootyng woulde haue a bowe made.

Thys woode as it is nowe generall and common amonges Englyshe men, so hath it continewed from longe tyme and had in moost price for bowes, amõges the Romaynes, as doth apere in this halfe verse of Vyrgill.

Taxi torquentur in arcus.

i.

Ewe fit for a bowe to be made on.

Virgilius.
Georg. 2.

Nowe as I saye, a bowe of Ewe must be hadde for perfecte shootinge at the prickes, whiche marke, bycause it is certayne, & moste certaine rules may be gyuen of it, shall serue for our cõmunication, at this time. A good bowe is knowen, much what as good counsayle is knowen, by the ende and proofe of it, & yet bothe a bowe and good counsell, maye be made bothe better and worse, by well or yll handlynge of them : as often-tymes chaũceth. And as a man both muste and wyll take counsell, of a wyse and honeste man, though he se not the ende of it, so must a shooter of necessitie, truste an honest and good bowyer for a bowe, afore he knowe the proofe of it. And as a wyse man wyll take plentye of counsel afore hand what soeuer need, so a shooter shulde haue alwayes .iii. or .iiii. bowes, in store, what so euer chaunce. PHI. But if I truste bowyers alwayes, sometyme I am lyke to be deceyued. TOX. There-fore shall I tell you some tokens in a bowe, that you shal be the seeldomer deceyued. If you come into a shoppe, and fynde a bowe that is small, long, heauy and strong, lyinge st[r]eyght, not windyng, not marred with knot gaule, wyndeshake, wem, freat or pynche, bye that bowe of my warrant. The beste colour of a bowe yᵗ I fynde, is whan the backe and the bellye in woorkynge, be muche what after one maner, for such often-tymes in wearyng, do proue lyke virgin wax or golde, hauynge a fine longe grayne, euen from the one ende of the bowe, to the other : the short graine although suche proue well somtyme, are for yᵉ most parte, very brittle. Of the makynge of the bowe, I wyll not greatly meddle, leste I shoulde seeme to enter into an other mannes occupation, whyche I can no skyll of. Yet I woulde desyre all bowyers to season theyr staues well, to woorke them and synke them well, to giue thē heetes conuenient, and tyllerynges plentye. For thereby they shoulde bothe get them selues a good name, (And a good name encreseth a mannes

profyt muche) and also do greate cōmodite to the hole Realme.
If any men do offend in this poynte, I am afrayde they be those
iourny mē whiche labour more spedily to make manye bowes
for theyr owne monye sake, than they woorke dilligently to
make good bowes, for the common welth sake, not layinge
before theyr eyes, thys wyse prouerbe.

Sone ynough, if wel ynough.

Wherwyth euere honest handye craftes man shuld measure, as
it were wyth a rule, his worke withal. He that is a iourney
man, and rydeth vpon an other mannes horse, yf he ryde an
honest pace, no manne wyll dysalowe hym : But yf he make
Poste haste, bothe he that oweth the horse, and he peraduenture
also that afterwarde shal bye the horse, may chaūce to curse
hym.

Suche hastinesse I am afrayde, maye also be found amonges
some of thē, whych through out yᵉ Realme in diuerse places
worke yᵉ kinges Artillarie for war, thinkynge yf they get a
bowe or a sheafe of arrowes to some fashion, they be good
ynough for bearynge gere. And thus that weapon whiche is
the chiefe defence of the Realme, verye ofte doth lytle seruyce
to hym that shoulde vse it, bycause it is so negligentlye wrought
of him that shuld make it, when trewlye I suppose that nether
yᵉ bowe can be to good and chefe woode, nor yet to well
seasoned or truly made, wyth hetynges and tillerynges, nether
that shafte to good wood or to thorowely wrought, with the
best pinion fedders that can be gotten, wherwith a man shal
serue his prince, defende his countrie, and saue hym selfe frome
his enemye. And I trust no man wyll be angrye wyth me for
spekynge thus, but those which finde them selfe touched
therin : which ought rather to be angrye wyth them selfe for
doynge so, than to be miscontent wyth me for saynge so. And
in no case they ought to be displeased wyth me, seinge this is
spoken also after that sorte, not for the notynge of anye person
seuerallye, but for the amendynge of euerye one generallye.
But turne we agayne to knowe a good shootynge bowe for
oure purpose.

Euerye bowe is made eyther of a boughe, of a plante or of
the boole of the tree. The boughe cōmonlye is verye knotty,
and full of pinnes, weak, of small pithe, and sone wyll folowe

the stringe, and seldome werith to anye fayre coloure, yet for chyldren & yonge beginners it maye serue well ynoughe. The plante proueth many times wel, yf it be of a good and clene groweth, and for the pith of it is quicke ynoughe of cast, it wyl plye and bow far afore it breake, as al other yōge thinges do. The boole of yᵉ tree is clenest wᵗout knot or pin, hauinge a faste and harde woode by reasonne of hys full groweth, stronge and myghtye of cast, and best for a bow, yf the staues be euen clouen, and be afterwarde wroughte not ouerwharte the woode, but as the graine and streyght growyng of the woode leadethe a man, or elles by all reason it must sone breake, & that in many shiuers. This must be considered in the roughe woode, & when the bow staues be ouerwrought and facioned. For in dressing and pikynge it vp for a bow, it is to late to loke for it But yet in these poyntes as I sayd before you muste truste an honest bowyer, to put a good bow in youre hand, somewhat lookinge your selfe to those tokens whyche I shewed you. And you muste not sticke for a grote or .xii. d. more than a nother man would giue yf it be a good bowe. For a good bow twise paide for is better than an ill bowe once broken.

Thus a shooter muste begyn not at the makynge of hys bowe lyke a bower, but at the byinge of hys bow lyke an Archere. And when his bow is bought and brought home, afore he truste muche vpon it, let hym trye and trym it after thys sorte.

Take your bow in to the feeld, shote in hym, sinke hym wyth deade heauye shaftes, looke where he cōmethe moost, prouyde for that place betymes, leste it pinche and so freate : whē you haue thus shot in him, and perceyued good shootynge woode in hym, you must haue hym agayne to a good cunnynge, and trustie woorkeman, whyche shall cut hym shorter, and pike hym and dresse hym fytter, make hym comme rounde compace euery where, and whippyng at the endes, but with discretion, lest he whyp in sunder or els freete, soner than he is ware of, he must also lay hym streght, if he be caste or otherwise nede require, and if he be flatte made, gather hym rounde, and so shall he bothe shoote the faster, for farre shootynge, and also the surer for nere pryckynge. PHI. What yf I come into a shoppe, and spye oute a bow, which shal both than please

me very wel whan I by him, and be also very fit and meete for
me whan I shote in hym : so that he be both weake ynoughe for
easye shootynge, and also quycke and spedye ynoughe for farre
castynge, than I woulde thynke I shall nede no more businesse
wyth him, but be contente wyth hym, and vse hym well ynoughe,
and so by that meanes, auoyde bothe great trouble, and also
some cost whiche you cunnynge archers very often put your
selues vnto, beynge verye Englyshe men, neuer ceasynge
piddelynge about your bowe & shaftes whan they be well, but
eyther with shorting and pikynge your bowes, or els with newe
fetheryng, peecynge and headinge your shaftes, can neuer haue
done vntyll they be starke nought. TOX. Wel *Philologe*,
surelye if I haue any iudgement at all in shootyng, it is no very
great good token in a bowe, whereof nothyng whan it is newe
and fresshe, nede be cutte away, euen as Cicero sayeth of a
yonge mānes wit and style, which you knowe better than I.
For euerye newe thynge muste alwayes haue more than it
neadeth, or elles it wyll not waxe better and better, but euer
decaye, and be worse and worse. Newe ale if it runne not
ouer the barrell whan it is newe tunned, wil sone lease his pith,
and his head afore he be longe drawen on.

    And lyke wyse as that colte whyche at the fyrste takynge
vp, nedeth lytle breakyng and handlyng, but is fitte and gentle
ynoughe for the saddle, seeldome or neuer proueth well, euen so
that bowe whyche at the fyrste byinge, wythout any more
proofe & trimmynge, is fit and easie to shoote in, shall neyther
be profitable to laste longe, nor yet pleasaunt to shoote well.
And therfore as a younge horse full of corage, wyth handlynge
and breakinge, is brought vnto a sure pace and goynge, so shall
a newe bowe fresshe and quicke of caste, by sinkyng &
cuttyng, be brought to a stedfast shootyng. And an easie and
gentle bow whan it is newe, is not muche vnlyke a softe spirited
boye when he is younge. But yet as of an vnrulie boye with
right handlyng, proueth oftenest of al a well ordered man : so
of an vnfit and staffysh bow with good trimming, muste nedes
folowe alwayes a stedfast shotynge bowe.

    And suche a perfite bowe, whiche neuer wyll deceyue a
man, excepte a man deceyue it, muste be had for that perfecte
ende, whyche you looke for in shootinge. PHI. Well
Toxophile, I see wel you be cunninger in this gere than I :

but put case that I haue thre or fower suche good bowes, pyked
and dressed, as you nowe speke of, yet I do remember y^t manye
learned men do saye, that it is easier to gette a good thynge,
than to saue and keepe a good thyng, wherfore if you can teache
me as concernyng that poynte, you haue satisfyed me plentifullye,
as concernynge a bowe. TOX. Trulye it was the nexte
thyng that I woulde haue come vnto, for so the matter laye.

When you haue broughte youre bowe to suche a poynte, as
I spake of, than you must haue an herdē or wullen cloth waxed,
wherw^t euery day you must rubbe and chafe your bowe, tyll it
shyne and glytter withall. Whyche thynge shall cause it bothe
to be cleane, well fauoured, goodlye of coloure, and shall also
bryng as it were a cruste, ouer it, that is to say, shall make it
euery where on the outsyde, so slyppery and harde, that neyther
any weete or wether can enter to hurte it, nor yet any freat or
pynche, be able to byte vpon it : but that you shal do it great
wrong before you breake it. This must be done oftentimes but
specially when you come from shootynge.

Beware also whan you shoote, of youre shaft hedes, dagger,
knyues or agglettes, lest they race your bowe, a thing as I sayde
before, bothe vnsemely to looke on, and also daūgerous for
freates. Take hede also of mistie and dankyshe dayes, whiche
shal hurte a bowe, more than any rayne. For then you muste
eyther alway rub it, or els leaue shootynge.

Your bowecase (this I dyd not promise to speake of, bycause
it is without the nature of shootynge, or els I
shoulde truble me wyth other thinges infinite   *Bowecase.*
more : yet seing it is a sauegarde for the bowe, somthynge I wyll
saye of it) youre bowecase I saye, yf you ryde forthe, muste
neyther be to wyde for youre bowes, for so shall one clap vpon
an other, and hurt them, nor yet so strayte that scarse they
can be thrust in, for that woulde laye them on syde & wynde
them A bowecase of ledder, is not the best, for that is ofttymes
moyste which hurteth the bowes very much. Therfore I haue
sene good shooters which would haue for euerye bowe, a sere
case made of wollen clothe, and than you maye putte .iii. or .iiii.
of them so cased, in to a ledder case if you wyll. This wollen
case shall bothe kepe them in sunder, and also wylle kepe a
bowe in his full strengthe, that it neuer gyue for any wether.
At home these wood cases be verye good for bowes to stande in.

But take hede y^t youre bowe stande not to nere a stone wall, for that wyll make hym moyste and weke, nor yet to nere any fier for that wyll make him shorte and brittle. And thus muche as concernyng the sauyng and keping of [y]our bowe: nowe you shall heare what thynges ye must auoyde, for feare of breakyng your bowe.

A shooter chaunseth to breake his bowe commonly .iiii. wayes, by the strynge, by the shafte, by drawyng to far, & by freates : By the stryng as I sayde afore, whan the strynge is eyther to shorte, to long, not surely put on, wyth one wap, or put croked on, or shorne in sundre wyth an euell nocke, or suffered to tarye ouer longe on. Whan the stryng fayles the bowe muste nedes breake, and specially in the myddes; because bothe the endes haue nothyng to stop them; but whippes so far backe, that the belly must nedes violentlye rise vp, the whyche you shall well perceyue in bendyng of a bowe backward. Therfore a bowe that foloweth the strynge is least hurt with breakyng of strynges. By the shafte a bowe is brokē ether when it is to short, and so you set it in your bow or when the nocke breakes for lytlenesse, or when the strynge slyppes wythoute the nocke for wydenesse, than you poule it to your eare and lettes it go, which must nedes breake the shafte at the leaste, and putte stringe and bow & al in ieopardy, bycause the strength of the bowe hath nothynge in it to stop the violence of it.

Thys kynde of breakynge is mooste perilouse for the standers by, for in such a case you shall se some tyme the ende of a bow flye a hoole score from a mā, and that moost commonly, as I haue marked oft the vpper ende of the bowe. The bow is drawne to far .ii. wayes. Eyther when you take a longer shafte then your owne, or els when you shyfte your hand to low or to hye for shootynge far. Thys waye pouleth the backe in sunder, and then the bowe fleethe in manye peces.

So when you se a bowe broken, hauynge the bellye risen vp both wayes or tone, the stringe brake it. When it is broken in twoo peces in a maner euen of and specyallye in the vpper ende, the shafte nocke brake it.

When the backe is pouled a sunder in manye peeces, to farre drawynge brake it.

These tokens eyther alwayes be trewe or els verye seldome mysse.

The fourthe thyng that breketh a bow is fretes, whych make a bowe redye and apte to breake by any of the .iii. wayes afore sayde. Freetes be in a shaft *Freates.* as well as in a bowe, and they be muche lyke a Canker, crepynge and encreasynge in those places in a bowe, whyche be weaker then other. And for thys purpose must your bowe be well trymmed and piked of a cōning man that it may come rounde in trew compasse euery where. For freetes you must beware, yf youre bow haue a knot in the backe, lest the places whyche be nexte it, be not alowed strong ynoughe to bere w^t the knotte, or elles the stronge knotte shall freate the weake places nexte it. Freates be fyrst litle pinchese, the whych whē you perceaue, pike the places about the pinches, to make them somewhat weker, and as well commynge as where it pinched, and so the pinches shall dye, and neuer encrease farther in to great freates.

Freates begynne many tymes in a pin, for there the good woode is corrupted, that it muste nedes be weke, and bycause it is weake, therfore it freates. Good bowyers therfore do rayse euery pyn & alowe it moore woode for feare of freatynge.

Agayne bowes moost commonlye freate vnder the hande, not so muche as some men suppose for the moistnesse of the hande, as for the heete of the hand : the nature of heate sayeth Aristotle is to lowse, and not to knyt fast, and the more lowser the more weaker, the weaker, the redier to freate. A bowe is not well made, whych hath not wood plentye in the hande. For yf the endes of the bowe be staffyshe, or a mans hande any thynge hoote the bellye must nedes sone frete. Remedie for fretes to any purpose I neuer hard tell of any, but onelye to make the freated place as stronge or stronger then any other. To fill vp the freate with lytle sheuers of a quill and glewe (as some saye wyll do wel) by reason must be starke nought.

For, put case the freete dyd cease then, yet the cause whiche made it freate a fore (and that is weakenesse of the place) bicause it is not taken away must nedes make it freate agayne. As for cuttyng out of freates wythe all maner of pecynge of bowes I wyll cleane exclude from perfite shootynge. For peced bowes be muche lyke owlde housen, whyche be more chargeable to repayre, than commodiouse to dwell in. Agayne to swadle a bowe much about wyth bandes, verye seldome dothe anye good, excepte it be to kepe downe a spel in the backe, otherwyse bandes ether nede not when the bow is any thinge worthe, or els boote not whē it is marde & past best. And although I knowe meane and poore shooters, wyll vse peced and banded bowes sometyme bycause they are not able to get better when they woulde, yet I am sure yf they consyder it well, they shall fynde it, bothe lesse charge and more pleasure to ware at any tyme a couple of shyllynges of a new bowe than to bestowe .x. d of peacynge an olde bowe. For better is coste vpon somewhat worth, than spence vpon nothing worth. And thys I speke also bycause you woulde haue me referre all to perfitnesse in shootynge.

Moreouer there is an other thynge, whyche wyl sone cause a bowe be broken by one of the .iii. wayes whych be first spoken of, and that is shotyng in winter, when there is any froste. Froste is wheresoeuer is any waterish humour, as is in al woodes, eyther more or lesse, and you knowe that al thynges frosen and Isie, wyl rather breke than bende. Yet if a man must nedes shoote at any suche tyme, lette hym take hys bowe, and brynge it to the fyer, and there by litle and litle, rubbe and chafe it with a waxed clothe, whiche shall bring it to that poynt, yᵗ he maye shote safelye ynough in it. This rubbyng with waxe, as I sayde before, is a great succour, agaynst all wete and moystnesse.

In the fyeldes also, in goyng betwyxt the pricks eyther wyth your hande, or elles wyth a clothe you muste keepe your bowe in suche a temper. And thus muche as concernynge youre bowe, howe fyrste to knowe what wood is best for a bowe, than to chose a bowe, after to trim a bowe, agayne to keepe it in goodnesse, laste of al, howe to saue it from al harm and euylnesse.

And although many men can saye more of a bow yet I trust these thynges be true, and almoste sufficient for the knowlege of a perfecte bowe. PHI. Surelye I beleue so, and yet I coulde haue hearde you talke longer on it: althogh I can not se, what maye be sayd more of it. Therfore excepte you wyll pause a whyle, you may go forwarde to a shafte.

TOX. What shaftes were made of, in oulde tyme authours *Hero. eute[r]p.* do not so manifestlye shewe, as of bowes. Herodotus doth tel, that in the flood of Nilus, ther was a beast, called a water horse, of whose skinne after it was dried, the Egyptians made shaftes, and dartes on. The tree called *Cornus* was so common to make shaftes of, that in good authours of yᵉ latyn tongue, *Cornus* is taken for a shafte, as in Seneca, and that place of Virgill,

Sen. Hipp.

Volat Itala Cornus.   *Virg. enei.* 9

Yet of all thynges that euer I warked of olde authours, either greke or latin, for shaftes to be made of, there is nothing so cōmon as reedes. Herodotus in describynge the mightie hoost of Xerxes doth tell that thre great contries vsed shaftes made of a rede, the Aethiopians, the Lycians (whose shaftes lacked fethers, where at I maruayle moste of all) and the men of Inde. The shaftes in Inde were verye longe, a yarde and an halfe, as Arrianus doth saye, or at the least a yarde, as Q. Curtius doth saye, and therfore they gaue yᵉ greater strype, but yet bycause they were so long, they were the more vnhansome, and lesse profitable to the men of Inde, as Curtius doeth tell.

In Polym.

Arrianus. 8.

Q. Curt. 8.

In Crete and Italie, they vsed to haue their shaftes of rede also. The best reede for shaftes grewe in Inde, and in Rhenus a flood of Italy.

Pli. 16. 36.

But bycause suche shaftes be neyther easie for Englishe men to get, and yf they were gotten scarse profitable for them to vse, I wyll lette them passe, and speake of those shaftes whyche Englysh men at this daye moste cōmonly do approue and allowe.

A shaft hath three principall partes, the stele, the fethers, and the head: whereof euerye one muste be seuerallye spoken of.

❡ Steles be made of dyuerse woodes, as,

Brasell.
Turkie wood.
Fusticke.
Sugercheste.
Hardbeame.
Byrche.
Asshe.
Ooke.

Seruis tree.
Hulder.
Blackthorne.
Beche.
Elder.
Aspe.
Salow.

These wooddes as they be most commonly vsed, so they be mooste fit to be vsed : yet some one fytter then an other for diuers mennes shotinge, as shalbe toulde afterwarde. And in this pointe as in a bowe you muste truste an honest fletcher. Neuerthelesse al thoughe I can not teache you to make a bowe or a shafte, whiche belongeth to a bowyer and a fletcher to cōme to theyr lyuyng, yet wyll I shewe you some tokens to knowe a bowe & a shafte, whiche pertayneth to an Archer to come to good shootynge.

A stele muste be well seasoned for Castinge, and it must be made as the grayne lieth & as it groweth or els it wyl neuer flye clene, as clothe cut ouertwhart and agaynste the wulle, can neuer hoose a manne cleane. A knottye stele maye be suffered in a bygge shafte, but for a lytle shafte it is nothynge fit, bothe bycause it wyll neuer flye far, and besydes that it is euer in danger of breakynge, it flieth not far bycause the strengthe of the shoote is hindred and stopped at the knotte, euen as a stone cast in to a plaine euen stil water, wyll make the water moue a greate space, yet yf there be any whirlynge plat in the water, the mouynge ceasethe when it commethe at the whyrlynge plat, whyche is not muche vnlyke a knotte in a shafte yf it be cōsidered wel. So euery thyng as it is plaine and streight of hys owne nature so is it fittest for far mouynge. Therfore a stele whyche is harde to stāde in a bowe, without knotte, and streighte (I meane not artificiallye streyghte as the fletcher dothe make it, but naturally streight as it groweth in the wood) is best to make a shaft of, eyther to go cleane, fly far or stand surely in any wedder. Now howe big, how small, how heuye, how lyght, how longe, how short, a shafte shoulde be particularlye for euerye man (seynge we must taulke of the generall nature of shootyng) can not be toulde no more than you Rhethoricians can appoynt any one kynde of wordes, of sentences, of fygures fyt for euery matter, but euen as the man and the matter requyreth so the fyttest to be vsed. Therfore as concernynge those contraryes in a shafte, euery man muste auoyde them and draw to the meane of them, whyche meane is best in al thynges. Yet yf a man happen to offende in any of the extremes it is better to offend in want and scantnesse, than in to muche and outragiouse excedynge. As it is better to haue a shafte a lytle to shorte than ouer longe, somewhat to lyght, than ouer lumpysshe, a lytle to small, than a greate deale to big, whiche thyng is not onely trewlye sayde in shootynge, but in all other thynges that euer man goeth aboute, as in eatynge, taulkynge, and all other thynges lyke, whych matter was onse excellentlye disputed vpon, in the Scooles, you knowe when.

And to offend, in these contraryes cōmeth much yf men take not hede, throughe the kynd of wood, wherof the shaft is made : For somme wood belōges to yᵉ excedyng part, some to yᵉ scāt part, some to yᵉ meane, as Brasell, Turkiewood, Fusticke, Sugar cheste, & such lyke, make deade, heuy lūpish, hobblyng shaftes Againe Hulder, black thorne, Serues tree, Beche, Elder, Aspe, and Salowe, eyther for theyr wekenes or lyghtenesse, make holow, starting, scudding, gaddynge shaftes. But Birche, Hardbeme, some Ooke, and some Asshe, beynge bothe stronge ynoughe to stande in a bowe, and also lyght ynoughe to flye far, are best for a meane, whiche is to be soughte oute in euery thinge. And althoughe I knowe that some mē shoote so stronge, that the deade woodes be lyghte ynoughe for them, and other some so weeke, that the lowse woodes be lykewyse for them bigge ynoughe yet generally for the moost parte of men, the meane is the best. And so to conclude, that is alwayes beste for a man, whiche is metest for him. Thus no wood of his owne nature, is eyther to lyght or to heuy, but as the shooter is him selfe whyche dothe vse it. For that shafte whiche one yeare for a man is to lyghte and scud-dinge, for the same selfe man the next yeare may chaunce be to heuy and hobblynge. Therfore can not I expresse, excepte generally, what is best wood for a shaft, but let euery mā when he knoweth his owne strength and the nature of euery wood, prouyde and fyt himselfe thereafter. Yet as concerning sheaffe Arrouse for war (as I suppose) it were better to make them of good Asshe, and not of Aspe, as they be now a dayes. For of all other woodes that euer I proued Asshe being big is swiftest and agayne heuy to giue a greate stripe with all, whyche Aspe shall not doo. What heuynes doth in a stripe euery man by experience can tell, therfore Asshe being both swyfter and heuier is more fit for sheafe Arroes thē Aspe, & thus muche for the best wood for shaftes.

Agayne lykewyse as no one wood can be greatlye meet for all kynde of shaftes, no more can one facion of the stele be fit for euery shooter. For those that be lytle brested and big toward the hede called by theyr lykenesse taperfashiō, reshe growne, and of some merrye fellowes bobtayles, be fit for them whiche shote vnder hande bycause they shoote wyth a softe lowse, and stresses not a shaft muche in the breste where the weyghte of the bowe lyethe as you maye perceyue by the werynge of euery shafte.

Agayne the bygge brested shafte is fytte for hym, which shoteth right afore him, or els the brest being weke shoulde neuer wythstande that strong piththy kynde of shootynge, thus the vnderhande must haue a small breste, to go cleane awaye oute of the bowe, the forehande muste haue a bigge breste to bere the great myghte of the bowe. The shafte must be made rounde nothynge flat wyth out gal or wemme, for thys purpose. For bycause roundnesse (whether you take example in heauen or in earthe) is fittest shappe and forme both for fast mouing and also for sone percynge of any thynge. And therfore Aristotle saythe that nature hath made the raine to be round, bycause it shoulde the easelyer enter throughe the ayre.

The nocke of the shafte is dyuersly made, for some be greate and full, some hansome & lytle, some wyde, some narow, some depe, some shalowe, some round, some longe, some wyth one nocke, some wyth a double nocke, wherof euery one hathe hys propertye.

The greate and full nocke, maye be well felte, and many wayes they saue a shafte from brekynge. The hansome and lytle nocke wyll go clene awaye frome the hand, the wyde nocke is noughte, both for breakyng of the shafte and also for soden slyppynge oute of the strynge when the narrowe nocke doth auoyde bothe those harmes. The depe and longe nocke is good in warre for sure kepyng in of the strynge. The shalow, and rownde nocke is best for our purpose in prickyng for cleane delyueraunce of a shoote. And double nockyng is vsed for double suerty of the shaft And thus far as concernynge a hoole stele.

Peecynge of a shafte with brasell and holie, or other heauy woodes, is to make yᵉ ende compasse heauy with the fethers in fliyng, for the stedfaster shotyng. For if the ende were plumpe heauy wyth lead and the wood nexte it lyghte, the head ende woulde euer be downwardes, and neuer flye strayght.

Two poyntes in peecing be ynough, lest the moystnes of the earthe enter to moche into the peecinge, & so leuse the glue. Therfore many poyntes be more plesaunt to the eye, than profitable for the vse.

Sūme vse to peece theyr shaftes in the nocke wyth brasel, or holye, to counterwey, with the head, and I haue sene sūme for the same purpose, bore an hole a lytle bineth the nocke, and put leade in it. But yet none of these wayes be anye thing needful at al, for yᵉ nature of a fether in flying, if a man marke it wel, is able to bear vp a wonderful weyght: and I thīke suche peecing came vp first, thus: whan a good Archer hath broken a good shafte, in the fethers, & for the fantasie he hath had to it, he is lothe to leese it, & therfore doeth he peece it. And than by and by other eyther bycause it is gaye, or elles because they wyll haue a shafte lyke a good archer, cutteth theyre hole shaftes, and peeceth them agayne: A thynge by my iudgement, more costlye than nedefull.

And thus haue you heard what wood, what fasshion, what nockynge, what peecynge a stele muste haue: Nowe foloweth the fetherynge.

PHI. I woulde neuer haue thought you could haue sayd halfe so muche of a stele, and I thynke as concernyng the litle fether and the playne head, there is but lytle to saye. TOX. Lytle, yes trulye: for there is no one thing, in al shoting, so-moche to be loked on as the fether. For fyrste a question maye be asked, whether any other thing besyde a fether, be fit for a shaft or no? if a fether onelye be fit, whether a goose fether onely, or no? yf a goose fether be best, then whether there be any difference, as concernynge the fether of an oulde goose, and a younge goose: a gander, or a goose: a fennye goose, or an vplandish goose. Againe which is best fether in any goose, the ryght wing or the left wing, the pinion fether, or any other

fether : a whyte, blacke, or greye fether ? Thirdly, in settyng
on of your fether, whether it be pared or drawen w^t a thicke
rybbe, or a thinne rybbe (the rybbe is ye hard quill whiche
deuydeth the fether) a long fether better or a shorte, set on nere
the nocke, or farre from the nocke, set on streight, or som what
bowyng ? & whether one or two fethers runne on the bowe.
Fourthly in couling or sheryng, whether high or lowe, whether
somewhat swyne backed (I muste vse shoters wordes) or sadle
backed, whether rounde, or square shorne ? And whether a
shaft at any tyme ought to be plucked, and how to be plucked.
PHI. Surely Toxophile, I thynke manye fletchers (although
daylye they haue these thinges in vre) if they were asked
sodeynly, what they coulde saye of a fether, they could not
saye so moch. But I praye you let me heare you more at large,
expresse those thynges in a fether, the whiche you packed vp in
so narrowe a rowme. And fyrst whether any other thyng may
be vsed for a fether or not. TOX. That was ye fyrste poynte
in dede, and bycause there foloweth many after, I wyll hye
apace ouer them, as one that had manye a myle to ride. Shaftes
to haue had alwayes fethers Plinius in Latin, and
Pl. 16. 36.
I. Pol. 1. 10. Iulius Pollux in Greke, do playnlye shewe, yet
Her. Polym. onely the Lycians I reade in Herodotus to haue
vsed shaftes without fedders. Onelye a fedder is
fit for a shafte for .ii. causes, fyrste bycause it is leathe weake to
giue place to the bowe, than bycause it is of that nature, that it
wyll starte vp after ye bow So, Plate, wood or horne can not
serue, bycause the[y] wil not gyue place. Againe, Cloth, Paper,
or Parchment can not serue, bycause they wyll not ryse after
the bowe, therfore a fedder is onely mete, bycause it onelye wyl
do bothe. Nowe to looke on the fedders of all maner of birdes,
you shal se some so lowe weke and shorte, some so course, stoore
and harde, and the rib so brickle, thin and narrow, that it can
nether be drawen, pared, nor yet well set on, that except it be
a swan for a dead shafte (as I knowe some good Archers haue
vsed) or a ducke for a flyghte whiche lastes but one shoote, there
is no fether but onelye of a goose that hath all commodities in
it. And trewelye at a short but, which some mā doth vse, y^e
Pecock fether doth seldome kepe vp ye shaft eyther ryght or
leuel, it is so roughe and heuy, so that many mē which haue
taken them vp for gayenesse, hathe layde them downe agayne

for profyte, thus for our purpose, the Goose is best fether, for the best shoter.   PHI. No that is not so, for the best shoter that euer was vsed other fethers.   TOX. Ye are you so cunninge in shootynge I praye you who was that.   PHI. Hercules whyche had hys shaftes fethered with Egles fethers as Hesiodus dothe saye.   TOX. Well as for *Hesiod. in* *Scuto. Her.* Hercules, seynge nether water nor lande, heauen nor hell, coulde scarse contente hym to abyde in, it was no meruell thoughe a sely poore gouse fether could not plese him to shoote wythal, and agayne as for Egles they flye so hye and builde so far of, yᵗ they be very hard to cōe by.   Yet welfare the gentle gouse which bringeth to a man euen to hys doore so manye excedynge commodities.   For *A Gouse.* the gouse is mās cōforte in war & in peace slepynge and wakynge. What prayse so euer is gyuen to shootynge the gouse may chalenge the beste parte in it.   How well dothe she make a man fare at his table?   Howe easelye dothe she make a man lye in hys bed?   How fit euen as her fethers be onelye for shootynge, so be her quylles fytte onelye for wrytyng.   PHILO. In deade Toxophyle that is the beste prayse you gaue to a gouse yet, and surelye I would haue sayde you had bene to blame yf you had ouerskypte it.   TOX. The Romaynes I trowe Philologe not so muche bycause a gouse wyth cryinge saued theyr Capitoliū and head toure wyth their golden Iupiter as Propertius doth say very pretely in thys verse.

Anseris et tutum uoce fuisse Iouem.   *Propertius.*
Id est.
Theues on a night had stolne Iupiter, had a gouse not a kekede.

Dyd make a golden gouse and set hir in the top of yᵉ Capitoliū, & appoynted also the Censores to alow out of yᵉ common hutche yearly stipēdes for yᵉ *Liui⁹ 1.* *Dec. 5.* findinge of certayne Geese, yᵉ Romaynes did not I saye giue al thys honor to a gouse for yᵗ good dede onely, but for other infinit mo which cōme daylye to a man by Geese, and surely yf I should declame in yᵉ prayse of any maner of beest lyuyng, I would chose a gouse.   But the gouse hath made vs flee to farre from oure matter.   Now sir ye haue hearde howe a fether must be had, and that a goose fether onely.   It foloweth of a yong gose and an oulde, and the residue belonging to a fether:

which thing I wyll shortlye course ouer : wherof, when you knowe the properties, you maye fitte your shaftes accordyng to your shotyng, which rule you must obserue in all other thynges too, bycause no one fashion or quantitie can be fitte for euery man, nomore than a shooe or a cote can be.   The oulde goose fether is styffe and stronge, good for a wynde, and fyttest for a deed shaft : the yonge goose fether is weake and fyne, best for a swyfte shaft, and it must be couled at the first shering, somewhat hye, for with shoting, it wyll sattle and faule very moche.   The same thing (although not so moche) is to be cōsydered in a goose and a gander.   A fenny goose, euen as her flesh is blacker, stoorer, vnholsomer, so is her fether for the same cause courser stoorer & rougher, & therfore I haue heard very good fletchers saye, that the seconde fether in some place is better then the pinion in other some.   Betwixt the winges is lytle differēce, but that you must haue diuerse shaftes of one flight, fethered with diuerse winges, for diuerse windes : for if the wynde and the fether go both one way the shaft wyl be caryed to moche.   The pinion fether as it hath the firste place in the winge, so it hath the fyrst place in good fetheringe.   You maye knowe it afore it be pared, by a bought whiche is in it, and agayne when it is colde, by the thinnesse aboue, and the thicknesse at the grounde, and also by the stifnes and finesse which wyll cary a shaft better, faster and further, euen as a fine sayle cloth doth a shyppe.

The coulour of the fether is leste to be regarded, yet som what to be looked on : lest for a good whyte you haue sometyme an yll greye.   Yet surelye it standeth with good reasō to haue the cocke fether black or greye, as it were to gyue a man warning to nocke ryght.   The cocke fether is called that which stādeth aboue in right nocking, which if you do not obserue the other fethers must nedes run on the bowe, and so marre your shote.   And thus farre of the goodnesse and choyse of your fether : now foloweth the setting on.   Wherin you must looke that your fethers be not drawen for hastinesse, but pared euen and streyghte with diligence.   The fletcher draweth a fether when he hath but one swappe at it with his knyfe, and then playneth it a lytle, with rubbynge it ouer his knyfe.   He pareth it when he taketh leysure and hede to make euery parte of the ryb apt to stand streight, and euen on vpon the stele.

This thing if a man take not heede on, he maye chaunce haue cause to saye so of his fletcher, as in dressinge of meate is communelye spoken of Cookes: and that is, that God sendeth vs good fethers, but the deuyll noughtie Fletchers. Yf any fletchers heard me saye thus, they wolde not be angrye with me, except they were yll fletchers: and yet by reason, those fletchers too, ought rather to amend them selues for doing yll, then be angry with me for saying truth. The ribbe in a styffe fether may be thinner, for so it wyll stande cleaner on: but in a weake fether you must leaue a thicker ribbe, or els yf the ryb which is the foundacion and grounde, wherin nature hath set euerye clefte of the fether, be taken to nere the fether, it muste nedes folowe, that the fether shall faule, & droupe downe, euen as any herbe doeth whyche hath his roote to nere taken on with a spade. The lengthe and shortnesse of the fether, serueth for diuers shaftes, as a long fether for a long heauy, or byg shafte, the shorte fether for the contrary. Agayne the shorte may stande farther, the longe nerer the nocke. Youre fether muste stande almooste streyght on, but yet after that sorte, y^t it maye turne rounde in flyinge. And here I consider the wonderfull nature of shootynge, whiche standeth all togyther by that fashion, which is moste apte for quicke mouynge, and that is by roundenesse. For firste the bowe must be gathered rounde, in drawyng it must come rounde compasse, the strynge muste be rounde, the stele rounde, the beste nocke rounde, the feather shorne somwhat rounde, the shafte in flyenge, muste turne rounde, and if it flye far, it flyeth a round compace. For eyther aboue or benethe a rounde cōpace, hyndereth the flyinge. Moreouer bothe the fletcher in makynge your shafte, and you in nockynge your shafte, muste take heede that two fethers equallye runne on the bowe. For yf one fether runne alone on the bowe, it shal quickely be worne, and shall not be able to matche with the other fethers, and agayne at the lowse, yf the shafte be lyght, it wyl starte, if it be heuye, it wil hoble. And thus as concernyng settyng on of your fether. Nowe of coulynge.

To shere a shafte hyghe or lowe, muste be as the shafte is heauy or lyght, great or lytle, long or short The swyne backed fashion, maketh the shaft deader, for it gathereth more ayer than the saddle backed, & therfore the saddle backe is surer for

daunger of wether, & fitter for smothe fliing. Agayn to shere
a shaft rounde, as they were wount somtime to do, or after the
triangle fashion, whyche is muche vsed nowe a dayes, bothe be
good. For roundnesse is apte for fliynge of his owne nature,
and all maner of triangle fashion, (the sharpe poynte goyng
before) is also naturally apte for quycke entrynge, and therfore
De nat. deor.   sayth Cicero, that cranes taught by nature, obserue
in flyinge a triangle fashion alwayes, bycause it is
so apt to perce and go thorowe the ayer wythall. Laste of all
pluckynge of fethers is noughte, for there is no suerty in it,
therfore let euery archer haue such shaftes, that he maye bothe
knowe them and trust them at euery chaunge of wether. Yet
if they must nedes be plucked, plucke them as litle as can be, for
so shal they be the lesse vnconstante. And thus I haue knit vp
in as shorte a roume as I coulde, the best fethers fetheringe and
coulinge of a shafte. PHI. I thynke surelye you haue so taken
vp the matter wyth you, y^t you haue lefte nothynge behinde
you. Nowe you haue brought a shafte to the head, whiche if
it were on, we had done as concernyng all instrumentes belongyng to shootynge.

TOX. Necessitie, the inuentour of all goodnesse (as all
authours in a maner, doo saye) amonges all other thinges
inuented a shaft heed, firste to saue the ende from breakyng,
then it made it sharpe to stycke better, after it made it of strŏg
matter, to last better : Last of all experience and wysedome of
men, hathe brought it to suche a perfitnesse, that there is no
one thing so profitable, belongyng to artillarie, either to stryke
a mannes enemye sorer in warre, or to shoote nerer the marke
at home, then is a fitte heed for both purposes. For if a shaft
lacke a heed, it is worth nothynge for neither vse. Therfore
seinge heedes be so necessary, they must of necessitie, be wel
looked vpon Heedes for warre, of longe tyme haue ben made,
not onely of diuers matters, but also of diuers fashions The
Troians had heedes of yron, as this verse spoken of Pandarus,
sheweth:

Vp to the pappe his string did he pull, his shaft to the harde yron.
Iliados. 4.

The Grecians had heedes of brasse, as Vlysses shaftes were

heeded, when he slewe Antinous, and the other wowers of
Penelope.

Quite through a dore, flewe a shafte with a brasse heed.
Odysse. 21.

It is playne in Homer, where Menelaus was wounded of
Pandarus shafte, y^t the heedes were not glewed on, but tyed on
with a string, as the cōmentaries in Greke playnelye tell. And therfore shoters at that tyme to   *Iliados.* 4.
cary their shaftes withoute heedes, vntill they occupyed them,
and than set on an heade as it apereth in Homer the .xxi. booke
Odyssei, where Penelope brought Vlixes bowe downe amonges
the gentlemen, whiche came on wowing to her, that he whiche
was able to bende it and drawe it, might inioye
her, and after her folowed a mayde sayth Homer,   *Odysse.* 21.
carienge a bagge full of heades, bothe of iron and brasse.

The men of Scythia, vsed heades of brasse. The men of
Inde vsed heades of yron The Ethiopians vsed heades of a
harde sharpe stone, as bothe Herodotus and Pollux
do tel. The Germanes as Cornelius Tacitus   *Clio.*
doeth saye, had theyr shaftes headed with bone,   *Hero*
and many countryes bothe of olde tyme and nowe,   *Polym*
vse heades of horne, but of all other yrō and style muste nedes
be the fittest for heades.

Iulius Pollux calleth otherwyse than we doe, where the
fethers be the head, and that whyche we call the
head, he calleth the poynte.   *I. Pol.* 1 : 10.

Fashion of heades is diuers and that of olde tyme : two
maner of arrowe heades sayeth Pollux, was vsed in olde tyme.
The one he calleth ὄγκινος descrybynge it thus, hauyng two
poyntes or barbes, lookyng backewarde to the stele and the
fethers, which surely we call in Englishe a brode arrowe head
or a swalowe tayle. The other he calleth γλωχὶς, hauing .ii.
poyntes stretchyng forwarde, and this Englysh men do call
a forkehead : bothe these two kyndes of heades, were vsed in
Homers dayes, for Teucer vsed forked heades, sayinge thus to
Agamemnon.

Eighte good shaftes haue I shot sithe I came, eche one wyth a
forke heade.   *Iliad.* 8.

Pandarus heades and Vlysses heades were broode arrow

heades, as a man maye learne in Homer that woulde be curiouse in knowyng that matter. Hercules vsed forked heades, but yet they had thre pointes or forkes, when other mennes *Plutarchus in Crasso.* had but twoo. The Parthyans at that great battell where they slewe ritche Crassus and his sonne vsed brode Arrowe heades, whyche stacke so sore that the Romaynes could not poule them out agayne. Commodus the Emperoure vsed forked heades, whose facion Herodiane doeth *Herodia.* ı. lyuely and naturally describe, sayinge that they were lyke the shap of a new mone wherewyth he would smite of the heade of a birde and neuer misse, other facion of heades haue not I red on. Our Englyshe heades be better in war than eyther forked heades, or brode arrowe heades. For firste the ende beynge lyghter they flee a great deele the faster, and by the same reason gyueth a far sorer stripe. Yea & I suppose if ye same lytle barbes which they haue, were clene put away, they shuld be far better. For thys euery mā doth graunt, y^t a shaft as lōg as it flyeth, turnes, and whā it leueth turnyng it leueth goyng any farther. And euery thynge that enters by a turnynge and boring facion, the more flatter it is, the worse it enters, as a knife thoughe it be sharpe yet because of the edges, wil not bore so wel as a bodkin, for euery rounde thynge enters beste & therefore nature, sayeth Aristotle, made the rayne droppes rounde for quicke percynge the ayre. Thus, eyther shaftes turne not in flyeng, or els our flatte arrowe heades stoppe the shafte in entrynge. PHI. But yet Toxophile to holde your communication a lytle I suppose the flat heade is better, bothe bycause it maketh a greter hoole, and also bycause it stickes faster in. TOX. These two reasons as they be bothe trewe, so they be both nought. For fyrst the lesse hoole, yf it be depe, is the worst to heale agayn : whē a man shoteth at hys enemy, he desyreth rather y^t it should enter far, than stick fast. For what remedye is it I praye you for hym whych is smitten w^t a depe wounde to poull out the shaft quickely, except it be to haste his death spedely ? thus heades whyche make a lytle hole & depe, be better in war, than those which make a great hole and sticke fast in.

Iulius Pollux maketh mencion of certayne kindes of *Pollux.* 7. heades for war which bear fyre in them, and *Psal.* 7. scripture also speaketh somwhat of the same.

Herodotus doth tell a wonderfull pollicy to be done by
Xerxses what tyme he beseged the great Toure in
Athenes : He made his Archers binde there shafte *Hero. Vran*
heades aboute wyth towe, and than set it on fyre and shoote
thē, whych thyng done by many Archers set all the places on
fyre, whych were of matter to burne : and besydes that dased
the men wythin, so yᵗ they knewe not whyther to turne them.
But to make an ende of all heades for warre I woulde wyshe
that the head makers of Englande shoulde make their sheafe
arrowe heades more harder poynted then they be : for I my selfe
haue sene of late suche heades set vpō sheafe Arrowes, as yᵉ
officers yf they had sene them woulde not haue bene content
wyth all.

Now as concernyng heades for pryckyng, which is oure
purpose, there be dyuerse kyndes, some be blonte heades, some
sharpe, some bothe blonte and sharpe. The blont heades men
vse bycause they perceaue them to be good, to kepe a lengthe
wyth all, they kepe a good lengthe, bycause a man poulethe
them no ferder at one tyme than at another. For in felynge
the plompe ende alwayes equallye he may lowse them. Yet in
a winde, and agaynste the wynd the wether hath so much power
on the brode end, yᵗ no man can kepe no sure lengthe, wyth
such a heade. Therfore a blont hede in a caulme or downe
a wind is very good, otherwyse none worse.

Sharpe heades at the ende wythout anye shoulders (I call
that the shoulder in a heade whyche a mans finger shall feele
afore it come to the poynte) wyll perche quycklye throughe
a wynde, but yet it hath .ii. discommodities, the one that it
wyll kepe no lengthe, it kepeth no lengthe, bycause no manne
can poule it certaynly as far one tyme as at an other : it is not
drawen certaynlye so far one tyme as at an other, bycause it
lackethe shouldrynge wherwyth as wyth a sure token a man
myghte be warned when to lowse, and also bycause menne are
afrayde of the sharpe poynt for settyng it in yᵉ bow. The
seconde incōmoditie is when it is lyghted on yᵉ ground, yᵉ smal
poynte shall at euerye tyme be in ieopardye of hurtynge, whyche
thynge of all other wyll sonest make the shafte lese the lengthe.
Now when blonte heades be good to kepe a lengthe wythall,
yet noughte for a wynde, sharpe heades good to perche the
wether wyth al, yet nought for a length, certayne headmakers

dwellyng in London perceyuynge the commoditie of both kynde
of heades ioyned wyth a discommoditie, inuented newe files and
other instrumentes where wyth [t]he[y] broughte heades for
pryckynge to such a perfitnesse, that all the commodities of the
twoo other heades should be put in one heade wyth out anye
discommoditie at all.   They made a certayne kynde of heades
whyche men call hie rigged, creased, or shouldred heades, or
syluer spone heades, for a certayne lykenesse that suche heades
haue wyth the knob ende of some syluer spones.

These heades be good both to kepe a length withal and also
to perche a wynde wythal, to kepe a length wythall bycause a
man maye certaynly poule it to the shouldrynge euery shoote
and no farther, to perche a wynde wythall bycause the pointe
from the shoulder forwarde, breketh the wether as al other
sharpe thynges doo.   So the blonte shoulder seruethe for a sure
lengthe kepynge, the poynte also is euer fit, for a roughe and
greate wether percyng.   And thus much as shortlye as I could,
as concernyng heades both for war & peace.   PHI.   But is
there no cunning as concerning setting on of ye head?   TOX.
Wel remēbred.   But that poynt belongeth to fletchers, yet you
may desyre hym to set youre heade, full on, and close on.   Ful
on is whan the wood is be[n]t hard vp to the ende or stoppynge
of the heade, close on, is when there is lefte wood on euerye
syde the shafte, ynoughe to fyll the head withall, or when it is
neyther to little nor yet to greate.   If there be any faulte in
anye of these poyntes, ye head whan it lyghteth on any hard
stone or grounde wil be in ieoperdy, eyther of breakynge, or els
otherwyse hurtynge.   Stoppynge of heades eyther wyth leade,
or any thynge els, shall not nede now, bycause euery siluer
spone, or showldred head is stopped of it selfe.   Shorte heades
be better than longe : For firste the longe head is worse for the
maker to fyle strayght compace euery waye : agayne it is worse
for the fletcher to set strayght on : thyrdlye it is alwayes in
more ieoperdie of breakinge, whan it is on.   And nowe I
trowe Philologe, we haue done as concernynge all Instrumentes
belongyng to shootynge, whiche euery sere archer ought to
prouyde for hym selfe.   And there remayneth .ii. thynges
behinde, whiche be generall or cōmon to euery man the Wether
& the Marke, but bicause they be so knit wyth shootynge
strayght, or kepynge of a lengthe, I wyll deferre them to that

place, and now we will come (God wyllyng) to handle oure instrumentes, the thing that euery man desireth to do wel. PHI. If you can teache me so well to handle these instrumētes as you haue described them, I suppose I shalbe an archer good ynough. TOX. To learne any thing (as you knowe better than I Philologe) & speciallye to do a thing w^t a mannes handes, must be done if a man woulde be excellent, in his youthe. Yonge trees in gardens, which lacke al senses, and beastes w^{t}out reson, when they be yong, may with handling and teaching, be brought to wonderfull thynges. And this is not onely true in natural thinges, but in artificiall thinges to, as the potter most connyngly doth cast his pottes whan his claye is softe & workable, and waxe taketh printe whan it is warme, & leathie weke, not whan claye and waxe be hard and oulde: and euen so, euerye man in his youthe, bothe with witte and body is moste apte and pliable to receyue any cunnyng that shulde be taught hym.

This cōmunication of teaching youthe, maketh me to remember the right worshipfull and my singuler good mayster, Sir Humfrey Wingfelde, to whom nexte God, I ought to refer for his manifolde benefites bestowed on me, the poore talent of learnyng, whiche god hath lent me: & for his sake do I owe my seruice to all other of the name & noble house of the Wyngfeldes, bothe in woord and dede. Thys worshypfull man hath euer loued and vsed, to haue many children brought vp in learnynge in his house amonges whome I my selfe was one. For whom at terme tymes he woulde bryng downe from Londō bothe bowe and shaftes. And when they shuld playe he woulde go with them him selfe in to the fyelde, & se them shoote, and he that shot fayrest, shulde haue the best bowe and shaftes, and he that shot ilfauouredlye, shulde be mocked of his felowes, til he shot better.

Woulde to god all Englande had vsed or wolde vse to lay the foundacion of youth, after the example of this worshipful man in bringyng vp chyldren in the Booke and the Bowe: by whiche two thynges, the hole common welth both in peace and warre is chefelye ruled and defended wythall.

But to our purpose, he that muste come to this high perfeƈtnes in shootyng whiche we speake of, muste nedes begin to learne it in hys youthe, the omitting of whiche thinge in

Englande, bothe maketh fewer shooters, and also euery man that is a shoter, shote warse than he myght, if he were taught. PHI. Euen as I knowe that this is true, whiche you saye, euen so Toxophile, haue you quyte discouraged me, and drawen my minde cleane from shootynge, seinge by this reason, no man y^t hath not vsed it in his youthe can be excellent in it. And I suppose the same reson woulde discourage many other mo, yf they hearde you talke after this sorte. TOX. This thyng Philologe, shall discourage no man that is wyse. For I wyll proue y^t wisdome maye worke the same thinge in a man, that nature doth in a chylde.

A chylde by thre thinges, is brought to excellencie. By Aptnesse, Desire, and Feare : Aptnesse maketh hym pliable lyke waxe to be formed and fashioned, euen as a man woulde haue hym. Desyre to be as good or better, than his felowes : and Feare of them whome he is vnder, wyl cause hym take great labour and payne with diligent hede, in learnynge any thinge, wherof procedeth at the laste excellency and perfeſt-nesse.

A man maye by wisdome in learnyng any thing, and specially to shoote, haue thre lyke commodities also, wherby he maye, as it were become younge agayne, and so attayne to excellencie. For as a childe is apte by naturall youth, so a man by vsyng at the firste weake bowes, far vnderneth his strength, shal be as pliable and readye to be taught fayre shotyng as any chylde : and daylye vse of the same, shal both kepe hym in fayer shotyng, and also at ye last bryng hym to stronge shootynge.

And in stede of the feruente desyre, which prouoketh a chylde to be better than hys felowe, lette a man be as muche stirred vp with shamefastnes to be worse than all other. And the same place that feare hathe in a chylde, to compell him to take peyne, the same hath loue of shotyng in a man, to cause hym forsake no labour, withoute whiche no man nor chylde can be excellent. And thus whatsoeuer a chylde may be taught by Aptnesse, Desire, & Feare, the same thing in shootynge, maye a man be taughte by weake bowes, Shame-fastnesse and Loue.

And hereby you may se that that is true whiche Cicero sayeth, that a man by vse, may be broughte to a newe nature.

And this I dare be bould to saye, that any man whiche will wisely begynne, and constantlye perseuer in this trade of learnyng to shote, shall attayne to perfeꞔtnesse therin. PHI. This communication Toxophile, doeth please me verye well, and nowe I perceyue that moste generally & chefly youthe muste be taughte to shoote, and secondarilye no man is debarred therfrom excepte it be more thorough his owne negligence for bicause he wyll not learne, than any disabilitie, bicause he can not lerne. Therfore seyng I wyll be glad to folowe your coūsell in chosynge my bowe and other instrumentes, and also am ashamed that I can shote no better thā I can, moreouer hauynge suche a loue toward shotynge by your good reasons to day, that I wyll forsake no labour in the exercise of the same, I beseche you imagyn that we had bothe bowe and shaftes here, and teache me how I should handle them, and one thynge I desyre you, make me as fayre an Archer as you can.

For thys I am sure in learnynge all other matters, nothynge is broughte to the moost profytable vse, which is not handled after the moost cumlye fasiō. As masters of fēce haue no stroke fit ether to hit an other or els to defende hym selfe, whyche is not ioyned wyth a wonderfull cumlinesse. A Cooke cā not chop hys herbes neither quickelye nor hansomlye excepte he kepe suche a mesure wyth hys choppynge kniues as woulde delyte a manne bothe to se hym and heare hym.

Euerye hand craft man that workes best for hys owne profyte, workes most semelye to other mens sight. Agayne in buyldynge a house, in makynge a shyppe, euery parte the more hansomely they be ioyned for profyt and laste, the more cumlye they be fashioned to euery mans syght and eye. Nature it selfe taught men to ioyne alwayes welfauourednesse wᵗ profytablenesse. As in man, that ioynt or pece which is by anye chaunce depriued of hys cumlynesse the same is also debarred of hys vse and profytablenesse.

As he that is gogle eyde and lokes a squinte hath both hys countenaunce clene marred, and hys sight sore blemmyshed, and so in all other members lyke. Moreouer what tyme of the yeare bryngeth mooste profyte wyth it for mans vse, the same also couereth and dekketh bothe earthe and trees wyth moost cūlynesse for mans pleasure. And that tyme whych takethe awaye the pleasure of the grounde, carieth w[t] hym also the profyt of the grounde, as euery man by experience knoweth in harde and roughe winters. Some thynges there be whych haue no other ende, but onely cumlynesse, as payntyng, and Daunsing. And vertue it selfe is nothynge eles but cumlynesse, as al Philosophers do agree in opinion, therfore seynge that whych is best done in anye matters, is alwayes moost cumlye done as both Plato and Cicero in manye places do proue, and daylye experience dothe teache in other thynges, I praye you as I sayde before teatche me to shoote as fayre, and welfauouredly as you can imagen.

TOX. Trewlye Philologe as you proue verye well in other matters, the best shootynge, is alwayes the moost cumlye shootynge but thys you know as well as I that Crassus shewethe in Cicero that as cumlinesse is the chefe poynt, & most to be sought for in all thynges, so cumlynesse onlye, can neuer be taught by any Arte or craft. But may be perceyued well when it is done, not described wel how it should be done.

Yet neuerthelesse to comme to it there be manye waye whych wayes men haue assayde in other matters, as yf a man would folowe in learnynge to shoote faire, the noble paynter Zeuxes in payntyng Helena, whyche to make his Image bewtifull dyd chose out .v. of the fayrest maydes in al the countrie aboute, and in beholdynge them conceyued & drewe out suche an Image that it far exceded al other, bycause the comelinesse of them al was broughte in to one moost perfyte comelinesse : So lykewyse in shotynge yf a man, woulde set before hys eyes .v. or .vi. of the fayrest Archers that euer he saw shoote, and of one learne to stande, of a nother to drawe, of an other to lowse, and so take of euery man, what euery man coulde do best, I dare saye he shoulde come to suche a comlynesse as neuer man came to yet. As for an example, if the moost comely poynte in shootynge that Hewe Prophete the Kynges seruaunte hath and as my frendes Thomas and Raufe Cantrell doth vse w[t] the moost semelye facyons that .iii. or iiii. excellent Archers haue beside, were al ioyned in one, I am sure all men woulde wonder at y[e] excellencie of it. And this is one waye to learne to shoote fayre. PHI. This is very wel truly, but I praye you teache me somewhat of shootyng fayre youre selfe. TOX. I can teache you to shoote fayre, euen as

Socrates taught a man ones to knowe God, for when he axed hym what was God : naye sayeth he I can tell you better what God is not, as God is not yll, God is vnspeakeable, vnsearche-able and so forth : Euen lykewyse can I saye of fayre shootyng, it hath not this discommodite with it nor that discommoditie, and at last a man maye so shifte all the discommodities from shootynge that there shall be left no thynge behynde but fayre shootynge. And to do this the better you must remember howe that I toulde you when I descrybed generally the hole nature of shootyng that fayre shotyng came of these thynges, of standynge, nockynge, drawynge, howldynge and lowsynge, the whych I wyll go ouer as shortly as I can, describynge the dis-commodities that men cōmonlye vse in all partes of theyr bodies, that you yf you faulte in any such maye knowe it & so go about to amend it. Faultes in Archers do excede the number of Archers, whyche come wyth vse of shootynge wythoute teachynge. Vse and custome separated from knowlege and learnynge, doth not onely hurt shootynge, but the moost weyghtye thynges in the worlde beside : And therfore I maruayle moche at those people whyche be the mayneteners of vses wᵗoute knowledge hauynge no other worde in theyr mouthe but thys vse, vse, custome, custome. Suche men more wylful than wyse, beside other discommo[di]ties, take all place and occasion from al amendmēt. And thys I speake generally of vse and custome.

Whych thynge yf a learned man had it in hande yᵗ woulde applye it to any one matter, he myght handle it wonderfullye. But as for shootyng, vse is the onely cause of all fautes in it and therfore chylderne more easly and soner maye be taught to shote excellentlye then men, bycause chylderne may be taught to shoote well at the fyrste, men haue more payne to vnlearne theyr yll vses, than they haue laboure afterwarde to come to good shootynge.

All the discommodities whiche ill custome hath graffed in archers, can neyther be quycklye poulled out, nor yet sone reckened of me, they be so manye.

Some shooteth, his head forwarde as though he woulde byte the marke : an other stareth wyth hys eyes, as though they shulde flye out : An other winketh with one eye, and loketh with the other : Some make a face with writhing theyr mouthe and countenaunce so, as though they were doyng you wotte what: An other blereth out his tonge: An other byteth his lyppes: An other holdeth his necke a wrye. In drawyng some set suche a compasse, as thoughe they woulde tourne about, and blysse all the feelde: Other heaue theyr hand nowe vp nowe downe, that a man can not decerne wherat they wolde shote, an other waggeth the vpper ende of his bow one way, the neyther ende an other waye. An other wil stand poyntinge his shafte at the marke a good whyle and by and by he wyll gyue hym a whip, and awaye or a man wite. An other maketh suche a wrestling with his gere, as thoughe he were able to shoote no more as longe as he lyued. An other draweth softly to ye middes, and by and by it is gon, you can not knowe howe.

An other draweth his shafte lowe at the breaste, as thoughe he woulde shoote at a rouynge marke, and by and by he lifteth his arme vp pricke heyghte. An other maketh a wrynchinge with hys backe, as though a manne pynched hym behynde.

An other coureth downe, and layeth out his buttockes, as though he shoulde shoote at crowes.

An other setteth forwarde hys lefte legge, and draweth backe wyth head and showlders, as thoughe he pouled at a rope, or els were afrayed of ye marke. An other draweth his shafte well, vntyll wythin .ii. fyngers of the head, and than he stayeth a lyttle, to looke at hys marke, and that done, pouleth it vp to the head, and lowseth: whych waye although sūme excellent shooters do vse, yet surely it is a faulte, and good mennes faultes are not to be folowed.

Summe men drawe to farre, summe to shorte, sūme to slowlye, summe to quickely, summe holde ouer longe, summe lette go ouer sone.

Summe sette theyr shafte on the grounde, and fetcheth him vpwarde. An other poynteth vp towarde the skye, and so bryngeth hym downewardes.

Ones I sawe a manne whyche vsed a brasar on his cheke, or elles he had scratched all the skynne of the one syde, of his face, with his drawynge hand.

An other I sawe, whiche at euerye shoote, after the loose, lyfted vp his ryght legge so far, that he was euer in ieoperdye of faulyng.

Summe stampe forwarde, and summe leape backwarde.
All these faultes be eyther in the drawynge, or at the loose :
w^t many other mo whiche you may easelye perceyue, and so go
about to auoyde them.

Nowe afterwarde whan the shafte is gone, men haue manye
faultes, whyche euell Custome hath broughte them to, and
specially in cryinge after the shafte, & speakynge woordes scarce
honest for suche an honest pastyme.

Suche woordes be verye tokens of an ill mynde, and
manifeste signes of a man that is subiecte to inmesurable
affections. Good mennes eares do abhor them, and an honest
man therfore wyl auoyde them. And besydes those whiche
muste nedes haue theyr tongue thus walkynge, other men vse
other fautes as some will take theyr bowe and writhe & wrinche
it, to poule in his shafte, when it flyeth wyde, as yf he draue
a carte. Some wyl gyue two or .iii. strydes forwarde, daunsing
and hoppynge after his shafte, as long as it flyeth, as though he
were a mad man. Some which feare to be to farre gone, runne
backewarde as it were to poule his shafte backe. Another
runneth forwarde, whan he feareth to be short, heauynge after
his armes, as though he woulde helpe his shafte to flye. An
other writhes or runneth a syde, to poule in his shafte strayght.
One lifteth vp his heele, and so holdeth his foote still, as longe
as his shafte flyeth. An other casteth his arme backewarde
after the lowse. And an other swynges hys bowe aboute hym,
as it were a man with a staffe to make roume in a game place.
And manye other faultes there be, whiche nowe come not to
my remēbraunce. Thus as you haue hearde, many archers
wyth marrynge theyr face and countenaunce, wyth other
partes, of theyr bodye, as it were menne that shoulde daunce
antiques, be farre from the comelye porte in shootynge, whiche
he that woulde be excellent muste looke for.

Of these faultes I haue verie many my selfe, but I talke
not of my shootynge, but of the generall nature of shootynge.
Nowe ymagin an Archer that is cleane wythout al these
faultes & I am sure euerye man would be delyted to se hym
shoote.

And althoughe suche a perfyte cumlynesse can not be
expressed wyth any precepte of teachyng, as Cicero and other
learned menne do saye, yet I wyll speake (accordyng to my

lytle knowlege) that thing in it, whych yf you folowe, althoughe you shall not be wythout fault, yet your fault shal neyther quickly be perceued, nor yet greatly rebuked of them that stande by. Standyng, nockyng, drawyng, holdyng, lowsyng, done as they shoulde be done, make fayre shootynge.

The fyrste poynte is when a man shoulde shote, to take *Standynge.* suche footyng and standyng as shal be both cumlye to the eye and profytable to hys vse, settyng hys countenaunce and al the other partes of hys bodye after suche a behauiour and porte, that bothe al hys strengthe may be employed to hys owne moost auaūtage, and hys shoot made and handled to other mens pleasure and delyte. A man must not go to hastely to it, for that is rashnesse, nor yet make to much to do about it, for y^t is curiositie, ye one fote must not stande to far from the other, leste he stoupe to muche whyche is vnsemelye, nor yet to nere together, leste he stande to streyght vp, for so a man shall neyther vse hys strengthe well, nor yet stande stedfastlye.

The meane betwyxt bothe must be kept, a thing more pleasaunte to beholde when it is done, than easie to be taught howe it shoulde be done.

To nocke well is the easiest poynte of all, and there in is *Nockynge.* no cunninge, but onelye dylygente hede gyuyng, to set hys shaft neyther to hye nor to lowe, but euen streyght ouertwharte hys bowe. Vnconstante nockynge maketh a man leese hys lengthe.

And besydes that, yf the shafte hande be hye and the bowe hande lowe, or contrarie, bothe the bowe is in ieopardye of brekynge, and the shafte, yf it be lytle, wyll start: yf it be great it wyll hobble. Nocke the cocke fether vpward alwayes as I toulde you whē I described the fether. And be sure alwayes y^t your stringe slip not out of the nocke, for than al is in ieopardye of breakynge.

Drawynge well is the best parte of shootyng. Men in *Drawynge.* oulde tyme vsed other maner of drawynge than we do. They vsed to drawe low at the brest, to the ryght pap and no farther, and this to be trew is playne *Iliad.* 4. in Homer, where he descrybeth Pandarus shootynge.

Vp to the pap his stringe dyd he pul, his shafte to the hard heed.

The noble women of Scythia vsed the same fashyon of shootyng low at the brest, and bicause their lefte pap hindred theyr shootynge at the lowse they cut it of when they were yonge, and therfore be they called in lackynge theyr pap Amazones. Nowe a dayes contrarye wyse we drawe to the ryghte eare and not to the pap. Whether the olde waye in drawynge low to the pap, or the new way to draw a loft to the eare be better, an excellente wryter in Greke called Procopius doth saye hys mynde, *Procopius Hist. Pers.* shewyng y^t the oulde fashyon in drawing to ye pap was nought, of no pithe, and therfore saith Procopius : is Artyllarye dispraysed in Homer whych calleth it οὐτιδανόν. I. Weake and able to do no good. Drawyng to the eare he prayseth greatly, whereby men shoote both stronger and longer : drawynge therfore to the eare is better than to drawe at the breste. And one thyng commeth into my remembraunce nowe Philologe when I speake of drawyng, that I neuer red of other kynde of shootyng, than drawing wyth a mãs hand ether to the breste or eare : This thyng haue I sought for in Homer Herodotus and Plutarch, and therfore I meruayle how cros- bowes came fyrst vp, of the which I am sure a *Crosbowes.* man shall finde lytle mention made on in any good Authour. Leo the Emperoure woulde haue hys souldyers drawe quycklye in warre, for that maketh a shaft flie a pace. In shootynge at the pryckes, hasty and quicke drawing is neyther sure nor yet cumlye. Therfore to drawe easely and vniformely, that is for to saye not waggyng your hand, now vpwarde, now downewarde, but alwayes after one fashion vntil you come to the rig or shouldring of ye head, is best both for profit & semelinesse. Holdynge must not be longe, *Holding.* for it bothe putteth a bowe in ieopardy, & also marreth a mans shoote, it must be so lytle y^t it maye be perceyued better in a mans mynde when it is done, than seene w^t a mans eyes when it is in doyng.

Lowsynge muste be muche lyke. So quycke and hard y^t it be wyth oute all girdes, so softe and gentle that *Lowsynge.* the shafte flye not as it were sente out of a bow case. The meane betwixt bothe, whyche is perfyte lowsynge is not so hard to be folowed in shootynge as it is to be descrybed in teachyng. For cleane lowsynge you must take

hede of hyttynge any thynge aboute you. And for the same
purpose Leo the Emperour would haue al Archers
in war to haue both theyr heades pouled, and
there berdes shauen leste the heare of theyr heades shuld stop
the syght of the eye, the heere of theyr berdes hinder the
course of the strynge.

Leo.

And these preceptes I am sure Philologe yf you folowe in
standyng, nockyng, drawynge, holdynge, and lowsynge, shal
bryng you at the last to excellent fayre shootynge. PHI. All
these thynges Toxophile althoughe I bothe nowe perceyue them
thorowlye, and also wyll remember them dilligently: yet to
morowe or some other day whē you haue leasure we wyll go to
the pryckes, and put them by lytle and lytle in experience.
For teachynge not folowed, doeth euen as muche good as
bookes neuer looked vpon. But nowe seing you haue taught
me to shote fayre, I praye you tel me somwhat, how I should
shoote nere leste that prouerbe myght be sayd iustlye of me
sometyme. He shootes lyke a gentle man fayre & far of.
TOX. He that can shoote fayre, lacketh nothyng but
shootyng streyght and kepyng of a length wherof commeth
hyttynge of the marke, the ende both of shootyng and also of
thys our communication. The handlyng of yᵉ wether & the
mark bicause they belōg to shootyng streyghte, and kepynge
of a lengthe, I wyll ioyne them togyther, shewinge what thinges
belonge to kepynge of a lengthe, and what to shootynge streyght.

The greatest enemy of shootyng is the wynde and the
wether, wherby true kepyng a lengthe is chefely
hindered. If this thing were not, men by teaching
might be brought to wonderful neare shootynge.
It is no maruayle if the litle poore shafte being sent alone, so
high in to the ayer, into a great rage of wether, one wynde
tossinge it that waye, an other thys waye, it is no maruayle
I saye, thoughe it leese the lengthe, and misse that place, where
the shooter had thought to haue founde it. Greter matters
than shotynge are vnder the rule and wyll of the wether, as
saylynge on the sea. And lykewise as in sayling, the chefe
poynt of a good master, is to knowe the tokens of chaunge of
wether, the course of the wyndes, that therby he maye the
better come to the Hauen : euen so the best propertie of a good
shooter, is to knowe the nature of the wyndes, with hym and

wynde and wether.

agaynste hym, that thereby he maye the nerer shote at hys marke. Wyse maysters whan they canne not winne the beste hauen, they are gladde of the nexte: Good shooters also, y^t can not whan they would hit the marke, wil labour to come as nigh as they can. All thinges in this worlde be vnperfite and vnconstant, therfore let euery man acknowlege hys owne weakenesse, in all matters great and smal, weyghtye and merye, and glorifie him, in whome only perfyte perfitnesse is. But nowe, sir, he that wyll at all aduentures vse the seas knowinge no more what is to be done in a tempest than in a caulme, shall soone becumme a marchaunt of Eele skinnes: so that shoter whiche putteth no difference, but shooteth in all lyke, in rough wether and fayre, shall always put his wynninges in his eyes.

Lytle botes and thinne boordes, can not endure the rage of a tempest. Weake bowes, & lyght shaftes can not stande in a rough wynde. And lykewyse as a blynde man which shoulde go to a place where he had neuer ben afore, that hath but one strayghte waye to it, and of eyther syde hooles and pyttes to faule into, nowe falleth in to this hole and than into that hole, and neuer cōmeth to his iourney ende, but wandereth alwaies here and there, farther and farther of: So that archer which ignorauntly shoteth considering neyther fayer nor foule, standynge nor nockynge, fether nor head, drawynge nor lowsyng, nor yet any compace, shall always shote shorte and gone, wyde and farre of, and neuer cumme nere, excepte perchaunce he stumble sumtyme on the marke. For ignoraunce is nothynge elles but mere blyndenesse.

A mayster of a shippe first learneth to knowe the cummyng of a tempest, the nature of it, and howe to behaue hym selfe in it, eyther with chaungynge his course, or poullynge downe his hye toppes and brode sayles, beyng glad to eschue as muche of the wether as he can: Euen so a good archer wyl fyrste wyth diligent vse and markynge the wether, learne to knowe the nature of the wynde, and with wysedome, wyll measure in hys mynde, howe muche it wyll alter his shoote, eyther in lengthe kepynge, or els in streyght shotynge, and so with chaunging his standynge, or takynge an other shafte, the whiche he knoweth perfytlye to be fitter for his pourpose, eyther bycause it is lower fethered, or els bycause it is of a better

wyng, wyll so handle w^t discretion hys shoote, that he shall
seeme rather to haue the wether vnder hys rule, by good hede
gyuynge, than the wether to rule hys shafte by any sodayne
chaungyng.

Therefore in shootynge there is as muche difference betwixt
an archer that is a good wether man, and an other that knoweth
and marketh nothynge, as is betwixte a blynde man, and he
that can se.

Thus, as concernynge the wether, a perfyte archer muste
firste learne to knowe the sure flyghte of his shaftes, that he may
be boulde alwayes, to trust them, than muste he learne by
daylye experience all maner of kyndes of wether, the tokens of
it, whan it wyl cumme, the nature of it whan it is cūme,
the diuersitie and alteryng of it, whan it chaungeth, the
decrease & diminishing of it, whā it ceaseth. Thirdly these
thinges knowen, and euery shoote diligentlye marked, than
must a man cōpare alwayes, the wether and his footyng
togyther, and with discretion measure them so, that what so
euer the roughe wether shall take awaye from hys shoote the
same shal iuste footynge restore agayne to hys shoote.

Thys thynge well knowen, and discretelye handeled in
shootynge, bryngeth more profite and commendation and prayse
to an Archer, than any other thynge besydes.

He that woulde knowe perfectly the winde and wether,
muste put differences betwixte tymes. For diuersitie of tyme
causeth diuersitie of wether, as in the whole yeare, Sprynge
tyme, Somer, Faule of the leafe, and Winter: Lykewyse in one
day Mornynge, Noonetyme, Afternoone, and Euentyde, bothe
alter the wether, and chaunge a mānes bowe wyth the
strength of man also.   And to knowe that this is so, is ynough for
a shoter & artillerie, and not to serche the cause, why it shoulde
be so : whiche belongeth to a learned man and Philosophie.

In consydering the tyme of the yeare, a wyse Archer wyll
folowe a good Shipman.   In Winter & rough wether, smal
bootes and lytle pinkes forsake the seas: And at one tyme of
the yeare, no Gallies come abrode; So lykewyse weake Archers,
vsyng small and holowe shaftes, with bowes of litle pith, muste
be content to gyue place for a tyme.

And this I do not saye, eyther to discōmende or discourage
any weake shooter : For lykewyse, as there is no shippe better

than Gallies be, in a softe and a caulme sea, so no man shooteth cumlier or nerer hys marke, than some weake archers doo, in a fayre and cleare daye.

Thus euery archer must knowe, not onelye what bowe and shafte is fittest for him to shoote withall, but also what tyme & season is best for hym to shote in. And surely, in al other matters to, amonge al degrees of men, there is no man which doth any thing eyther more discretely for his commendation, or yet more profitable for his aduauntage, than he which wyll knowe perfitly for what matter and for what tyme he is moost apte and fit. Yf men woulde go aboute matters whych they should do and be fit for, & not suche thynges whyche wylfullye they desyre & yet be vnfit for, verely greater matters in the cōmon welthe than shootyng shoulde be in better case than they be. This ignorauncie in men whyche know not for what tyme, and to what thynge they be fit, causeth some wyshe to be riche, for whome it were better a greate deale to be poore: other to be medlynge in euery mans matter, for whome it were more honestie to be quiete and styll. Some to desire to be in the Courte, whiche be borne and be fitter rather for the carte. Somme to be maysters and rule other, whiche neuer yet began to rule them selfe: some alwayes to iangle and taulke, whych rather shoulde heare and kepe silēce. Some to teache, which rather should learne. Some to be prestes, whiche were fytter to be clerkes. And thys peruerse iudgement of yᵉ worlde, when men mesure them selfe a misse, bringeth muche mysorder and greate vnsemelynesse to the hole body of the common wealth, as yf a manne should were his hoose vpon his head, or a woman go wyth a sworde and a buckeler euery man would take it as a greate vncumlynesse although it be but a tryfle in respecte of the other.

Thys peruerse iudgement of men hindreth no thynge so much as learnynge, bycause commonlye those whych be vnfittest foɪ learnyng, be cheyfly set to learnynge.

As yf a man nowe a dayes haue two sonnes, the one impotent, weke, sickly, lispynge, stuttynge, and stamerynge, or hauynge any misshape in hys bodye: what doth the father of suche one commonlye saye? This boye is fit for nothynge els, but to set to lernyng and make a prest of, as who would say, yᵉ outcastes of the worlde, hauyng neyther countenaūce tounge nor wit (for of a peruerse bodye cũmeth commonly a peruerse mynde) be good ynough to make those men of, whiche shall be appoynted to preache Goddes holye woorde, and minister hys blessed sacramentes, besydes other moost weyghtye matters in the common welthe put ofte tymes, and worthelye to learned mennes discretion and charge : whan rather suche an offyce so hygh in dignitie, so godlye in administration, shulde be committed to no man, whiche shulde not haue a countenaunce full of cumlynesse to allure good menne, a bodye ful of manlye authoritie to feare ill men, a witte apte for al learnynge with tongue and voyce, able to perswade all men. And although fewe suche men as these can be founde in a common wealthe, yet surely a godly disposed man, will bothe in his mynde thyncke fit, and with al his studie labour to get such men as I speke of, or rather better, if better can be gotten for suche an hie administration, whiche is most properlye appoynted to goddes owne matters and businesses.

This peruerse iugement of fathers as concernynge the fitnesse and vnfitnesse of theyr chyldren causeth the cõmon wealthe haue many vnfit ministers: And seyng that ministers be, as a man woulde say, instrumentes wherw^t the cõmon wealthe doeth worke all her matters w^{t}all, I maruayle howe it chaũceth y^t a pore shomaker hath so much wit, y^t he will prepare no instrument for his science neither knyfe nor aule, nor nothing els whiche is not very fitte for him: the cõmon wealthe can be content to take at a fonde fathers hande, the rifraffe of the worlde, to make those instrumentes of, wherw^{t}al she shoulde worke ye hiest matters vnder heauen. And surely an aule of lead is not so vnprofitable in a shomakers shop, as an vnfit minister, made of grosse metal, is vnsemely in ye cõmõ welth. Fathers in olde time among ye noble Persians might not do w^t theyr childrẽ as they thought good, but as the iudgement of the cõmon wealth al wayes thought best. This fault of fathers bringeth many a blot w^t it, to the great deformitie of the common wealthe: & here surely I can prayse gentlewomen which haue alwayes at hande theyr glasses, to se if any thinge be amisse, & so will amende it, yet the cõmon wealth hauing ye glasse of knowlege in euery mans hand, doth se such vncumlines in it: & yet winketh at it. This faulte & many suche lyke, myght be sone wyped awaye, yf fathers woulde bestow their children on y^t thing alwayes, whervnto nature hath ordeined them moste apte & fit. For if youth be grafted streyght, & not awrye, the hole cōmon welth wil florish therafter. Whan this is done, than muste euery man beginne to be more ready to amende hym selfe, than to checke an other, measuryng their matters with that wise prouerbe of Apollo, *Knowe thy selfe* : that is to saye, learne to knowe what thou arte able, fitte, and apte vnto, and folowe that.

This thinge shulde be bothe cumlie to the common wealthe, and moost profitable for euery one, as doth appere very well in all wise mennes deades, & specially to turne to our communication agayne in shootynge, where wise archers haue always theyr instrumentes fit for theyr strength, & wayte euermore suche tyme and wether, as is most agreable to their gere. Therfore if the wether be to sore, and vnfit for your shootynge, leaue of for that daye, and wayte a better season. For he is a foole y^t wyl not go, whome necessitie driueth. PHI. This cōmunication of yours pleased me so well Toxophile, that surelye I was not hastie to calle you, to descrybe forthe the wether but with all my harte woulde haue suffered you yet to haue stande longer in this matter. For these thinges touched of you by chaunse, and by the waye, be farre aboue the matter it selfe, by whose occasion ye other were broughte in. TOX. Weyghtye matters they be in dede, and fit bothe in an other place to be spoken : & of an other man than I am, to be handled. And bycause meane men must meddle wyth meane matters, I wyl go forwarde in descrybyng the wether, as concernynge shooting: and as I toulde you before, In the hole yere, Spring tyme, Somer, Fal of the leafe, and Winter: and in one day, Morning, Noone tyme, After noone, and Euentyde, altereth the course of the wether, the pith of the bowe, the strength of the man. And in euery one of these times the wether altereth, as sumtyme wyndie, sumtyme caulme, sumtyme cloudie, sumtyme clere, sumtyme hote, sumtyme coulde, the wynde sumtyme moistye and thicke, sumtyme drye and smothe. A litle winde in a moystie day, stoppeth a shafte more than a good whiskynge wynde in a clere daye. Yea, and I haue sene whan there hath bene no winde at all, the ayer so mistie and thicke, that both the markes haue ben wonderfull great. And ones, whan the Plage was in Cambrige, the downe

winde twelue score marke for the space of .iii. weekes, was
.xiii. score, and an halfe, and into the wynde, beynge not very
great, a great deale aboue .xiiii. score.

The winde is sumtyme playne vp and downe, whiche is
commonly moste certayne, and requireth least knowlege,
wherin a meane shoter with meane geare, if he can shoote
home, maye make best shifte.   A syde wynde tryeth an archer
and good gere verye muche.   Sumtyme it bloweth a lofte,
sumtyme hard by the grounde: Sumtyme it bloweth by blastes,
& sumtyme it continueth al in one: Sumtyme ful side wynde,
sumtyme quarter with hym and more, and lykewyse agaynst
hym, as a man with castynge vp lyght grasse, or els if he take
good hede, shall sensibly learne by experience.   To se the
wynde, with a man his eyes, it is vnpossible, the nature of it is
so fyne, and subtile, yet this experience of the wynde had
I ones my selfe, and that was in the great snowe that fell .iiii.
yeares agoo: I rode in the hye waye betwixt Topcliffe vpon
Swale, and Borowe bridge, the waye beyng sumwhat trodden
afore, by waye fayrynge men.   The feeldes on bothe sides were
playne and laye almost yearde depe with snowe, the nyght
afore had ben a litle froste, so y^t the snowe was hard and
crusted aboue.   That morning the sun shone bright and clere,
the winde was whistelinge a lofte, and sharpe accordynge to the
tyme of the yeare.   The snowe in the hye waye laye lowse
and troden wyth horse feete : so as the wynde blewe, it toke
the lowse snow with it, and made it so slide vpon the snowe in
the felde whyche was harde and crusted by reason of the frost
ouer nyght, that therby I myght se verye wel, the hole nature
of the wynde as it blewe y^t daye.   And I had a great delyte &
pleasure to marke it, whyche maketh me now far better to
remember it.   Sometyme the wynd would be not past .ii.
yeardes brode, and so it would carie the snowe as far as I could
se.   An other tyme the snow woulde blowe ouer halfe the
felde at ones.   Sometyme the snowe woulde tomble softly, by
and by it would flye wonderfull fast.   And thys I perceyued
also that ye wind goeth by streames & not hole togither.   For
I should se one streame wyth in a Score on me, thā the space
of .ii. score no snow would stirre, but after so muche quātitie
of grounde, an other streame of snow at the same very tyme
should be caryed lykewyse, but not equally.   For the one

would stande styll when the other flew a pace, and so contynewe somtyme swiftlyer sometime slowlyer, sometime broder, sometime narrower, as far as I coulde se. Nor it flewe not streight, but sometyme it crooked thys waye sometyme that waye, and somtyme it ran round aboute in a compase. And somtyme the snowe wold be lyft clene from the ground vp in to the ayre, and by & by it would be al clapt to the grounde as though there had bene no winde at all, streightway it woulde rise and flye agayne.

And that whych was the moost meruayle of al, at one tyme .ii. driftes of snowe flewe, the one out of the West into yᵉ East, the other out of the North in to yᵉ East: And I saw .ii. windes by reasō of yᵉ snow the one crosse ouer the other, as it had bene two hye wayes. And agayne I shoulde here the wynd blow in the ayre, when nothing was stirred at the groūd. And when all was still where I rode, not verye far frō me the snow should be lifted wonderfully. This experiēce made me more meruaile at yᵉ nature of the wynde, than it made me conning in yᵉ knowlege of yᵉ wynd: but yet therby I learned perfitly that it is no meruayle at al thoughe men in a wynde lease theyr length in shooting, seying so many wayes the wynde is so variable in blowynge.

But seynge that a Mayster of a shyp, be he neuer so cunnynge, by the vncertayntye of the wynde, leeseth many tymes both lyfe and goodes, surelye it is no wonder, though a ryght good Archer, by the self same wynde so variable in hys owne nature, so vnsensyble to oure nature, leese manye a shoote and game.

The more vncertaine and disceyuable the wynd is, the more hede must a wyse Archer gyue to know the gyles of it.

He yᵗ doth mistrust is seldome begiled. For although therby he shall not attayne to that which is best, yet by these meanes he shall at leaste auoyde yᵗ whyche is worst. Besyde al these kindes of windes you must take hede yf you se anye cloude apere and gather by lytle and litle agaynst you, or els yf a showre of raine be lyke to come vpon you: for than both the dryuing of the wether and the thyckynge of the ayre increaseth the marke, when after yᵉ showre al thynges are contrary clere and caulme, & the marke for the most parte new to begyn agayne. You must take hede also yf euer you shote where one

of the markes or both stondes a lytle short of a hye wall, for
there you may be easlye begyled. Yf you take grasse and
caste it vp to se howe the wynde standes, manye tymes you
shal suppose to shoote downe the wynde, when you shote cleane
agaynste the wynde.   And a good reasō why.   For the wynd
whych commeth in dede against you, redoundeth bake agayne
at the wal, and whyrleth backe to the prycke and a lytle farther
and than turneth agayne, euen as a vehement water doeth
agaynste a rocke or an hye braye, whyche example of water as
it is more sensible to a mãs eyes, so it is neuer a whyt the
trewer than this of the wynde.   So that the grasse caste vp
shall flee that waye whyche in dede is the longer marke and
disceyue quycklye a shooter that is not ware of it.

This experience had I ones my selfe at Norwytch in the
chapel felde wythin the waulles.   And thys waye I vsed in
shootynge at those markes.

When I was in the myd way betwixt the markes whyche
was an open place, there I toke a fether or a lytle lyght grasse
and so as well as I coulde, learned how the wynd stoode, that
done I wente to the prycke as faste as I coulde, and according
as I had foūde yᵉ wynde when I was in the mid waye, so I was
fayne than to be content to make the best of my shoote that I
coulde.   Euen suche an other experiēce had I in a maner at
Yorke, at the prickes, lying betwixte the castell and Ouse syde.
And although you smile Philologe, to heare me tell myne owne
fondenes : yet seing you wil nedes haue me teach you somwhat
in shotyng, I must nedes somtyme tel you of myne owne
experience, & the better I may do so, bycause Hippocrates in

*Hippo. De
morb. vulg.*

teachynge physike, vseth verye muche the same
waye.   Take heede also when you shoote nere
the sea cost, although you be .ii. or .iii. miles from
the sea, for there diligent markinge shall espie in the moste
clere daye wonderfull chaunginge.   The same is to be cōsidered
lykewyse by a riuer side speciallie if it ebbe & flowe, where he
yᵗ taketh diligent hede of yᵉ tide & wether, shal lightly take
away al yᵗ he shooteth for.   And thus of yᵉ nature of windes
& wether according to my marking you haue hearde Philologe :
& hereafter you shal marke farre mo your selfe, if you take hede.
And the wether thus marked as I tolde you afore, you muste
take hede, of youre stãding, yᵗ therby you may win as much

as you shal loose by the wether. PHI. I se well it is no
maruell though a man misse many tymes in shootyng, seing y^e
wether is so vnconstant in blowing, but yet there is one thing
whiche many archers vse, y^t shall cause a man haue lesse nede
to marke the wether, & that is Ame gyuing. TOX. Of
gyuyng Ame, I can not tel wel, what I shuld say. For in
a straunge place it taketh away al occasion of foule game, which
is ye only prayse of it, yet by my iudgemēt, it hīdreth y^e
knowlege of shotyng, & maketh men more negligente: ye which
is a disprayse. Though Ame be giuē, yet take hede, for at an
other mãs shote you can not wel take Ame, nor at your owne
neither, bycause the wether wil alter, euen in a minute, & at
the one marke & not at the other, & trouble your shafte in the
ayer, when you shal perceyue no wynde at the ground, as I my
selfe haue sene shaftes tumble a lofte, in a very fayer daye.
There may be a fault also, in drawing or lowsynge, and many
thynges mo, whiche all togyther, are required to kepe a iust
length. But to go forward the nexte poynte after the markyng
of your wether, is the takyng of your standyng. And in a side
winde you must stand sumwhat crosse in to the wynde, for so
shall you shoote the surer. Whan you haue taken good footing,
than must you looke at your shafte, y^t no earthe, nor weete be
lefte vpon it, for so should it leese the lengthe. You must loke
at the head also, lest it haue had any strype, at the last shoote.
A stripe vpon a stone, many tymes will bothe marre the head,
croke the shafte, and hurte the fether, wherof the lest of them
all, wyll cause a man lease his lengthe. For suche thinges
which chaunce euery shoote, many archers vse to haue sūme
place made in theyr cote, fitte for a lytle fyle, a stone, a Hun-
fyshskin, and a cloth to dresse the shaft fit agayne at all nedes.
Thys must a man looke to euer when he taketh vp his shaft.
And the heade maye be made to smothe, which wil cause it flye
to far: when youre shafte is fit, than must you take your bow
euen in the middes or elles you shall both lease your lengthe,
and put youre bowe in ieopardye of breakynge. Nockynge
iuste is next, which is muche of the same nature. Than drawe
equallye, lowse equallye, wyth houldynge your hande euer of
one heighte to kepe trew compasse. To looke at your shafte
hede at the lowse, is the greatest helpe to kepe a lengthe that
can be, whych thyng yet hindreth excellent shotyng, bicause

a man can not shote streight perfitlye excepte he looke at his marke : yf I should shoote at a line and not at the marke, I woulde alwayes loke at my shaft ende, but of thys thyng some what afterwarde. Nowe if you marke the wether diligentlye, kepe your standynge iustely, houlde and nocke trewlye, drawe and lowse equallye, and kepe youre compace certaynelye, you shall neuer misse of your lengthe. PHI. Then there is nothyng behinde to make me hit ye marke but onely shooting streight. TOX. No trewlye. And fyrste I wyll tel you what shyftes Archers haue founde to shoote streyght, thā what is the best waye to shoote streyght. As the wether belongeth specially to kepe a lengthe (yet a side winde belongeth also to shote streight) euen so the nature of the pricke is to shote streight. The lengthe or shortnesse of the marke is alwayes vnder the rule of the wether, yet sumwhat there is in ye marke, worthye to be marked of an Archer. Yf the prickes stand of a streyght playne groūd they be ye best to shote at. Yf ye marke stād on a hyl syde or ye groūd be vnequal w^t pittes & turninge wayes be-twyxte the markes, a mans eye shall thynke that to be streight whyche is croked : The experience of this thing is sene in payntynge, the cause of it is knowen by learnynge.

And it is ynoughe for an archer to marke it and take hede of it. The cheife cause why men can not shoote streight, is bicause they loke at theyr shaft : and this fault commeth bycause a mā is not taught to shote when he is yong. Yf he learne to shoote by himselfe he is a frayde to pull the shafte throughe the bowe, and therfore looketh alwayes at hys shafte : yll vse con-firmeth thys faulte as it doth many mo.

And men continewe the longer in thys faulte bycause it is so good to kepe a lengthe wyth al, and yet to shote streight, they haue inuēted some waies, to espie a tree or a hill beyonde the marke, or elles to haue sūme notable thing betwixt ye markes : & ones I sawe a good archer whiche did caste of his gere, & layd his quiuer w^t it, euen in the midway betwixt ye prickes. Sūme thought he dyd so, for sauegarde of his gere : I suppose he did it, to shoote streyght w^tall. Other men vse to espie sūme marke almoost a bow wide of ye pricke, and than go about to kepe him selfe on y^t hande that the prycke is on, which thing howe muche good it doth, a man wil not beleue, that doth not proue it. Other & those very good archers in drawyng, loke at the marke vntill they come almost to ye head, than they looke at theyr shafte, but at ye very lowse, w^t a seconde sight they fynde theyr marke agayne. This way & al other afore of me rehersed are but shiftes & not to be folowed in shotyng streyght. For hauyng a mans eye alwaye on his marke, is the only waye to shote streght, yea & I suppose so redye & easy a way yf it be learned in youth & confirmed w^t vse, y^t a man shall neuer misse therin. Men doubt yet ī lokīg at ye mark what way is best whether betwixt the bowe & the stringe, aboue or beneth hys hand, & many wayes moo: yet it maketh no great matter which way a man looke at his marke yf it be ioyned w^t comly shotynge. The diuersite of mens standyng and drawing causeth diuerse mē loke at theyr marke diuerse wayes: yet they al lede a mās hand to shoote streight yf nothyng els stoppe. So that cumlynesse is the only iudge of best lokyng at the marke. Some men wonder why in casting a mans eye at ye marke, the hande should go streyght. Surely yf he consydered the nature of a mans eye, he wolde not wonder at it: For this I am certayne of, that no seruaunt to hys mayster, no chylde to hys father is so obedient, as euerye ioynte and pece of the body is to do what soeuer the eye biddes. The eye is the guide, the ruler & the succourer of al the other partes. The hāde, the foote & other members dare do nothynge w^tout the eye, as doth appere on the night and darke corners. The eye is the very tonge wherw^t wyt & reasō doth speke to euery parte of the body, & the wyt doth not so sone signifye a thynge by the eye, as euery part is redye to folow, or rather preuent the byddyng of the eye. Thys is playne in many thinges, but most euident in fence and feyghtynge, as I haue heard men saye. There euery part standynge in feare to haue a blowe, runnes to the eye for helpe, as yonge chyldrē do to ye mother: the foote, the hand, & al wayteth vpō the eye. Yf the eye byd ye hād either beare of, or smite, or the foote ether go forward, or backeward, it doth so: And that whyche is moost wonder of all the one man lookynge stedfastly at the other mans eye and not at his hand, wyl, euē as it were, rede in his eye where he purposeth to smyte nexte, for the eye is nothyng els but a certayne wyndowe for wit to shote oute hir hede at.

Thys wonderfull worke of god in makynge all the members so obedient to the eye, is a pleasaunte thynge to remember and

loke vpon : therfore an Archer maye be sure in learnyng to
looke at hys marke when he is yong, always to shoote streyghte.
The thynges that hynder a man whyche looketh at hys marke,
to shote streyght, be these : A syde wynde, a bowe either to
stronge, or els to weake, an ill arme, whan a fether runneth on
the bowe to much, a byg brested shafte, for hym that shoteth
vnder hande, bycause it wyll hobble : a little brested shafte for
hym y^t shoteth aboue ye hande, bicause it wyl starte : a payre
of windynge prickes, and many other thinges mo, which you
shal marke your selfe, & as ye knowe thē, so learne to amend
them.   If a man woulde leaue to looke at his shafte, and learne
to loke at his marke, he maye vse this waye, whiche a good
shooter tolde me ones that he did.   Let him take his bowe on
the nyght, and shoote at .ii. lightes, and there he shall be
compelled to looke always at his marke, & neuer at his
shafte : This thing ones or twyse vsed wyl cause hym forsake
lokynge at hys shafte.   Yet let hym take hede of settynge his
shaft in the bowe.

Thus Philologe to shoote streyght is the leaste maysterie of
all, yf a manne order hym selfe thereafter, in hys youthe.   And
as for keypynge a lengthe, I am sure the rules whiche I gaue
you, wil neuer disceyue you, so that there shal lacke nothynge,
eyther of hittinge the marke alwayes, or elles verye nere
shotynge, excepte the faulte be onely in youre owne selfe,
whiche maye come .ii. wayes, eyther in hauing a faynt harte or
courage, or elles in sufferynge your selfe ouer muche to be led
with affection : yf a mans mynde fayle hym, the bodye whiche
is ruled by the mynde, can neuer doe his duetie, yf lacke of
courage were not, men myght do mo mastries than they do, as
doeth appere in leapynge and vaultinge.

All affections and specially anger, hurteth bothe mynde and
bodye.   The mynde is blynde therby : and yf the mynde be
blynde, it can not rule the bodye aright.   The body both blood
and bone, as they say, is brought out of his ryght course by
anger : Wherby a man lacketh his right strengthe, and therfore
can not shoote wel.   Yf these thynges be auoyded (wherof I
wyll speake no more, both bycause they belong not properly to
shoting, & also you can teache me better, in them, than I you)
& al the preceptes which I haue gyuen you, diligently marked,
no doubt ye shal shoote as well as euer man dyd yet, by the

grace of God. Thys communication handled of me Philologe, as I knowe wel not perfytly, yet as I suppose truelye you must take in good worthe, wherin if diuers thinges do not all togyther please you, thanke youre selfe, whiche woulde haue me rather faulte in mere follye, to take that thynge in hande whyche I was not able for to perfourme, than by any honeste shamefastnes withsay your request & minde, which I knowe well I haue not satisfied. But yet I wyl thinke this labour of mine the better bestowed, if to morow or some other daye when you haue leysour, you wyl spende as much tyme with me here in this same place, in entreatinge the question *De origine animę,* and the ioynyng of it with the bodye, that I maye knowe howe far Plato, Aristotle, & the Stoiicians haue waded in it.

PHI. How you haue handeled this matter Toxoph. I may not well tel you my selfe nowe, but for your gentlenesse and good wyll towarde learnyng & shotyng, I wyll be content to shewe you any pleasure whensoeuer you wyll : and nowe the sunne is doune therfore if it plese you, we wil go home and drynke in my chambre, and there I wyll tell you playnelye what I thinke of this cōmunication and also, what daye we will appoynt at your request for the other matter, to mete here agayne.

Deo gratias.

☛ LONDINI. ☜

In ædibus Edouardi VVhytchurch.

Cum priuilegio ad impri-
mendum solum.

1545.

❧ A REPORT

and Discourse written by
Roger Ascham, of the affaires
and state of Germany and the
Emperour Charles his court,
duryng certaine yeares
while the sayd Roger
was there.

AT LONDON.

¶ Printed by Iohn Daye,
dwelling ouer Aldersgate.

¶ *Cum Gratia & Priuilegio Regiæ*
Maiestatis, per Decennium.

∂ *John Astely to R. Ascham.*

I Now finde true by experience, which I haue oft heard of
others, & sometymes read my selfe : that mē make no such
accompt of commodities when they haue thē, as when they
want thē.   I meane this by our frendly fellowshyp together at
Cheston Chelsey, and here at *Hatfield* her graces house : our
pleasant studies in readyng together *Aristotles* Rethorike, *Cicero*,
and *Liuie* : our free talke mingled alwayes with honest mirth :
our trimme cōferences of that present world : and to true
iudgementes of the troublesome tyme that followed.

These commodities I now remēber with some grief, which
we then vsed with much pleasure, besides many other fruites of
frendshyp that faythfull good will could affourd.   And these
thinckynges cause me oft to wish, either you to be here with
vs, or me to be there with you : but what wishyng is nothyng
els but a vayne waylyng for that which will wanteth, I wil
cease from wishyng, and seeke the true remedy for this sore.
And that is whilest we mete agayne in deede, in the meane-
while to ease our desires with oft writyng the one to the other :
I would in deede I had bene partaker in your company, of that
your pleasaunt absence out of your countrey : And because I
was not, I pray you let me be partaker by your letters of some
fruite of that your iourney.

We heare of great sturres in those parties : and how the
Emperour a Prince of great wisedome and great power hath
bene driuen to extreme shiftes, and that by the pollicie of mean
men who were thought to be hys frendes, and not by the
puisantnes of others who were knowne to be his open enemyes.   I

know your wont in markyng diligently and notyng truely all such
great affaires: And you know lykewise how desirous I am always
to read any thing that you write.　Write therfore I pray you,
that we your frendes beyng at home may en-
ioye by your letters a pleasant memory of
you in this tyme whilest you be absent a-
broad. Farewell in Christ from Hatfield. xix. Octobris. 1552.

♄ R. Ascham, to Iohn Asteley.

SAlutem Plurimam in Christo Iesu. That part of your letters from *Hatfield, decimo nono Octob.* renewing a most pleasaunt memory of our frēdly fellowship together, & full of your wonted good will towardes me : I aunswered immediatly from *Spires* by *Fraunces* the post : whiche letter if it be not yet come to your hand, ye might haue heard tell of it in M. Secretary *Cicels* chamber in the Court.

As concernyng the other part of your letter, for your wish, to haue bene with me, in this mine absence from my countrey : and for your request, to be made partaker by my letters of the sturre of these times here in *Germany*. Surely I would you had your wish : for then should not I now nede to bungle vp yours so great a request, when presently you should haue sene with much pleasure, which now peraduēture you shall read with some doubt, lesse thynges may encrease by writyng which were so great in doyng, as I am more afrayd to leaue behind me much of the matter, then to gather vp more then hath sprong of the trouth.

Your request conteineth few wordes but cōprehendeth both great and diuers matters. As first the causes of the open inuasion by the *Turke* : of the secret workyng for such soddeyne brechesse in *Italy*, and *Germany* : of the fine fetches in the *French* practises : of the double dealyng of *Rome* with all partes : thē more particularly why Duke *Octauio*, the Prince of *Salerne*, Marches *Albert*, and Duke *Maurice* brake so out with the Emperour, which were all so fast knit vnto hym as the bondes of affinitie, loyaltie, bloud, and benefites could assure him of them : *Octauio* being his sonne in law, the Prince one of hys priuy chamber, Marches *Albert* hys kynsman, and Duke *Maurice* so inhaunsed with honor and enriched with benefites by hym, as the Duke could not haue wished greater in hope, then the Emperour performed in deede. Here is stuffe plenty to furnish well vp a trimme history if a workeman had it in handlyng. When you and I read *Liuie* together if you do remember, after some reasonyng we cōcluded both what was in our opinion to be looked for at his hand that would well and aduisedly write an history : First, point was, to write nothyng false : next, to be bold to say any truth, wherby is auoyded two great faultes, flattery and hatred : For which

C. Cæsar.
P. Iouius.

two pointes *Cæsar* is read to his great prayse, and *Iouius* the *Italian* to hys iust reproch. Then to marke diligently the causes, coūsels, actes, and issues in all great attemptes : And in causes, what is iust or vniust : in coūsels, what is purposed wisely or rashly : in actes, what is done couragiously or fayntly : And of euery issue, to note some generall lesson of wisedome & warines, for lyke

Polibius.
Phi. Co-
mines.

matters in time to come : wherin *Polibius* in *Greeke* and *Phillip Comines* in *French* haue done the duties of wyse and worthy writers. Diligence also must be vsed in kepyng truly the order of tyme : and describyng lyuely, both the site of places and nature of persons not onely for the outward shape of the body : but also

Thucidi-
des.
Homer.

for the inward dispositiō of the mynde as *Thucidides* doth in many places very trimly, and *Homer* euery where and that alwayes most excellently, which obseruation is chiefly to be marked in hym. And our

Chaucer.

Chaucer doth the same, very praise worthely : marke hym well and conferre hym with any other that writeth of our tyme in their proudest toung whosoeuer lyst. The stile must be alwayes playne and open : yet sometime higher and lower as matters do ryse and fall : for if proper and naturall wordes, in well ioyned sentences do lyuely expresse the matter, be it troublesome, quyet, angry or pleasant, A man shal thincke not to be readyng but present in doyng

Titus Li-
uius.

of the same. And herein *Liuie* of all other in any toung, by myne opiniō carieth away the prayse.

Syr *Thomas More* in that pamphlet of *Richard* the thyrd,

Tho. Mo-
rus.

doth in most part I beleue of all these pointes so content all men, as if the rest of our story of England were so done, we might well compare with *Fraunce*, *Italy*, or *Germany* in that behalfe. But see how the pleasant remembraunce of our old talke together hath caried me farther then I thought to go. And as for your request to know

the cause and maner of these late sturres here ye shall not looke
for such precise order now in writyng, as we talked on then. No
it is not all one thing to know perfectly by reading and to
performe perfectly in doyng I am not so vnaduised to take so
much vpō me, nor you so vnfrendly to looke for so much from
me. But that you may know that I haue not bene altogether
idle in this my absence, and that I will not come home as one
that can say nothing of that he hath sene and heard abroad :
I will homely and rudely (yet not altogether disorderly) part
priuately vnto you such notes of affaires as I priuately marked
for my selfe : which I either felt and saw, or learned in such
place and of such persōs as had willes to seeke for, and wayes
to come by, and wittes to way the greatest matters that were
to be marked in all these affaires. For no wieke almost hath
past in the which there hath not commonly come to my hand
for the most part of the notable thynges that haue bene
attempted in *Turky*, *Hungary*, *Italy*, *Fraunce*, and *Germany*.
In declaryng to you these thyngs I will obserue onely the first
two pointes of our wont communication : that is to my writyng
I will set forward nothyng that is false, nor yet keepe backe
any thyng that is true. For I playing no part of no one side,
but sittyng downe as indifferent looker on, neither Imperiall
nor Frēch, but flat English do purpose with troth to report the
matter. And seyng I shall lyue vnder such a Prince, as kyng
Edward is, and in such a countrey as Englād is (I thanke God)
I shall haue neither neede to flatter the one side for profite, nor
cause to feare the other side for displeasure. Therefore let my
purpose of reportyng the troth as much content you, as the
meane handlyng of the matter may mislike you. Yet speakyng
thus much of trouth, I meane not such a hid trouth as was
onely in the brest of Monsieur *d'Arras* on the Emperours side,
or in Baron *Hadeck* on Duke *Maurice* side, with whom and
with on other of his counsell he onely conferred all his purposes
three yeares before he brake out with yᵉ Emperour : but
I meane such a troth as by conference and common cōsent
amongest all the Ambassadors and Agentes in this Court and
other witty & indifferent heades beside was generally conferred
and agreed vpō. What better cōmoditie to know the trouth
any writer in *Greeke Latine* or other toung hath had, I can not
perceiue, except onely *Xenophon*, *Cæsar*, and *Phillip Comines* :

which two first worthy writers wrote their owne actes so wisely, and so without all suspicion of parcialitie, as no mā hetherto by mine opinion hath borne him selfe so vprightly in writyng the histories of others : The thyrd hauyng in a maner yᵉ like oportunitie hath not deserued lyke commendations, at least as I suppose. Englād hath matter & Englād hath mē furnished with all abilitie to write : who if they would might bryng both lyke prayse vnto them selues, & like profite to others, as these two noble mē haue done. They lay for their excuse the lacke of leysure which is true in deede : But if we cōsider the great affaires of *Cæsar* we may iudge hee was worthy to winne all praise that was so willing & wittie to winne such time when his head & his handes night and day were euer most full, would to God that these our mē as they are ready to prayse hym were euen as willyng to follow hym, and so to wynne like prayse them selues.

And to keepe you no longer with my priuate talke from the matter it selfe, I will begyn at the spryng of the matter from whence all these mischiefes dyd flow, the which now hath so ouerflowed the most part of Christendome, as God onely from heauen must make an end of this miserable tragedie, wherein these two great Princes take such pleasure still to play. In Religion & libertie were sayd to be of many men the very causes of all these sturres : yet in myne opinion & as the matter it selfe shall well proue it, vnkyndnes was the very sede, whereof all these troubles dyd grow. A Knight of England of worthy memorie for wit learnyng and experience old Syr *Thomas Wiat* wrote to his sonne that the greatest mischief amongest men and least punished is vnkyndnes : the greatest mischief truly & least punished also by any ordinary law & sentence, yet as I haue sene here by experience, vnkyndnes hath so wrought with men, as the meane were not affrayd to attempt their reuēge, nor the Emperour able to withstand their displease. Yea vnkyndnes was onely the hoke, which *Henry* the *French* kyng hath vsed these late yeares to plucke from the Emperour and draw to hym selfe, so many Princes and great cōmodities as he hath : with this hoke bayted with money the bayte of all mischief, the *French* kyng hath not ceased to angle at as many harts in *Italy* and *Germany* as

The cause of yᵉ sturres in Italy & Germany.

Unkyndnes.

he knew any matter of vnkyndnes to bee ministred vnto, by the Emperour. There be few Princes in all the Empire but if I had leysure, I could particularly proue, and when I come home in our priuate talke I wil fully declare that some good big matter of vnkindnes hath bene offred vnto them by the Emperour. Yea *Ferdinando* his brother, *Maximilian* his nephew and sonne in law, the Dukes of *Bauarie* and *Cleues* which haue maried his nieces haue bene shrewdly touched therwith. Also yᵉ Papisticall Byshops as *Mentz*, *Pamburge*, *Herbipolis*, *Saltz-burge*, and diuers others haue felt their part herein. Few Princes or states, Protestantes or Papistes, but haue bene troubled therwith. But euen as a quaterne in the begynnyng is a wanderyng disease in the body vnknowne what it wil turne vnto, and yet at last it draweth to certaine dayes & houres : euen so these grieues in the whole body of the Empire dyd first worke secretly and not appeare openly, vntill this melancholy vnkyndnes did so swell in mens stomaches that at length in *Insburgh* it brast out into a shrewd sicknes, whereof the first fit was felt to be so daūgerous, that if the Emperour and we had not more spedely chaunged the ayre, I am affrayed and sure I am we were wel affrayd then, the sickenes would haue proued also to vs that were present with hym very contagious. Well this grief growyng this to certaine fittes, and I my selfe beyng not greatly greued at yᵉ hart with it but had leysure enough with small ieoperdy (I thanke God) to looke quietly vpon them that were sicke, because I would not be idle amongst them I began dayly to note the workyng of this sickenes, and namely from the xix. of May .1552. when we ranne from *Insburgh* till the first of next January whē the siege of *Metz* was abādoned. Neuertheles before I come to these ordinary dayes I will shortly touch how the Emperour beyng in peace with all the world .1550. when we came to his Court, had soone after so many enemyes as hee knew not which way to turne hym.

¶ *The Turke.*

THe date of peace betwixt the Emperour and the *Turke* had to expire an.1551. The Emperour hearyng what preparation the *Turke* had made the yeare before for warre and specially by Sea, which must needes

The brech with the *Turke.*

be agaynst Christendome, thought it better for him to ende
the peace with some aduauntage, thē that the *Turke* should
begyn the warre with too much strength & therfore in
sommer .1550. he sent *Iohn de Vega* Viceroy of *Cicile* &
Andrea Dorea into *Barbaria*, who wan the strong towne of
Affrica from *Dragut Raies* sometyme a Pirate and now the
Turkes chief doer in all the affaires of *Affrike* and *mare
mediteraneo*. This Court raised vp other rumors of this brech
with the *Turke* how that this enterprice was made for *Seripho*
sake a hethen kyng. But the Emperours frend in *Barbaria*
to whom *Dragat Rayes* had done great wrong, yet men that
knew the troth, and are wont also to say it, haue told me that
the towne of *Affrica* stode so fit to annoy *Spayne* for the *Turke*
when he list, that the Emperour was compelled to seeke by all
meanes to obtaine it, much fearyng, lest when he was absent
in *Germany*, the *Turke* would be too nigh and to homely a gest
with hym in *Spayne* whensoeuer the peace should be expired.
The whole story of winnyng *Affrica* ye may read whē you
list beyng wel written in *Latin* by a *Spaniard* that was present
at it.

Affrica was earnestly required agayne by the *Turke*, and
fayre promised agayne by the Emperour, but beyng in deede
not deliuered, the *Turke* for a reuenge the next yeare, first
assaulted *Malta* and after wan *Tripoly* from whence the *Turke*
may easely and soddenly whensoeuer hee list set vpon *Cicelie*,
Naples, or any cost of *Italie* or *Spayne* and most commodiously,
what soeuer the Emperour doth hold in *Barbary* : so that the
gayne of *Affrica* is thought nothyng comparable with the losse
of *Tripoly*.

When *Tripoly* was besieged by the *Turkes*, *Monsieur Daramont* was sent Ambassadour to *Constantinople* from the *French*
kyng : and ariuyng by the way at *Malta*, hee was desired by
the great master of the order to go to *Tripoly*, and for the
frendshyp that was betwene *Fraunce* and the *Turke* to treat for
the Christians there. *Daramont* did so and had leaue of the
Turkes generall to enter the towne and talke with the Captaine.
And by this meanes they within yelded, on this condition
to part safe with bag and baggage which was graunted by the
generall. But assoone as the *Turkes* entred the towne they put
old & yong, man, woman, and child to the sword sauing two

hundred of the strongest men to be their Galley slaues for euer. The generall beyng asked why he kept no promise made this aunswere : If the Emperour had kept faith with my master for *Affrica* I would not haue broken with them of *Tripoly*, and therfore (sayth he) with Christen men which care for no trothe promises may iustly be broken. This *Turkish* crueltie was reuenged this last yeare in *Hungary*, when lyke promise of lyfe was made, and yet all put to the sword the Christians biddyng the *Turkes* remember *Tripoly*. To such beastly crueltie the noble feates of armes be come vnto betwixt the Christen men and the *Turkes*. And one fact of either side is notable to bee knowen, yet horrible to be told and fouler to be followed : and it is pitie that mãs nature is such, as will commonlie commend good thynges in readyng and yet will as commonly follow ill thynges in doyng.

The *Bassa* of *Buda*, tooke in a skirmish a gētleman of the kyng of *Romanes* : for whose deliuery men for entreaty and money for hys raunsome were sent to *Buda*. The *Bassa* appointed a day to geue them aunswere, and at time and place assigned, called for them and sent for the gentleman likewise. And soddenly came out two hangmen bare armed with great butchers kniues in theyr handes bringing with them certaine bandogges musled kept hungry without meate of purpose : the *Bassa* bad them do their feate : who commyng to the gentleman stripped him naked, and bound him to a piller, after with their kniues they cut of his flesh by gobbets and flang it to the dogges. Thus yᵉ poore gentlemã suffred grief great for yᵉ payne, but greater for the spight : nor so tormēted in feelyng his fleshe mangled with kniues, as in seyng him selfe peece meale deuoured by dogges. And thus as long as hee felt any payne they cut him in collops, and after they let their dogges lose vpon him to eate vp the residue of him, that yᵉ grief which was ended in him being dead might yet continue in his frendes lookyng on. They were bad depart and tell what they saw, who ye may be sure were in care enough to cary home with them such a cruell message.

An horrible fact.

Not long after this, three *Turkes* of good estimation and place, were taken by the Christen men : for whose raunsome great summes of gold were offred. Aunswere was made to the messenger that all the gold in *Turky* should not saue thē. And because ye *Turkes* will eate no swines flesh, you shall see if swine will eate any *Turkish* fleshe. And so likewise great bores were kept hungry, & in sight of the messenger the three *Turkes* were cut in collops and throwne amongest them.

For these foule deedes I am not so angry with the *Turkes* that began them as I am sory for the Christen men that follow them. I talked with a worthy gentleman this day both for his great experience and excellent learnyng *Marc Anthonio d'Anula*

The great *Turke*.

Ambassadour of *Venice* with the Emperour: who told me that the great *Turke* him selfe (Religion excepted) is a good and mercyfull, iust and liberall Prince, wise in makyng and true in performyng any couenant, and as sore a reuenger of troth not kept. He prayed God to

Mustapha the *Turkes* eldest sonne

kepe him long aliue: for his eldest sonne *Mustapha* is cleane contrary, geuē to all mischief cruell, false, gettyng he careth not how vniustly, and spendyng he careth not how vnthriftely what soeuer he may lay hand on, wilye in makyng for his purpose, & ready to breake for his profite all couenantes, he is wery of quietnes and peace, a seeker of strife and warre, a great mocker of meane men, a sore oppressor of poore men, openly contemnyng God, and a bent enemy agaynst Christes name and Christen men. But to go forward with my purpose. The *Turke* beyng onest disclosed an open enemy to the Emperour, many meane men begā to be the bolder to put out their heades to seeke some open remedy for theyr priuate iniuries: *Fraunce* beyng at euery

Brech of *Italie*.

mans elbow to harten and to helpe, whosoeuer had cause to be aggreued with the Emperour. And first *Octauio* Duke of *Parma*, much agreued as nature well required with his fathers death & besides that fearing the losse not onely of his state, but also of his lyfe, fell from the Emperour in the end of the yeare .1550.

Pietro Aloysio Farnesio sonne to *Papa Paulo tercio* Duke of

Octauio.

Placētia: father to this Duke *Octauio* Duke of *Parma* which maried the Emperors base daughter, and to *Horatio* Duke of *Castro*, who of late hath maried also the *French* kynges base daughter, and the two Cardinals *Alexandro* and *Ramusio Farnesy*, was slaine men say by the meanes of *Ferranto Gonzaga* gouernour of *Millan* by

whose death the state of *Placentia* belōging then to the house
of *Fernesia* came into the Emperour handes. The whole
processe of this mans death is at length set out in the stories of
Italie : my purpose is onely to touch it, because hereby rose
such a heate betwixt the whole famely of *Fernesia* and *Don
Ferranto Gonzaga* as hath stirred vp such a smoke in *Italy*
betwixt the Emperour and *Fraunce*, as is not like to be
quenched but with many a poore mans bloud, as *Horace* noteth
wittely out of *Homer*, saying :

> *What follies so euer great Princes make* :
> *The people therfore go to wrake.*

Octauio beyng sorest greeued with his fathers death and
beyng best able to reuenge it was so feared of *Gonzaga* that
he thought hym selfe neuer assured for *Petro Luis* death as long
as *Octauio* his sonne should lyue : for men neuer loue whē
they haue iust cause to feare, but must nedes still mistrust
without all hope of reconcilyng whom they haue before hurt
beyōd all remedy of amendes. And yet I heard a gentlemā
of *Millan* say (who was sent hether to the Emperour by
Gonzaga) that *Octauio* is such a Prince for good nature and
gentle behauiour that he supposed there was not one in *Italy*
but did loue hym except it were his maister *Gonzaga*. These
two Princes beyng neighbours the one at *Millan* the other at
Parma shewed smal frendshyp the one to the other. But
Octauio was euermore wrong to the worse by many and sundry
spites, but chiefly with dayly feare of hys life by poysoning :
for the which fact certain persons in *Parma* were taken and
layd fast. Neuertheles *Octauios* nature is so farre from seekyng
bloud and reuenge and so geuen to pitie and gentlenes, that
although they went about not onely to geue away his state by
treason, but also to take away his life by poysonyng, yea, and
after that the deede was proued playnly on them, and sentence
of death pronounced openly agaynst them, yet he gaue them
lyfe and libertie which would haue taken both from hym.

And when *Monsieur Thermes* earnestly told him that where
the euill were not kept in with feare of Iustice, the good should
neuer lyue in suretie and quietnes : his aunswere was that he
so abhorred the sheddyng of bloud in others as he would neuer
wash his handes in any : let his enemies do to him the worst

they could. Addyng, that he thought it his most honor to be
vnlykest such for his gentlenes which were misliked of all
mē for their crueltie : wherby he hath wonne that he which of
good nature can hurt none, is now of right loued of all and
onely hated of him whō no man in *Italy* for his cruelty doth
loue. And this talke is so true that it was told in an other
language but in the selfe same termes at an honorable table
here in *Bruxels* by a gentleman of *Millan* an agent in the
Court, a doer for *Gonzaga*, who the same tyme was prisoner
in *Parma*.

And although *Octauio* by good nature was harmeles in not
seekyng reuenge, yet he was not careles by good reason in
seekyng hys remedy but made oft & great cōplaintes of his
grieues to the Emperour, which were not so hotely made, but
they were as coldly heard, that at lēgth *Octauio* findyng least
comfort, where of right he looked for most ayde, & seyng that
displeasures could not be ended in *Gonzaga* nor could not be
amended by the Emperour : then he compelled agaynst his
nature turned his hate due to *Gonzaga* to reuenge this vndeserued
vnkyndnes in the Emperour, euen as *Pausanias* dyd with *Phillip*
kyng of *Macedonie*, who conqueryng with pollicie and power
all outward enemyes, was slayne when and where, he thought
him selfe most sure of his dearest frēd, for vnkindnes, because
Phillip ought and would not reuēge *Pausanias* on him that had
done him a foule displeasure.

Octauio seyng what was done to his father euen when hys
graundfather was Byshop of *Rome*, thought, that now as his
house decayed, so his iopardy encreased. And therfore agaynst
a desperate euill began to seeke for a desperate remedie, which
was fet from *Rome* a shop alwayes open to any mischief as you
shall perceiue in these few leaues if you marke them well.

Octauio cōplained to *Iulio tercio* of the wrōges of *Gonzaga*
& of the vnkindnes of the Emperour, desirying that by his
wisedome and authoritie, he would now succor him or els not
onely he should leese his life but also the Church of *Rome*
should lose her right in *Parma*, as she had done before in
Placentia. The Byshop gaue good eare to this talke, for he
spied that hereby should be offred vnto him, a fit occasion to set
the Emperour and *Fraunce* together by the eares. He thought
the Emperour was to bigge in *Italy* hauyng on ye one side of

Rome Naples vnder his obedience, on the other side *Siena*, *Florence* and *Genoa* at his commaundement, besides *Placentia*, *Millan*, *Monteferrato*, and a great part of *Piemount*.

The Emperour beyng thus strong in *Italy*, the Byshop thought his own state to be his so lōg as it pleased the Emperour to let him haue it: & therfore if *Parma* were not left an entry for *Fraunce* to come into *Italy*, he might ouersoone be shut vp in present miserie when all outward ayde should be shut out from him.

The Popes counsel was that *Octauio* should put him selfe vnder the *French* kynges protection whom hee knew would most willingly receiue him : *Parma* lying so fit for the *French* kyng, when soeuer he would set vpon the enterprice of *Millan*. This practise of the Pope *Monsieur de Thermes* the *French* kynges Ambassadours dyd vtter before the consistorie of Cardinals at *Rome* : prouing that the Pope, not the kyng his master was the occasion of that warre.

When *Octauio* with the whole house of *Farnesia* became thus *Frēch*, the Emperour more fearyng the state of *Millan* then lamentyng the losse of *Octauio* persuaded on his side the Byshop of *Rome* to require *Parma* as the Churches right, & to punish *Octauio* as the Churches rebell, promising that he him selfe as an obedient sonne of the Church would stretch out his arme and open his purse in that recouery of the Churches right : neuertheles the Byshop must beare the name of the warre because hee might not breake peace with *Fraunce*. Thus Princes openly cōtenācing quietnes & priuily brewyng debate although they got others to broch it, yet God commōly suffreth thē selues to drinke most of the misery thereof in the end. The Byshop seyng that he must either begyn the mischief or els it would not on so fast as he wished to haue it, set lustely vpon it : and first cited *Octauio*, after excommunicated him, and shortly after besieged *Parma* ayded both with mē and money by the Emperour : which thyng the *French* kyng began to stomach, thinckyng that yᵉ Emperour dyd offer him both wrong & dishonor in not suffring him beyng a kyng to helpe a poore man that fled to his ayde. And thus these two Princes first helpyng others began by litle and litle to fall out them selues. And that the Pope dyd set these two Princes together, a *Pasquill*

Breach wᵗ *Fraunce.*

made at *Rome* and sent to this Court doth well declare. And seyng that you so well vnderstand the *Italian* toung and that if it were turned into English it would leese the whole grace therof, I will recite it in the toung that it was made in.

Interlocutori Pasquillo et Romano.

Pasq. *HAnno vn bel gioco il Re, et l' Imperatore*
per terzo el Papa, e giocano à Primera.
Rom. *che v' e d' invito?* Pasq. *Italia tutta intera.*
Rom. *Chi vi l' ha messa?* Pasq. *il coglion del pastore.*
Rom. *Che tien in mano il Re?* Pasq. *Ponto magiore.*
e'l Papa ha cinquant' vno, e se despera.
Rom. *Cæsar che Ponto s'a?* Pasq. *lui sta a Primera.*
Rom. *che gli manca?* Pasq. *danari a far fauore.*
Il Papa dice, à vol, e vuol Partito :
Cæsar Pensoso sta Sopra di questo,
teme à Scoprir di [non] trouar moneta
Il Re dice, no, no, Scoprite Presto,
che io tengo Ponto, a guadagnar l' invito
l' ho li danari, et Cæsar se gli aspeta.

¶ *Tutti stanno a vedetta*

Chi di lor due guadagni. Rom. *il Papa?* Pas. *è fuora,*
vinca chi vuol, lui Perde, in sua mal' hora.

¶ *L' Imperatore anchora*

Teme, e tien stretto, e Scopre Pian le carte,
e quì la sorte gioca, più che l' Arte.

¶ *Metta questi in disparte.*

Stabilito è nel Ciel quello, che esser dè,
ne gioua 'l nostro dir, questo Sarà questo è.

The *French* king in the sommer .1551. proclaimed warre against *Charles* kyng of *Spayne*, abusing that name for a sottlety to separate ye whole quarell from the Empire : when the Emperour would not be persuaded at *Augusta* that either the *Turke* would, or the *French* kyng durst make him open warre, or that any Prince in *Italy* or *Germany* could be entised to breake out with him.

Monsieur Mariliacke the *French* Ambassadour at *Augusta* euer bare the Emperour in hand that such rumors of war were raysed of displeasure & that his master intended nothyng so much as the continuance of amitie, yea this he durst do, when many in ye Emperours court knew that the war was already proclaimed in *Fraunce.*

The Emperour blinded with the ouer good opinion of his own wisedome, likyng onely what him selfe listed, and contemnyng easely all aduise of others (which selfe will condition doth commonly follow, and as commonly doth hurt all great wittes) dyd not onely at this tyme suffer him selfe thus to be abused : but also afterward more craftely by the Pope for the continuaunce of warre at *Parma*, & more boldly by Duke *Maurice* for his repayre to *Inspruke*, and not the least of all, now lately at *Metz* by some of his owne counsellours for the recouery of that towne.

But Princes and great personages whiche will heare but what and whom they list, at the length fayle when they would not, and commonly blame whom they should not : But it is well done that as great men may by authoritie contemne the good aduise of others : so God doth prouide by right iudgement that they haue leaue in the ende to beare both the losse and shame therof them selues.

Thus ye see how the Pope was both the brewer and brocher and also bringer of ill lucke to both these Princes, and as it came wel to passe dranke well of it him selfe both with expences of great treasures, and with the losse of many lyues and specially of two noble gentlemen, the Prince of *Macedonia* and *Il Seigñ. Giouan Baptista di Monte* his owne nephew : but the Popes care was neither of money nor men, so that he might set the two Princes surely together. And therfore was not onely content (as a man might say) to hasard *Parma* on the meyne chaūce : but to make the two Princes better sporte & fresher game, set also euē then *Mirandula* on a bye chaunce that mischief enough might come together.

When the Princes were well in and the one so lusty with good lucke that hee had no lust to leaue, aud the other so chafed with leesyng, that still he would venture. Besides their playing in sporte for the Pope at *Parma* and *Mirandula*, they fell

Pope.
Parma.
Mirādula.

to it a good them selues in *Piemoūt*, *Loraigne*, *Flaunders* and
Picardy, the *French* kyng robbyng by Sea and spoyling by
land, with calling in the *Turke*, and sturryng vp all Princes
and states that had any occasion to beare any grudge to the
Emperour.   Of all their neighbours onely our noble kyng,
and the wise senate of *Venize* would be lookers on.

And when the Pope saw they were so hote at it as he well
knew as the one would not start in so great good lucke : so y^e
other could not leaue by so much shame of losse.   And
although it did him good to see them cope so lustely together :
neuertheles he thought it scarce his surety that they should play
so nere his elbow so earnestly, least if they fell to farre out and
the one should winne to much of the other, then he peraduenture would compell at length the Pope him selfe which
begā the play to kepe him sport afterward for that that he had
in *Italy*.   And therfore very craftely he gat them to play in an

The Po-
pes prac-
tice.

other place, and tooke vp the game for *Parma*
and *Mirandula* taking truce with *Fraunce* for
certaine yeares, and bad them make what sport
they would farther of in *Loraigne* & *Picardy*.   And that there
should lacke neither iniurie nor spite in the Popes doynges, whē
the Emperour saw that whether hee would or no, the Pope
would needes fall in with *Fraunce*, then he desired the Pope
that such bastilians and fortes of fence as were made about
Mirandula when it was besieged might either be deliuered to
hys mens handes or els defaced that the *Frenchmen* might not
haue them, which request was very reasonable seyng the
Emperour had bene at all the charge in makyng of them : But
they were neither deliuered nor defaced, nor left indifferēt, but
so put into the *French mens* handes, that *Mirandula* now is
made very strong to the *French* faction by Emperours money
and the Popes falsehode.

This fact was very wrongfull of the Pope for the deede :
but more spitefull for the tyme : for euen when Duke *Maurice*
had wonne *Augusta*, euen then the Pope gaue vp the siege of
Mirandula and fell in with *Fraunce* that care enough might
come vppon the Emperour together both out of *Germany*, and
out of *Italy* at once.   And euē this day .25. June .1553. when
I was writyng this place, commeth newes to *Bruxells*, that the
Pope hath of new played with the Emperour more foule play

at *Siena*, then he dyd before at *Mirandula*: For whē the
Emperour had bene at passing charges in kepyng a great host,
for the recouery of *Siena* from December last vnto June: the
Pope would needes become stickler in that matter betwene the
Emperour, the *French* kyng and *Siena* promising such conditions
to all, as neither of the Princes should lose honour and yet
Siena should haue had liberties. The Emperour good man yet
agayne trustyng him who so spightfully had deceaued hym
before dismissed hys hoste, which done *Siena* was left still in
the *French mēs* hādes: who therby haue such oportunitie to
fortifie it, as yᵉ Emperor is not like by force to recouer it.
Piramus Secretary to yᵉ Emperor told this tale to Syr *Phillip
Hobby* & the Byshop of Westminster openly at yᵉ table: which
Piramus is a Papist for his life: & beyng asked how he could
excuse the Popes vnkyndnes agaynst his master yᵉ Emperour:
Hee aunswered smilyng *Iulius tercius* is a knaue but yᵉ Pope is
an honest mā, which saying is cōmō in this court. And
although they wil vnderstād both yᵉ spight of yᵉ pope, & yᵉ
shame of their master, yet are they cōtent stil to speake of yᵉ
pope though he neuertheles still do ill to yᵉ Emperour.

And thus to returne to my purpose how the Pope set the
two Princes together, & shift his owne necke a while out of
the halter, leauyng most vnfrendly the Emperour when he was
farthest behynd hand: and how *Octauio* for feare of *Gonzaga*,
and vnkyndnes of the Emperour fell with all hys famely to be
French, I haue briefly passed over for the bast I haue to come
to the matters of *Germany*.

¶ *The Prince of Salerne.*

THe Emperour beyng thus set vpon by the *Turke* and
Fraunce with open warre, and troubled by the house of
Fernesia with so soddeyne breaches, and most of all encombred
with the feare of the sturres in *Germany* which secretly were
then in workyng: the Prince of *Salerne* also declared hym selfe
an open enemy.

This Prince in this court is much beloued for his gētlenes
and openly praysed for his wisedome, & greatly lamented for
his fortune, who before tyme hath done so good and faythfull

seruice to the Emperour : that I haue heard some in this Court say, which loue the Emperour well and serue him in good place, that their master hath done the Prince so much wrong, as he could do no lesse then he dyd : who being so vniustly hãdled by his enemies, the Viceroy of *Naples*, and so vnkyndly dealt with all by hys master yᵉ Emperour, was driuen by necessitie to seeke an vnlawfull shift.

The Viceroy *Don Pietro de Toledo* vncle to yᵉ Duke of *Alua*, & father in law to yᵉ duke of *Florẽce* vsed him selfe with much cruelty ouer yᵉ people of *Naples* by exactions of money without measure, by Inquisition of mens doyngs without order, & not onely of mens doynges, but also of mẽs outward lookyngs, & inward thinkynges, vsing the least suspicion for a sufficiẽt witnes to spoyle & to kill whõ soeuer he lysted. Mẽ that had sutes vnto him, had as leue bene away with the losse of their right, as haue come to his presence to abyde his lokes & taũts : And (as I heard a wise gẽtlemã of *Italy* say) he gaue audiẽce in such tyme & place, as he may easlyer in this Court speake with *Monsieur d'Arras* then he could in *Naples* with the Viceroyes Porter. And commõly he would not heare them whilest an hundred suters should come at once, and then the Porter let them in by one and by one euen as he fauoured not as the matter required, commaũdyng then, to be short or els they should come short in the next tyme. And so mens sutes were pulled frõ cõmon law to priuate will, & were heard not in place open to Iustice but in priuate Parlors shit vp to all that came not in by fauour or money. And therfore iudgements were allotted not as law appointed, but as the Viceroy listed. This fault (*Cicero* sayth) vndyd *Cæsar* who drew the commõ law into his own house, & so in hauing other mẽs goods lost all mẽs hartes and not long after his owne lyfe : for euen those that dyd helpe him plucke down *Pompey*, dyd after kill him for pulling downe the lawes : So we see that Princes not in gatheryng much money, nor in bearing ouer great swinge but in keping of frendes & good lawes lyue most merely & raigne most surely. But such as gape alwayes for other mens goods cõmõly neuer enioy yᵉ fruite of their owne : for they neuer cease to win by wrõg till at length they leese by right goodes lyfe & all. And therfore it is notable yᵗ *Dion.* in *Plato* writeth to *Dionisius* yᵉ tyraũt, how *Euripides* in euery

tragedy bringeth for some great vice one or other great Prince
to ruine & yet not one doth cōplaine thus :

> *Out out alas alas, I dye for lacke of goodes.*

But euery one singeth this song :

> *Out out alas alas, I dye for lacke of frendes.*

For a Prince that will take mēs goods when he listeth
without order shall want mens hartes whē he needeth wᵗout
pitie : but in hauyng their hartes he shall neuer lacke their
goodes, as the good kyng *Cirus* sayd to the rich kyng *Cræsus*.
And to haue the peoples hartes the next way is to be gentle to
euery one, iust to all and liberall to many and especially to such
as either by excellency of wit or good will in true seruice do
well deserue it. Also to set his chiefest ioy not in priuate
pleasure like *Sardanapalus*, but in commō wealth as we haue
example of *Titus Vespasianus* : and to thinke his treasure
greatest, not when his coffers be fullest as *Cræsus* dyd, but when
his subiectes be richest as *Cyrus* dyd & that through hys wisedome and care as all prayse worthy princes haue euer hetherto
done. And what will the people rēder agayn to such a Prince?
A small subsidy, with a great grudge? no, but their whole hartes
to loue him : their whole goodes to ayde hym : theyr handes
ready to defende hym, and theyr lyues as ready to dye for hym
when soeuer he shall haue neede. A Prince that thus doth
lyue and thus is loued at home may be enuyed with much
prayse, and hated with smal hurte of any power abroad.

And therfore haue I heard wisemen discommend the
gouernement in *Fraunce* in makyng theyr people almost slaues,
and from thence a cōmon saying of some in ⸱ Syr John
England, that would haue the people neither witty ⸱ Gates
nor wealthy when wit is the meare gift of G O D : ⸱ wish.
So that to wish men lesse wit that haue it, is to count God
scarse wise that gaue it. And wealth of the people as Scripture
sayth : is the glory of a Prince, and surety of hys raigne.
But suspition in all gouerning breedeth such sayinges, when
wrong doth beare such swynge, as ill conscience doth alwayes
wish that men should lacke either wit to perceaue or habilitie
to amende what soeuer is done amisse. But God send such
Achitophels better ende then their counsels doth deserue which

would seme wise by other mens folly, and would be rich by other mens pouertie.

To returne to the Viceroy of *Naples* the common opinion of those in this Court which haue priuate cause to say wel on him do speake it boldly and openly, that he was such a one as neuer could content his couetousnes with money, nor neuer satisfie his crueltie with bloud : And so by this foule meane many gentlemē in *Naples* haue lost some theyr liues but moe theyr liuynges, and almost all theyr libertie. And there be at this day as men say here that know it a good sort of thousandes *Neapolitanes*, named *Foriensuti*, who beyng spoyled at home by violence, robbe other abroad for neede, which comber so the passage betwixt *Rome* and *Naples*, as no man departeth commonly from *Rome* without company which commeth to *Naples* without robbyng.

The whole body of the kyngdome of *Naples* was so distempered inwardly with this misorder, with a litle outward occasion it would easely haue burst forth into a foule sore. A lesse matter then the rauishyng of *Lucrece*, A meaner ayde then the helpe of *Brutus*, was thought sufficient to haue stirred vp this inward grudge to open reuenge. But see how God prouided for the Emperour and the quyet of that kingdome : For God in takyng away one *Spanyard* hath made *Naples* now more strong, then if the Emperour had set xx. thousand of the best in *Spayne* there : for euen this last Lent .1553. *Don Pietro di Toledo* dyed at *Florence* by whose goyng away mens hartes in *Naples* be so come agayne to the Emperour, as he shall now haue lesse neede either to care for the fyne fetches of *Fraunce*, or to feare the great power of the *Turke*. A gentleman of this Court a true seruaunt to the Emperour sayd merely in a company where I was, that his master the Emperour had won more in *Naples* by the death of the Viceroy, then he had lost in *Lorraigne* by the forgyng of *Metz*.

But to my purpose not many yeares agoe diuers in *Naples* made their cōplaint to the Prince of *Salerne* of their griefes, who was thought would be most willyng for his good nature, and best able for his authoritie to seeke some remedie for them by way of intercessiō to the Emperour.

The Prince beyng here at *Bruxels* humbly besought hys Maiestie to pitie the miserie of hys poore subiectes : who by this sute gat of the Emperour for hys cliantes, wordes without hope : and of the Viceroy for him selfe hatred without ende. The Prince yet alwayes bare hym selfe so wisely, that he could not without some sturre be thrust downe openly : and ridyng on his iourney he was once shot with a dagge secretly.

Thus he seyng no ende of displeasure in the Viceroy no hope of remedy in the Emperour, when he saw the *Turke* on the Sea, the *French* kyng in the field, Duke *Maurice* and the Marches vp, and a good part of *Italy* either risen, or ready to rise, thinkyng the tyme come of theyr most hope for helpe by the Princes, and of least feare of punishment by the Emperour, came forth to play his part also amongest the rest : who whē flying first to the *French* kyng and after by hys counsell as it is sayd to the *Turke*, is compelled to venture vppon many hard fortunes. And what succes he shall haue either of helpe in *Fraunce* or comfort of the *Turke*, or mercy of the Emperour I can not yet write. But this last winter he hath lyen in the Ile of *Cio*, and now I heare say this sommer he is on the Sea with 63. Gallyes of the *Turkes* at his commaundement, what enterprice he will make, or what successe he shall haue when we shall heare of the matter, I trust I shal either by some priuate letter from hence or by present talke at home fully satisfie you therin.

¶ *Albert Marches of Bradenburge.*

ALbert Marches of *Bradenburge* in the begynnyng of his sturre .1552. wrote a booke and set it Print wherin he declared the causes of hys fallyng from the Emperour wittely alledgyng common misery as a iust pretence of hys priuate enterprise makyng other mens hurtes, his remedy to heale his own sores and common wronges hys way to reuenge priuate displeasures : shewyng liberty to be lost, and Religion to be defaced, in all *Germany*, lamentyng the long captiuitie of the two great Princes : and all the dispossessyng of hys father in law Duke *Otto Henrick* : sore enueyng against the pride of the *Spanyardes* and the authoritie of straungers, which had now in their handes the seale of the Impiere, and in theyr swynge the doyng of all thynges, and at their cōmaundement all such mens voyces as were to be

Marches Albertes booke and the cōtents therof.

Sore and iust com-playntes.

called the Imperiall Dietes : cōpellyng the *Germanes* in their owne countrey to vse straunge toungs for their priuate sutes, wherin they could say nothyng at all, or nothyng to the purpose : vsing *Camera Imperialis* at *Spires* for a common key to open all mens coffers when they listed and these were the chiefest points in Marches booke.

The Marches also sore enueyed agaynst *Luice de Auila* for writyng, and agaynst the Emperour for suffring such a booke as *Luice de Auila* wrote : wherein the honor of *Germany* and the Princes therof & by name Marches *Albert*, who was in yᵉ first warres on the Emperours side, was so defamed to all the world : yea the Marches was so throughly chafed with this boke, yᵗ when I was in the Emperours court he offred yᵉ combat with *Luice de Auila*, which the Emperour for good wil and wise respectes would in no case admit.

The booke of *Luice de Auila*.

Not onely the Marches but also the Princes at the Diet of *Passan* this last yeare made a common complaint of this booke. I knew also the good old Prince *Fredericke Palsgraue* of yᵉ *Rhene* in September last when the Emperour lay at *Landaw* beside *Spires*, goyng with his great army to *Metz*, complayned to the Emperour hym selfe and to his counsell of a certaine spightfull place in that booke against him : The good prince told me this tale him selfe at hys house in *Heldibirge* whē I caried vnto him kyng *Edwardes* letters, the Lord Ambassadour him selfe beyng sicke at *Spires*.

And wise men say that the Duke of *Bauiere*, also is euill contented for that which is written in that booke agaynst his father when he deserued of the Imperials, to haue bene rewarded rather with prayse and thankes then with any vnkynde note of blame and dishonour : of whom the Emperour in his warres agaynst the *Lansgraue* and the Duke of *Saxonie* receiued such kindnes, as no Prince in *Germany* for all respectes in yᵗ case was able to affourde hym : as first he had his whole countrey of *Bauiere* for a sure footyng place, to begyn the warre in : and had also both men and vittaile of hym what he would, and at lēgth should haue had that countrey his onely refuge, if that in warre he had come to any vnderdele as he was like enough to haue done. But it was Gods secret will and pleasure to haue

The duke of *Bauiere* vnkyndly handled.

the matter then go as it did : And for that cause men say Duke
Albert of *Bauiere* that now is that hath maryed the Emperours
niece, was more straunge this last yeare to the Emperour, when
he was driuen to that extremitie to flye away on the night from
Inspurge and was more familiar with duke *Maurice*, and more
frendly to the Princes confederate then els peraduenture he
would haue done.

And here a writer may learne, of Princes affaires a good
lesson to beware of parcialitie either in flattery, or spight : For
although thereby a man may please his owne Prince presently
yet he may perchaunce as much hurt hym in the end as *Luis de*
Auila dyd hurt ye Emperour his master in writyng of this
booke.   In deede this booke was not ye chiefest cause of this
sturre in *Germany* : but sure I am that many Princes in
Germany were sore agreeued w^t it, as the Emperour wāted both
theyr hartes & their handes whē he stode in most nede of
frendes : Iust reprehension of all vices as folie, vniust dealyng,
cowardice, and vicious liuyng, must be frely and franckly vsed,
yet so with that moderate discression as no purposed malice or
bēt hatred, may seeme to be the breeder of any false reproch.
Which humor of writyng followeth so full, in *Paulus Iouius*
bookes, and that by that iudgement of his owne frendes, as
I haue heard wise and well learned men say : that his whole
study and purpose is spent on these pointes, to deface the
Emperour, to flatter *Fraunce*, to spite England, to belye
Germany, to prayse the *Turke*, to keepe vp the Pope, to pull
downe Christ and Christes Religion, as much as lyeth in him.
But to my purpose agayne.

The matters before of me briefly rehearsed, were at large
declared in Marches *Albertes* booke : yet that you may know
what secret workyng went before this playne writyng and open
doyng, and because the Marches part hath bene so notable in
all this pastime, I will by more particular circumstaunces lead
you to this generall complaintes.

There be at this day fiue Marchesses of *Bradenburge* :
Ioachimus Elector, *Iohānes* his brother who for Ciuile seruice is
Imperiall with might and mayne, & yet in Religion a Christian
Prince with hart toung & honesty of lyfe : Doctour *Christopher*
Monte, both a learned and wise man, our kynges Maiestie
seruaunt and his Agent in the affaires of *Germany* hath told me

diuers tymes, that this Marches *Iohn* and the Duke of *Swaburg*, be two of the worthiest Princes in all the Empier either in considering wisely, or executing courageously any great affaire. The thyrd is Marches *George* who dwelleth in *Franconia* not farre from *Noremberg*. The fourth Marches *Albert* the elder the mighty Duke of *Prusia* hable for his power to cope with any Prince, and xv. yeares together he dyd stoutly withstand in continuall warre the strength of the kyng of *Pole*. He hath so fully banished Papistry and so surely established the doctrine of the Gospell in *Prusia*, as no where hetherto in *Germany* is more diligently done, he loueth learnyng and honoreth learned men, and therfore .an. 1544. he founded a new Vniuersitie in *Prusia* called *Mons Regius* bryngyng thether with plentyfull thynges excellent learned men in all tounges and sciences. He is vncle to this notable Marches *Albert*, and lackyng children hath made him his heyre, and hath already inuestured hym in the Dukedome of *Prusia*.

Duke of *Prusia*.

The fift is Marches *Albert* of whom I purpose to write on : whose father was *Cassimirus* descended from the kynges of *Pole*, and for his noblenes agaynst the *Turke* called *Achilles Germanicus* : and therfore might very well engender such a hoate *Pirrhus*. Marches *Albert* in hys young yeares as I haue heard wise men say, was rude in hys maners, nor did not shew any token of towardnes likely to attempt any such affaires as in deede he hath done. It might be either for the lacke of learnyng and good bringyng vp (a great and common fault in great Princes of *Germany*) or els for his bashfull nature in youth, which propertie *Xenophon* wittely fayned to be in *Cyrus* at like yeares iudgyng bashfulnes in youth to be a great token of vertue in age.

Xenoph. a´ κυρ૪.

Marches *Albert* is now at this day about xxxi. yeares old : of a good stature, neither very high, nor very low, thicke without grosenes : rather wel boned for strength, then ouerloded with flesh : his face fayre, bewtifull, brode, sterne, and manly : somewhat resemblyng my Lord Marches of *Northt.* when he was of the same yeares, his eyes great and rowlyng, makyng his countenance cherefull when he talketh : and yet whē he geueth eare to other he kepeth both a sadde looke without signe of suspicion, and also a well set eye without token of malice : And this behauiour I marked well in hym when I dyned in his company at the siege of *Metz*, in the County *Iohn* of *Nassaus* tent, his voyce is great and his wordes not many, more ready to here other then to talke him selfe. And when he talketh he so frameth hys toung to agree with hart, as speakyng and meanyng seemeth to be alwayes at one in hym, and herein he may be well called the sonne of *Achilles* whom *Homer* wittely doth fayne to haue such a free open nature : whose saying in *Greeke* is excellent, but beyng turned in the wrong side into English, it shall lesse delight you yet thus much it signifieth :

> *Who either in earnest or in sport,*
> *doth frame hym selfe after such sort :*
> *This thyng to thincke and that to tell,*
> *my hart abhorreth as gate to hell.*

Homer, meanyng hereby that a Prince of noble courage should haue his hart, his looke, hys toung, and his handes so alwayes agreeyng together in thinkyng, pretendyng, and speakyng, and doyng, as no one of these foure should at any tyme be at iarre with an other, which agreeyng together in their right tune, do make a pleasaunt melody in all mens eares both sweetest and loudest, called in English (honor) and most fitly in *Greeke* Τιμη, the price and prayse of vertue.

And though the Marches be free to say what he thinketh, yet he is both secret in purposyng & close in workyng what soeuer hee goeth about. Now very skillfull to do harme to others, and as ware to keepe hurte from hym selfe, yet first bet vnto it with his own rod : for in yᵉ former warres of *Germany* being on yᵉ Emperours side he fell into the handes of Duke *Iohn Fridericke* of *Saxony*, which chaūce he is charged sore withall by *Luice de Auila* and that with so spightfull and open a mouth, as moued the Marches to offer hym the combat as I sayd before. He is now most courageous in hardest ad- uentures, most cherefull in present ieoperdy, and most paynefull in greatest labours : hauyng no souldier vnder him, that can better away with heate and cold or longer suffer hunger and thrist then he him selfe. His apparell is souldier like, better knowen by his fearce doynges then by his gay goyng : His souldiours feare him for his stoutnes, and loue him for his liberalitie : which winneth to him authoritie fit for a stout Captaine, and worketh in them obediēce due to good souldiours.

This last yeare a litle before hys agreement w^t the Emperour hys souldiours for lacke of money & meate fell to mutenyng and then fell the Marches fastest to hangyng, not hidyng him selfe for feare, but cōming abroad with courage, did protest that neither the proudest should make misorder without punishmēt nor yet the prodest should lacke as long as either he had peny in hys purse or loafe of bread in his tent.   And after this sort of outward behauiour and inward condition in Marches *Albert*, as I haue marked his person my selfe and as I haue learned hys doynges by such as by experience knew them well & for theyr honesty would reporte them right and now how he fell frō the Emperour I wil as briefly declare.

The Marches serued the Emperour as I said before in the former warres in *Germany* agaynst the *Lansgraue* and the Duke of *Saxony*, where he lost some honour and spent much money. The Emperour shortly after came downe hether to *Bruxels* hauyng the Marches in his company, who lookyng for a great recompēce of hys costes, and receiuyng litle, and seyng his honor not onely defaced in the field presently when he was taken prisoner, but also defamed for euer by writing cōfirmed by the Emperours priuiledge to grow abroad in the world began to take the matter so vnkindly, that he left comming to the Court, and kept his owne house : rising euery day very early : and writing all the forenoone very diligently yet what he did no man knew : so that his absence breed a talke in the Court, and his soddein and secret study wrought a wonderfull gelousy of his doynges in the Emperours head : for he knew the Marches to haue courage enough to attēpt matters ouer great : and therfore sent *Mōsieur Granduill* vnto the Marches house as of hym selfe to grope out his doynges, who declared vnto the Marches ye Emperours great goodwil towards hym, shewyng that his Maiestie was purposed to make him a great personage, & to begyn withall had in mynde to geue hym a goodly and profitable office in all his Mintes.

The Marches aunswered roundly and plainly to the first, that the Emperour could not make him greater then he was, beyng Marches of *Bradenburge* : And as for ye office in the Minte, he said smiling, he vsed not oft to tell his owne money, & therefore he thought not to make the accōpt of others & so made nothing of the Emperours offer : onely hee desired

Grandeuill that the Emperour would geue him leaue to go home
to his owne, which he obtained : And at his departure y^e
Emperour gaue him a patent of 4000. crownes by ye yeare :
But ye Marches was not well foure miles out of *Bruxels*, when
he sent the patent by post to ye Emperour agayne saying : his
Maiestie might better bestow it on some that had more neede
of it.   And in deede the Marches is as loth to receiue of his
frendes by beneuolence, as he is ready to take frō hys enemies
by violēce which commeth somewhat of to stout a courage.

Thus the Marches came home not best contented as it may
well appeare : nor saw not the Emperour after till he met hym
at the siege of *Metz*. *Casmirus* his father and the Marches hym
selfe were great spenders and deepe detters: the one for his
stoutnes in warre, the other for his lustines in youth.   And
therefore became quicke borrowers & slow payers, which thyng
brought the Marches into such trouble as hee had with the City
of *Noremberge* with his neighbours the Bishop of *Herbipolis* and
with his Godfather the Byshop of *Pamberge*.

The Marches was no sooner come home, but these Byshops
spying their tyme, when he had left the Emperours Court, and
had quite lost or much lessened his frendship there, begā to
trouble him with new suites for old debtes in *Camera Imperiali*,
at *Spires*, where the Marches because hee lacked either fauour
in the Court, or experience in young yeares, or good matter on
his side, was alwayes wrong to the worst, and to stuffe vp his
stomach with more matter of vnkindnes against the Emperour,
it is sayd that letters from the greatest in the Emperours Court
were neuer lackyng at *Spires* to helpe forward processe agaynst
the Marches.

Shortly after this tyme begā the siege of *Madenburg* where
Duke *Maurice* by the Emperour was appoynted generall.
The Marches either weery of leesyng at home by sutes, or
desirous to winne abroad by warre, or els purposing to practise
some way to reuenge his displeasures made him ready to serue
against *Madenburg* with 500. horse.   And in the begynnyng
of the spryng of the yeare .1551. he set forward and in his way
went to visite *Ernestus* his cosin Duke of *Saxony* brother to *Iohn
Fridericke* thē prisoner with the Emperour.   The selfe same
time *Lazarus Swendy* was sent from the Emperour as Commissary to duke *Ernestus* with earnest commaundement that the

Duke and all his, should receiue the doctrine of the *Interim*. And that I may accomplish my purpose, which is to paynt out as cruelly as I can, by writyng, the very Image of such persons as haue played any notable part in these affaires : and so you beyng absent shall with some more pleasure read their doynges.

Lazarus Swendy. This *Lazarus Swendy* is a tall and a comely personage, and beyng brought vp in learnyng vnder *Oecolampadius* at *Basile* makyng (as it was told me by an honest man that was throughly acquainted with hym there) more accompt of his tall stature, thē of any bewty of the mynde, began to be wery of learnyng, and became desirous to beare some bragge in the world : and so made a souldiour, mard a scholer, & because he would make a lusty chaunge from the feare of God and knowledge of Christs doctrine, he fell to be a peruerse and bloudy Papist : euer at hand in any cruell execution agaynst the poore Protestantes as commonly all such do which so wittingly shake of Christ, and his Gospell : such a Commissary you may be sure would cruelly enough execute his office.

Duke *Ernestus* told the Commissary that he his landes and lyfe were at his Maiesties commaundement, his Maiestie knew how quietly he bare him selfe alwayes, & therfore his trust was as he willingly serued the Emperour with true obedience : so he might as freely serue God with right conscience : for he would rather leaue hys landes and goodes and all to the Emperour, and go beg with his wife & children, then they would forsake the way of the Gospell which God hath commaunded them to follow.

And marke how euidently God dyd declare both how much such a Cōmission sent out abroad in *Germany* agaynst him and hys word dyd displease him : and also how much the prayers and sighyng hartes of iust men do in tyme preuayle with hym : for as a man of much honesty & great knowledge in all the matters of *Germany* did tell me, assoone as this Commissiō was once abroad, the practises in *Germany* began to styrre, yet not so openly as the Emperour might haue iust cause to withstand them, nor so couertly but he had occasion enough to mistrust them : and thereby he both lacked helpe for open remedy, and wanted no displeasure for inward grief.

Duke *Ernestus*, Marches *Albert*, and *Lazarus Swendy* sate at supper togethers : & as they were talkyng of yᵉ *Interim*, the Marches soddenly brast out into a fury saying : what deuill? will yᵉ Emperour neuer leaue striuyng with God in defacyng true Religiō and tossyng the world in debarryng all mēs liberties? addyng, that he was a Prince vnkynd to euery man, and kept touch with no mā, that could forget all mens merites, & would deceiue whom soeuer he promised.

The Duke liked not this hoate talke in hys house and at his table, but sayd : Cosin you speake but merely, and not as you thincke, adding much the prayse of the Emperours gentlenes shewed to many, and of his promise kept withall. Well (quoth the Marches) if he had bene either kynde where men haue deserued or would haue performed that hee promised : neither should I at this tyme accuse hym, nor you haue sit here in this place to defende hym, for he promised to geue me this house with all the landes that thereto belongeth : but ye be affrayd Cosin (quoth yᵉ Marches) lest this talke be to loud, and so heard to farre of : when in deede if the Commissarie here, be so honest a man as I take him, and so true to his master as he should be, he will not fayle to say what he hath heard, and on the same cōdition Commissary I bryng thee good lucke, and drancke of vnto hym a great glasse of wine. *Lazarus Swendyes* talke then sounded gētly and quietly, for he was sore affrayed of the Marches. But he was no soner at home with the Emperour, but word was sent straight to Duke *Maurice* that the Marches who was as thē come to *Madenburg* if he would needes serue there, should serue without wages.

Ye may be sure the Marches was chafed a new with this newes who already had lost a great sort of hys men and now must leese hys whole labour thether, and all his wages there, besides the losse of hys honour in takyng such shame of hys enemies, & receiuyng such vnkyndnes of the Emperour.

The Marches was not so greeued but Duke *Maurice* was as well contented with this commaundement : for euen then was Duke *Maurice* Secretary practisyng by Baron *Hadeckes* aduise with the *French* kyng for the sturre which dyd follow : and therfore was glad when he saw the Marches might be made hys so easely whiche came very soone to passe : so that the Marches for the same purpose in the ende of the same yeare went into *Fraunce* secretly, and was there with *Shertly* as a commõ Launce Knight, and named hymselfe Captaine *Paul*, lest the Emperour spials should get out hys doynges : where by the aduise of *Shertly* hee practised with the *French* kyng for the warres which followed after. This matter was told vnto me by *Iohn Mecardus* one of the chief Preachers in *Augusta*, who beyng banished the Empiere, when and how ye shall heare after was fayne to flye, and was with *Shertly* the same yeare in *Fraunce*.

The Marches came out of *Fraunce* in the begynnyng of the yeare .1552. and out of hand gathered vp men, but his purpose was not knowne, yet the Emperour mistrusted the matter, beyng at *Insburg*, sent *Doct. Hasius* one of hys counsell, to know what cause he had to make such sturre. This *Doct. Hasius* was once an earnest protestãt, and wrote a booke on that side, & was one of the *Palsgraues* priuy counsell : But for hope to clime higher, he was very ready to be entised by yᵉ Emperour to forsake first his master & then God : By whõ the Emperour knew much of all yᵉ Princes Protestants purposes, for he was commonly one whom they had vsed in all their Dietes and priuate practises : which thing caused the Emperour to seeke to haue hym : that by his head he might the easelyer ouerthrow the Protestantes, & with them God and hys word in all *Germany*.

This man is very lyke *M. Parrie* her graces cofferer in head, face, legges and bellye. What aũswere *Hasius* had I can not tell, but sure I am the Marches then both wrote his booke of complayntes agaynst the Emperour, and set it out in Printe. And also came forward with banner displayed, and tooke *Dillyng* upon *Danuby* the Cardinall of *Augustus* towne, which Cardinall with a few Priestes fled in post to the Emperour at *Inspurg*, where he found so cold cheare, and so litle comfort, that forthwith in all hast, he posted to *Rome*.

Horsemen and footemen in great companies still gathered to the Marches : and in the ende of March he marched forward to *Augusta*, where he, Duke *Maurice*, the young *Lansgraue*, the duke of *Mechelburg*, *George*, and *Albert*, with *William* Duke of *Brunswycke*, and other Princes confederate met together and besieged that Citie, Where I will leaue the Marches till I haue brought Duke *Maurice* and hys doinges to the same time, and to the same place.

¶ *Duke Maurice.*

NOt many yeares agoe whole *Saxony* was chiefly vnder two Princes : the one duke *Iohn Fredericke* borne Elector, who yet liueth, defender of *Luther*, a noble setter out, and as true a follower of Christ and his Gospell : The other hys kynsman Duke *George* who is dead, Knight of the order of the Golden Fleece, a great mā of the Emperour, a mayntainer of *Cocleus*, and a notable piller of Papistry.

Duke *Iohn Fredericke* is now 50. yeares of age, so byg of personage as a very strong horse is scarse able to beare hym & yet is he a great deale bygger in all kynde of vertues, in wisedome, iustice, liberalitie, stoutnes, temperancy in hym self, and humanitie *Iohn Fredericke Duke of Saxon.* towardes others, in all affaires, and either fortunes vsing a singular trouth and stedfastnes : so that *Luice de Auila*, and the Secretary of *Ferrare* who wrote the story of the first warres in *Germany*, and professe to be his ernest enemies both for matters of state and also of Religion, were so compelled by his worthynes to say the truth as though theyr onely purpose had bene to write his prayse. He was fiue yeares prisoner in this Court, where he wan such loue of all men, as the *Spanyardes* now say : they would as gladly fight to set hym vp agayne as euer they dyd to pull hym downe : For they see that he is wise in all his doynges, iust in all hys dealynges, lowly to the meanest, princely with the biggest, and excellyng gentle to all, whom no aduersitie could euer moue, nor pollicy at any tyme entice to shrincke from God and his word. And here I must needes commend the Secretary of *Ferrare*, who beyng a Papist, and writyng the history of the late warres in *Germany*, doth not kepe backe a goodly testimony of Duke *Frederickes* constancy toward God and hys Religion.

When the Emperour had taken the Duke prisoner he came shortly after before the Citie of *Witemberg* : and beyng aduised by some bloudy coūsellours that Duke *Frederickes* death should, by the terrour of it turne all the Protestantes from theyr Religion, caused a write to be made for the Duke to be executed the next mornyng vppon a solemne scaffold in the sight of his wife, children, and the whole Citie of *Wittemberg*.

This write signed with the Emperours own hand was sent

ouer night to the Duke, who whē the write came vnto hym
was in hys tent playing at Chesse with his Cosin and fellow
prisoner the *Lansgraue* of *Lithenberg*, and readyng it aduisedly
ouer layd it downe quietly beside and made no countenance at
all at yᵉ matter, but sayd Cosin take good heede to your game,
and returnyng to his play as quietly as though he had receiued
some priuate letter of no great importance dyd geue the
Lansgraue a trim mate.

The Emperour (I doubt not) chiefly moued by God :
secondly of his great wisedome and naturall clemency, when
he vnderstode his merueilous constancie chaunged his purpose
and reuoked the write, and euer after gaue him more honour,
and shewed him more humanitie then any Prince that euer
I haue read of haue hetherto done to his prisoner.

He is also such a louer of learnyng as his Librarie furnished
with bookes of all tounges and sciēces, passeth all other
Libraries which are yet gathered in Christendome : For my
frend *Ieronimus Wolfius* who translated *Demosthenes* out of *Greeke*
into *Latine*, who had sene the *Frēch* kings Library at *Augusta*,
hath told me that though in six monethes he was not able onely
to write out the titles of the bookes in the *Fuggers* Library, yet
was it not so byg as Duke *Frederickes* was which he saw in
Saxony. I thinke he vnderstandeth no straunge toung saue
somewhat the *Latin* and a litle the *French* : And yet it is
merueilous that my frend *Iohannes Sturmius* doth report by
writyng, what he heard *Phillip Melanĉthon* at a tyme say of this
noble Duke : that he thought the Duke did priuately read &
write more euery day thē did both he and *D. Aurifaber* which
two were counted in all mens iudgementes to be the greatest
readers and writers in all the Vniuersitie of *Wittemberg*.

And as hee doth thus read with such diligence, euen so he
can report with such a memory what soeuer he doth read, and
namely histories, as at his table on euery new occasion he is
accustomed to recite some new story which hee doth with such
pleasure and vtterance as men be content to leaue their meat to
heare him talke : and yet hee hym selfe is not disdaynfull to
heare the meanest nor will ouerwhart any mans reason. He
talketh without tauntyng, and is mery without scoffyng,
deludyng no man for sport, nor nippyng no man for spight.

Two kindes of men as his Preachers did tell me at *Vilacho*

he will neuer lōg suffer to be in his house : the one a commō
mocker, who for his pride thincketh so wel of his owne wit as
his most delight is to make other mē fooles, and where God of
his prouidence hath geuen small wit he for his sport wil make it
none, and rather then he should leese his pleasure, he would an
other should leese his wit : as I heare say was once done in
England, and that by the sufferaunce of such as I am sorry for
the good wil I beare them to heare such a report : the other a
priuy whisperer a pickthācke a tale teller medling so with other
mēs matters, as he findeth no leysure to looke to his owne : one
such in a great house is able to turne and tosse the quietnes of
all. Such two kinde of men sayth the Duke besides the present
troubling of others neuer or seldome come to good end them
selues. He loueth not also bold and thicke skinned faces,
wherein the meanyng of the hart doth neuer appeare. Nor
such hid talke as lyeth in wayte for other mens wittes. But
would, yᵗ wordes should be so framed with the toung, as they
be alwayes ment in the hart.

And therfore the Duke him selfe thincketh nothyng which
he dare not speake, nor speaketh nothyng whiche
hee will not do. Yet hauyng thoughtes grounded A noble na-
ture.
vppon wisedome, his talke is always so accom-
panied with discression and his deedes so attende vppon true dealyng, as he neither biteth with wordes, nor wringeth with deedes,
except impudency follow the fault, which *Xenophon* wittely calleth
the farthest point in al doyng, and then he vseth to speake home
as he did to a *Spanyard* this last yeare at *Villacho*, who beyng of
the Dukes garde, when he was prisoner, and now preasyng to
sit at his table when he was at libertie, Because many nobles of
yᵉ Court came that day to dine with the duke, The gentleman
Husher gently desired the *Spanyard* to spare his rowme for that
day for a great personage : But hee countenancyng a braue
Spanish bragge, sayd, *Seignor* ye know me well enough, and so
sat him downe.

The Duke heard him, and preuentyng hys mans aunswere
sayd : In deede you be to well knowen, by the same tokē the
last tyme you were here you tooke a gobblet away with you, &
therfore when you haue dyned you may go without farewell,
and haue leaue to come agayne when ye be sent for. In the
meane while an honest man may occupy your place. But in

remembryng so good a Prince I haue gone to farre from my matter : And yet the remembraunce of him is neuer out of place, whose worthynes is neuer to be forgotten.

Duke *George* of *Saxony* a litle before he dyed hauyng no child did disinherite Duke *Henry* his brother by his last wil because he was a Protestant, and gaue away his whole inheritaunce to *Ferdinando* kyng of *Romaines*.

But Duke *Iohn Fredericke* by force of armes set and kept his Cosin Duke *Henry* in his right : And he dying soone after left behynd hym two sonnes Duke *Maurice* and Duke *Augustus*, who likewise in their youth were defended in theyr right by the wisedome and force of Duke *Iohn Fredericke*. Duke *Maurice* was brought vp in Duke *Iohn Frederickes* house as if hee had bene hys owne sonne and maryed the *Lansgraues* daughter.

After it came to passe that the Emperour attempted to establish Papistry in *Germany* with the sword, agaynst which purpose the *Lansgraue* and duke *Iohn Fredericke* armed them selues not to resist the Emperour as the Papistes say, but to kepe Gods Religion vp, if any by violence would pull it downe, refusing neuer, but requiryng always to referre them and theyr doctrine to a lawfull and free generall Councell where truth in Religion might be fully tryed in the hearyng of euen and

Εν ίσοις καὶ ὁμοίοις, wordes alwayes vsed in *Thucidides* in decidyng cōmon controuersies.

*equall iudges and that by the touchstone of Gods Canonicall Scriptures.

Duke *Maurice* in the begynnyng of his warre was suspected neither of the *Lansgraue* nor of Duke *Fredericke* beyng sonne in law to the one and nighe kinsman to the other and agreeyng in Religiō with both. Yea he was not onely not suspected, but as I heard skilful mē say he was ready with his counsell & promised his ayde to helpe forward yᵉ enterprice, or els *Hance Fredericke* beyng a Prince of such wisedome would not haue left at home behind hym an enemy of such a force.

Francisco Duke *Maurice* Agent with the Emperour was asked, I beyng by at *Augusta*, how he could excuse his masters vnkindnes towards *Iohn Fredericke* who had bene such a father vnto him. He graunted that Duke *Fredericke* had bene great frend vnto him, and might haue a greater if he had would, and thē lesse strife had followed then did. And troth it is (sayd he) as Duke *Fredericke* kept my master in his right, so afterward he put him from part of his right, when in his yong yeares hee chopped and chaunged landes with him when he listed : which thing my master comming to mans state much misliked, and oft complaynyng could neuer obtayne remedy therein. Kyndnes should rather haue kyndly encreased, so vnkyndly haue decayed specially when the one was trusted withall, and the other of such yeares, as he had neither wit to perceiue nor power to amend if any iniurie were offred vnto hym. Troth also it is that my master was brought vp in Duke *Frederickes* house : but he hath more cause to cōplaine on them that brought him thether, then to thanke such as brought him vp there, where he had alwayes plentie of drinke and as much scant of good teachyng to come to such vertue and learnyng as dyd belong to a Prince of his state.

Now whether this talke was altogether true, or, an ill excuse was made to couer a foule fact I can not tell : but sure I am *Francisco* sayd thus. I haue heard wise men say that it is not lyke, that for such a priuate strife Duke *Maurice* would haue so forsaken not onely his frend and kinsman, but also his father in law or would for the losse a litle, or rather for the chaūge of a peece haue so hassarded his whole estate, which was once in the first warre all gone saue *Lypsia*, and one other towne, beside the losse of loue in whole *Germany* and his good name amongst all Protestantes, in the middest of whom all hys liuinges do lye.

Well surely there was some great cause that could sturre vp so great a strife, and that was as wise men and wel willyng on Duke *Maurice* side in myne opinion haue truly iudged, the foule vice of ambition.

O Lord how many worthy men hath this one vice beareft from good common weales, which for all other respectes were most vnworthy of that end they came vnto. My hart weepes for those noble men of England, whose valiantnes in warre, whose wisedome in peace this Realme shall want and wayle and wish and wish for in tyme to come, which of late by this onely vice haue bene taken from vs. Examples, lesse for our grief and as fit for this purpose be plenty enough in other states.

Why Duke *Maurice* left hys dearest frendes and fell in with the Emperour. Ambition.

Ouer many experiences do teach vs, though a Prince be wise stout liberall gentle mercyfull and excellently learned, though he deserue all the prayse, that vertue nature and fortune cā affourd him, yea that wit it selfe can wish for as we read that noble *Iulius Cæsar* had, and that by the testimony of those that loued him not, neuertheles if these two foule verses of *Euripides*.

> *Do right alway and wrong refraine,*
> *Except onely for rule and raigne.*

If these verses say I do not onely sound well in his eare, but sincke deepe also in his hart, surely there is neither kindred, frendship, law, othe, obedience, countrey, God, nor his owne life, but he will hassard to leese all rather then to pursue this foule vice : For *Polynices*, for whom· this verse was first made in *Greeke*, did fill not onely his owne countrey full of dead carcasses, but also whole *Greece* full of weepyng widdowes. And *Cæsar* for whom the same verse was turned into *Latin* did not onely turne vpside down the goodliest common wealth that euer G O D suffred to stand vpon the earth : but also tossed the whole world with battayle and slaughter euen almost from the sunne setting vnto the sunne rising.   And did not stop to bryng souldiours to do mischief further then any man now dare iourney by land either for pleasure or profite.

But see the fruite and end which this vngodly great growing bringeth men vnto : Both these Princes were slaine the one by his brother the other by his owne sonne, of whom in life, nature & benefites would they should haue taken most cōfort of. But men that loue to clime to hye haue alwayes least feare, and therefore by reason fall most soddenly and also fardest downe : yea the very bowghes that helped hym vp will now whip him in fallyng downe : For who so in climyng trusteth when he is goyng vp any bough at all ouer much, though hee seeme to tread neuer so surely vppon it yet if he once begyn to slyp the same selfe bough is reddiest to beat him that seemed before surest to beare him.   Examples hereof be seen dayly and forgotten hereby.

An other mischief chaunceth commonly to these high climers : that they will heare no man so gladly as such which are euer hartenyng them to clime still.   If wise and good men durst speake more freely then they do : great men should do both others and them selues lesse harme thē they are wont to do. He hateth him selfe and hasteth his owne hurt that is content to heare none so gladly as either a foole or a flatterer. A wonderfull follie in a great man him selfe and some peace of miserie in a whole common wealth, where fooles chiefly, and flatterers may speake freely what they will and wise men and good men shal commonly be shent, if they speake what they should.

And how commeth this to passe ? it is the very plague of God for great mens sinnes, and the plaine high way to their iust punishment. And when God suffreth them so willingly to graunt freedome to follie and so gladly to geue hearyng to flattery : But see when the great man is gone and hath playd his part, fooles and flatterers be stil vpon the stage. Such liue in all worldes, such laugh in all miseries : such *Daui* and *Getæ*, haue alwayes the longest partes : and go out who shal they tary in place still. I know also many a good *mitio*, which haue played long partes whom I pray God kepe long still vpon the stage. And I trust no man will be miscontent with my generall saying except conscience do pricke him of his owne priuate ill doyng.

There be common wealthes where freedome in speakyng truth hath kept great mē from boldnes in doyng ill : for free and frendly aduise is the trimmest glasse that any great man can vse to spye his owne fault in : which taken away they runne commonly so farre in foule doyng, as some neuer stay till they passe all remedy saue onely to late repentaunce. And as I would haue no flattery but wish for freedome : So in no wise do I commend ouermuch boldnes, or any kind of rayling. But that libertie in speakyng should be so mingled with good will and discretion, as no great person should be vnhonorably spoken vpō, or any meane man touched out of order either for sport or spite : as some vnquiet heades neuer contented with any state are euer procuryng either secretly with raylyng billes, or openly with tauntyng songes, or els some scoffing common play.

An other kynd of to bold talkers surpasse all these selly rumors, who are called, and so will be, commō discoursers of all Princes affaires. These make a great accompt of them selues

and will be commonly formost in any prease, and lustly with
out blushing shoulder backe others : These will seeme to see
further needes, in any secret affayre then the best and wisest
coūsellor a Prince hath.   These be the open flatterers and
priuy mislikers of all good counsellors doynges.   And one
common note, the most part of this brotherhode of discoursers
commōly cary with them where they be bold to speake : to like
better *Tullies* Offices, then S. Paules Epistles : and a tale in
Bocace, then a story of the Bible.

And therfore for any Religion earnest setters forth of
present tyme : with consciences confirmed with *Machiauelles*
doctrine to thincke say and do what soeuer may serue best for
profite or pleasure.   But as concernyng flatterers and raylers to
say mine opinion whether I like worse, surely as I haue read
few men to haue bene hurt with bitter poysons : so haue
I heard of as few great men to haue bene greatly harmed with
sharpe talke : but are so ware therin, that commonly they wil
complaine of theyr hurt before they feele harme.   And flattery
agayne is so sweete, that it pleaseth best, when it hurteth most,
and therfore is alwayes to be feared : because it alwayes de-
lighteth, but in lookyng aside to these hye climers, I haue
gone out of the way, of mine owne matter.

To returne to Duke *Maurice*, he saw that Duke *Frederickes*
fallyng might be his rising, and perchaunce was moued with
some old iniuries, but beyng of young yeares and of nature full
of desire and courage he was a trimme pray for old practises
to be easely caryed away with fayre new promises sounding
altogether to honor and profite, and so he forsoke his father and
his frend, and became wholy the Emperours till hee had brought
both them into prison.   Duke *Fredericke* was taken in the field
and so became the Emperours iust prisoner.   Yet as long as the
Lansgraue was abroad, the Emperour thought his purpose neuer
atchieued, and therefore practised a new with duke *Maurice* to
get him also into his hāds.

Duke *Maurice* with *Ioachim* Elector of *Bradenburge* became
meanes betwixt the *Lansgraue* and the Emperour.   Conditions
both of mercy from the one, and of amendes from the other
were drawen out.   *Maurice* and the Marches bound them
selues sureties to the *Lāsgraues* children, for their fathers safe
returne : for amongest the rest of cōditions this was one of the

chiefest, that he should come in no prison. And so at *Hala* in *Saxony*, he came boldly to the Emperours presence, who receiued him not very cherefully, nor gaue him not his hand which in *Germany* is the very token of an assured reconsiliation.

The Duke of *Alua* made the *Lansgraue* a supper, and called also thether Duke *Maurice*, and the Marches of *Bradeburg* where they had great chere : but after supper it was told Duke *Maurice* and the Marches, that they might depart for the *Lansgraue* must lodge there that night.

On the morrow, they reasoned of the matter wholly to this purpose that the Emperours promises not the *Lansgraues* person ought to be kept. Aunswere was made that the Emperour went no further then conditions led him which were that he should not be kept in euerlastyng prison : and they agayne replyed he ought to be kept in no prison. When I was at *Villacho* in *Carinthia* I asked Duke *Frederickes* Preacher what were the very wordes in *Dutch*, wherby the *Lansgraue* agaynst his lookyng was kept in prison. He sayd the fallacion was very pretty and notable and tooke his penne and wrote in my booke the very wordes wherin the very controuersie stode, duke *Maurice* sayd it was.

Nicht in einig gefengknes .i. Not in any prison.
The Imperials sayd no, but thus.

Nicht in ewig gefengknes .i. Not in euerlastyng prison. And how soone *einig*, may be turned into *ewig*, not with scrape of knife, but with the least dash of a pen so that it shall neuer be perceiued, a man that will proue, may easely see.

Moreouer *Luice d'Auila* in his booke doth reioyce that the *Lansgraue* did so deceaue hym selfe with his owne conditions in makyng of which as *d'Auila* saith, he was wont to esteeme his own wit aboue all other mens. Well, how so euer it came to passe the *Lansgraue* was kept in prison. And from that houre Duke *Maurice* fell from the Emperour thinckyng hym selfe most vnkyndly hādled, that he by whose meanes chiefly the Emperour had won such honor in *Saxony*, must now be rewarded with shame in all *Germany*, and be called a traytor to GOD, and hys countrey, his father, and his frend. And though he was greeued inwardly at the hart, yet he bare all thynges quietly in coūtenance purposing though he had lost will yet

would he not leese his profite, and so hiding his hurt presently,
whilest some fitter time should discouer some better remedy,
he went with the Emperour to *Augusta*, where accordyng to
hys promise he was made Elector.   Yet the same night after
hys solemne creation, two verses set vppon his gate might more
greue him, then all that honour could delight hym, which were
these.

> *Seu Dux, seu Princeps, seu nunc dicaris Elector.*
> *Mauricij Patriæ proditor ipse tui.*

After that he had gotten that he looked for, he gat him
home into his countrey : from whence afterward the Emperour
with no pollicie could euer bryng hym, he alwayes alledgyng,
the feare that he had of some sturre by Duke *Frederickes*
children.

Hetherto the *Germaines* much mislyked the doynges of Duke
Maurice.   But after that he had felt him selfe so vnkyndly
abused as for his good seruice to be made the betrayer of his
father, he tooke such matters in hand & brought them so to
passe, as he recouered the loue of his countrey and purchased
such hate of his enemyes, as the *Spanyardes* tooke their displeasure from all other, and bestowed wholly vppon the Duke
Maurice : and yet he bare him selfe with such wit, and courage
agaynst them, as they had alwayes cause to feare hym and neuer
occasion to contemne hym :   Yea if he had liued he would
sooner men thinke haue driuen all *Spanyardes* out of *Germany*,
then they should haue hurt hym in *Saxony*, for he had ioyned
vnto him such strength, and there was in him such pollicie, as
they durst neuer haue come vppon him with power, nor neuer
should haue gone beyond hym with wit.   He had so displeased
the Emperour as he knew wel neither his lādes : nor his life
could make amendes whē x. poundes of Benefites which he
was able to do, could not way with one ounce of displeasure
that he had already done : and therefore neuer after sought to
seeke his loue which he knew could neuer be gotten : but gaue
him selfe wholy to set vp *Maximiliā*, who beyng him selfe of
great power, and of all other most beloued for his worthynes in
all *Germany*, and now vsing the head and hand of duke *Maurice*
and his frendes, and hauyng the helpe of as many as hated the
Spanyardes, that is to say almost all Protestantes and Papistes to

in *Germany*, he should easely haue obtained what soeuer he had gone about. But that bonde is now broken: for euen this day when I was writyng this place, came word to this Court, that Marches *Albert*, and Duke *Maurice* had fought, where the Marches had lost the field, and Duke *Maurice* had lost his life: which whole battaile because it is notable, I would here at length describe, but that I should wander to farre from my purposed matter: and therfore I in an other place, or els some other with better oportunitie shall at large report the matter.

Ye see the cause why and the time whē Duke *Maurice* fell from the Emperour. And because he was so notable a Prince, I will describe also the maner how he proceded in all these doyngs, as I learned amongest them that did not greatly loue him. And because it were small gayne to flatter him that is gone, and great shame to lye vppon him that is dead, for pleasyng any that be alyue, I so will report on hym as his doynges since my commyng to this Court haue deserued.

He was now of the age of xxxij. yeares well faced in countenance complection fauour and beard not much vnlike to Syr *Raffe Sadler* but some deale higher, and well and strong made to beare any labour and payne. He was once (men say) geuen to drinckyng, but now he had cleane left it, contented with small diet and litle sleepe in this last yeares, and therefore had a wakyng and workyng head: and became so witty and secret, so hardy and ware, so skillfull of wayes, both to do harme to others, and keepe hurt from him selfe, as he neuer tooke enterprise in hand wherein he put not his aduersary always to the worse. And to let other matter of *Germany* passe, euen this last yeare within the compasse of eight monethes he professed him selfe open enemy agaynst foure the greatest powers that I know vpon earth. The *Turke*, the *Pope*, the *Emperour*, & the *French* king, & ob- | The Turke.
tained his purpose and wan prayse agaynst thē all foure: For he in person and pollicie & courage dispatched the *Turkes* purpose and power this last yeare in *Hungary*.

The Councell at *Trent* which the Pope & the Emperour went so about to establish he onely brought to | The Pope.
none effect: first by open protestatiō agaynst that Councell, and after by his commyng with his army to *Insburge*, he brought such feare to the Bishops there gathered, that they

ran euery one farre away frō thence, with such speed as they neuer durst hetherto speake of meeting there agayne. And how he delt with yᵉ Emperour, both in forcyng him to flye from *Insburge*, and compellyng him to such a peace at *Passo*, my whole *Diarium* shall at full instruct you.

The Emperour.

And of all other he serued the *Frēch* kyng best, who fayre pretendyng the deliuery of the ij. Princes captiues, and the maintenaunce of Religion & libertie in *Germany*, purposed in very deede nothyng els, but yᵉ destruction of the Emperor, & the house of *Austria* : for what cared he for religion abroad, who at home not onely followeth none him selfe priuately in his life, but also persecuteth the trouth in others openly with the sword. But I do him wrong to say he followeth none, who could for his purpose be cōtent at one time to embrace all : & for to do hurt enough to the Emperor would become at once by solemne league, Protestāt, Papish, Turkish, & deuillish. But such Princes that cary nothyng els but the name of bearing vp Gods word, deserue the same prayse and the same end that that Prince dyd, who semed so ready to beare vp yᵉ Arke of the Lord, & yet otherwise pursued Gods true Prophetes & his word.

French kyng.

Agayne how much the *French* kyng cared for the libertie of *Germany* he well declared in stealyng away so vnhonorably from the Empire the Citie of *Metz*. But he thinckyng to abuse Duke *Maurice* for his ambitious purpose, in very deede & in the end Duke *Maurice* vsed him as he should : for first he made him pay well for yᵉ whole warres in *Germany* as it is sayd .200000. crownes a moneth : And after when the *French* kyng fell to catching of Cities, duke *Maurice* tendryng yᵉ state of his countrey brake of with hym, and began to parle wᵗ the good kyng of *Romanes* at *Luiz*, which thyng whē the *Frēch* kyng heard came within ij. miles of the *Rhene*, he straight way hyed more hastly & with more disorder, for all his great hast, out of *Germany*, as they say that were there, then the Emperour being sicke without company and pressed by his enemy dyd go from *Insburg*.

And see how nobly Duke *Maurice* did which for yᵉ loue of his coūtrey, durst fall from the *Frēch* kyng before he atchieued any thyng agaynst the Emperour. And rather thē *Germany*

should leese her Cities so by the *French* king, he had leuer
hassard, both the leesing of his enterprice, & also the leauyng
of hys father in law still in prison with the Emperour.   But
as he had wit to take money plēty of the *French* kyng : so had
he wit also to furnish him selfe so frō home as he durst first
fall out with the *French* kyng, & durst also after to set vpō the
Emperour till he had brought his honest purpose to passe.   For
there is not almost any in this Court but they will say duke
Maurice did honestly in deliuering his father by strong hand,
which before left no fayre meane vnproued to do that humbly
by entreaty, which after, was cōpelled to bryng to passe stoutly
by force.   And I pray you first marke well what he did and
then iudge truly if any thing was done that he ought not to
do.

  For first he him selfe with yᵉ Marches of *Bradenburge* most
humbly by priuate sute laboured for the *Lansgraues* deliuery
offring to the Emperour, princely offers, and not to be refused :
as a huge summe of money : a fayre quantitie of great
ordinaunce, certaine holdes of his, some to be
defaced, some geuē to yᵉ Emperour : and also
personall pledges of great houses for hys good
haberaunce all the residue of his life.

Duke
Maurice
offer for the
Lāsgraues
deliuery.

  After whē this sute was not regarded they
againe procured all yᵉ Princes & states of *Germany* beyng at yᵉ
Diet at *Augusta* .an. 1548. to be hūble intercessors for him,
offring yᵉ selfe same cōditions rehearsed before addyng this more
to become sureties them selues in any bande to his Maiestie for
his due obedience for tyme to come.

  Thirdly by the Prince of *Spayne* Duke *Maurice* neuer left
to entreat yᵉ Emperour, yea he was so carefull of yᵉ matter,
that his Ambassadors followed the Prince euen to his shipping
at *Genoa :* who had spokē oftē presently before, & wrote
earnestly frō thence to his father for yᵉ *Lansgraues* deliuery, &
it would not be.   And wise mē may say it was not yᵉ wisest
deede that euer yᵉ Emperor did, to deny yᵉ prince this sute :
for if yᵉ Prince had bene made yᵉ deliuerer of yᵉ ij. princes out
of captiuity, he had won therby such fauor in all *Germany*, as
wᵗout all doubt he had bene made coadiutor wᵗ the k. of
Romaines his vncle, And afterward yᵉ Emperor.   Which thing
was lustly denyed to yᵉ Emperor by the Electors, though he

laboured in y^t matter so sore as he neuer dyd in any other before.

Fourthly this last yeare a litle before the open warres duke *Maurice* procured once agayne, not onely all ye Princes and free Estates of *Germany*, but also the kyng of *Romaines Ferdinand*, *Maximilian* his sonne king of *Boeme*, the kyng of *Pole*, the kyng of *Dēmarke* the king of *Sweden*, to send also their Ambassadors for this suite, so that at once xxiiij. Ambassadours came before the Emperour together at *Insburge*. To whom whē the Emperour had geuen very fayre wordes in effect cōcernyng a double meanyng aunswere, & that was this : That it did him good to see so noble an Ambassage at once. And therfore so many Princes should well vnderstand y^t he would make a good accompt of their sute. Neuertheles because duke *Maurice* was the chiefest partie herein he would with speede send for him, and vse his head for the better endyng of this matter. But Duke *Maurice* seyng that all these Ambassadors wēt home without him, and that the matter was referred to his present talke who was neuer heard in the matter before, he wisely met with this double meaning aunswere of the Emperours with a double meanyng *replica* agayne : for he promised the Emperour to come, and at last in deede came so hastly and so hotely as the Emperour could not abide the heat of his breath : For when duke *Maurice* saw that all humble sutes, all quiet meanes were spent in vayne, & had to beare him iust witnes therin all ye Princes of *Germany:* First with close pollicie, after open power both wittely and stoutly, he atchieued more by force then he required by suite : For the Emperour was glad to condiscend (which surely in an extreme aduersitie was done like a wise Prince) without money, without artillery, without defacyng of holdes, w^{t}out receiuyng of pledges, to send the *Lansgraue* home, honorably accōpanied with (at the Emperors charges) the nobilitie of *Brabant* & *Flaunders*.

This last day I dined with the Ambassadour of *Venice* in cōpany of many wise heades, where duke *Maurice* was greatly praysed of some for his wit : of other for ye execution of his purposes. Well sayth a lusty *Italian* Priest, I can not much prayse his wit, which might haue had the Emperour in his handes & would not. Loe such be these *Machiauels* heades, who thincke no mā to haue so much wit as he should, except he do more mischief then he neede. But Duke *Maurice* purposing to do no harme to the Emperour, but good to his father in law, obtainyng yᵉ one pursued not the other. Yea I know it to be most true whē we fled from *Insburg* so hastly, Duke *Maurice* sent a post to yᵉ good kyng of *Romanes*, & bad him will the Emperor to make no such speede for he purposed not to hurt his person : but to helpe his frend, whereupon the Diet at *Passo* immediatly folowed.

I cōmend rather the iudgement of *Iohn Baptist Gascaldo*, the Emperours man and yᵉ kyng of *Romanes* generall ın *Hungary*, who is not wont to say better, or loue any mā more then he should specially *Ger-* *maines*, & namely Protestantes. And yet this last winter he wrote to the Emperour that he had marked Duke *Maurice* well in all his doynges agaynst the *Turke*, and of all men that euer he had sene, he had a head to forecast the best with pollicie and wit, and a hart to set vppon it with courage and speed, & also a discressiō to stay most wisely vpon the very pricke of aduauntage.

Marches *Marignan* told some in this Court foure yeares ago that Duke *Maurice* should become the greatest enemy to the Emperour that euer the Emperour had : which thing he iudged (I beleue) not of any troublesome nature which he saw in Duke *Maurice*, but of the great wronges that were done to Duke *Maurice*, knowyng that he had both wit to perceiue them quietly and also a courage not to beare them ouer long.

Some other in this court that loued not duke *Maurice*, & hauyng no hurt to do him by power, went about to say him some for spight & therfore wrote these two spightfull verses agaynst him.

Iugurtham Maurus prodit Mauricius vltra,
Henricum, Patruum, Socerum, cum Cæsare, Gallum.

He that gaue me this verse added thereunto this his iudgement, well (sayth he) he that could finde in his hart to betray his frend Duke *Henry* of *Brunswicke*, his nigh kinsman Duke *Fredericke*, his father in law the *Lansgraue*, his soueraigne Lord the Emperour, his confederate the *French* kyng, breakyng all bondes of frendshyp, nature, law, obediēce, and othe, shall besides all these, deceaue all men if at length he do not deceaue hym selfe. This verse and this sentence, the one made of spight, the other spoken of displeasure be here commended as men be affectioned. For my part as I can not accuse him for all: so will I not excuse him for part. And yet since I came

Duke Maurice. to this Court I should do him wrong if I did not cōfesse that which as wise heades as be in this Court haue iudged on him, euen those that for countrey & Religion were not his frendes, that is, to haue shewed him selfe in all these affayres betwixt the Emperour and him: first, humble in intreatyng, diligent in pursuyng, witty in purposing, secret in workyng, fearce to foresee by open warre, ready to parle for common peace, wise in choyse of conditions, and iust in performyng of couenaunts.

And I know he offended the Emperour beyond all remedy of amēdes: So would I be loth to see as I haue once sene, his Maiestie fall so agayne into any enemyes handes: leste peraduenture lesse gentlenes would be found in him then was found in Duke *Maurice*, who when he was most able to hurt, was most ready to hold hys hād and that agaynst such an enemy, as he knew well would neuer loue him, and should alwayes be of most power to reuenge. If Duke *Maurice* had had a *Machiauels* head or a cowardes hart, he would haue worne a bloudyer sword thē he did, which he neuer drew out in all these sturres, but once at yᵉ *Cluce* & yᵗ was to saue yᵉ Emperors mē.

Hetherto I haue followed the order of persons which hath caused me somewhat to misorder both tyme & matter, yet where diuers great affaires come together, a man shall write confusedly for the matter, & vnpleasantly for yᵉ reader, if he vse not such an apt kinde of partitiō as yᵉ matter will best affourde, which thyng (*Plato* sayth) who cā not do, knoweth not how to write. Herein *Herodotus* deserueth in myne opinion a great deale more prayse then *Thucidides*, although he wrote of a matter more confused for places, time, and persons, then the other did.

In this point also *Appianus Alexandrinus* is very commendable, and not by chaunce but by skil doth follow this order, declaryng in his Prologue iust causes why he should do so. Our writers in later tyme, both in *Latin* & other tounges commonly confound to many matters together, and so write well of no one. But see master *Astley* I thincking to be in some present talke with you, after our old wont do seeme to forget both my selfe and my purpose.

For the rest that is behind I will vse a grose & homely kind of talke with you : for I will now as it were cary you, out of England with me, & will lead you the same way that I went euen to the Emperours Court beyng at *Augusta* .an. 1550. And I will let you see in what case it stode, and what thyngs were in doyng when we came first thether. After I wil cary you and that a pace, because the chiefest matters be throughly touched in this my former booke, through the greatest affaires of ij. yeares in this Court. Yet in order till we haue brought Duke *Maurice* (as I promised you) to ioyne with Marches *Albert* in besiegyng *Augusta*. And thē because priuy practises brast out into open sturres I might better marke thynges dayly then I could before. And so we will depart with the Emperour from *Insburg*, and see dayly what chaunces were wrought by feare and hope in this Court till hys Maiestie left the siege of *Metz*, and came downe hether to *Bruxels* : where then all things were shut vp into secret practises till lastly of all, they brake forth into new mis-chiefes, betwixt the Emperour and *Fraunce* in *Picardy*, & also betwixt Duke *Maurice*, and the Marches in hyghe *Germany* which thynges I trust some other shall marke and describe a great deale better then I am hable to doe.

¶ FINIS.

THE

SCHOLEMASTER

Or plaine and perfite way of tea-
chyng children, to vnderstand, write, and
speake, the Latin tong, but specially purposed
for the priuate brynging vp of youth in Ientle-
men and Noble mens houses, and commodious
also for all such, as haue forgot the Latin
tonge, and would, by themselues, with-
out à Scholemaster, in short tyme,
and with small paines, recouer à
sufficient habilitie, to vnder-
stand, write, and
speake Latin.

¶ By Roger Ascham.

¶ *An.* 1570.

AT LONDON.

Printed by Iohn Daye, dwelling
ouer Aldersgate.

¶ *Cum Gratia & Priuilegio Regiæ Maiestatis,*
per Decennium.

❡ To the honorable Sir William

Cecill Knight, principall Secretarie to
the Quenes most excellent Maiestie.

SOndry and reasonable be the causes why learned men haue vsed to offer and dedicate such workes as they put abrode, to some such personage as they thinke fittest, either in respeƈt of abilitie of defense, or skill for iugement, or priuate regard of kindenesse and dutie. Euery one of those considerations, Syr, moue me of right to offer this my late husbands M. Aschams worke vnto you. For well remembryng how much all good learnyng oweth vnto you for defense therof, as the Vniuersitie of Cambrige, of which my said late husband was a member, haue in chosing you their worthy Chaunceller acknowledged, and how happily you haue spent your time in such studies & caried the vse therof to the right ende, to the good seruice of the Quenes Maiestie and your contrey to all our benefites, thyrdly how much my sayd husband was many wayes bound vnto you, and how gladly and comfortably he vsed in hys lyfe to recognise and report your goodnesse toward hym, leauyng with me then hys poore widow and a great sort of orphanes a good comfort in the hope of your good continuance, which I haue truly found to me and myne, and therfore do duely and dayly pray for you and yours: I could not finde any man for whose name this booke was more agreable for hope [of] protection, more mete for submission to iudgement, nor more due for respeƈt of worthynesse of your part and thankefulnesse of my husbandes and myne. Good I trust it shall do, as I am put in great hope by many very well learned that can well iudge therof. Mete therefore I compt it that such good as my husband was able to doe and leaue to the common weale, it should

*be receiued vnder your name, and that the world should owe thanke
therof to you, to whom my husband the authour of it was for good
receyued of you, most dutiefully bounden.   And so besechyng you, to
take on you the defense of this booke, to auaunce the good that may
come of it by your allowance and furtherance to publike vse and
benefite, and to accept the thankefull recognition of me and my poore
children, trustyng of the continuance of your good memorie of* M. Ascham *and his, and dayly commen-
dyng the prosperous estate of you and yours to*
God *whom you serue and whoes you
are, I rest to trouble you.*

Your humble Margaret
Ascham.

❧ *A Præface to the Reader.*

WHen the great plage was at London, the yeare 1563. the Quenes Maiestie Queene *Elizabeth*, lay at her Castle of Windsore: Where, vpon the 10. day of December, it fortuned, that in Sir *William Cicells* chamber, hir Highnesse Principall Secretarie, there dined togither these personages, M. Secretarie him selfe, Syr *William Peter*, Syr *J. Mason*, D. *Wotton*, Syr *Richard Sackuille* Treasurer of the Exchecker, Syr *Walter Mildmaye* Chauncellor of the Exchecker, M. *Haddon* Master of Requestes, M. *John Astely* Master of the Iewell house, M. *Bernard Hampton*, M. *Nicasius*, and *J.* Of which number, the most part were of hir Maiesties most honourable priuie Counsell, and the reast seruing hir in verie good place. I was glad than, and do reioice yet to remember, that my chance was so happie, to be there that day, in the companie of so manie wise & good men togither, as hardly than could haue beene piked out againe, out of all England beside.

M. Secretarie hath this accustomed maner, though his head be neuer so full of most weightie affaires of the Realme, yet, at diner time he doth seeme to lay them alwaies aside: and findeth euer fitte occasion to taulke pleasantlie of other matters, but most gladlie of some matter of learning: wherein, he will curteslie heare the minde of the meanest at his Table.

Not long after our sitting doune, I haue strange newes brought me, sayth M. Secretarie, this morning, that diuerse Scholers of Eaton, be runne awaie from the Schole, for feare of beating. Whereupon, M. Secretarie tooke occasion, to wishe, that some $\quad$ M. *Secreta-rie.*

more discretion were in many Scholemasters, in vsing correction, than commonlie there is. Who many times, punishe rather, the weakenes of nature, than the fault of the Scholer. Whereby, many Scholers, that might else proue well, be driuen to hate learning, before they knowe, what learning meaneth: and so, are made willing to forsake their booke, and be glad to be put to any other kinde of liuing.

M. *Peter*, as one somewhat seuere of nature, said plainlie,

M. *Peter.* that the Rodde onelie, was the sworde, that must keepe, the Schole in obedience, and the Scholer

M. *Wotton.* in good order. M. *Wotton*, à man milde of nature, with soft voice, and fewe wordes, inclined to M. Secretaries iudgement, and said, in mine opinion, the Schole-

Ludus li- house should be in deede, as it is called by name,
terarum. the house of playe and pleasure, and not of feare

Plato de and bondage: and as I do remember, so saith
Rep. 7. *Socrates* in one place of *Plato*. And therefore, if a Rodde carie the feare of à Sworde, it is no maruell, if those that be fearefull of nature, chose rather to forsake the Plaie, than to stand alwaies within the feare of a Sworde in a fonde

M. *Mason.* mans handling. M. *Mason*, after his maner, was verie merie with both parties, pleasantlie playing, both, with the shrewde touches of many courste boyes, and with the small discretion of many leude Scholemasters. M. *Haddon*

M. *Haddon.* was fullie of M. *Peters* opinion, and said, that the best Scholemaster of our time, was the greatest beater, and named the Person. Though, quoth I, it

The Author of was his good fortune, to send from his Schole,
this booke. vnto the Vniuersitie, one of the best Scholers in deede of all our time, yet wise men do thinke, that that came so to passe, rather, by the great towardnes of the Scholer, than by the great beating of the Master: and whether this be true or no, you your selfe are best witnes. I said somewhat farder in the matter, how, and whie, yong children, were soner allured by loue, than driuen by beating, to atteyne good learning: wherein I was the bolder to say my minde, bicause M. Secretarie curteslie prouoked me thereunto: or else, in such à companie, and namelie in his præsence, my wonte is, to be more willing, to vse mine eares, than to occupie my tonge.

Syr *Walter Mildmaye*, M. *Astley*, and the rest, said verie litle: onelie Syr *Rich. Sackuill*, said nothing at all.   After dinner I went vp to read with the Queenes Maiestie.   We red than together in the Greke tongue, as I well remember,   Demost. that noble Oration of *Demosthenes* against *Æschines*,   περὶ πα- for his false dealing in his Ambassage to king   ραπρεσβ. *Philip* of Macedonie.   Syr *Rich. Sackuile* came vp sone after: and finding me in hir Maiesties priuie chamber, he   Syr *R.* tooke me by the hand, & carying me to à   *Sackuiles* windoe, said, M. *Ascham*, I would not for à good   communi- deale of monie, haue bene, this daie, absent from   cation with   the Author diner.   Where, though I said nothing, yet I gaue   of this as good eare, and do consider as well the taulke,   booke. that passed, as any one did there.   M. Secretarie said very wisely, and most truely, that many yong wittes be driuen to hate learninge, before they know what learninge is.   I can be good witnes to this my selfe : For à fond Scholemaster, before I was fullie fourtene yeare olde, draue me so, with feare of beating, from all loue of learninge, as nowe, when I know, what difference it is, to haue learninge, and to haue litle, or none at all, I feele it my greatest greife, and finde it my greatest hurte, that euer came to me, that it was my so ill chance, to light vpon so lewde à Scholemaster.   But seing it is but in vain, to lament thinges paste, and also wisdome to looke to thinges to cum, surely, God willinge, if God lend me life, I will make this my mishap, some occasion of good hap, to litle *Robert Sackuile* my sonnes sonne.   For whose bringinge vp, I would gladlie, if it so please you, vse speciallie your good aduice.   I heare saie, you haue à sonne, moch of his age : we wil deale thus togither.   Point you out à Scholemaster, who by your order, shall teache my sonne and yours, and for all the rest, I will prouide, yea though they three do cost me a couple of hundred poundes by yeare: and beside, you shall finde me as fast à Frend to you and yours, as perchance any you haue.   Which promise, the worthie Ientleman surelie kept with me, vntill his dying daye.

We had than farther taulke togither, of bringing vp of children : of the nature, of quicke, and hard wittes: The cheife of the right choice of à good witte : of Feare, and   pointes of loue in teaching children.   We passed from   this booke.

children and came to yonge men, namely, Ientlemen: we
taulked of their to moch libertie, to liue as they lust: of their
letting louse to sone, to ouer moch experience of ill, contrarie to
the good order of many good olde common welthes of the
Persians and Grekes: of witte gathered, and good fortune
gotten, by some, onely by experience, without learning.   And
lastlie, he required of me verie earnestlie, to shewe, what I
thought of the common goinge of Englishe men into Italie.
But, sayth he, bicause this place, and this tyme, will not suffer
so long taulke, as these good matters require, therefore I pray
you, at my request, and at your leysure, put in some order of
writing, the cheife pointes of this our taulke, concerning the
right order of teachinge, and honestie of liuing, for the good
bringing vp of children & yong men.   And surelie, beside
contentinge me, you shall both please and profit verie many
others.   I made some excuse by lacke of habilitie, and weakenes
of bodie: well, sayth he, I am not now to learne, what you can
do.   Our deare frende, good M. *Goodricke*, whose iudgement I
could well beleue, did once for all, satisfye me fullie therein.
Againe, I heard you say, not long agoe, that you may thanke
Syr *John Cheke*, for all the learninge you haue: And I know
verie well my selfe, that you did teach the Quene.   And
therefore seing God did so blesse you, to make you the Scholer
of the best Master, and also the Scholemaster of the best
Scholer, that euer were in our tyme, surelie, you should please
God, benefite your countrie, & honest your owne name, if you
would take the paines, to impart to others, what you learned
of soch à Master, and how ye taught such à scholer.   And, in
vttering the stuffe ye receiued of the one, in declaring the
order ye tooke with the other, ye shall neuer lacke, neither
matter, nor maner, what to write, nor how to write in this
kinde of Argument.

I beginning some farther excuse, sodeinlie was called to
cum to the Queene.   The night following, I slept litle, my
head was so full of this our former taulke, and I so mindefull,
somewhat to satisfie the honest request of so deare à frend,
I thought to præpare some litle treatise for a New yeares gift
that Christmas.   But, as it chanceth to busie builders, so, in
building thys my poore Scholehouse (the rather bicause the forme
of it is somewhat new, and differing from others) the worke

rose dailie higher and wider, than I thought it would at the beginninge.

And though it appeare now, and be in verie deede, but a small cotage, poore for the stuffe, and rude for the workemanship, yet in going forward, I found the site so good, as I was lothe to giue it ouer, but the making so costlie, outreaching my habilitie, as many tymes I wished, that some one of those three, my deare frendes, with full pursses, Syr *Tho. Smithe*, M. *Haddon*, or M. *Watson*, had had the doing of it. M. {Smith. Haddō. Watson. }
Yet, neuerthelesse, I my selfe, spending gladlie that litle, that I gatte at home by good Syr *Iohn Cheke*, and that that I borrowed abroad of my frend *Sturmius*, beside somewhat that was left me in Reuersion by my olde Masters, *Plato, Aristotle*, and *Cicero*, I haue at last patched it vp, as I could, Syr *I. Cheke. I. Sturmius. Plato. Aristotle. Cicero.*
and as you see. If the matter be meane, and meanly handled, I pray you beare, both with me, and it: for neuer worke went vp in worse wether, with mo lettes and stoppes, than this poore Scholehouse of mine. Westminster Hall can beare some witnesse, beside moch weakenes of bodie, but more trouble of minde, by some such sores, as greue me to toche them my selfe, and therefore I purpose not to open them to others. And, in middes of outward iniuries, and inward cares, to encrease them withall, good Syr *Rich. Sackuile* dieth, that worthie Ientleman: That earnest fauorer and furtherer of Gods true Religion: Syr *R. Sackuill.*
That faithfull Seruitor to his Prince and Countrie: A louer of learning, & all learned men : Wise in all doinges : Curtesse to all persons : shewing spite to none : doing good to many : and as I well found, to me so fast à frend, as I neuer lost the like before. Whan he was gone, my hart was dead. There was not one, that woare à blacke gowne for him, who caried à heuier hart for him, than I. Whan he was gone, I cast this booke àwaie : I could not looke vpon it, but with weping eyes, in remembring him, who was the onelie setter on, to do it, and would haue bene, not onelie à glad commender of it, but also à sure and certaine comfort, to me and mine, for it. Almost two yeares togither, this booke lay scattered, and neglected, and had bene quite giuen ouer of me, if the goodnesse of one had not giuen me some life and spirite againe. God, the

mouer of goodnesse, prosper alwaies him & his, as he hath
many times comforted me and mine, and, I trust to God, shall
comfort more and more. Of whom, most iustlie I may saie,
and verie oft, and alwaies gladlie, I am wont to say, that
sweete verse of *Sophocles,* spoken by *Oedipus* to worthie *Theseus.*

Soph. in
Oed. Col.   ἔχω [γὰρ] ἄχω διὰ σὲ, κοὐκ ἄλλον βροτῶν.

Thys hope hath helped me to end this booke: which, if he
allowe, I shall thinke my labours well imployed, and shall not
moch æsteme the misliking of any others. And I trust, he
shall thinke the better of it, bicause he shall finde the best part
thereof, to cum out of his Schole, whom he, of all men loued
and liked best.

Yet some men, frendly enough of nature, but of small
iudgement in learninge, do thinke, I take to moch paines, and

Plato in
initio
Theagis.
οὐ γὰρ ἔστι
περὶ ὅτου
θειοτέρου
ἄνθρωπος
ἂν βουλεύ-
σαιτο, ἢ
περὶ παι-
δείας, καὶ
τῶν αὑτοῦ,
καὶ τῶν
οἰκείων.

spend to moch time, in setting forth these
childrens affaires. But those good men were
neuer brought vp in *Socrates* Schole, who saith
plainlie, that no man goeth about a more godlie
purpose, than he that is mindfull of the good
bringing vp, both of hys owne, and other mens
children.

Therfore, I trust, good and wise men, will
thinke well of this my doing. And of other, that
thinke otherwise, I will thinke my selfe, they are
but men, to be pardoned for their follie, and
pitied for their ignoraunce.

In writing this booke, I haue had earnest respecte to three
speciall pointes, trothe of Religion, honestie in liuing, right order
in learning. In which three waies, I praie God, my poore
children may diligently waulke: for whose sake, as nature
moued, and reason required, and necessitie also somewhat
compelled, I was the willinger to take these paines.

For, seing at my death, I am not like to leaue them any
great store of liuing, therefore in my life time, I thought good
to bequeath vnto thē, in this litle booke, as in my Will and
Testament, the right waie to good learning: which if they
followe, with the feare of God, they shall verie well cum to
sufficiencie of liuinge.

I wishe also, with all my hart, that yong M. *Rob. Sackuille,*

may take that fru&te of this labor, that his worthie Grauntfather
purposed he should haue done: And if any other do take, either
proffet, or pleasure hereby, they haue cause to thanke M.
Robert Sackuille, for whom speciallie this my Scholemaster was
prouided.

And one thing I would haue the Reader consider in
readinge this booke, that bicause, no Scholemaster hath charge
of any childe, before he enter into hys Schole, therefore I
leauing all former care, of their good bringing vp, to wise and
good Parentes, as à matter not belonging to the Scholemaster,
I do appoynt thys my Scholemaster, than, and there to begin,
where his office and charge beginneth. Which charge lasteth
not long, but vntill the Scholer be made hable to go to the
Vniuersitie, to procede in Logike, Rhetoricke, and other kindes
of learning.

Yet if my Scholemaster, for loue he beareth to hys
Scholer, shall teach hym somewhat for hys furtherance,
and better iudgement in learning, that may serue
him seuen yeare after in the Vniuersitie, he
doth hys Scholer no more wrong, nor deserueth no worse name therby, than he
doth in London, who sellinge silke
or cloth vnto his frend, doth
giue hym better measure,
than either hys pro-
mise or bargaine
was.

Farewell in Christ.

The first booke for the youth.

AFter the childe hath learned perfitlie the eight partes of
speach, let him then learne the right ioyning togither of
substantiues with adiectiues, the nowne with the verbe, the
relatiue with the antecedent. And in learninge farther hys
Syntaxis, by mine aduice, he shall not vse the common order
in common scholes, for making of latines: wherby, the childe
commonlie learneth, first, an euill choice of wordes,
Cic. de (and right choice of wordes, saith *Cæsar*, is the
Cla. or. foundation of eloquence) than, a wrong placing
of wordes: and lastlie, an ill framing of the sentence, with
a peruerse iudgement, both of wordes and sentences. These
Making of faultes, taking once roote in yougthe, be neuer, or
Lattines hardlie, pluckt away in age. Moreouer, there is
marreth no one thing, that hath more, either dulled the
Children. wittes, or taken awaye the will of children from
learning, then the care they haue, to satisfie their masters, in
making of latines.

For, the scholer, is commonlie beat for the making, whē
the master were more worthie to be beat for the mending, or
rather, marring of the same: The master many times, being
as ignorant as the childe, what to saie properlie and fitlie to the
matter.

Two scholemasters haue set forth in print, either of them
Horman. a booke, of soch kinde of latines, *Horman* and
Whitting- *Whittington.*
ton. A childe shall learne of the better of them,
that, which an other daie, if he be wise, and cum to iudgement,
he must be faine to vnlearne againe.

There is a waie, touched in the first booke of *Cicero De Oratore*, which, wiselie brought into scholes, truely taught, and cōstantly vsed, would not _{I. De Or.} onely take wholly away this butcherlie feare in making of latines, but would also, with ease and pleasure, and in short time, as I know by good experience, worke a true choice and placing of wordes, a right ordering of sentences, an easie vnderstandyng of the tonge, a readines to speake, a facultie to write, a true iudgement, both of his owne, and other mens doinges, what tonge so euer he doth vse.

The waie is this. After the three Concordances learned, as I touched before, let the master read vnto hym the Epistles of *Cicero*, gathered togither and chosen out by *Sturmius*, for the capacitie of children.

First, let him teach the childe, cherefullie and plainlie, the cause, and matter of the letter : then, let him construe it into Englishe, so oft, as the childe may _{The order of teaching.} easilie carie awaie the vnderstanding of it : Lastlie, parse it ouer perfitlie. This done thus, let the childe, by and by, both construe and parse it ouer againe : so, that it may appeare, that the childe douteth in nothing, that his master taught him before. After this, the childe must take a paper booke, and sitting in some place, where no man shall prompe him, by him self, let him translate into Englishe his former lesson. Then shewing it to his master, let the master take from him his latin booke, and _{Two paper bokes.} pausing an houre, at the least, than let the childe translate his owne Englishe into latin againe, in an other paper booke. When the childe bringeth it, turned into latin, the master must compare it with *Tullies* booke, and laie them both togither : and where the childe doth well, either in chosing, or true placing of *Tullies* wordes, let the master _{Children learne by prayse.} praise him, and saie here ye do well. For I assure you, there is no such whetstone, to sharpen a good witte and encourage a will to learninge, as is praise.

But if the childe misse, either in forgetting a worde, or in chaunging a good with a worse, or misordering the sentence, I would not haue the master, either froune, or chide with him, if the childe haue done his diligence, and vsed no trewandship

therein. For I know by good experience, that a childe shall
take more profit of two fautes, ientlie warned of,
then of foure thinges, rightly hitt. For than, the
master shall haue good occasion to saie vnto him.

Ientlenes
in teaching.

N. *Tullie* would haue vsed such a worde, not this : *Tullie*
would haue placed this word here, not there : would haue vsed
this case, this number, this person, this degree, this gender : he
would haue vsed this moode, this tens, this simple, rather than
this compound : this aduerbe here, not there : he would haue
ended the sentence with this verbe, not with that nowne or
participle. etc.

   In these fewe lines, I haue wrapped vp, the most tedious
part of Grammer : and also the ground of almost all the Rewles,
that are so busilie taught by the Master, and so hardlie learned
by the Scholer, in all common Scholes : which after this sort,
the master shall teach without all error, and the scholer shall
learne without great paine : the master being led by so sure
a guide, and the scholer being brought into so plaine and easie
a waie.   And therefore, we do not contemne Rewles, but we
gladlie teach Rewles : and teach them, more plainlie, sensiblie,
and orderlie, than they be commonlie taught in common
Scholes.   For whan the Master shall compare *Tullies* booke
with his Scholers translation, let the Master, at the first,
lead and teach his Scholer, to ioyne the Rewles of his Grammer
booke, with the examples of his present lesson, vntill the
Scholer, by him selfe, be hable to fetch out of his Grammer,
euerie Rewle, for euerie Example : So, as the Grammer booke
be euer in the Scholers hand, and also vsed of him, as a
Dictionarie, for euerie present vse.   This is a liuely and perfite
waie of teaching of Rewles : where the common waie, vsed in
common Scholes, to read the Grammer alone by it selfe, is
tedious for the Master, hard for the Scholer, colde and vn-
cumfortable for them bothe.

   Let your Scholer be neuer afraide, to aske you any dout,
but vse discretlie the best allurements ye can, to encorage him
to the same : lest, his ouermoch fearinge of you, driue him
to seeke some misorderlie shifte : as, to seeke to be helped
by some other booke, or to be prompted by some other
Scholer, and so goe aboute to begile you moch, and him selfe
more.

With this waie, of good vnderstanding the mater, plaine construinge, diligent parsinge, dailie translatinge, cherefull admonishinge, and heedefull amendinge of faultes : neuer leauinge behinde iuste praise for well doinge, I would haue the Scholer brought vp withall, till he had red, & translated ouer yᵉ first booke of Epistles chosen out by *Sturmius*, with a good peece of a Comedie of *Terence* also.

All this while, by mine aduise, the childe shall vse to speake no latine : For, as *Cicero* saith in like mater, with like wordes, *loquendo, male loqui discunt.* And, that excellent learned man, *G. Budæus*, in his Greeke Commentaries, sore complaineth, that whan he began to learne the latin tonge, vse of speaking latin at the table, and elsewhere, vnaduisedlie, did bring him to soch an euill choice of wordes, to soch a crooked framing of sentences, that no one thing did hurt or hinder him more, all the daies of his life afterward, both for redinesse in speaking, and also good iudgement in writinge.

Latin
speakyng.
G. Budæus.

In very deede, if childrē were brought vp, in soch a house, or soch a Schole, where the latin tonge were properlie and perfitlie spoken, as *Tib.* and *Ca. Gracci* were brought vp, in their mother *Cornelias* house, surelie, than the dailie vse of speaking, were the best and readiest waie, to learne the latin tong. But, now, commonlie, in the best Scholes in England, for wordes, right choice is smallie regarded, true proprietie whollie neglected, confusion is brought in, barbariousnesse is bred vp so in yong wittes, as afterward they be, not onelie marde for speaking, but also corrupted in iudgement : as with moch adoe, or neuer at all, they be brought to right frame againe.

Yet all men couet to haue their children speake latin : and so do I verie earnestlie too. We bothe, haue one purpose : we agree in desire, we wish one end : but we differ somewhat in order and waie, that leadeth rightlie to that end. Other would haue them speake at all aduentures : and, so they be speakinge, to speake, the Master careth not, the Scholer knoweth not, what. This is, to seeme, and not to bee : except it be, to be bolde without shame, rashe without skill, full of wordes without witte. I wish to haue them speake so, as it may well appeare, that the braine doth gouerne the tonge, and that reason leadeth forth the taulke. *Socrates* doctrine is true in *Plato*, and well

Plato.
Horat.
marked, and truely vttered by *Horace* in *Arte Poetica*, that, where so euer knowledge doth accompanie the witte, there best vtterance doth alwaies awaite vpon the tonge : For, good vnderstanding must first be bred

Much writyng breedeth ready speakyng.
in the childe, which, being nurished with skill, and vse of writing (as I will teach more largelie hereafter) is the onelie waie to bring him to iudgement and readinesse in speakinge : and that in farre shorter time (if he followe constantlie the trade of this litle lesson) than he shall do, by common teachinge of the cōmon scholes in England.

But, to go forward, as you perceiue, your scholer to goe better and better on awaie, first, with vnderstanding his lesson more quicklie, with parsing more readelie, with translating more spedelie and perfitlie then he was wonte, after, giue him longer lessons to translate : and withall, begin to teach him,

The secōd degree and order in teachyng.
both in nownes, & verbes, what is *Proprium*, and what is *Translatum*, what *Synonymum*, what *Diuersum*, which be *Contraria*, and which be most notable *Phrases* in all his lecture.

As :

Proprium.	{ *Rex Sepultus est magnificè.*
Translatum.	{ *Cum illo principe, Sepulta est & gloria et Salus Reipublicæ.*
Synonyma.	{ *Ensis, Gladius. Laudare, prædicare.*
Diuersa.	{ *Diligere, Amare. Calere, Exardescere. Inimicus, Hostis.*
Contraria.	{ *Acerbum & luctuosum bellum. Dulcis & læta Pax.*
Phrases.	{ *Dare verba. abjicere obedientiam.*

Your scholer then, must haue the third paper booke: in the which, after he hath done his double transla- The thyrd paper boke. tion, let him write, after this sort foure of these forenamed sixe, diligentlie marked out of euerie lesson.

Quatuor.
$$\begin{cases} Propria. \\ Translata. \\ Synonyma. \\ Diuersa. \\ Contraria. \\ Phrases. \end{cases}$$

Or else, three, or two, if there be no moe: and if there be none of these at all in some lecture, yet not omitte the order, but write these.

$$\begin{cases} Diuersa\ nulla. \\ Contraria\ nulla.\ etc. \end{cases}$$

This diligent translating, ioyned with this heedefull marking, in the foresaid Epistles, and afterwarde in some plaine Oration of *Tullie*, as, *pro lege Manil: pro Archia Poeta*, or in those three *ad C. Cæs*: shall worke soch a right choise of wordes, so streight a framing of sentences, soch a true iudgement, both to write skilfullie, and speake wittlelie, as wise men shall both praise, and maruell at.

If your scholer do misse sometimes, in marking rightlie these foresaid sixe thinges, chide not hastelie: for that shall, both dull his witte, and discorage his diligence: Ientlenes in teaching. but monish him gentelie: which shall make him, both willing to amende, and glad to go forward in loue and hope of learning.

I haue now wished, twise or thrise, this gentle nature, to be in a Scholemaster: And, that I haue done so, neither by chance, nor without some reason, I will now declare at large, why, in mine opinion, loue is Loue. Feare. fitter then feare, ientlenes better than beating, to bring vp a childe rightlie in learninge.

With the common vse of teaching and beating in common scholes of England, I will not greatlie contend: which if I did, it were but a small grammaticall Common Scholes. controuersie, neither belonging to heresie nor

treason, nor greatly touching God nor the Prince : although in
very deede, in the end, the good or ill bringing vp of children,
doth as much serue to the good or ill seruice, of God, our
Prince, and our whole countrie, as any one thing doth beside.

I do gladlie agree with all good Scholemasters in these
pointes : to haue children brought to good perfitnes in learning :
to all honestie in maners : to haue all fautes rightlie amended :
to haue euerie vice seuerelie corrected : but for the order and
waie that leadeth rightlie to these pointes, we somewhat differ.

Sharpe Schole-masters.
For commonlie, many scholemasters, some, as
I haue seen, moe, as I haue heard tell, be of so
crooked a nature, as, when they meete with a
hard witted scholer, they rather breake him, than bowe him,
rather marre him, then mend him. For whan the scholemaster
is angrie with some other matter, then will he sonest faul to
beate his scholer : and though he him selfe should be punished
for his folie, yet must he beate some scholer for his pleasure :
though there be no cause for him to do so, nor yet fault in the
scholer to deserue so. These ye will say, be fond scholemasters,
and fewe they be, that be found to be soch. They be fond in
deede, but surelie ouermany soch be found euerie where. But

Nature punished.
this will I say, that euen the wisest of your great
beaters, do as oft punishe nature, as they do
correcte faultes. Yea, many times, the better
nature, is sorer punished : For, if one, by quicknes of witte,
take his lesson readelie, an other, by hardnes of witte, taketh it
not so speedelie : the first is alwaies commended, the other is
commonlie punished : whan a wise scholemaster, should rather
discretelie consider the right disposition of both their natures,
and not so moch wey what either of them is able to do now,

Quicke wittes for learnyng.
as what either of them is likelie to do hereafter.
For this I know, not onelie by reading of bookes
in my studie, but also by experience of life,
abrode in the world, that those, which be commonlie the
wisest, the best learned, and best men also, when they be olde,
were neuer commonlie the quickest of witte, when they were
yonge. The causes why, amongest other, which be many, that
moue me thus to thinke, be these fewe, which I will recken.
Quicke wittes commonlie, be apte to take, vnapte to keepe :
soone hote and desirous of this and that : as colde and sone

wery of the same againe : more quicke to enter spedelie, than hable to pearse farre : euen like ouer sharpe tooles, whose edges be verie soone turned. Soch wittes delite them selues in easie and pleasant studies, and neuer passe farre forward in hie and hard sciences. And therfore the quickest wittes commonlie may proue the best Poetes, but not the wisest Orators : readie of tonge to speake boldlie, not deepe of iudgement, either for good counsell or wise writing. Also, for maners and life, quicke wittes commonlie, be, in desire, newfangle, in purpose, vnconstant, light to promise any thing, readie to forget euery thing: both benefite and iniurie: and therby neither fast to frend, nor fearefull to foe : inquisitiue of euery trifle, not secret in greatest affaires : bolde, with any person : busie, in euery matter : sothing, soch as be present : nipping any that is absent : of nature also, alwaies, flattering their betters, enuying their equals, despising their inferiors : and, by quicknes of witte, verie quicke and readie, to like none so well as them selues.

Quicke wittes, for maners & lyfe.

Moreouer commonlie, men, very quicke of witte, be also, verie light of conditions : and thereby, very readie of disposition, to be caried ouer quicklie, by any light cumpanie, to any riot and vnthriftines when they be yonge : and therfore seldome, either honest of life, or riche in liuing, when they be olde. For, quicke in witte, and light in maners, be, either seldome troubled, or verie sone wery, in carying a verie heuie purse. Quicke wittes also be, in most part of all their doinges, ouerquicke, hastie, rashe, headie, and brainsicke. These two last wordes, Headie, and Brainsicke, be fitte and proper wordes, rising naturallie of the matter, and tearmed aptlie by the condition, of ouer moch quickenes of witte. In yougthe also they be, readie scoffers, priuie mockers, and euer ouer light and mery. In aige, sone testie, very waspishe, and alwaies ouer miserable : and yet fewe of them cum to any great aige, by reason of their misordered life when they were yong : but a great deale fewer of them cum to shewe any great countenance, or beare any great authoritie abrode in the world, but either liue obscurelie, men know not how, or dye obscurelie, mē marke not whan. They be like trees, that shewe forth, faire blossoms & broad leaues in spring time, but bring out small and not long lasting fruite in haruest time : and that onelie soch, as fall, and rotte, before they be ripe, and so, neuer, or seldome, cum to any good at all. For this ye shall finde most true by experience, that amongest a number of quicke wittes in youthe, fewe be found, in the end, either verie fortunate for them selues, or verie profitable to serue the common wealth, but decay and vanish, men know not which way: except a very fewe, to whom peraduenture blood and happie parentage, may perchance purchace a long standing vpon the stage. The which felicitie, because it commeth by others procuring, not by their owne deseruinge, and stand by other mens feete, and not by their own, what owtward brag so euer is borne by them, is in deed, of it selfe, and in wise mens eyes, of no great estimation.

Some wittes, moderate enough by nature, be many tymes marde by ouer moch studie and vse of some sciences, namelie, Musicke, Arithmetick, and Geometrie. Thies sciences, as they sharpen mens wittes ouer moch, so they change mens maners ouer sore, if they be not moderatlie mingled, & wiselie applied to som good vse of life. Marke all Mathematicall heades, which be onely and wholy bent to those sciences, how solitarie they be thēselues, how vnfit to liue with others, & how vnapte to serue in the world. This is not onelie knowen now by common experience, but vttered long before by wise mens Iudgement and sentence. *Galene* saith, moch Musick marreth mens maners: and *Plato* hath a notable place of the same thing in his bookes *de Rep.* well marked also, and excellentlie translated by *Tullie* himself. Of this matter, I wrote once more at large, xx. yeare a go, in my booke of shoting: now I thought but to touch it, to proue, that ouer moch quicknes of witte, either giuen by nature, or sharpened by studie, doth not commonlie bring forth, eyther greatest learning, best maners, or happiest life in the end.

Contrariewise, a witte in youth, that is not ouer dulle, heauie, knottie and lumpishe, but hard, rough, and though somwhat staffishe, as *Tullie* wisheth *otium, quietum, non languidum*: and *negotium cum labore, non cum periculo*, such a witte I say, if it be, at the first well handled by the mother, and rightlie smothed and wrought as it

Marginal notes:

Som sciences hurt mēs wits, and mar mens maners.

Mathematicall heades.

Galen.
Plato.

Hard wits in learning.

should, not ouerwhartlie, and against the wood, by the scholemaster, both for learning, and hole course of liuing, proueth
alwaies the best. In woode and stone, not the softest, but
hardest, be alwaies aptest, for portrature, both fairest for pleasure,
and most durable for proffit. Hard wittes be hard to receiue,
but sure to keepe : painefull without werinesse, hedefull without
wauering, constant without newfanglenes : bearing heauie
thinges, thoughe not lightlie, yet willinglie : entring hard
thinges, though not easelie, yet depelie, and so cum to that
perfitnes of learning in the ende, that quicke wittes, seeme in
hope, but do not in deede, or else verie seldome, Hard wits
euer attaine vnto. Also, for maners and life, hard in maners
wittes commonlie, ar hardlie caried, either to and lyfe.
desire euerie new thing, or else to meruell at euery strange
thinge : and therfore they be carefull and diligent in their own
matters, not curious and busey in other mens affaires : and so,
they becum wise them selues, and also ar counted honest by
others. They be graue, stedfast, silent of tong, secret of hart.
Not hastie in making, but constant in keping any promise.
Not rashe in vttering, but ware in considering euery matter :
and therby, not quicke in speaking, but deepe of iudgement,
whether they write, or giue counsell in all waightie affaires.
And theis be the mē, that becum in the end, both most happie
for themselues, and alwaise best estemed abrode in the world.
I haue bene longer in describing, the nature, the good or ill
success, of the quicke and hard witte, than perchance som will
thinke, this place and matter doth require. But The best
my purpose was hereby, plainlie to vtter, what wittes dri-
iniurie is offered to all learninge, & to the common uen from
welthe also, first, by the fond father in chosing, learnyng,
but chieflie by the lewd scholemaster in beating to other li-
                                                    uyng.
and driuing away the best natures from learning. A childe
that is still, silent, constant, and somwhat hard of witte, is
either neuer chosen by the father to be made a scholer, or else,
when he commeth to the schole, he is smally regarded, little
looked vnto, he lacketh teaching, he lacketh coraging, he lacketh
all thinges, onelie he neuer lacketh beating, nor any word, that
may moue him to hate learninge, nor any deed that may driue
him from learning, to any other kinde of liuing.
And when this sadde natured, and hard witted child, is bette

from his booke, and becummeth after eyther student of
the common lawe, or page in the Court, or
seruingman, or bound prentice to a merchant,
or to som handiecrafte, he proueth in the ende,
wiser, happier and many tymes honester too, than
many of theis quick wittes do, by their learninge.

Learning is, both hindred and iniured to, by the ill choice
of them, that send yong scholers to the vniuersities. Of whom
must nedes cum all oure Diuines, Lawyers, and Physicions.

Thies yong scholers be chosen commonlie, as yong apples be
chosen by children, in a faire garden about *S.
Iames* tyde: a childe will chose a sweeting, because it
is presentlie faire and pleasant, and refuse a Runnet,
because it is than grene, hard, and sowre, whan the
one, if it be eaten, doth breed, both wormes and ill humors:
the other if it stand his tyme, be ordered and kepte as it should, is
holsom of it self, and helpeth to the good disgestion of other meates:
Sweetinges, will receyue wormes, rotte, and dye on the tree, and
neuer or seldom cum to the gathering for good and lasting store.

For verie greafe of harte I will not applie the similitude:
but hereby, is plainlie seen, how learning is robbed of hir best
wittes, first by the greate beating, and after by the ill chosing
of scholers, to go to the vniuersities. Whereof cummeth
partelie, that lewde and spitefull prouerbe, sounding to the
greate hurte of learning, and shame of learned men, that, the
greatest Clerkes be not the wisest men.

And though I, in all this discourse, seem plainlie to prefer,
hard and roughe wittes, before quicke and light wittes, both for
learnyng and maners, yet am I not ignorant that som quicknes
of witte, is a singuler gifte of God, and so most rare emonges
men, and namelie such a witte, as is quicke without lightnes,
sharpe without brittlenes, desirous of good thinges without
newfanglenes, diligēt in painfull thinges without werisomnes,
and constant in good will to do all thinges well, as I know was
in Syr *Iohn Cheke*, and is in som, that yet liue, in whome all
theis faire qualities of witte ar fullie mette togither.

But it is notable and trewe, that *Socrates* saith in *Plato* to
his frende *Crito*. That, that number of men is
fewest, which far excede, either in good or ill, in
wisdom or folie, but the meane betwixt both, be

the greatest number: which he proueth trewe in diuerse other thinges: as in greyhoundes, emonges which fewe are found, exceding greate, or exceding litle, exceding swift, or exceding slowe: And therfore, I speaking of quick and hard wittes, I ment, the common number of quicke and hard wittes, emonges the which, for the most parte, the hard witte, proueth manie times, the better learned, wiser and honester man: and therfore, do I the more lament, that soch wittes commonlie be either kepte from learning, by fond fathers, or bet from learning by lewde scholemasters.

Verie good, or verie ill men, be fewest in number.

And speaking thus moche of the wittes of children for learning, the opportunitie of the place, and goodnes of the matter might require to haue here declared the most speciall notes of a good witte for learning in a childe, after the maner and custume of a good horsman, who is skilfull, to know, and hable to tell others, how by certein sure signes, a man may choise a colte, that is like to proue an other day, excellent for the saddle. And it is pitie, that commonlie, more care is had, yea and that emonges verie wise men, to finde out rather a cunnynge man for their horse, than a cunnyng man for their children. They say nay in worde, but they do so in deede. For, to the one, they will gladlie giue a stipend of 200. Crounes by yeare, and loth to offer to the other, 200. shillinges. God, that sitteth in heauen laugheth their choice to skorne, and rewardeth their liberalitie as it should: for he suffereth them, to haue, tame, and well ordered horse, but wilde and vnfortunate Children: and therfore in the ende they finde more pleasure in their horse, than comforte in their children.

Horsemen be wiser in knowledge of a good Colte, than scholemasters be, in knowledge of a good witte.

A good Rider better rewarded thā a good Scholemaster.

Horse well broken, children ill taught.

But concerning the trewe notes of the best wittes for learning in a childe, I will reporte, not myne own opinion, but the very iudgement of him, that was counted the best teacher and wisest man that learning maketh mention of, and that is *Socrates* in *Plato*, who expresseth orderlie thies seuen plaine notes to choise a good witte in a child for learninge.

Plato in 7. de Rep.

1 Εὐφυής.
2 Μνήμων.
3 Φιλομαθής.
4 Φιλόπονος.
5 Φιλήκοος.
6 Ζητητικός.
7 Φιλέπαινος.

Trewe notes of a good witte.

And bicause I write English, and to Englishemen, I will plainlie declare in Englishe both, what thies wordes of *Plato* meane, and how aptlie they be linked, and how orderlie they folow one an other.

1. Εὐφυής.

Is he, that is apte by goodnes of witte, and appliable by readines of will, to learning, hauing all other qualities of the minde and partes of the bodie, that must an other day serue learning, not trobled, māgled, and halfed, but sounde, whole, full, & hable to do their office: as, a tong, not stamering, or ouer hardlie drawing forth wordes, but plaine, and redie to deliuer the meaning of the minde : a voice, not softe, weake, piping, womannishe, but audible, stronge, and manlike : a countenance, not werishe and crabbed, but faire and cumlie : a personage, not wretched and deformed, but taule and goodlie : for surelie, a cumlie countenance, with a goodlie stature, geueth credit to learning, and authoritie to the person : otherwise commonlie, either, open contempte, or priuie disfauour doth hurte, or hinder, both person and learning. And, euen as a faire stone requireth to be sette in the finest gold, with the best workmanshyp, or else it leseth moch of the Grace and price, euen so, excellencye in learning, and namely Diuinitie, ioyned with a cumlie personage, is a meruelous Iewell in the world. And how can a cumlie bodie be better employed, than to serue the fairest exercise of Goddes greatest gifte, and that is learning. But commonlie, the fairest bodies, ar bestowed on the foulest purposes. I would it were not so : and with examples herein I will not medle : yet I wishe, that

Witte. Will. The tong. The voice. Face. Stature. Learnyng ioyned with a cumlie personage.

those shold, both mynde it, & medle with it, which haue most occasion to looke to it, as good and wise fathers shold do, and greatest authoritie to amend it, as good & wise magistrates ought to do: And yet I will not let, openlie to lament the vnfortunate case of learning herein.

For, if a father haue foure sonnes, three faire and well formed both mynde and bodie, the fourth, wretched, lame, and deformed, his choice shalbe, to put the worst to learning, as one good enoughe to becum a scholer. I haue spent the most parte of my life in the Vniuersitie, and therfore I can beare good witnes that many fathers commonlie do thus: wherof, I haue hard many wise, learned, and as good men as euer I knew, make great, and oft complainte: a good horseman will choise no soch colte, neither for his own, nor yet for his masters sadle. And thus moch of the first note.

Deformed creatures commonlie set to lear-nyng.

2 Μνήμων.

Good of memorie, a speciall parte of the first note εὐφυής, and a mere benefite of nature: yet it is so necessarie for learning, as *Plato* maketh it a separate and perfite note of it selfe, and that so principall a note, as without it, all other giftes of nature do small seruice to learning. *Afranius*, that olde Latine Poete maketh Memorie the mother of learning and wisedome, saying thus.

Memorie.

Aul. Gel.

Vsus me genuit, Mater peperit memoria, and though it be the mere gifte of nature, yet is memorie well preserued by vse, and moch encreased by order, as our scholer must learne an other day in the Vniuersitie: but in a childe, a good memorie is well known, by three properties: that is, if it be, quicke in receyuing, sure in keping, and redie in deliuering forthe againe.

Three sure signes of a good me-morie.

3 Φιλομαθής.

Giuen to loue learning: for though a child haue all the giftes of nature at wishe, and perfection of memorie at wil, yet if he haue not a speciall loue to learning, he shall neuer attaine to moch learning. And therfore *Isocrates,* one of the noblest scholemasters, that is in memorie of learning, who taught Kinges and Princes, as *Halicarnassæus* writeth, and out of whose schole, as *Tullie* saith, came forth, mo noble Capitanes, mo wise Councelors, than did out of *Epeius* horse at *Troie*. This *Isocrates*, I say, did cause to be writtē, at the entrie of his schole, in golden letters, this golden sentence, ἐὰν ἦς φιλομαθὴς, ἔση πολυμαθής which excellentlie said in *Greeke*, is thus rudelie in Englishe, if thou louest learning, thou shalt attayne to moch learning.

4. Φιλόπονος.

Is he, that hath a lust to labor, and a will to take paines. For, if a childe haue all the benefites of nature, with perfection of memorie, loue, like, & praise learning neuer so moch, yet if he be not of him selfe painfull, he shall neuer attayne vnto it. And yet where loue is present, labor is seldom absent, and namelie in studie of learning, and matters of the mynde: and therfore did *Isocrates* rightlie iudge, that if his scholer were φιλομαθής he cared for no more. *Aristotle*, variing from *Isocrates* in priuate affaires of life, but agreing with *Isocrates* in common iudgement of learning, for loue and labor in learning, is of the same opiniō, vttered in these wordes, in his Rhetorike *ad Theodecten*. Libertie kindleth loue: Loue refuseth no labor: and labor obteyneth what so euer it seeketh. And yet neuerthelesse, Goodnes of nature may do little good: Perfection of memorie, may serue to small vse: All loue may be employed in vayne: Any labor may be sone graualed, if a man trust alwaies to his own singuler witte, and will not be glad somtyme to heare, take aduise, and learne of an other: And therfore doth *Socrates* very notablie adde the fifte note.

2 Rhet. ad Theod.

5. Φιλήκοος.

He, that is glad to heare and learne of an other. For otherwise, he shall sticke with great troble, where he might go easelie forwarde: and also catche hardlie a verie litle by his owne toyle, whan he might gather quicklie a good deale, by an nothers mans teaching. But now there be some, that haue great loue to learning, good lust to labor, be willing to learne of others, yet, either of a fonde shamefastnes, or else of a proud folie, they dare not, or will not, go to learne of an nother: And therfore doth *Socrates* wiselie adde the sixte note of a good witte in a childe for learning, and that is.

6. Ζητητικός.

He, that is naturallie bold to aske any question, desirous to searche out any doute, not ashamed to learne of the meanest, not affraide to go to the greatest, vntill he be perfitelie taught, and fullie satisfiede. The seuenth and last poynte is.

7. Φιλέπαινος.

He, that loueth to be praised for well doing, at his father, or masters hand. A childe of this nature, will earnestlie loue learnyng, gladlie labor for learning, willinglie learne of other, boldlie aske any doute. And thus, by *Socrates* iudgement, a good father, and a wise scholemaster, shold chose a childe to make a scholer of, that hath by nature, the foresayd perfite qualities, and cumlie furniture, both of mynde and bodie: hath memorie, quicke to receyue, sure to keape, and readie to deliuer: hath loue to learning: hath lust to labor: hath desire to learne of others: hath boldnes to aske any questiō: hath mynde holie bent, to wynne praise by well doing.

The two firste poyntes be speciall benefites of nature: which neuerthelesse, be well preserued, and moch encreased by good order. But as for the fiue laste, loue, labor, gladnes to learne of others, boldnes to aske doutes, and will to wynne praise, be wonne and maintened by the onelie wisedome and discretiō of the scholemaster. Which fiue poyntes, whether a scholemaster shall worke soner in a childe, by fearefull beating, or curtese handling, you that be wise, iudge.

Yet some men, wise in deede, but in this matter, more by seueritie of nature, thā any wisdome at all, do laugh at vs, when we thus wishe and reason, that yong children should rather be allured to learning by ientilnes and loue, than compelled to learning, by beating and feare: They say, our reasons serue onelie to breede forth talke, and passe a waie tyme, but we neuer saw good scholemaster do so, nor neuer red of wise man that thought so.

Yes forsothe: as wise as they be, either in other mens opinion, or in their owne conceite, I will bring the contrarie iudgement of him, who, they them selues shall confesse, was as wise as they are, or else they may be iustlie thought to haue small witte at all: and that is *Socrates*, whose iudgement in Plato is plainlie this in these wordes: which, bicause they be verie notable, I will recite them in his owne tong, οὐδὲν μάθημα μετὰ δουλείας χρὴ μανθάνειν: οἱ μὲν γὰρ τοῦ σώματος πόνοι βίᾳ πονούμενοι χεῖρον οὐδὲν τὸ σῶμα ἀπεργάζονται; ψυχῇ δέ, βίαιον οὐδὲν ἔμμονον μάθημα: in Englishe thus, No learning ought to be learned with bondage: For, bodelie labors, wrought by compulsion, hurt not the bodie: but any learning learned by cōpulsion, tarieth not lōg in the mynde: And why? For what soeuer the mynde doth learne vnwillinglie with feare, the same it doth quicklie forget without care. And lest proude wittes, that loue not to be contraryed, but haue lust to wrangle or trifle away troth, will say, that *Socrates* meaneth not this of childrens teaching, but of som other higher learnyng, heare, what *Socrates* in the same place doth more plainlie say: μὴ τοίνυν βίᾳ, ὦ ἄριστε, τοὺς παῖδας ἐν τοῖς μαθήμασιν, ἀλλὰ παίζοντας τρέφε, that is to say, and therfore, my deare frend, bring not vp your children in learning by compulsion and feare, but by playing and pleasure. And you, that do read *Plato*, as ye shold, do well perceiue, that these be no Questions asked by *Socrates*, as doutes, but they be Sentences, first affirmed by *Socrates*, as mere trothes, and after, giuen forth by *Socrates*, as right Rules, most necessarie to be marked, and fitte to be folowed of all them, that would haue children taughte, as they should. And in this counsell, iudgement, and authoritie of *Socrates* I will repose my selfe, vntill I meete with a man of the contrarie mynde, whom I may iustlie take to be wiser, than I thinke *Socrates* was. Fonde scholemasters, neither can vnderstand, nor will folow this good counsell of *Socrates*, but wise ryders, in their office, can and will do both: which is the onelie cause, that cōmonly, the yong ientlemen of England, go so vnwillinglie to schole, and run so fast to the stable: For in verie deede fond scholemasters, by feare, do beate into thē, the hatred of learning, and wise riders, by ientle allurements, do breed vp in

Plato in 7. de Rep.

The right readyng of *Plato*.

Yong Ientlemen, be wiselier taught to ryde, by cōmon ryders, than to learne, by common Scholemasters.

them, the loue of riding. They finde feare, & bondage in scholes, They feele libertie and freedome in stables: which causeth them, vtterlie to abhore the one, and most gladlie to haunt the other. And I do not write this, that in exhorting to the one, I would dissuade yong ientlemen from the other: yea I am sorie, with all my harte, that they be giuen no more to riding, then they be: For, of all outward qualities, Ryding. to ride faire, is most cumelie for him selfe, most necessarie for his contrey, and the greater he is in blood, the greater is his praise, the more he doth excede all other therein. It was one of the three excellent praises, amongest the noble ientlemen the old *Percians,* Alwaise to say troth, to ride faire, and shote well: and so it was engrauen vpon *Darius* tumbe, as *Strabo* beareth witnesse. Strabo. 15.

Darius the king, lieth buried here,
Who in riding and shoting had neuer peare.

But, to our purpose, yong men, by any meanes, leesing the loue of learning, whan by tyme they cum to their owne rule, they carie commonlie, from the schole with them, a perpetuall hatred of their master, and a continuall contempt of learning. If ten Ientlemen be asked, why they forget so sone in Court, that which they were learning so long in schole, eight of them, or let me be blamed, will laie the fault on their ill handling, by their scholemasters.

Cuspinian doth report, that, that noble Emperor *Maximilian,* would lament verie oft, his misfortune herein.

Yet, some will say, that children of nature, loue pastime, and mislike learning: bicause, in their kinde, the Pastime. one is easie and pleasant, the other hard and werisom: which is an opinion not so trewe, as Learnyng. some men weene: For, the matter lieth not so much in the disposition of them that be yong, as in the order & maner of bringing vp, by them that be old, nor yet in the differēce of learnyng and pastime. For, beate a child, if he daunce not well, & cherish him, though he learne not well, ye shall haue him, vnwilling to go to daunce, & glad to go to his booke. Knocke him alwaies, when he draweth his shaft ill, and fauor him againe, though he faut at his booke, ye shall haue hym verie loth to be in the field, and verie willing to be in the schole.

Yea, I saie more, and not of my selfe, but by the iudgemēt of those, from whom few wisemen will gladlie dissent, that if euer the nature of man be giuen at any tyme, more than other, to receiue goodnes, it is, in innocencie of yong yeares, before, that experience of euill, haue taken roote in hym. For, the pure cleane witte of a sweete yong babe, is like the newest wax, most hable to receiue the best and fayrest printing: and like a new bright siluer dishe neuer occupied, to receiue and kepe cleane, anie good thyng that is put into it.

And thus, will in children, wiselie wrought withall, maie

Will. ⎫
        ⎬ in Children.
Witte. ⎭

easelie be won to be verie well willing to learne. And witte in childrē, by nature, namelie memorie, the onelie keie and keper of all learning, is readiest to receiue, and surest to kepe anie maner of thing, that is learned in yougth: This, lewde and learned, by common experiēce, know to be most trewe. For we remember nothyng so well when we be olde, as those things which we learned when we were yong: And this is not straunge, but

Yōg yeares
aptest for
learnyng.

common in all natures workes. Euery man sees, (as I sayd before) new wax is best for printyng: new claie, fittest for working: new shorne woll, aptest for sone and surest dying: new fresh flesh, for good and durable salting. And this similitude is not rude, nor borowed of the larder house, but out of his scholehouse, of whom, the wisest of England, neede not be ashamed to learne. Yong Graftes grow not onelie sonest, but also fairest, and bring alwayes forth the best and sweetest frute : yong whelpes learne easelie to carie: yong Popingeis learne quicklie to speake: And so, to be short, if in all other thinges, though they lacke reason, sens, and life, the similitude of youth is fittest to all goodnesse, surelie nature, in mankinde, is most beneficiall and effectuall in this behalfe.

Therfore, if to the goodnes of nature, be ioyned the wisedome of the teacher, in leading yong wittes into a right and plaine waie of learnyng, surelie, children, kept vp in Gods feare, and gouerned by his grace, maie most easelie be brought well to serue God and contrey both by vertue and wisedome.

But if will, and witte, by farder age, be once allured frō innocencie, delited in vaine sightes, filed with foull taulke, crooked with wilfulnesse, hardned with stubburnesse, and let

louse to disobedience, surelie it is hard with ientlenesse, but vnpossible with seuere crueltie, to call them backe to good frame againe. For, where the one, perchance maie bend it, the other shall surelie breake it: and so in stead of some hope, leaue an assured desperation, and shamelesse contempt of all goodnesse, the fardest pointe in all *Xen. 1. Cy-*
mischief, as *Xenophon* doth most trewlie and most *ri Pæd.*
wittelie marke.

Therfore, to loue or to hate, to like or contemne, to plie this waie or that waie to good or to bad, ye shall haue as ye vse a child in his youth.

And one example, whether loue or feare doth worke more in a child, for vertue and learning, I will gladlie report: which maie be hard with some pleasure, and folowed with more profit. Before I went into *Germanie*, I came to Brodegate in Leceter-
shire, to take my leaue of that noble Ladie *Iane*
Grey, to whom I was exceding moch beholdinge. *Lady Iane*
Hir parentes, the Duke and Duches, with all the *Grey.*
houshould, Gentlemen and Gentlewomen, were huntinge in the Parke: I founde her, in her Chamber, readinge *Phædon Platonis* in Greeke, and that with as moch delite, as som ientleman wold read a merie tale in *Bocase.* After salutation, and dewtie done, with som other taulke, I asked hir, whie she wold leese soch pastime in the Parke? smiling she answered me: I wisse, all their sporte in the Parke is but a shadoe to that pleasure, that I find in *Plato*: Alas good folke, they neuer felt, what trewe pleasure ment. And howe came you Madame, quoth I, to this deepe knowledge of pleasure, and what did chieflie allure you vnto it: seinge, not many women, but verie fewe men haue atteined thereunto. I will tell you, quoth she, and tell you a troth, which perchance ye will meruell at. One of the greatest benefites, that euer God gaue me, is, that he sent me so sharpe and seuere Parentes, and so ientle a scholemaster. For whē I am in presence either of father or mother, whether I speake, kepe silence, sit, stand, or go, eate, drinke, be merie, or sad, be sowyng, plaiyng, dauncing, or doing anie thing els, I must do it, as it were, in soch weight, mesure, and number, euen so perfitelie, as God made the world, or else I am so sharplie taunted, so cruellie threatened, yea presentlie some tymes, with pinches, nippes, and bobbes, and other waies, which

I will not name, for the honor I beare them, so without measure misordered, that I thinke my selfe in hell, till tyme cum, that I must go to *M. Elmer*, who teacheth me so ientlie, so pleasantlie, with soch faire allurementes to learning, that I thinke all the tyme nothing, whiles I am with him. And when I am called from him, I fall on weeping, because, what soeuer I do els, but learning, is ful of grief, trouble, feare, and whole misliking vnto me: And thus my booke, hath bene so moch my pleasure, & bringeth dayly to me more pleasure & more, that in respect of it, all other pleasures, in very deede, be but trifles and troubles vnto me. I remember this talke gladly, both bicause it is so worthy of memorie, & bicause also, it was the last talke that euer I had, and the last tyme, that euer I saw that noble and worthie Ladie.

I could be ouer long, both in shewinge iust causes, and in recitinge trewe examples, why learning shold be taught, rather by loue than feare. He that wold see a perfite discourse of it,

Sturmius de Inst. Princ.

let him read that learned treatese, which my frende *Ioan. Sturmius* wrote *de institutione Principis*, to the Duke of *Cleues*.

Qui parcit virgæ, odit filiū.

The godlie counsels of *Salomon* and *Iesus* the sonne of *Sirach*, for sharpe kepinge in, and bridleinge of youth, are ment rather, for fatherlie correction, then masterlie beating, rather for maners, than for learninge: for other places, than for scholes. For God forbid, but all euill touches, wantonnes, lyinge, pickinge, slouthe, will, stubburnnesse, and disobedience, shold be with sharpe chastisemēt, daily cut away.

This discipline was well knowen, and diligentlie vsed, among the *Græcians*, and old *Romanes*, as doth appeare in *Aristophanes*, *Isocrates*, and *Plato*, and also in the Comedies of *Plautus*: where we see that children were vnder the rule of three persones: *Præceptore*, *Pædagogo*, *Parente*: the scholemaster

1. Scholemaster.
2. Gouernour.
3. Father.

taught him learnyng with all ientlenes: the Gouernour corrected his maners, with moch sharpenesse: The father, held the sterne of his whole obedience: And so, he that vsed to teache, did not commōlie vse to beate, but remitted that ouer to an other mans charge. But what shall we saie, whan now in our dayes, the scholemaster is vsed, both for *Præceptor* in learnyng, and *Pædagogus* in maners. Surelie, I wold he shold not cōfound their offices, but discretelie vse the dewtie of both so, that neither ill touches shold be left vnpunished, nor ientlesse in teaching anie wise omitted. And he shall well do both, if wiselie he do appointe diuersitie of tyme, & separate place, for either purpose: vsing alwaise soch discrete modera- tion, as the scholehouse should be counted a sanctuarie against feare: and verie well learning, a common perdon for ill doing, if the fault, of it selfe be not ouer heinous.

The schole house.

And thus the children, kept vp in Gods feare, and preserued by his grace, finding paine in ill doing, and pleasure in well studiyng, shold easelie be brought to honestie of life, and perfitenes of learning, the onelie marke, that good and wise fathers do wishe and labour, that their children, shold most buselie, and carefullie shot at.

There is an other discommoditie, besides crueltie in schole- masters in beating away the loue of learning from childrē, which hindreth learning and vertue, and good bringing vp of youth, and namelie yong ientlemen, verie moch in England. This fault is cleane contrary to the first. I wished before, to haue loue of learning bred vp in children:

Youth of England brought vp with to much li- bertie.

I wishe as moch now, to haue yong men brought vp in good order of liuing, and in some more seuere discipline, thē commonlie they be. We haue lacke in England of soch good order, as the old noble *Persians* so carefullie vsed: whose children, to the age of xxi. yeare, were brought vp in learnyng, and exercises of labor,

Xen. 7. Cyri Ped.

and that in soch place, where they should, neither see that was vncumlie, nor heare that was vnhonest. Yea, a yong ientlemā was neuer free, to go where he would, and do what he liste him self, but vnder the kepe, and by the counsell, of some graue gouernour, vntill he was, either maryed, or cald to beare some office in the common wealth.

And see the great obedience, that was vsed in old tyme to fathers and gouernours. No sonne, were he neuer so old of yeares, neuer so great of birth, though he were a kynges sonne, might not mary, but by his father and mothers also consent. *Cyrus* the great, after he had conquered *Babylon*, and subdewed

Riche king *Crœsus* with whole *Asia minor*, cummyng tryumph-
antlie home, his vncle *Cyaxeris* offered him his daughter to
wife. *Cyrus* thanked his vncle, and praised the maide, but for
mariage he answered him with thies wise and sweete wordes, as

they be vttered by *Xenophon*, ὦ κυαξάρη, τό
τε γένος ἐπαινῶ, καὶ τὴν παῖδα, καὶ δῶρα·
βούλομαι δέ, ἔφη, σὺν τῇ τοῦ πατρὸς γνώμῃ
καὶ [τῇ] τῆς μητρὸς ταῦτά σοι συναινέσαι, &c., that is to say :
Vncle *Cyaxeris*, I commend the stocke, I like the maide, and
I allow well the dowrie, but (sayth he) by the counsell and
consent of my father and mother, I will determine farther ot
thies matters.

Strong *Samson* also in Scripture saw a maide that liked him,
but he spake not to hir, but went home to his father, and his
mother, and desired both father and mother to make the
mariage for him. Doth this modestie, doth this obedience,
that was in great kyng *Cyrus*, and stoute *Samson*, remaine in
our yongmen at this daie ? no surelie : For we liue not
longer after them by tyme, than we liue farre different from
them by good order. Our tyme is so farre from that old
discipline and obedience, as now, not onelie yong ientlemen, but
euen verie girles dare without all feare, though not without
open shame, where they list, and how they list, marie them
selues in spite of father, mother, God, good order, and all.
The cause of this euill is, that youth is least looked vnto, when
they stand [in] most neede of good kepe and regard. It auail-
eth not, to see them well taught in yong yeares, and after whā
they cum to lust and youthfull dayes, to giue them licence to
liue as they lust them selues. For, if ye suffer the eye of a
yong Ientleman, once to be entangled with vaine sightes, and
the eare to be corrupted with fond or filthie taulke, the mynde
shall quicklie fall seick, and sone vomet and cast vp, all the
holesome doctrine, that he receiued in childhoode, though he
were neuer so well brought vp before. And being ons inglutted
with vanitie, he will streight way loth all learning, and all good
counsell to the same. And the parentes for all their great cost

Xen. 8. Cy-
ri Pæd.

Great mēs
sonnes
worst
brought
vp.

and charge, reape onelie in the end, the frute
of grief and care.

This euill, is not common to poore men, as God
will haue it, but proper to riche and great mens

children, as they deserue it. In deede from seuen, to seuentene, yong ientlemen commonlie be carefullie enough brought vp : But from seuentene to seuen and twentie (the most dangerous tyme of all a mans life, and most slipperie to stay well in) they haue commonlie the reigne of all licens in their owne Wise men hand, and speciallie soch as do liue in the Court. fond fa-And that which is most to be merueled at, thers. commonlie, the wisest and also best men, be found the fondest fathers in this behalfe. And if som good father wold seick some remedie herein, yet the mother (if the house hold of our Lady) had rather, yea, & will to, haue her sonne cunnyng & bold, in making him to lyue trimlie when he is yong, than by learning and trauell, to be able to serue his Prince and his contrie, both wiselie in peace, and stoutelie in warre, whan he is old.

The fault is in your selues, ye noble mens sonnes, and therefore ye deserue the greater blame, that Meane commonlie, the meaner mens children, cum to m̄es sonnes be, the wisest councellours, and greatest doers, come to in the weightie affaires of this Realme. And great au-why ? for God will haue it so, of his prouidence : thoritie. bicause ye will haue it no otherwise, by your negligence.

And God is a good God, & wisest in all his doinges, that will place vertue, & displace vice, in those Nobilitie kingdomes, where he doth gouerne. For he without knoweth, that Nobilitie, without vertue and wisedome. wisedome, is bloud in deede, but bloud trewelie, without bones & sinewes : & so of it selfe, without the other, verie weeke to beare the burden of weightie affaires.

The greatest shippe in deede commonlie carieth the greatest burden, but yet alwayes with the greatest ieoperdie, not onelie for the persons and goodes committed vnto it, Nobilitie but euen for the shyppe it selfe, except it be with wise-gouerned, with the greater wisdome. dome.

But Nobilitie, gouerned by learning and wisedome, is in deede, most like a faire shippe, hauyng tide and winde at will, vnder the reule of a skilfull master : whan contrarie wise, a shippe, caried, yea with the hiest tide & greatest winde, | Nobilite with { Wisedom. | Out wise-dome.

lacking a skilfull master, most commonlie, doth either, sinck it selfe vpō sandes, or breake it selfe vpon rockes.   And euen so, how manie haue bene, either drowned in vaine pleasure, or ouerwhelmed by stout wilfulnesse, the histories of England be able to affourde ouer many examples vnto vs.   Therfore, ye great and noble mens children, if ye will haue rightfullie that praise, and enioie surelie that place, which your fathers haue, and elders had, and left vnto you, ye must kepe it, as they gat it, and that is, by the onelie waie, of vertue, wisedome, and worthinesse.

Vaine plea-sure, and stoute wil-fulnes, two greatest enemies to Nobilitie.

For wisedom, and vertue, there be manie faire examples in this Court, for yong Ientlemen to folow.   But they be, like faire markes in the feild, out of a mans reach, to far of, to shote at well.   The best and worthiest men, in deede, be somtimes seen, but seldom taulked withall: A yong Ientleman, may somtime knele to their person, smallie vse their companie, for their better instruction.

But yong Ientlemen ar faine commonlie to do in the Court, as yong Archers do in the feild : that is take soch markes, as be nie them, although they be neuer so foule to shote at.   I meene, they be driuen to kepe companie with the worste : and what force ill companie hath, to corrupt good wittes, the wisest men know best.

Ill compa-nie marreth youth.

And not ill companie onelie, but the ill opinion also of the most part, doth moch harme, and namelie of those, which shold be wise in the trewe de-cyphring, of the good disposition of nature, of cumlinesse in Courtlie maners, and all right doinges of men.

The Court iudgeth worst of the best natures in youth.

But error and phantasie, do commonlie occupie, the place of troth and iudgement.   For, if a yong ientleman, be demeure and still of nature, they say, he is simple and lacketh witte : if he be bashefull, and will soone blushe, they call him a babishe and ill brought vp thyng, when *Xenophon* doth preciselie note in *Cyrus*, that his bashfulnes in youth, was ye verie trewe signe of his vertue & stoutnes after : If he be innocent and ignorant of ill, they say, he is rude, and hath no grace, so

Xen. in 1. Cyr. Pæd.

The Grace in Courte.

vngraciouslie do som gracelesse men, misuse the faire and godlie word G R A C E.

But if ye would know, what grace they meene, go, and looke, and learne emonges them, and ye shall see that it is: First, to blush at nothing. And blushyng in youth, sayth *Aristotle* is nothyng els, but feare to do ill: which feare beyng once lustely fraid away from youth, thē foloweth, to dare do any mischief, to cōtemne stoutly any goodnesse, to be busie in euery matter, to be skilfull in euery thyng, to acknowledge no ignorance at all. To do thus in Court, is coūted of some, the chief and greatest grace of all: and termed by the name of a vertue, called Corage & boldnesse, whan *Crassus* in *Cicero* teacheth the cleane contrarie, and that most wittelie, saying thus: *Audere, cum bonis etiam rebus coniunctum, per seipsum est magnopere fugiendum.* Which is to say, to be bold, yea in a good matter, is for it self, greatlie to be exchewed.

Grace of Courte.

Cic. 3. *de Or.*

Boldnes yea in a good matter, not to be praised.

Moreouer, where the swing goeth, there to follow, fawne, flatter, laugh and lie lustelie at other mens liking. To face, stand formest, shoue backe: and to the meaner man, or vnknowne in the Court, to seeme somwhat solume, coye, big, and dangerous of looke, taulk, and answere: To thinke well of him selfe, to be lustie in contemning of others, to haue some trim grace in a priuie mock. And in greater presens, to beare a braue looke: to be warlike, though he neuer looked enimie in the face in warre: yet som warlike signe must be vsed, either a slouinglie busking, or an ouerstaring frounced hed, as though out of euerie heeres toppe, should suddenlie start out a good big othe, when nede requireth, yet praised be God, England hath at this time, manie worthie Capitaines and good souldiours, which be in deede, so honest of behauiour, so cumlie of conditions, so milde of maners, as they may be examples of good order, to a good sort of others, which neuer came in warre. But to retorne, where I left: In place also, to be able to raise taulke, and make discourse of euerie rishe: to haue a verie good will, to heare him selfe speake: To be seene

More Grace of Courte.

Men of warre, best of conditions.

Palmistrie.

in Palmestrie, wherby to conueie to chast eares, som fond or filthie taulke :

And, if som Smithfeild Ruffian take vp, som strange going : som new mowing with the mouth : som wrinchyng with the shoulder, som braue prouerbe : som fresh new othe, that is not stale, but will rin round in the mouth : som new disguised garment, or desperate hat, fond in facion, or gaurish in colour, what soeuer it cost, how small soeuer his liuing be, by what shift soeuer it be gotten, gotten must it be, and vsed with the first, or els the grace of it, is stale and gone : som part of this gracelesse grace, was discribed by me, in a little rude verse long ago.

> *To laughe, to lie, to flatter, to face :*
> *Foure waies in Court to win men grace.*
> *If thou be thrall to none of thiese,*
> *Away good Peek goos, hens Iohn Cheese :*
> *Marke well my word, and marke their dede,*
> *And thinke this verse part of thy Crede.*

Would to God, this taulke were not trewe, and that som mens doinges were not thus : I write not to hurte any, but to proffit som : to accuse none, but to monish soch, who, allured by ill counsell, and folowing ill example, cōtrarie to their good bringyng vp, and against their owne good nature, yeld ouermoch to thies folies and faultes : I know many seruing men, of good order, and well staide : And againe, I heare saie, there be som seruing men do but ill seruice to their yong masters. Yea, rede *Terence* and *Plaut.* aduisedlie ouer, and ye shall finde in those two wise writers, almost in euery commedie, no vnthriftie yong man, that is not brought there vnto, by the sotle inticement of som lewd seruant. And euen now in our dayes *Getæ* and *Daui*, and manie bold bawdie *Phormios* to, be preasing in, to pratle on euerie stage, to medle in euerie matter, whan honest *Parmenos* shall not be hard, but beare small swing with their masters. Their companie, their taulke, their ouer great experience

Side notes:

Ill { Councell. / Cōpany. }

Seruinge men.

Terentius.
Plautus.

Serui corruptelæ iuuenum.

Gnatos and

Multi Getæ pauci Parmenones.

in mischief, doth easelie corrupt the best natures, and best brought vp wittes.

But I meruell the lesse, that thies misorders be emonges som in the Court, for commonlie in the contrie also euerie where, innocencie is gone : Bashful-nesse is banished : moch presumption in yougthe : small authoritie in aige : Reuerence is negleƈted : dewties be confounded : and to be shorte, disobedience doth ouerflowe the bankes of good order, almoste in euerie place, almoste in euerie degree of man.

Misorders in the coun-trey.

Meane men haue eies to see, and cause to lament, and occasion to complaine of thies miseries : but other haue authoritie to remedie them, and will do so to, whan God shall think time fitte. For, all thies misorders, be Goddes iuste plages, by his sufferance, brought iustelie vpon vs, for our sinnes, which be infinite in nomber, and horrible in deede, but namelie, for the greate abhominable sin of vn-kindnesse : but what vnkindnesse ? euen such vnkindnesse as was in the Iewes, in contemninge Goddes voice, in shrinking frõ his woorde, in wishing backe againe for *Ægypt*, in committing aduoultrie and hordom, not with the women, but with the doctrine of Babylon, did bring all the plages, destructions, and Captiuities, that fell so ofte and horriblie, vpon Israell.

Contempt of Gods trewe Re-ligion.

We haue cause also in England to beware of vnkindnesse, who haue had, in so fewe yeares, the Candel of Goddes woorde, so oft lightned, so oft put out, and yet will venture by our vnthankfulnesse in doctrine and sinfull life, to leese againe, lighte, Candle, Candlesticke and all.

Doctrina Mores.

God kepe vs in his feare, God grafte in vs the trewe knowledge of his woorde, with a forward will to folowe it, and so to bring forth the sweete fruites of it, & then shall he preserue vs by his Grace, from all maner of terrible dayes.

The remedie of this, doth not stand onelie, in making good common lawes for the hole Realme, but also, (and perchance cheiflie) in obseruing priuate discipline euerie man care-fullie in his own house : and namelie, if speciall regard be had to yougth : and that, not so moch,

Publicæ Leges.

Domestica disciplina.

Cognitio boni.

in teaching them what is good, as in keping them from that, that is ill.

Therefore, if wise fathers, be not as well waare in weeding from their Children ill thinges, and ill companie, *Ignoratio* as they were before, in graftinge in them *mali.* learninge, and prouiding for them good schole-masters, what frute, they shall reape of all their coste & care, common experience doth tell.

Here is the place, in yougthe is the time whan som *Some* ignorance is as necessarie, as moch knowledge, *ignorance,* and not in matters of our dewtie towardes God, *as good as* as som wilful wittes willinglie against their owne *knowledge.* knowledge, perniciouslie againste their owne conscience, haue of late openlie taught. In deede *S. Chryso-* *Chrisost. de* *stome,* that noble and eloquent Doctor, in a *Fato.* sermon *contra fatum,* and the curious serchinge of natiuities, doth wiselie saie, that ignorance therein, is better than knowledge: But to wring this sentence, to wreste thereby out of mens handes, the knowledge of Goddes doctrine, is without all reason, against common sence, contrarie to the iudgement also of them, which be the discretest men, and best learned, on their own side. I know, *Iulianus* *Iulia. Apo-* *Apostata* did so, but I neuer hard or red, that any *stat.* auncyent father of the primitiue chirch, either thought or wrote so.

But this ignorance in yougthe, which I spake on, or rather this simplicitie, or most trewlie, this innocencie, *Innocency* is that, which the noble *Persians,* as wise *Xenophon* *in youth.* doth testifie, were so carefull, to breede vp their yougth in. But Christian fathers commonlie do not so. And I will tell you a tale, as moch to be misliked, as the *Persians* example is to be folowed.

This last somer, I was in a Ientlemans house: where *A childe ill* a yong childe, somewhat past fower yeare olde, *brought* cold in no wise frame his tonge, to saie, a litle *vp.* shorte grace: and yet he could roundlie rap out, so manie vgle othes, and those of the newest facion, as som good man of fourescore yeare olde hath neuer hard named *Ill Pa-* before: and that which was most detestable of *rentes.* all, his father and mother wold laughe at it. I moche doubte, what comforte, an other daie, this childe shall bring vnto them. This Childe vsing moche the companie of seruinge men, and geuing good eare to their taulke, did easelie learne, which he shall hardlie forget, all daies of his life hereafter : So likewise, in the Courte, if a yong Ientleman will ventur him self into the companie of Ruffians, it is ouer greate a ieopardie, lest, their facions, maners, thoughtes, taulke, and deedes, will verie sone, be euer like. The confounding of companies, breedeth confusion of good maners Ill compa- both in the Courte, and euerie where else. nie.

And it maie be a great wonder, but a greater shame, to vs Christian men, to vnderstand, what a heithen writer, *Isocrates*, doth leaue in memorie of writing, concerning the *Isocrates.* care, that the noble Citie of *Athens* had, to bring vp their yougthe, in honest companie, and vertuous discipline, whose taulke in Greke, is, to this effect, in Englishe.

" The Citie, was not more carefull, to see their Children
" well taughte, than to see their yong men well
" gouerned : which they brought to passe, not so In Orat.
" much by common lawe, as by priuate discipline. Ariopag.
" For, they had more regard, that their yougthe, by good order
" shold not offend, than how, by lawe, they might be punished :
" And if offense were committed, there was, neither waie to
" hide it, neither hope of pardon for it. Good natures, were
" not so moche openlie praised as they were secretlie marked,
" and watchfullie regarded, lest they should lease the goodnes
" they had. Therefore in scholes of singing and dauncing, and
" other honest exercises, gouernours were appointed, more
" diligent to ouersee their good maners, than their masters were,
" to teach them anie learning. It was som shame to a yong
" man, to be seene in the open market : and if for businesse, he
" passed throughe it, he did it, with a meruelous modestie, and
" bashefull facion. To eate, or drinke in a Tauerne, was not
" onelie a shame, but also punishable, in a yong man. To
" contrarie, or to stand in termes with an old man, was more
" heinous, than in som place, to rebuke and scolde with his
" owne father: with manie other mo good orders, and faire disciplines, which I referre to their reading, that haue lust to looke vpon the description of such a worthie common welthe.

And to know, what worthie frute, did spring of soch
Good sede,
worthie
frute. worthie seade, I will tell yow the most meruell
of all, and yet soch a trothe, as no man shall
denie it, except such as be ignorant in knowledge
of the best stories.

Athens, by this discipline and good ordering of yougthe, did
Athenes. breede vp, within the circute of that one Citie,
within the compas of one hondred yeare, within
the memorie of one mans life, so manie notable Capitaines in
warre, for worthinesse, wisdome and learning, as be scarse
Roma. matchable no not in the state of Rome, in the
compas of those seauen hondred yeares, whan it
florished moste.

And bicause, I will not onelie saie it, but also proue it, the
The noble
Capitaines
of Athens. names of them be these. *Miltiades, Themistocles,
Xantippus, Pericles, Cymon, Alcybiades, Thrasybulus,
Conon, Iphicrates, Xenophon, Timotheus, Theopompus,
Demetrius,* and diuers other mo: of which euerie one, maie
iustelie be spoken that worthie praise, which was geuen to
Scipio Africanus, who, *Cicero* douteth, whether he were, more
noble Capitaine in warre, or more eloquent and wise councelor
in peace. And if ye beleue not me, read dili-
Æmil.
Probus.
Plutarchus. gentlie, *Æmilius Probus* in Latin, and *Plutarche*
in Greke, which two, had no cause either to
flatter or lie vpon anie of those which I haue
recited.

And beside nobilitie in warre, for excellent and matchles
The lear-
ned of A-
thenes. masters in all maner of learninge, in that one
Citie, in memorie of one aige, were mo learned
men, and that in a maner altogether, than all
tyme doth remember, than all place doth affourde, than all other
tonges do conteine. And I do not meene of those Authors,
which, by iniurie of tyme, by negligence of men, by crueltie of
fier and sworde, be lost, but euen of those, which by Goddes
grace, are left yet vnto us: of which I thank God, euen my
poore studie lacketh not one. As, in Philosophie, *Plato, Aristotle, Xenophon, Euclide* and *Theophrast*: In eloquens and Ciuill
lawe, *Demosthenes, Æschines, Lycurgus, Dinarchus, Demades,
Isocrates, Isæus, Lysias, Antisthenes, Andocides*: In histories, *Herodotus, Thucydides, Xenophon*: and which we lacke, to our

great losse, *Theopompus* and *Eph[orus]* : In Poetrie, *Æschylus,*
Sophocles, Euripides, Aristophanes, and somwhat of *Menander,*
Demosthenes sister sonne.

Now, let Italian, and Latin it self, Spanishe, French,
Douch, and Englishe bring forth their lerning, Learnyng,
and recite their Authors, *Cicero* onelie excepted, chiefly con-
and one or two moe in Latin, they be all patched teined in
cloutes and ragges, in comparison of faire wouen the Greke,
broade clothes. And trewelie, if there be any ther tong.
good in them, it is either lerned, borowed, or
stolne, from some one of those worthie wittes of *Athens.*

The remembrance of soch a common welthe, vsing soch
discipline and order for yougthe, and thereby bringing forth to
their praise, and leauing to vs for our example, such Capitaines
for warre, soch Councelors for peace, and matcheles masters,
for all kinde of learninge, is pleasant for me to recite, and not
irksum, I trust, for other to heare, except it be soch, as make
neither counte of vertue nor learninge.

And whether, there be anie soch or no, I can not well tell :
yet I heare saie, some yong Ientlemen of oures, Contem-
count it their shame to be counted learned : and ners of
perchance, they count it their shame, to be learnyng.
counted honest also, for I heare saie, they medle as litle with the
one, as with the other. A meruelous case, that Ientlemen
shold so be ashamed of good learning, and neuer a whit ashamed
of ill maners : soch do saie for them, that the Ientlemen
Ientlemen of France do so : which is a lie, as of France.
God will haue it. *Langæus,* and *Bellæus* that be
dead, & the noble *Vidam* of Chartres, that is aliue, and infinite
mo in France, which I heare tell of, proue this to be most false.
And though som, in France, which will nedes be Ientlemen,
whether men will or no, and haue more ientleshipe in their hat,
than in their hed, be at deedlie feude, with both learning and
honestie, yet I beleue, if that noble Prince, king *Francis* the
first were aliue, they shold haue, neither place in Franciscus
his Courte, nor pension in his warres, if he had i. Nobilis.
knowledge of them. This opinion is not French, Francorū
but plaine Turckishe : from whens, some Frenche Rex.
fetche moe faultes, than this : which, I praie God, kepe out of

England, and send also those of oures better mindes, which bend them selues againste vertue and learninge, to the contempte of God, dishonor of their contrie to the hurt of manie others, and at length, to the greatest harme, and vtter destruction of themselues.

Som other, hauing better nature, but lesse witte, (for ill commonlie, haue ouer moch witte) do not vtterlie dispraise learning, but they saie, that without learning, common experience, knowledge of all facions, and haunting all companies, shall worke in yougthe, both wisdome, and habilitie, to execute anie weightie affaire. Surelie long experience doth proffet moch, but moste, and almost onelie to him (if we meene honest affaires) that is diligentlie before instructed with preceptes of well doinge. For good precepts of learning, be the eyes of the minde, to looke wiselie before a man, which waie to go right, and which not.

Experience without learnyng.

Learning teacheth more in one yeare than experience in twentie: And learning teacheth safelie. when experience maketh mo miserable then wise. He hasardeth sore, that waxeth wise by experience. An vnhappie Master he is, that is made cunning by manie shippewrakes: A miserable merchant, that is neither riche or wise, but after som bankroutes. It is costlie wisdom, that is bought by experience. We know by experience it selfe, that it is a meruelous paine, to finde oute but a short waie, by long wandering. And surelie, he that wold proue wise by experience, he maie be wittie in deede, but euen like a swift runner, that runneth fast out of his waie, and vpon the night, he knoweth not whither. And verilie they be fewest of number, that be happie or wise by vnlearned experience. And looke well vpon the former life of those fewe, whether your example be old or yonge, who without learning haue gathered, by long experience, a litle wisdom, and som happines: and whan you do consider, what mischeife they haue committed, what dangers they haue escaped (and yet xx. for one, do perishe in the aduenture) than thinke well with your selfe, whether ye wold, that your owne son, should cum to wisdom and happines, by the waie of soch experience or no.

Learnyng.

Experiēce.

It is a notable tale, that old Syr *Roger Chamloe*, sometime

cheife Iustice, wold tell of him selfe. When he was Auncient
in Inne of Courte, Certaine yong Ientlemen
were brought before him, to be corrected for   *Syr Roger*
certaine misorders : And one of the lustiest saide :   *Chamloe.*
Syr, we be yong ientlemen, and wisemen before vs, haue
proued all facions, and yet those haue done full well : this they
said, because it was well knowen, that Syr *Roger* had bene a
good feloe in his yougth. But he aunswered them verie wiselie.
In deede saith he, in yougthe, I was, as you ar now : and I
had twelue feloes like vnto my self, but not one of them came
to a good ende. And therfore, folow not my example in yougth,
but folow my councell in aige, if euer ye thinke to cum to this
place, or to thies yeares, that I am cum vnto, lesse ye meete
either with pouertie or Tiburn in the way.

Thus, experience of all facions in yougthe, beinge, in profe,
alwaise daungerous, in isshue, seldom lucklie, is
a waie, in deede, to ouermoch knowledge, yet   *Experiēce.*
vsed commonlie of soch men, which be either caried by som
curious affection of mynde, or driuen by som hard necessitie of
life, to hasard the triall of ouer manie perilous aduentures.

Erasmus the honor of learning of all oure time, saide
wiselie that experience is the common schole-   *Erasmus.*
house of foles, and ill men : Men, of witte and
honestie, be otherwise instructed. For there be,   Experiēce,
that kepe them out of fier, and yet was neuer   the schole-
burned : That beware of water, and yet was neuer   house of
                                                     Foles, and
nie drowninge : That hate harlottes, and was   ill men.
neuer at the stewes : That abhorre falshode, and neuer brake
promis themselues.

But will ye see, a fit Similitude of this aduentured experience.
A Father, that doth let louse his son, to all experiences, is most
like a fond Hunter, that letteth slippe a whelpe to the hole
herde. Twentie to one, he shall fall vpon a rascall, and let
go the faire game. Men that hunt so, be either ignorant
persones, preuie stealers, or night walkers.

Learning therefore, ye wise fathers, and good bringing vp,
and not blinde & dangerous experience, is the next and readiest
waie, that must leede your Children, first, to wisdom, and than
to worthinesse, if euer ye purpose they shall cum there.

And to saie all in shorte, though I lacke Authoritie to giue

counsell, yet I lacke not good will to wisshe, that the yougthe
How expe-
rience may
proffet.
in England, speciallie Ientlemen, and namelie nobilitie, shold be by good bringing vp, so grounded
in iudgement of learninge, so founded in loue of
honestie, as, whan they shold be called forthe to the execution
of great affaires, in seruice of their Prince and contrie, they
might be hable, to vse and to order, all experiences, were they
good were they bad, and that, according to the square, rule, and
line, of wisdom learning and vertue.

And, I do not meene, by all this my taulke, that yong
Diligent
learninge
ought to be
ioyned with
pleasant
pastimes,
namelie in a
ientleman.
Ientlemen, should alwaies be poring on a booke,
and by vsing good studies, shold lease honest
pleasure, and haunt no good pastime, I meene
nothing lesse: For it is well knowne, that I both
like and loue, and haue alwaies, and do yet still
vse, all exercises and pastimes, that be fitte for my
nature and habilitie. And beside naturall disposition, in iudgement also, I was neuer, either Stoick in doctrine,
or Anabaptist in Religion, to mislike a merie, pleasant, and
plaifull nature, if no outrage be committed, against lawe,
mesure, and good order.

Therefore, I wold wishe, that, beside some good time, fitlie
appointed, and constantlie kepte, to encrease by readinge, the
knowledge of the tonges and learning, yong ientlemen shold
Learnyng
ioyned with
pastimes.
vse, and delite in all Courtelie exercises, and
Ientlemanlike pastimes. And good cause whie:
For the self same noble Citie of Athenes, iustlie
commended of me before, did wiselie and vpon great consideration, appoint, the Muses, *Apollo,* and *Pallas,* to be patrones of
Musæ.
learninge to their yougthe. For the Muses,
besides learning, were also Ladies of dauncinge,
Apollo.
mirthe and ministrelsie: *Apollo,* was god of shooting,
Pallas.
and Author of cunning playing vpō Instrumentes:
Pallas also was Laidie mistres in warres. Wher-
bie was nothing else ment, but that learninge shold be alwaise
mingled, with honest mirthe, and cumlie exercises: and that
warre also shold be gouerned by learning, and moderated by
wisdom, as did well appeare in those Capitaines of *Athenes*
named by me before, and also in *Scipio* & *Cæsar,* the two
Diamondes of Rome.

And *Pallas*, was no more feared, in weering *Ægida*, thā she was praised, for chosing *Oliua*: whereby shineth the glory of learning, which thus, was Gouernour & Mistres, in the noble Citie of *Athenes*, both of warre and peace.

Therefore, to ride cumlie: to run faire at the tilte or ring: to plaie at all weapons: to shote faire in bow, or surelie in gon: to vaut lustely: to runne: to leape: to wrestle: to swimme: To daunce cumlie: to sing, and playe of instrumentes cunnyngly: to Hawke: to hunte: to playe at tennes, & all pastimes generally, which be ioyned with labor, vsed in open place, and on the day light, conteining either some fitte exercise for warre, or some pleasant pastime for peace, be not onelie cumlie and decent, but also verie necessarie, for a Courtlie Ientleman to vse.

But, of all kinde of pastimes, fitte for a Ientleman, I will, godwilling, in fitter place, more at large, declare fullie, in my booke of the Cockpitte: which I do write, to satisfie som, I trust, with som reason, that be more curious, in marking other mens doinges, than carefull in mendyng their owne faultes. And som also will nedes busie them selues in merueling, and adding thereunto vnfrendlie taulke, why I, a man of good yeares, and of no ill place, I thanke God and my Prince, do make choise to spend soch tyme in writyng of trifles, as the schole of shoting, the Cockpitte, and this booke of the first Principles of Grammer, rather, than to take some weightie matter in hand, either of Religion, or Ciuill discipline.

Wise men I know, will well allow of my choise herein: and as for such, who haue not witte of them selues, but must learne of others, to iudge right of mens doynges, let them read that wise Poet *Horace* in his *Arte Poetica*, who willeth wisemen to beware, of hie and loftie Titles. For, great shippes, require costlie tackling, and also afterward dangerous gouernment: Small boates, be neither verie chargeable in makyng, nor verie oft in great ieoperdie: and yet they cary many tymes, as good and costlie ware, as greater vessels do. A meane Argument, may easelie beare, the light burden of a small faute, and haue alwaise at hand, a ready excuse for ill handling: And, some praise it is, if it so chaunce, to be

The right choise, to chose a fitte Argument to write vpon.

Hor. in Arte Poet.

better in deede, than a man dare venture to seeme. A hye title, doth charge a man, with the heauie burden, of to great a promise: and therefore sayth *Horace* verie wittelie, that, that Poete was a verie foole, that began hys booke, with a goodlie verse in deede, but ouer proude a promise.

Fortunam Priami cantabo & nobile bellum,

And after, as wiselie.

Quantò rectiùs hic, qui nil molitur ineptè. etc.

Homers wisdom in choice of his Argument.

Meening *Homer*, who, within the compasse of a smal Argument, of one harlot, and of one good wife, did vtter so moch learning in all kinde of sciences, as, by the iudgement of *Quintilian*, he deserueth so hie a praise, that no man yet deserued to sit in the second degree beneth him. And thus moch out of my way, concerning my purpose in spending penne, and paper, & tyme, vpō trifles, & namelie to aunswere some, that haue neither witte nor learning, to do any thyng them selues, neither will nor honestie, to say well of other.

The Cortegian, an excellent booke for a ientleman.

To ioyne learnyng with cumlie exercises, *Conto Baldesær Castiglione* in his booke, *Cortegiano*, doth trimlie teache: which booke, aduisedlie read, and diligentlie folowed, but one yeare at home in England, would do a yong ientleman more good, I wisse, then three yeares trauell abrode spent in *Italie.* And I meruell this booke, is no more read in the Court, than it is, seyng it is so well translated into English by a worthie

Syr Tho. Hobbye.

Ientleman Syr *Th. Hobbie*, who was many wayes well furnished with learnyng, and very expert in knowledge of diuers tonges.

Examples better then preceptes.

And beside good preceptes in bookes, in all kinde of tonges, this Court also neuer lacked many faire examples, for yong ientlemen to folow: And surelie, one example, is more valiable, both to good and ill, than xx. preceptes written in bookes: and so *Plato*, not in one or two, but diuerse places, doth plainlie teach.

If kyng *Edward* had liued a litle longer, his onely example had breed soch a rase of worthie learned ientlemen, as this Realme neuer yet did affourde. *King Ed. 6.*

And, in the second degree, two noble Primeroses of Nobilitie, the yong Duke of Suffolke, and Lord H. *Matreuers*, were soch two examples to the Court for learnyng, as our tyme may rather wishe, than looke for agayne. *The yong Duke of Suffolke. L. H. Martreuers.*

At Cambrige also, in S. Iohns Colledge, in my tyme, I do know, that, not so much the good statutes, as two Ientlemen, of worthie memorie Syr *Iohn Cheke*, and Doctour *Readman*, by their onely example of excellency in learnyng, of godlynes in liuyng, of diligecie in studying, of councell in exhorting, of good order in all thyng, did breed vp, so many learned men, in that one College of S. Iohns, at one time, as I beleue, the whole Vniuersitie of *Louaine*, in many yeares, was neuer able to affourd. *Syr John Cheke. D. Readman.*

Present examples of this present tyme, I list not to touch: yet there is one example, for all the Ientlemen of this Court to folow, that may well satisfie them, or nothing will serue them, nor no example moue them, to goodnes and learning. *Queene Elisabeth.*

It is your shame, (I speake to you all, you yong Ientlemen of England) that one mayd should go beyond you all, in excellencie of learnyng, and knowledge of diuers tonges. Pointe forth six of the best giuen Ientlemen of this Court; and all they together, shew not so much good will, spend not so much tyme, bestow not so many houres, dayly orderly, & constantly, for the increase of learning & knowledge, as doth the Queenes Maiestie her selfe. Yea I beleue, that beside her perfit readines, in *Latin, Italian, French, & Spanish*, she readeth here now at Windsore more Greeke euery day, than some Prebendarie of this Chirch doth read *Latin* in a whole weeke. And that which is most praise worthie of all, within the walles of her priuie chamber, she hath obteyned that excellencie of learnyng, to vnderstand, speake, & write, both wittely with head, and faire with hand, as scarse one or two rare wittes in both the Vniuersities haue in many yeares reached vnto. Amongst all the benefites y^t God hath blessed me with all, next the knowledge of Christes true Religion, I counte this the greatest, that it pleased God to call me, to be one poore minister in settyng forward these excellent giftes of learnyng in this most excellent Prince. Whose onely example, if the rest of our

Ill Exam-
ples haue
more force,
then good
examples.
nobilitie would folow, than might England be, for learnyng and wisedome in nobilitie, a spectacle to all the world beside. But see the mishap of men: The best examples haue neuer such forse to moue to any goodnes, as the bad, vaine, light and fond, haue to all ilnes.

And one example, though out of the compas of learning, yet not out of the order of good maners, was notable in this Courte, not fullie xxiiij. yeares a go, when all the actes of Parlament, many good Proclamations, diuerse strait commaunde-mentes, sore punishment openlie, speciall regarde priuatelie, cold not do so moch to take away one misorder, as the example of one big one of this Courte did, still to kepe vp the same: The memorie whereof, doth yet remaine, in a common prouerbe of Birching lane.

Take hede therfore, ye great ones in ye Court, yea though

Great men
in Court,
by their
example,
make or
marre, all
other mens
maners.
ye be ye greatest of all, take hede, what ye do, take hede how ye liue. For as you great ones vse to do, so all meane men loue to do. You be in deed, makers or marrers, of all mens maners within the Realme. For though God hath placed yow, to be cheife in making of lawes, to beare greatest authoritie, to commaund all others: yet God doth order, that all your lawes, all your authoritie, all your commaundementes, do not halfe so moch with meane men, as

Example
in Religiō.
doth your example and maner of liuinge. And for example euen in the greatest matter, if yow your selues do serue God gladlie and orderlie for conscience sake, not coldlie, and somtyme for maner sake, you carie all the Courte with yow, and the whole Realme beside, earnestlie and orderlie to do the same. If yow do otherwise, yow be the onelie authors, of all misorders in Religion, not onelie to the Courte, but to all England beside. Infinite shall be made cold in Religion by your example, that neuer were hurt by reading of bookes.

And in meaner matters, if three or foure great ones in

Courte, will nedes outrage in apparell, in huge hose, in monstrous hattes, in gaurishe colers, let the Prince Proclame, make Lawes, order, punishe, commaunde euerie gate in London dailie to be watched, let all Example in apparell. good men beside do euerie where what they can, surelie the misorder of apparell in mean men abrode, shall neuer be amended, except the greatest in Courte will order and mend them selues first. I know, som greate and good ones in Courte, were authors, that honest Citizens of London, shoulde watche at euerie gate, to take misordered persones in apparell. I know, that honest Londoners did so: And I sawe, which I sawe than, & reporte now with some greife, that som Courtlie men were offended with these good men of London. And that, which greued me most of all, I sawe the verie same tyme, for all theis good orders, commaunded from the Courte and executed in London, I sawe I say, cum out of London, euen Masters, vnto the presence of the Prince, a great rable of Vshers, & meane and light persons, in apparell, for matter, Scholers against lawe, for making, against order, for facion, of fense. namelie hose, so without all order, as he thought himselfe most braue, that durst do most in breaking order and was most monsterous in misorder. And for all the great commaundementes, that came out of the Courte, yet this bold misorder, was winked at, and borne withall, in the Courte. I thought, it was not well, that som great ones of the Court, durst declare themselues offended, with good men of London, for doinge their dewtie, & the good ones of the Courte, would not shew themselues offended, with ill men of London, for breaking good order. I fownde thereby a sayinge of *Socrates* to be most trewe that ill men be more hastie, than good men be forwarde, to prosecute their purposes, euen as Christ himselfe saith, of the Children of light and darknes.

Beside apparell, in all other thinges to, not so moch, good lawes and strait commaundementes as the example and maner of liuing of great men, doth carie all meane men euerie where, to like, and loue, & do, as they do. For if but two or three noble men in the Court, wold but beginne to Example shoote, all yong Ientlemen, the whole Court, all in shoo- London, the whole Realme, wold straight waie tyng. exercise shooting.

What praise shold they wynne to themselues, what commoditie shold they bring to their contrey, that would thus
deserue to be pointed at : Beholde, there goeth, the author of
good order, the guide of good men. I cold say more, and yet
not ouermuch. But perchance, som will say, I haue stepte to
farre, out of my schole, into the common welthe, from teaching

Writtē not for great mē, but for great mens children. a yong scholer, to monishe greate and noble men:
yet I trust good and wise men will thinke and
iudge of me, that my minde was, not so moch,
to be busie and bold with them, that be great
now, as to giue trewe aduise to them, that may
be great hereafter. Who, if they do, as I wishe them to do,
how great so euer they be now, by blood and other mens
meanes, they shall becum a greate deale greater hereafter, by
learninge, vertue, and their owne desertes: which is trewe praise,
right worthines, and verie Nobilitie in deede. Yet, if som will
needes presse me, that I am to bold with great men, & stray to

Ad Philip. farre from my matter, I will aunswere them with
*S. Paul, siue perc ontētionem, siue quocunq̃ modo,
modò Christus prædicetur, &c.* euen so, whether in place, or out
of place, with my matter, or beside my matter, if I can hereby
either prouoke the good, or staye the ill, I shall thinke my
writing herein well imployed.

But, to cum downe, from greate men, and hier matters, to
my litle children, and poore scholehouse againe, I will, God
willing, go forwarde orderlie, as I purposed, to instructe
Children and yong men, both for learninge and maners.

Hitherto, I haue shewed, what harme, ouermoch feare
bringeth to children : and what hurte, ill companie, and ouermoch libertie breedeth in yougthe : meening thereby, that from
seauen yeare olde, to seauentene, loue is the best allurement to
learninge : from seauentene to seauen and twentie, that wise
men shold carefullie see the steppes of yougthe surelie staide by
good order, in that most slipperie tyme : and speciallie in the
Courte, a place most dangerous for yougthe to liue in, without
great grace, good regarde, and diligent looking to.

Syr *Richard Sackuile*, that worthy Ientleman of worthy

Trauelyng into Ita-lie. memorie, as I sayd in the begynnynge, in the
Queenes priuie Chamber at Windesore, after he
had talked with me, for the right choice of a good

witte in a child for learnyng, and of the trewe difference betwixt quicke and hard wittes, of alluring yong children by ientlenes to loue learnyng, and of the speciall care that was to be had, to keepe yong men from licencious liuyng, he was most earnest with me, to haue me say my mynde also, what I thought, concernyng the fansie that many yong Ientlemen of England haue to trauell abroad, and namely to lead a long lyfe in Italie. His request, both for his authoritie, and good will toward me, was a sufficient commaundement vnto me, to satisfie his pleasure, with vtteryng plainlie my opinion in that matter. Syr quoth I, I take goyng thither, and liuing there, for a yonge ientleman, that doth not goe vnder the kepe and garde of such a man, as both, by wisedome can, and authoritie dare rewle him, to be meruelous dangerous. And whie I said so than, I will declare at large now: which I said than priuatelie, and write now openlie, not bicause I do contemne, either the knowledge of strange and diuerse tonges, and namelie the Italian tonge, which next the Greeke and Latin   The Italian tong. tonge, I like and loue aboue all other: or else bicause I do despise, the learning that is gotten, or the experience that is gathered in strange contries: or for any priuate malice that beare to Italie: which contrie, and in it, namelie Rome, I haue alwayes speciallie   Italia. honored: bicause, tyme was, whan Italie and   Roma. Rome, haue bene, to the greate good of vs that now liue, the best breeders and bringers vp, of the worthiest men, not onelie for wise speakinge, but also for well doing, in all Ciuill affaires, that euer was in the worlde. But now, that tyme is gone, and though the place remayne, yet the olde and present maners, do differ as farre, as blacke and white, as vertue and vice. Vertue once made that contrie Mistres ouer all the worlde. Vice now maketh that contrie slaue to them, that before, were glad to serue it. All men seeth it: They themselues confesse it, namelie soch, as be best and wisest amongest them. For sinne, by lust and vanitie, hath and doth breed vp euery where, common contēpt of Gods word, priuate contention in many families, open factions in euery Citie: and so, makyng them selues bonde, to vanitie and vice at home, they are content to beare the yoke of seruyng straungers abroad. *Italie* now, is not that *Italie*, that it was wont to be: and therfore now, not so fitte a place, as some do counte it, for yong men to fetch either wisedome or honestie from thence. For surelie, they will make other but bad Scholers, that be so ill Masters to them selues. Yet, if a ientleman will nedes trauell into *Italie*, he shall do well, to looke on the life, of the wisest traueler, that euer traueled thether, set out by the wisest writer, that euer spake with tong, Gods doctrine onelie excepted : and that is *Vlysses* in

Vlysses. *Homere. Vlysses*, and his trauell, I wishe our
Homere. trauelers to looke vpon, not so much to feare
them, with the great daungers, that he many tymes suffered, as to instruct them, with his excellent wisedome, which he alwayes and euerywhere vsed. Yea euen those, that be learned and wittie trauelers, when they be disposed to prayse traueling, as a great commendacion, and the best Scripture they haue for it, they gladlie recite the third verse of *Homere*, in his first booke of *Odyssea*, conteinyng a great prayse of *Vlysses*, for

ὀδυς. α. the witte he gathered, & wisedome he vsed in
his traueling.

 Which verse, bicause, in mine opinion, it was not made at the first, more naturallie in *Greke* by *Homere*, nor after turned more aptelie into *Latin* by *Horace*, than it was a good while ago, in *Cambrige*, translated into English, both plainlie for the sense, and roundlie for the verse, by one of the best Scholers, that euer S. Iohns Colledge bred, *M. Watson*, myne old frend, somtime Bishop of Lincolne, therfore, for their sake, that haue lust to see, how our English tong, in auoidyng barbarous ryming, may as well receiue, right quantitie of sillables, and trewe order of versifiyng (of which matter more at large hereafter) as either *Greke* or *Latin*, if a cunning man haue it in handling, I will set forth that one verse in all three tonges, for an Example to good wittes, that shall delite in like learned exercise.

Homerus.

πολλῶν δ᾽ ἀνθρώπων ἴδεν ἄστεα καὶ νόον ἔγνω.

Horatius.

Qui mores hominum multorum vidit & vrbes.

M. Watson.

All trauellers do gladly report great prayse of Vlysses,
For that he knew many mens maners, and saw many Cities.

And yet is not *Vlysses* commended, so much, nor so oft, in *Homere*, bicause he was πολύτροπος, that is, skilfull in many mēs manners and facions, as bicause he was πολύμητις, that is, wise in all *Vlyss.* {πολύτροπος. πολύμητις.

purposes, & ware in all places : which wisedome and warenes will not serue neither a traueler, except *Pallas* be always at his elbow, that is Gods speciall grace *Pallas* from from heauen, to kepe him in Gods feare, in all heauen. his doynges, in all his ieorneye. For, he shall not always in his absence out of England, light vpon a ientle *Alcynous*, and walke in his faire gardens *Alcynous.* δδ. 2. full of all harmelesse pleasures : but he shall sometymes, fall, either into the handes of some cruell *Cyclops*, or into the lappe of some wanton *Cyclops.* δδ. ι. and dalying Dame *Calypso* : and so suffer the *Calypso.* δδ. ε. danger of many a deadlie Denne, not so full of perils, to distroy the body, as, full of vayne pleasures, to poyson the mynde. Some *Siren* *Sirenes.* shall sing him a song, sweete in tune, but sownding in the ende, to his vtter destruction. δδ. μ. If *Scylla* drowne him not, *Carybdis* may fortune *Scylla.* swalow hym. Some *Circes* shall make him, of *Caribdis.* a plaine English man, a right *Italian.* *Circes.* δδ. κ. And at length to hell, or to some hellish place, is he likelie to go : from whence is hard returning, although one *Vlysses*, and that by *Pallas* ayde, and good coūsell of *Tiresias* once δδ. λ. escaped that horrible Den of deadly darkenes.

Therfore, if wise men will nedes send their sonnes into *Italie*, let them do it wiselie, vnder the kepe and garde of him, who, by his wisedome and honestie, by his example and authoritie, may be hable to kepe them safe and sound, in the feare of God, in Christes trewe Religion, in good order and honestie of liuyng : except they will haue them run headling, into ouermany ieoperdies, as *Vlysses* had done many tymes, if *Pallas* had not always gouerned him : if he had not vsed, to stop his eares with waxe : to bind him selfe to δδ. μ. the mast of his shyp : to feede dayly, vpon that δδ. κ. swete herbe *Moly* with the blake roote and Moly Her- white floore, giuen vnto hym by Mercurie, to ba. auoide all the inchantmētes of *Circes.* Wherby, the Diuine

Poete *Homer* ment couertlie (as wise and Godly men do iudge)
that loue of honestie, and hatred of ill, which
Psal. 33. *Dauid* more plainly doth call the feare of God:
the onely remedie agaynst all inchantementes of sinne.

I know diuerse noble personages, and many worthie Ientlemen of England, whom all the *Siren* songes of *Italie*, could
neuer vntwyne from the maste of Gods word: nor no inchant-
ment of vanitie, ouerturne them, from the feare of God, and
loue of honestie.

But I know as many, or mo, and some, sometyme my
deare frendes, for whose sake I hate going into that coūtrey the
more, who, partyng out of England feruent in the loue of
Christes doctrine, and well furnished with the feare of God,
returned out of *Italie* worse transformed, than euer was any in
Circes Court. I know diuerse, that went out of England, men
of innocent life, men of excellent learnyng, who returned out
of *Italie*, not onely with worse maners, but also with lesse
learnyng: neither so willing to liue orderly, nor yet so hable to
speake learnedlie, as they were at home, before they went
abroad. And why? *Plato*, yᵗ wise writer, and worthy
traueler him selfe, telleth the cause why. He went into *Sicilia*,
a coūtrey, no nigher *Italy* by site of place, thā *Italie* that is
now, is like *Sicilia* that was thē, in all corrupt maners and
licēciousnes of life. *Plato* found in *Sicilia*, euery Citie full of
vanitie, full of factions, euen as *Italie* is now. And as *Homere*,
like a learned Poete, doth feyne, that *Circes*, by pleasant inchantmētes, did turne men into beastes, some into Swine, som
into Asses, some into Foxes, some into Wolues etc. euen so
Plat. ad *Plato*, like a wise Philosopher, doth plainelie
Dionys. declare, that pleasure, by licentious vanitie, that
Epist. 3. sweete and perilous poyson of all youth, doth
ingender in all those, that yeld vp themselues to her, foure
notorious properties.

The fruits
of vayne
pleasure.
{
1. λήθην
2. δυσμαθίαν
3. ἀφροσύνην
4. ὕβριν.
}

The first, forgetfulnes of all good thinges learned before:
Causes the second, dulnes to receyue either learnyng or
why men honestie euer after: the third, a mynde embracing

lightlie the worse opinion, and baren of discretion
to make trewe difference betwixt good and ill,
betwixt troth, and vanitie, the fourth, a proude
disdainfulnes of other good mē, in all honest
matters. *Homere* and *Plato*, haue both one
meanyng, looke both to one end. For, if a mā
inglutte himself with vanitie, or walter in filthines like a Swyne, all learnyng, all goodnes, is
sone forgotten : Than, quicklie shall he becum
a dull Asse, to vnderstand either learnyng or
honestie : and yet shall he be as sutle as a Foxe,
in breedyng of mischief, in bringyng in misorder,
with a busie head, a discoursing tōg, and a factious harte, in
euery priuate affaire, in all matters of state, with this pretie
propertie, always glad to commend the worse
partie, and euer ready to defend the falser
opiniō. And why? For, where will is giuē
from goodnes to vanitie, the mynde is sone caryed from right
iudgement, to any fond opinion, in Religion, in Philosophie, or
any other kynde of learning. The fourth fruite of vaine
pleasure, by *Homer* and *Platos* iudgement, is pride
in them selues, contempt of others, the very
badge of all those that serue in *Circes* Court. The trewe
meenyng of both *Homer* and *Plato*, is plainlie declared in one
short sentence of the holy Prophet of God
Hieremie, crying out of the vaine & vicious life
of the *Israelites*. This people (sayth he) be
fooles and dulhedes to all goodnes, but sotle, cunning and
bolde, in any mischiefe. &c.

The true medicine against the inchantmentes of *Circes*,
the vanitie of licencious pleasure, the inticementes of all sinne,
is, in *Homere*, the herbe *Moly*, with the blacke roote, and white
flooer, sower at the first, but sweete in the end : which,
Hesiodus termeth the study of vertue, hard and
irksome in the beginnyng, but in the end, easie
and pleasant. And that, which is most to be
marueled at, the diuine Poete *Homere* sayth plainlie that this
medicine against sinne and vanitie, is not found
out by man, but giuen and taught by God. And
for some one sake, that will haue delite to read

Side notes:
returne out
of Italie,
lesse lear-
ned and
worse ma-
nered.

Homer and
Plato ioy-
ned and ex-
pounded.

A Swyne.
An Asse.
A Foxe.

ἀφροσύνη,
Quid, et
vnde.

ὕβρις.

Hieremias
4. Cap.

Hesiodus
de virtute.

Homerus,
diuinus
Poeta.

that sweete and Godlie Verse, I will recite the very wordes of
Homere and also turne them into rude English metre.

χαλεπὸν δέ τ᾿ ὀρύσσειν
ἀνδράσι γε θνητοῖσι, θεοὶ δέ τε πάντα δύνανται.

In English thus.

No mortall mā, with sweat of browe, or toile of minde,
But onely God, who can do all, that herbe doth finde.

Plato also, that diuine Philosopher, hath many Godly
medicines agaynst the poyson of vayne pleasure, in many
places, but specially in his Epistles to *Dionisius* the tyrant of
Sicilie: yet agaynst those, that will nedes becum
beastes, with seruyng of *Circes*, the Prophet
Dauid, crieth most loude, *Nolite fieri sicut equus et
mulus*: and by and by giueth the right medicine, the trewe herbe *Moly*, *In camo & freno maxillas
eorum constringe*, that is to say, let Gods grace be the bitte,
let Gods feare be the bridle, to stay them from runnyng headlong into vice, and to turne them into the right way agayne.

Dauid in the second Psalme after, giueth the
same medicine, but in these plainer wordes,
Diuerte à malo, & fac bonum. But I am affraide, that ouer
many of our trauelers into *Italie*, do not exchewe the way to
Circes Court: but go, and ryde, and runne, and flie thether,
they make great hast to cum to her: they make great sute to
serue her: yea, I could point out some with my finger, that
neuer had gone out of England, but onelie to serue *Circes*, in
Italie. Vanitie and vice, and any licence to ill liuyng in
England was counted stale and rude vnto them. And so, beyng
Mules and Horses before they went, returned verie Swyne and
Asses home agayne: yet euerie where verie Foxes with suttle
and busie heades; and where they may, verie
wolues, with cruell malicious hartes. A meruelous monster, which, for filthines of liuyng, for
dulnes to learning him selfe, for wilinesse in
dealing with others, for malice in hurting without
cause, should carie at once in one bodie, the belie of a Swyne,
the head of an Asse, the brayne of a Foxe, the wombe of
a wolfe. If you thinke, we iudge amisse, and write to sore

*Plat. ad
Dio.*

Psal. 32.

Psal. 33.

A trewe
Picture of
a knight of
Circes
Court.

against you, heare, what the *Italian* sayth of the English man, what the master reporteth of the scholer: who vttereth playnlie, what is taught by him, and what learned by you, saying, *Englese Italianato, e vn diabolo incarnato,* that is to say, you remaine men in shape and facion, but becum deuils in life and condition.   This is not, the opinion of one, The Ita-
liãs iudge-
ment of
Englishmē
brought vp
in Italie.

for some priuate spite, but the iudgement of all, in a common Prouerbe, which riseth, of that learnyng, and those maners, which you gather in *Italie*: a good Scholehouse of wholesome doctrine : and worthy Masters of commendable Scholers, where the Master had rather diffame hym selfe for hys teachyng, than not shame his Scholer for his learning.   A good nature of the maister, and faire conditions of the The Ita-
lian diffa-
meth him
selfe, to
shame the
Englishe
man.

scholers.   And now chose you, you *Italian* English men, whether you will be angrie with vs, for calling you monsters, or with the *Italianes*, for callyng you deuils, or else with your owne selues, that take so much paines, and go so farre, to make your selues both.   If some yet do not well vnder-stand, what is an English man Italianated, I will plainlie tell him.   He, that by liuing, & traueling in *Italie*, bringeth home into Englãd out of *Italie*, An Eng-
lish man
Italiana-
ted.

the Religion, the learning, the policie, the experiēce, the maners of *Italie*.   That is to say, for Religion, Papistrie or worse : for learnyng, lesse commonly than they caried out with them : for pollicie, a factious hart, a discoursing head, a mynde to medle in all mens matters : for experience, plentie of new mischieues neuer knowne in England before : for maners, varietie of vanities, and chaunge of

The
1 Religion.
2 Learn-
   ing.
3 Pollicie.
4 Experi-
   ence.
5 Maners.
} gotten in
Italie.

filthy lyuing.   These be the inchantementes of *Circes*, brought out of *Italie*, to marre mens maners in England: much, by example of ill life, but more by preceptes of fonde bookes, of late translated out of *Italian* into English, sold in euery shop in London, com-mended by honest titles the soner to corrupt *Italian*
bokes trãs-
lated into
English.

honest maners : dedicated ouer boldlie to vertuous and honor-

able personages, the easielier to begile simple and innocēt wittes.
It is pitie, that those, which haue authoritie and charge, to allow and dissalow bookes to be printed, be no more circumspect herein, than they are. Ten Sermons at Paules Crosse do not so moch good for mouyng mē to trewe doctrine, as one of those bookes do harme, with inticing men to ill liuing. Yea, I say farder, those bookes, tend not so moch to corrupt honest liuyng, as they do, to subuert trewe Religion. Mo Papistes be made, by your mery bookes of *Italie*, than by your earnest bookes of *Louain*. And bicause our great Phisicians, do winke at the matter, and make no counte of this sore, I, though not admitted one of their felowshyp, yet hauyng bene many yeares a prentice to Gods trewe Religion, and trust to continewe a poore iorney man therein all dayes of my life, for the dewtie I owe, & loue I beare, both to trewe doctrine, and honest liuing, though I haue no authoritie to amend the sore my selfe, yet I will declare my good will, to discouer the sore to others.

S. Paul saith, that sectes and ill opinions, be the workes of the flesh, and frutes of sinne, this is spoken, no more trewlie for the doctrine, than sensiblie for the reason. And why? For, ill doinges, breed ill thinkinges. And of corrupted maners, spryng peruerted iudgementes. And

Ad Gal. 5.

Voluntas ⎫ ⎧ Bonum.
            ⎬ Respicit ⎨
Mens   ⎭ ⎩ Verum.

how? there be in man two speciall thinges: Mans will, mans mynde. Where will inclineth to goodnes, the mynde is bent to troth: Where will is caried from goodnes to vanitie, the mynde is sone drawne from troth to false opinion. And so, the readiest way to entangle the mynde with false doctrine, is first to intice the will to wanton liuyng. Therfore, when the busie and open Papistes abroad, could not, by their contentious bookes, turne men in England fast enough, from troth and right iudgement in doctrine, than the sutle and secrete Papistes at home, procured bawdie bookes to be translated out of the *Italian* tonge, whereby ouer many yong willes and wittes allured to wantonnes, do now boldly contemne all seuere bookes that sounde to honestie and godlines. In our forefathers tyme, whan Papistrie, as a standyng poole, couered and ouerflowed all England, fewe bookes were read in our tong, sauyng certaine bookes of Cheualrie, as they sayd, for pastime and pleasure, which, as some say, were made in Monasteries, by idle Monkes, or wanton Chanons: as one for example, *Morte Arthure*: the whole pleasure of which booke standeth in two speciall poyntes,

in open mans slaughter, and bold bawdrye: In which booke those be counted the noblest Knightes, that do kill most men without any quarell, and commit fowlest aduoulteries by sutlest shiftes: as Sir *Launcelote*, with the wife of king *Arthure* his master: Syr *Tristram* with the wife of king *Marke* his vncle: Syr *Lamerocke* with the wife of king *Lote*, that was his own aunte. This is good stuffe, for wise men to laughe at, or honest men to take pleasure at. Yet I know, when Gods Bible was banished the Court, and *Morte Arthure* receiued into the Princes chamber. What toyes, the dayly readyng of such a booke, may worke in the will of a yong ientleman, or a yong mayde, that liueth welthelie and idlelie, wise men can iudge, and honest mē do pitie. And yet ten *Morte Arthures* do not the tenth part so much harme, as one of these bookes, made in *Italie*, and translated in England. They open, not fond and common wayes to vice, but such subtle, cunnyng, new, and diuerse shiftes, to cary yong willes to vanitie, and yong wittes to mischief, to teach old bawdes new schole poyntes, as the simple head of an English man is not hable to inuent, nor neuer was hard of in England before, yea when Papistrie ouerflowed all. Suffer these bookes to be read, and they shall soone displace all bookes of godly learnyng. For they, carying the will to vanitie, and marryng good maners, shall easily corrupt the mynde with ill opinions, and false iudgement in doctrine: first, to thinke ill of all trewe Religion, and at last to thinke nothyng of God hym selfe, one speciall pointe that is to be learned in *Italie*, and *Italian* bookes. And that which is most to be lamented, and therfore more nedefull to be looked to, there be moe of these vngratious bookes set out in Printe within these fewe monethes, than haue bene sene in England many score yeare before. And bicause our English men made *Italians*, can not hurt, but certaine persons, and in certaine places, therfore these *Italian* bookes are made English, to bryng mischief enough openly and boldly, to all states great and meane, yong and old, euery where.

And thus yow see, how will intised to wantonnes, doth easelie allure the mynde to false opinions: and how corrupt maners in liuinge, breede false iudgement in doctrine: how sinne and fleshlines, bring forth sectes and heresies: And therefore suffer not vaine bookes to breede vanitie in mens willes, if yow would haue Goddes trothe take roote in mens myndes.

That Italian, that first inuented the Italian Prouerbe against our Englishe men Italianated, ment no more their vanitie in liuing, than their lewd opinion in Religion. For, in calling them Deuiles, he carieth them cleane from God: and yet he carieth them no farder, than they willinglie go themselues, that is, where they may freely say their mindes, to the open contempte of God and all godlines, both in liuing and doctrine.

The Italian prouerbe expounded.

And how? I will expresse how, not by a Fable of *Homere*, nor by the Philosophie of *Plato*, but by a plaine troth of Goddes word, sensiblie vttered by *Dauid* thus. Thies men, *abhominabiles facti in studijs suis*, thinke verily, and singe gladlie the verse before, *Dixit insipiens in Corde suo, non est Deus:* that is to say, they geuing themselues vp to vanitie, shakinge of the motions of Grace, driuing from them the feare of God, and running headlong into all sinne, first, lustelie contemne God, than scornefullie mocke his worde, and also spitefullie hate and hurte all well willers thereof. Than they haue in more reuerence, the triumphes of Petrarche: than the Genesis of Moses: They make more accounte of *Tullies* offices, than *S. Paules* epistles: of a tale in *Bocace*, than a storie of the Bible. Than they counte as Fables, the holie misteries of Christian Religion. They make Christ and his Gospell, onelie serue Ciuill pollicie: Than neyther Religion cummeth amisse to them: In tyme they be Promoters of both openlie: in place againe mockers of both priuilie, as I wrote once in a rude ryme.

Psa. 14.

Now new, now olde, now both, now neither,
To serue the worldes course, they care not with whether.

For where they dare, in cumpanie where they like, they

boldlie laughe to scorne both protestant and Papist. They care for no scripture: They make no coūte of generall councels : they contēne the consent of the Chirch: They passe for no Doctores: They mocke the Pope: They raile on *Luther*: They allow neyther side : They like none, but onelie themselues : The marke they shote at, the ende they looke for, the heauen they desire, is onelie, their owne present pleasure, and priuate proffit: whereby, they plainlie declare, of whose schole, of what Religion they be: that is, Epicures in liuing, and ἄθεοι in doctrine: this last worde, is no more vnknowne now to plaine Englishe men, than the Person was vnknown somtyme in England, vntill som Englishe man tooke peines, to fetch that deuelish opinion out of Italie. Thies men, thus Italianated abroad, can not abide our Godlie Italian Chirch at home: they be not of that Parish, they be not of that felowshyp: they like not yᵗ preacher: they heare not his sermons: Excepte somtymes for cōpanie, they cum thither, to heare the Italian tonge naturally spoken, not to hear Gods doctrine trewly preached.

The Ita-
liā Chirche
in London.

And yet, thies men, in matters of Diuinitie, openlie pretend a great knowledge, and haue priuatelie to them selues, a verie compendious vnderstanding of all, which neuertheles they will vtter when and where they liste: And that is this: All the misteries of *Moses*, the whole lawe and Cerimonies, the Psalmes and Prophetes, Christ and his Gospell, G O D and the Deuill, Heauen and Hell, Faith, Conscience, Sinne, Death, and all they shortlie wrap vp, they quickly expounde with this one halfe verse of *Horace*.

Credat Iudæus Appella.

Yet though in Italie they may freely be of no Religion, as they are in Englande in verie deede to, neuerthelesse returning home into England they must countenance the profession of the one or the other, howsoeuer inwardlie, they laugh to scorne both. And though, for their priuate matters they can follow, fawne, and flatter noble Personages, contrarie to them in all respectes, yet commonlie they allie themselues with the worst Papistes, to whom they be wedded, and do well agree togither in three proper opinions: In open contempte of Goddes worde: in a secret securitie of sinne: and in

Papistrie
and impie-
tie agree in
three opini-
ons.

a bloodie desire to haue all taken away, by sword or burning,
that be not of their faction. They that do
Pigius.   read, with indifferent iudgement, *Pygius* and
Machiaue-   *Machiauel*, two indifferent Patriarches of thies
lus.   two Religions, do know full well that I say trewe.

Ye see, what manners and doctrine, our Englishe men fetch
out of Italie: For finding no other there, they can bring no
Wise and   other hither. And therefore, manie godlie and
honest tra-   excellent learned Englishe men, not manie yeares
uelers.   ago, did make a better choice, whan open crueltie
draue them out of this contrie, to place themselues there, where
Germanie.   Christes doctrine, the feare of God, punishment
of sinne, and discipline of honestie, were had in
speciall regarde.

I was once in Italie my selfe: but I thanke God, my
abode there, was but ix. dayes: And yet I sawe
Venice.   in that litle tyme, in one Citie, more libertie to
sinne, than euer I hard tell of in our noble Citie of London in
ix. yeare. I sawe, it was there, as free to sinne,
London.   not onelie without all punishment, but also
without any mans marking, as it is free in the Citie of London,
to chose, without all blame, whether a man lust to weare Shoo
or pantocle. And good cause why: For being vnlike in troth
of Religion, they must nedes be vnlike in honestie of liuing.
Seruice of   For blessed be Christ, in our Citie of London,
God in   commonlie the commandementes of God, be more
England.   diligentlie taught, and the seruice of God more
reuerentlie vsed, and that daylie in many priuate mens houses,
Seruice of   than they be in Italie once a weeke in their
God in I-   common Chirches : where, masking Ceremonies,
talie.   to delite the eye, and vaine soundes, to please
the eare, do quite thrust out of the Chirches, all seruice of
The Lord   God in spirit and troth. Yea, the Lord Maior
Maior of   of London, being but a Ciuill officer, is com-
London.   monlie for his tyme, more diligent, in punishing
sinne, the bent enemie against God and good order, than all
The In-   the bloodie Inquisitors in Italie be in seauen yeare.
quisitors in   For, their care and charge is, not to punish
Italie   sinne, not to amend manners, not to purge
doctrine, but onelie to watch and ouersee that Christes trewe

Religion set no sure footing, where the Pope hath any Iurisdiction. I learned, when I was at *Venice*, that there it is counted good pollicie, when there be foure or fiue brethren of one familie, one, onelie to marie :   An ungod-
all the rest, to waulter, with as litle shame, in   lie pollicie.
open lecherie, as Swyne do here in the common myre. Yea, there be as fayre houses of Religion, as great prouision, as diligent officers, to kepe vp this misorder, as Bridewell is, and all the Masters there, to kepe downe misorder. And therefore, if the Pope himselfe, do not onelie graunt pardons to furder thies wicked purposes abrode in Italie, but also (although this present Pope, in the beginning, made som shewe of misliking thereof) assigne both meede and merite to the maintenance of stewes and brothelhouses at home in Rome, than let wise men thinke Italie a safe place for holsom doctrine, and godlie manners, and a fitte schole for yong ientlemen of England to be brought vp in.

Our Italians bring home with them other faultes from Italie, though not so great as this of Religion, yet a great deale greater, thā many good men can well beare. For commonlie they cum home, common contemners of mariage and readie persuaders of all other to the same :   Contempt
not because they loue virginitie, nor yet because   of mariage.
they hate prettie yong virgines, but, being free in Italie, to go whither so euer lust will cary them, they do not like, that lawe and honestie should be soch a barre to their like libertie at home in England. And yet they be, the greatest makers of loue, the daylie daliers, with such pleasant wordes, with such smilyng and secret countenances, with such signes, tokens, wagers, purposed to be lost, before they were purposed to be made, with bargaines of wearing colours, floures, and herbes, to breede occasion of ofter meeting of him and her, and bolder talking of this and that &c. And although I haue seene some, innocent of all ill, and stayde in all honestie, that haue vsed these thinges without all harme, without all suspicion of harme, yet these knackes were brought first into England by them, that learned thē before in *Italie* in *Circes* Court: and how Courtlie curtesses so euer they be counted now, yet, if the meaning and maners of some that do vse them, were somewhat

amended, it were no great hurt, neither to them selues, nor to others.

An other propertie of this our English *Italians* is, to be meruelous singular in all their matters: Singular in knowledge, ignorant of nothyng: So singular in wisedome (in their owne opinion) as scarse they counte the best Counsellor the Prince hath, comparable with them: Common discoursers of all matters: busie searchers of most secret affaires: open flatterers of great men: priuie mislikers of good men: Faire speakers, with smiling countenãces, and much curtessie openlie to all men. Ready bakbiters, sore nippers, and spitefull reporters priuilie of good men. And beyng brought vp in *Italie*, in some free Citie, as all Cities be there: where a man may freelie discourse against what he will, against whom he lust: against any Prince, agaynst any gouernement, yea against God him selfe, and his whole Religion: where he must be, either *Guelphe* or *Gibiline*, either *French* or *Spanish*: and always compelled to be of some partie, of some faction, he shall neuer be compelled to be of any Religion: And if he medle not ouer much with Christes true Religion, he shall haue free libertie to embrace all Religions, and becum, if he lust at once, without any let or punishment, Iewish, Turkish, Papish, and Deuillish.

A yong Ientleman, thus bred vp in this goodly schole, to learne the next and readie way to sinne, to haue a busie head, a factious hart, a talkatiue tonge, fed with discoursing of factions: led to contemne God and his Religion, shall cum home into England, but verie ill taught, either to be an honest man him self, a quiet subiect to his Prince, or willyng to serue God, vnder the obedience of trewe doctrine, or within the order of honest liuing.

I know, none will be offended with this my generall writing, but onelie such, as finde them selues giltie priuatelie therin: who shall haue good leaue to be offended with me, vntill they begin to amende them selues. I touch not them that be good: and I say to litle of them that be nought. And so, though not enough for their deseruing, yet sufficientlie for this time, and more els when, if occasion so require.

And thus farre haue I wandred from my first purpose of teaching a child, yet not altogether out of the way, bicause this whole taulke hath tended to the onelie aduauncement of trothe in Religion, and honestie of liuing: and hath bene wholie within the compasse of learning and good maners, the speciall pointes belonging in the right bringyng vp of youth.

But to my matter, as I began, plainlie and simplie
with my yong Scholer, so will I not leaue him,
God willing, vntill I haue brought him a perfite Scholer out of the Schole, and placed
him in the Vniuersitie, to becum a fitte
student, for Logicke and Rhetoricke:
and so after to Phisicke, Law, or
Diuinitie, as aptnes of nature, aduise of frendes, and
Gods   disposition   shall
lead him.

The ende of the first booke.

✒ *The second booke.*

AFter that your scholer, as I sayd before, shall cum in
deede, first, to a readie perfitnes in translating, than, to a
ripe and skilfull choice in markyng out hys six pointes, as,

1. *Proprium.*
2. *Translatum.*
3. *Synonymum.*
4. *Contrarium.*
5. *Diuersum.*
6. *Phrases.*

Than take this order with him: Read dayly vnto him,
some booke of *Tullie,* as the third booke of
Epistles chosen out by *Sturmius, de Amicitia,*
de *Senectute,* or that excellent Epistle conteinyng almost the
whole first booke *ad Q. fra*: some Comedie of
Terence or *Plautus*: but in *Plautus,* skilfull choice
must be vsed by the master, to traine his Scholler
to a iudgement, in cutting out perfitelie ouer old and vnproper
wordes: *Cæs. Commentaries* are to be read with
all curiositie, in specially without all exception to
be made, either by frende or foe, is seene, the vnspotted
proprietie of the Latin tong, euen whan it was, as the *Grecians*
say, in ἀκμῇ, that is, at the hiest pitch of all perfitenesse: or
some Orations of *T. Liuius,* such as be both longest
and plainest.

These bookes, I would haue him read now, a good deale at
euery lecture: for he shall not now vse dalie translation, but
onely construe againe, and parse, where ye suspect, is any nede:
yet, let him not omitte in these bookes, his former exercise, in

Cicero.

Terentius.
Plautus.

Iul. Cæsar.

T. Liuius.

marking diligently, and writyng orderlie out his six pointes.
And for translating, vse you your selfe, euery second or thyrd
day, to chose out, some Epistle *ad Atticum*, some notable
common place out of his Orations, or some other part of
Tullie, by your discretion, which your scholer may not know
where to finde: and translate it you your selfe, into plaine
naturall English, and than giue it him to translate into Latin
againe: allowyng him good space and tyme to do it, both with
diligent heede, and good aduisement. Here his witte shalbe
new set on worke: his iudgement, for right choice, trewlie
tried: his memorie, for sure reteyning, better exercised, than
by learning, any thing without the booke: & here, how much
he hath proffited, shall plainly appeare. Whan he bringeth it
translated vnto you, bring you forth the place of *Tullie*: lay
them together: compare the one with the other: commend his
good choice, & right placing of wordes: Shew his faultes iently,
but blame them not ouer sharply: for, of such missings, ientlie
admonished of, proceedeth glad & good heed taking: of good
heed taking, springeth chiefly knowledge, which after, groweth
to perfitnesse, if this order, be diligentlie vsed by the scholer &
iently handled by the master: for here, shall all the hard
pointes of Grāmer, both easely and surelie be learned vp:
which, scholers in common scholes, by making of Latines, be
groping at, with care & feare, & yet in many yeares, they
scarse can reach vnto them. I remember, whan I was yong,
in the North, they went to the Grammer schole, litle children:
they came from thence great lubbers: always learning, and
litle profiting: learning without booke, euery thing, vnder-
stādyng within the booke, litle or nothing: Their whole
knowledge, by learning without the booke, was tied onely to
their tong & lips, and neuer ascēded vp to the braine & head,
and therfore was sone spitte out of the mouth againe: They
were, as men, alwayes goyng, but euer out of the way: and
why? For their whole labor, or rather great toyle without
order, was euen vaine idlenesse without proffit. In deed,
they tooke great paynes about learning: but employed small
labour in learning: Whan by this way prescribed in this
booke, being streight, plaine, & easie, the scholer is alwayes
laboring with pleasure, and euer going right on forward with
proffit: Always laboring I say, for, or he haue cōstrued

parced, twise trãslated ouer by good aduisemēt, marked out his six pointes by skilfull iudgement, he shall haue necessarie occasion, to read ouer euery lecture, a dosen tymes, at the least. Which, bicause he shall do alwayes in order, he shall do it alwayes with pleasure: And pleasure allureth loue: loue hath lust to labor: labor alwayes obteineth his purpose, as most

Rhet. 2
In Oedip. Tyr.
Epist. lib. 7.

trewly, both *Aristotle* in his Rhetoricke & *Oedipus* in *Sophocles* do teach, saying, πᾶν γὰρ ἐκπονού-μενον ἅλισκε. *et cet.* & this oft reading, is the verie right folowing, of that good Counsell, which *Plinie* doth geue to his frende *Fuscus*, saying, *Multum, non multa.* But to my purpose againe:

Whan, by this diligent and spedie reading ouer, those forenamed good bokes of *Tullie, Terence, Cæsar,* and *Liuie,* and by this second kinde of translating out of your English, tyme shall breed skill, and vse shall bring perfection, than ye may trie, if you will, your scholer, with the third kinde of translation: although the two first wayes, by myne opinion, be, not onelie sufficent of them selues, but also surer, both for the Masters teaching, and scholers learnyng, than this third way is: Which is thus. Write you in English, some letter, as it were from him to his father, or to some other frende, naturallie, according to the disposition of the child, or some tale, or fable, or plaine narration, according as *Aphthonius* beginneth his exercises of learning, and let him translate it into Latin againe, abiding in soch place, where no other scholer may prompe him. But yet, vse you your selfe soch discretion for choice therein, as the matter may be within the compas, both for wordes and sentences, of his former learning and reading. And now take heede, lest your scholer do not better in some point, than you your selfe, except ye haue bene diligentlie exercised in these kindes of translating before:

I had once a profe hereof, tried by good experience, by a deare frende of myne, whan I came first from Cambrige, to serue the Queenes Maiestie, than Ladie *Elizabeth,* lying at worthie Syr *Ant. Denys* in Cheston. *Iohn Whitneye,* a yong ientleman, was my bedfeloe, who willyng by good nature and prouoked by mine aduise, began to learne the Latin tong, after the order declared in this booke. We began after Christmas: I read vnto him *Tullie de Amicitia,* which he did euerie day twise translate, out of Latin into English, and out of English into Latin agayne. About S. Laurence tyde after, to proue how he proffited, I did chose out *Torquatus* taulke *de Amicitia*, in the later end of the first booke *de finib.* bicause that place was, the same in matter, like in wordes and phrases, nigh to the forme and facion of sentences, as he had learned before in *de Amicitia.* I did translate it my selfe into plaine English, and gaue it him to turne into Latin : Which he did, so choislie, so orderlie, so without any great misse in the hardest pointes of Grammer, that some, in seuen yeare in Grammer scholes, yea, & some in the Vniuersities to, can not do halfe so well. This worthie yong Ientleman, to my greatest grief, to the great lamentation of that whole house, and speciallie to that most noble Ladie, now Queene *Elizabeth* her selfe, departed within few dayes, out of this world.

And if in any cause, a man may without offence of God speake somewhat vngodlie, surely, it was some grief vnto me, to see him hie so hastlie to God, as he did. A Court, full of soch yong Ientlemen, were rather a Paradise than a Court vpon earth. And though I had neuer Poeticall head, to make any verse, in any tong, yet either loue, or sorow, or both, did wring out of me than, certaine carefull thoughtes of my good will towardes him, which in my murning for him, fell forth, more by chance, than either by skill or vse, into this kinde of misorderlie meter.

Myne owne Iohn Whitney, now farewell, now death doth parte vs
  twaine,
No death, but partyng for a while, whom life shall ioyne agayne.
Therfore my hart cease sighes and sobbes, cease sorowes seede to sow,
Wherof no gaine, but greater grief, and hurtfull care may grow.
Yet, whan I thinke vpon soch giftes of grace as God him lent,
My losse, his gaine, I must a while, with ioyfull teares lament.
Yong yeares to yelde soch frute in Court, where seede of vice is sowne,
Is sometime read, in some place seene, amōgst vs seldom knowne.
His life he ledde, Christes lore to learne, with will to worke the
  same :
He read to know, and knew to liue, and liued to praise his name.
So fast to frende, so foe to few, so good to euery weight,
I may well wishe, but scarcelie hope, agayne to haue in sight.

The greater ioye his life to me, his death the greater payne :
His life in Christ so surelie set, doth glad my hearte agayne :
His life so good, his death better, do mingle mirth with care,
My spirit with ioye, my flesh with grief, so deare a frend to spare.
Thus God the good, while they be good, doth take, and leaues vs ill,
That we should mend our sinfull life, in life to tary still.
Thus, we well left, be better reft, in heauen to take his place,
That by like life, and death, at last, we may obteine like grace.
Myne owne Iohn Whiteney agayne fairewell, a while thus parte in
     twaine,
Whom payne doth part in earth, in heauen great ioye shall ioyne
     agayne.

In this place, or I procede farder, I will now declare, by
whose authoritie I am led, and by what reason I am moued, to
thinke, that this way of duble translation out of one tong into
an other, in either onelie, or at least chiefly, to be exercised,
speciallie of youth, for the ready and sure obteining of any
tong.
     There be six wayes appointed by the best learned men, for
the learning of tonges, and encreace of eloquence, as

> 1. *Translatio linguarum.*
> 2. *Paraphrasis.*
> 3. *Metaphrasis.*
> 4. *Epitome.*
> 5. *Imitatio.*
> 6. *Declamatio.*

All theis be vsed, and commended, but in order, and for
respectes : as person, habilitie, place, and tyme shall require.
The fiue last, be fitter, for the Master, than the scholer : for
men, than for children : for the vniuersities, rather than for
Grammer scholes : yet neuerthelesse, which is, fittest in mine
opinion, for our schole, and which is, either wholie to be
refused, or partlie to be vsed for our purpose, I will, by good
authoritie, and some reason, I trust perticularlie of euerie
one, and largelie enough of them all, declare orderlie vnto you.

¶ *Translatio Linguarum.*

Translation, is easie in the beginning for the scholer, and bringeth also moch learning and great iudgement to the Master.   It is most common, and most commendable of all other exercises for youth : most common, for all your constructions in Grammer scholes, be nothing els but translations : but because they be not double translations, as I do require, they bring forth but simple and single commoditie, and bicause also they lacke the daily vse of writing, which is the onely thing that breedeth deepe roote, both in yᵉ witte, for good vnderstanding, and in yᵉ memorie, for sure keeping of all that is learned.   Most commēdable also, & that by yᵉ iudgemēt of all authors, which intreate of theis exercises.
Tullie in the person of *L. Crassus*, whom he   1. de Or.
maketh his example of eloquence and trewe iudgement in learning, doth, not onely praise specially, and chose this way of translation for a yong man, but doth also discommend and refuse his owne former wont, in exercising *Paraphrasin &* *Metaphrasin.   Paraphrasis* is, to take some eloquent Oration, or some notable common place in Latin, and expresse it with other wordes :   *Metaphrasis* is, to take some notable place out of a good Poete, and turn the same sens into meter, or into other wordes in Prose.   *Crassus,* or rather *Tullie,* doth mislike both these wayes, bicause the Author, either Orator or Poete, had chosen out before, the fittest wordes and aptest composition for that matter, and so he, in seeking other, was driuen to vse the worse.

Quintilian also preferreth translation before all other exercises :   yet hauing a lust, to dissent, from   Quint. x.
Tullie (as he doth in very many places, if a man read his Rhetoricke ouer aduisedlie, and that rather of an enuious minde, than of any iust cause) doth greatlie commend *Paraphrasis,* crossing spitefullie *Tullies* iudgement in refusing the same :   and so do *Ramus* and *Talæus* euen at this day in *France* to.   But such singularitie, in dissenting from the best mens iudgementes, in liking onelie their owne opinions, is moch misliked of all them, that ioyne with learning, discretion, and wisedome.   For he, that can neither like *Aristotle* in Logicke and Philosophie, nor *Tullie* in Rhetoricke and

Eloquence, will, from these steppes, likelie enough presume, by like pride, to mount hier, to the misliking of greater matters : that is either in Religion, to haue a dissentious head, or in the common wealth, to haue a factious hart: as I knew one a student in Cambrige, who, for a singularitie, began first to dissent, in the scholes, from *Aristotle*, and sone after became a peruerse *Arrian*, against Christ and all true Religion : and studied diligentlie *Origene*, *Basileus*, and *S. Hierome*, onelie to gleane out of their workes, the pernicious heresies of *Celsus*, *Eunomius*, and *Heluidius*, whereby the Church of Christ, was so poysoned withall.

But to leaue these hye pointes of diuinitie, surelie, in this quiet and harmeles controuersie, for the liking, or misliking of *Paraphrasis* for a yong scholer, euen as far, as *Tullie* goeth beyond *Quintilian*, *Ramus*, and *Talæus*, in perfite Eloquence, euen so moch, by myne opinion, cum they behinde *Tullie*, for trew iudgement in teaching the same.

Plinius Secundus, a wise Senator, of great experiēce, excellentlie learned him selfe, a liberall Patrone of learned men, and the purest writer, in myne opinion, of all his age, I except not *Suetonius*, his two scholemasters *Quintilian* and *Tacitus*, nor yet his most excellent learned Vncle, the Elder *Plinius*, doth expresse in an Epistle to his frende *Fuscus*, many good wayes for order in studie : but he beginneth with translation, and preferreth it to all the rest : and bicause his wordes be notable, I will recite them.

Vtile in primis, vt multi præcipiunt, ex Græco in Latinum, & ex Latino vertere in Græcum : Quo genere exercitationis, proprietas splendorǵ verborum, apta structura sententiarum, figurarum copia & explicandi vis colligitur. Præterea, imitatione optimorum, facultas similia inueniendi paratur : & quæ legentem, fefellissent, transferentem fugere non possunt. Intelligentia ex hoc, & iudicium acquiritur.

Ye perceiue, how *Plinie* teacheth, that by this exercise of double translating, is learned, easely, sensiblie, by litle and litle, not onelie all the hard congruities of Grammer, the choice of

[margin notes:]
* Plinius Secundus. Plinius dedit Quintiliano præceptori suo, in matrimoniũ filiæ, 50000 numũ.

Epist. lib. 7, Epist. 9.

aptest wordes, the right framing of wordes and sentences, cumlines of figures and formes, fitte for euerie matter, and proper for euerie tong, but that which is greater also, in marking dayly, and folowing diligentlie thus, the steppes of the best Autors, like inuention of Argumentes, like order in disposition, like vtterance in Elocution, is ēaselie gathered vp : ~whereby your scholer shall be brought not onelie to like eloquence, but also, to all trewe vnderstanding and right iudgement, both for writing and speaking. And where *Dionys. Halicarnassæus* hath written two excellent bookes, the one, *de deleɛ̃u optimorum verborum,* the which, I feare, is lost, the other, of the right framing of wordes and sentences, which doth remaine yet in Greeke, to the great proffet of all them, that trewlie studie for eloquence, yet this waie of double translating, shall bring the whole proffet of both these bookes to a diligēt scholer, and that easelie and pleasantlie, both for fitte choice of wordes, and apt composition of sentences. And by theis authorities and reasons am I moued to thinke, this waie of double translating, either onelie or chieflie, to be fittest, for the spedy and perfit atteyning of any tong. And for spedy atteyning, I durst venture a good wager, if a scholer, in whom is aptnes, loue, diligence, & constancie, would but translate, after this sorte, one litle booke in *Tullie,* as *de seneɛ̃ute,* with two Epistles, the first *ad Q. fra :* the other *ad lentulum,* the last saue one, in the first booke, that scholer, I say, should cum to a better knowledge in the Latin tong, thā the most part do, that spend foure or fiue yeares, in tossing all the rules of Grammer in common scholes. In deede this one booke with these two Epistles, is not sufficient to affourde all Latin wordes (which is not necessarie for a yong scholer to know) but it is able to furnishe him fully, for all pointes of Grammer, with the right placing ordering, & vse of wordes in all kinde of matter. And why not ? for it is read, that *Dion. Prussæus,* that wise Philosopher, & excellēt orator of all his tyme, did cum to the great learning & vtterance that was in him, by reading and folowing onelie two bookes, *Phædon Platonis,* and *Demosthenes* most notable oration περὶ παραπρεσ-βείας. And a better, and nerer example herein, may be, our most noble Queene *Elizabeth,* who neuer toke yet, Greeke nor Latin Grammer in her hand, after the first declining of a nowne and a verbe, but onely by this double translating of

Demosthenes and *Isocrates* dailie without missing euerie forenone, and likewise som part of Tullie euery afternone, for the space of a yeare or two, hath atteyned to soch a perfite vnderstanding in both the tonges, and to soch a readie vtterance of the latin, and that wyth soch a iudgement, as they be fewe in nomber in both the vniuersities, or els where in England, that be, in both tonges, comparable with her Maiestie. And to conclude in a short rowme, the commodities of double translation, surelie the mynde by dailie marking, first, the cause and matter : than, the wordes and phrases : next, the order and composition : after the reason and argumentes : than the formes and figures of both the tonges : lastelie, the measure and compas of euerie sentence, must nedes, by litle and litle drawe vnto it the like shape of eloquence, as the author doth vse, which is red.

And thus much for double translation.

Paraphrasis.

Paraphrasis, the second point, is not onelie to expresse at large with moe wordes, but to striue and contend (as *Quintilian* saith) to translate the best latin authors, into other latin wordes, as many or thereaboutes.

Lib. x.

This waie of exercise was vsed first by *C. Crabo*, and taken vp for a while, by *L. Crassus*, but sone after, vpon dewe profe thereof, reiected iustlie by *Crassus* and *Cicero* : yet allowed and made sterling agayne by *M. Quintilian* : neuerthelesse, shortlie after, by better assaye, disalowed of his owne scholer *Plinius Secundus*, who termeth it rightlie thus *Audax contentio.* It is a bold comparison in deede, to thinke to say better, than that is best. Soch turning of the best into worse, is much like the turning of good wine, out of a faire sweete flagon of siluer, into a foule mustie bottell of ledder : or, to turne pure gold and siluer, into foule brasse and copper.

Soch kinde of *Paraphrasis*, in turning, chopping, and changing, the best to worse, either in the mynte or scholes, (though *M. Brokke* and *Quintilian* both say the contrary) is moch misliked of the best and wisest men. I can better allow an other kinde of *Paraphrasis*, to turne rude and barbarus, into proper and eloquent : which neuerthelesse is an exercise, not fitte for a scholer, but for a perfite master, who in plentie hath good choise, in copie hath right iudgement, and grounded skill, as did appeare to be in *Sebastian Castalio,* in translating *Kemppes* booke *de Imitando Christo.*

But to folow *Quintilianus* aduise for *Paraphrasis,* were euen to take paine, to seeke the worse and fowler way, whan the plaine and fairer is occupied before your eyes.

The olde and best authors that euer wrote, were content if occasion required to speake twise of one matter, not to change the wordes, but ῥητῶς, that is, worde for worde to expresse it againe. For they thought, that a matter, well expressed with fitte wordes and apt composition, was not to be altered, but liking it well their selues, they thought it would also be well allowed of others.

A scholemaster (soch one as I require) knoweth that I say trewe.

He readeth in *Homer,* almost in euerie booke, and speciallie in *Secundo et nono Iliados,* not onelie som verses, *Homerus.* but whole leaues, not to be altered with new, but to be vttered with the old selfe same wordes. ᾽Ιλ. { 2. } { 9. }

He knoweth, that *Xenophon,* writing twise of *Agesilaus,* once in his life, againe in the historie *Xenophō.* of the Greekes, in one matter, kepeth alwayes the selfe same wordes. He doth the like, speaking of *Socrates,* both in the beginning of his Apologie and in the last ende of ἀπομνημονευμάτων.

Demosthenes also in 4. *Philippica,* doth borow his owne wordes vttered before in his oration *de Chersoneso.* He doth the like, and that more at large, in his *Demosthenes.* orations, against *Androtion* and *Timocrates.*

In latin also, *Cicero* in som places, and *Virgil* in mo, do repeate one matter, with the selfe same wordes. *Cicero.* Thies excellent authors, did thus, not for lacke *Virgilius.* of wordes, but by iudgement and skill: whatsoeuer, other, more curious, and lesse skilfull, do thinke, write, and do.

Paraphrasis neuerthelesse hath good place in learning, but not, by myne opinion, for any scholer, but is onelie to be left to a perfite Master, eyther to expound openlie a good author withall, or to compare priuatelie, for his owne exercise, how some notable place of an excellent author, may be vttered with other fitte wordes: But if ye alter also, the composition, forme, and order than that is not *Paraphrasis*, but *Imitatio*, as I will fullie declare in fitter place.

The scholer shall winne nothing by *Paraphrasis*, but onelie, if we may beleue *Tullie*, to choose worse wordes, to place them out of order, to feare ouermoch the iudgement of the master, to mislike ouermuch the hardnes of learning, and by vse, to gather vp faultes, which hardlie will be left of againe.

The master in teaching it, shall rather encrease hys owne labor, than his scholers proffet: for when the scholer shall bring vnto his master a peece of *Tullie* or *Cæsar* turned into other latin, then must the master cum to *Quintilians* goodlie lesson *de Emendatione*, which, (as he saith) is the most profitable part of teaching, but not in myne opinion, and namelie for youthe in Grammer scholes. For the master nowe taketh double paynes: first, to marke what is amisse: againe, to inuent what may be sayd better. And here perchance, a verie good master may easelie both deceiue himselfe, and lead his scholer into error.

It requireth greater learning, and deeper iudgement, than is to be hoped for at any scholemasters hand: that is, to be able alwaies learnedlie and perfitelie

$$\left\{\begin{array}{l}\textit{Mutare quod ineptum est:}\\ \textit{Transmutare quod peruersum est:}\\ \textit{Replere quod deest;}\\ \textit{Detrahere quod obest:}\\ \textit{Expungere quod inane est.}\end{array}\right.$$

And that, which requireth more skill, and deaper consideracion

$$\left\{\begin{array}{l}\textit{Premere tumentia:}\\ \textit{Extollere humilia:}\\ \textit{Astringere luxuriantia:}\\ \textit{Componere dissoluta.}\end{array}\right.$$

The master may here onelie stumble, and perchance faull in teaching, to the marring and mayning of the Scholer in learning, whan it is a matter, of moch readyng, of great learning, and tried iudgement, to make trewe difference betwixt

$$\left\{\begin{array}{l} \textit{Sublime, et Tumidum:} \\ \textit{Grande, et immodicum:} \\ \textit{Decorum, et ineptum:} \\ \textit{Perfeǎum, et nimium.} \end{array}\right.$$

Some men of our time, counted perfite Maisters of eloquence, in their owne opinion the best, in other mens iudgements very good, as *Omphalius* euerie where, *Sadoletus* in many places, yea also my frende *Osorius*, namelie in his Epistle to the Queene & in his whole booke *de Iusticia*, haue so ouer reached thē selues, in making trew difference in the poyntes afore rehearsed, as though they had bene brought vp in some schole in *Asia*, to learne to decline rather then in *Athens* with *Plato, Aristotle*, and *Demosthenes*, (from whence *Tullie* fetched his eloquence) to vnderstand, what in euerie matter, to be spoken or written on, is, in verie deede, *Nimium, Satis, Parum*, that is for to say, to all considerations, *Decorum*, which, as it is the hardest point, in all learning, so is it the fairest and onelie marke, that scholers, in all their studie, must alwayes shote at, if they purpose an other day to be, either sounde in Religion, or wise and discrete in any vocation of the common wealth.

Agayne, in the lowest degree, it is no low point of learnyng and iudgement for a Scholemaster, to make trewe difference betwixt

$$\left\{\begin{array}{l} \textit{Humile \& depressum:} \\ \textit{Lene \& remissum:} \\ \textit{Siccum \& aridum:} \\ \textit{Exile \& macrum:} \\ \textit{Inaffeǎatum \& negleǎum.} \end{array}\right.$$

In these poyntes, some, louing *Melanǎhon* well, as he was well worthie, but yet not considering well nor wiselie, how he of nature, and all his life and studie by iudgement was wholly spent in *genere Disciplinabili*, that is, in teaching, reading, and expounding plainlie and aptlie schole matters, and therfore imployed thereunto a fitte, sensible, and caulme kinde of speaking and writing, some I say, with very well louyng, but not with verie well weying *Melanǎhones* doinges, do frame them selues a style, cold, leane, and weake, though the matter be neuer so warme & earnest, not moch vnlike vnto one, that had a pleasure, in a roughe, raynie, winter day, to clothe him selfe with nothing els, but a demie, bukram cassok, plaine without plites, and single with out lyning: which will neither beare of winde nor wether, nor yet kepe out the sunne, in any hote day.

Some suppose, and that by good reason, that *Melancthon* him selfe came to this low kinde of writing, by vsing ouer moch *Paraphrasis* in reading: For studying therbie to make euerie thing streight and easie, in smothing and playning all things to much, neuer leaueth, whiles the sence it selfe be left, both lowse and lasie. And some of those *Paraphrasis* of *Melancthon* be set out in Printe, as, *Pro Archia Poeta, & Marco Marcello*: But a scholer, by myne opinion, is better occupied in playing or sleping, than in spendyng time, not onelie vainlie but also harmefullie, in soch a kinde of exercise.

Paraphrasis in vse of teaching, hath hurt Melanchtons stile in writing.

If a Master woulde haue a perfite example to folow, how, in *Genere sublimi*, to auoide *Nimium*, or in *Mediocri*, to atteyne *Satis*, or in *Humili*, to exchew *Parum*, let him read diligently for the first, *Secundam Philippicam*, for the meane, *De Natura Deorum*, and for the lowest, *Partitiones*. Or, if in an other tong, ye looke for like example, in like perfection, for all those three degrees, read *Pro Ctesiphonte, Ad Leptinem, & Contra Olympiodorum*, and, what witte, Arte, and diligence is hable to affourde, ye shall plainely see.

Cicero.

Demosthenes.

For our tyme, the odde man to performe all three perfitlie, whatsoeuer he doth, and to know the way to do them skilfullie, whan so euer he list, is, in my poore opinion, *Ioannes Sturmius.*

Ioan. Stur.

He also councelleth all scholers to beware of *Paraphrasis*, except it be, from worse to better, from rude and barbarous, to proper and pure latin, and yet no man to exercise that neyther, except soch one, as is alreadie furnished with plentie of learning, and grounded with stedfast iudgement before.

All theis faultes, that thus manie wise men do finde with the exercise of *Paraphrasis*, in turning the best latin, into other, as good as they can, that is, ye may be sure, into a great deale worse, than it was, both in right choice for proprietie, and trewe placing, for good order is committed also commonlie in all

common scholes, by the scholemasters, in tossing and trobling
yong wittes (as I sayd in the beginning) with that boocherlie
feare in making of Latins.

Therefore, in place, of Latines for yong scholers, and of
Paraphrasis for the masters, I wold haue double translation
specially vsed. For, in double translating a perfite peece of
Tullie or *Cæsar*, neyther the scholer in learning, nor ye Master
in teaching can erre. A true tochstone, a sure metwand lieth
before both their eyes. For, all right cōgruitie : proprietie of
wordes : order in sentences : the right imitation, to inuent good
matter, to dispose it in good order, to confirme it with good
reason, to expresse any purpose fitlie and orderlie, is learned
thus, both easelie & perfitlie : Yea, to misse somtyme in this
kinde of translation, bringeth more proffet, than to hit right,
either in *Paraphrasi* or making of Latins. For though ye say
well, in a latin making, or in a *Paraphasis*, yet you being but
in doute, and vncertayne whether ye saie well or no, ye gather
and lay vp in memorie, no sure frute of learning thereby : But
if ye fault in translation, ye ar easelie taught, how perfitlie to
amende it, and so well warned, how after to exchew, all soch
faultes againe.

Paraphrasis therefore, by myne opinion, is not meete for
Grammer scholes : nor yet verie fitte for yong men in the
vniuersitie, vntill studie and tyme, haue bred in them, perfite
learning, and stedfast iudgement.

There is a kinde of *Paraphrasis*, which may be vsed, without
all hurt, to moch proffet : but it serueth onely the Greke and
not the latin, nor no other tong, as to alter *linguam Ionicam aut
Doricam* into *meram Atticam* : A notable example there is left
vnto vs by a notable learned man *Diony: Halicarn:* who, in his
booke, περὶ συντάξεως, doth translate the goodlie storie of
Candaules and *Gyges* in 1. *Herodoti*, out of *Ionica lingua*, into
Atticam. Read the place, and ye shall take, both pleasure and
proffet, in conference of it. A man, that is exercised in reading,
Thucydides, Xenophon, Plato, and *Demosthenes*, in vsing to turne,
like places of *Herodotus*, after like sorte, shold shortlie cum to
soch a knowledge, in vnderstanding, speaking, and writing the
Greeke tong, as fewe or none hath yet atteyned in England.
The like exercise out of *Dorica lingua* may be also vsed, if a
man take that litle booke of *Plato, Timæus Locrus, de Animo et*

natura, which is writtē *Dorice*, and turne it into soch Greeke, as *Plato* vseth in other workes. The booke, is but two leaues: and the labor wold be, but two weekes: but surelie the proffet, for easie vnderstanding, and trewe writing the Greeke tonge, wold conteruaile wyth the toile, that som men taketh, in otherwise coldlie reading that tonge, two yeares.

And yet, for the latin tonge, and for the exercise of *Paraphrasis*, in those places of latin, that can not be bettered, if some yong man, excellent of witte, corragious in will, lustie of nature, and desirous to contend euen with the best latin, to better it, if he can, surelie I commend his forwardnesse, and for his better instruction therein, I will set before him, as notable an example of *Paraphrasis*, as is in Record of learning. *Cicero* him selfe, doth contend, in two sondrie places, to expresse one matter, with diuerse wordes : and that is *Paraphrasis*, saith *Quintillian*. The matter I suppose, is taken out of *Panætius* : and therefore being translated out of Greeke at diuers times, is vttered for his purpose, with diuers wordes and formes: which kinde of exercise, for perfite learned men, is verie profitable.

2. De Finib.

a. *Homo enim Rationem habet à natura menti datam quæ, &* *causas rerum et consecutiones videt, & similitudines, transfert, &* *disiunɛ̃ta coniungit, & cum præsentibus futura copulat, omnemȝ* *compleɛ̃titur vitæ consequentis statum.* b. *Eademȝ ratio facit* *hominem hominum appetentem, cumȝ his, natura, & sermone in vsu* *congruentem: vt profeɛ̃tus à caritate domesticorū ac suorum, currat* *longius, & se implicet, primò Ciuiū, deinde omnium mortalium* *societati: vtȝ non sibi soli se natū meminerit, sed patriæ, sed suis,* *vt exigua pars ipsi relinquatur.* c. *Et quoniā eadem natura* *cupiditatem ingenuit homini veri inueniendi, quod facillimè apparet,* *cum vacui curis, etiam quid in cœlo fiat, scire auemus, &c.*

1. Officiorum.

a. *Homo autem, qui rationis est particeps, per quam conse-* *quentia cernit, & causas rerum videt, earumȝ progressus, et quasi* *antecessiones non ignorat, similitudines, comparat, rebusȝ præsentibus* *adiungit, atȝ anneɛ̃tit futuras, facile totius vitæ cursum videt, ad eamque degendam præparat res necessarias.* b. *Eademq̃ natura vt rationis hominem conciliat homini, & ad Orationis, & ad vitæ societatem : ingeneratq̃ imprimis præcipuum quendam amorem in eos, qui procreati sunt, impellitq̃ vt hominum cœtus & celebrari inter se, & sibi obediri velit, ob easq̃ causas studeat parare ea, quæ suppeditent ad cultum & ad victum, nec sibi soli, sed coniugi, liberis, cæterisq̃ quos charos habeat, tueriq̃ debeat.* c. *Quæ cura exsuscitat etiam animos, & maiores ad rem gerendam facit : imprimisq̃ hominis est propria veri inquisitio atq̃ inuestigatio : ita cum sumus necessarijs negocijs curisq̃ vacui, tum auemus aliquid videre, audire, addiscere, cognitionemq̃ rerum mirabilium. &c.*

The conference of these two places, conteinyng so excellent a peece of learning, as this is, expressed by so worthy a witte, as *Tullies* was, must needes bring great pleasure and proffit to him, that maketh trew counte, of learning and honestie. But if we had the *Greke* Author, the first Patterne of all, and therby to see, how *Tullies* witte did worke at diuerse tymes, how, out of one excellent Image, might be framed two other, one in face and fauor, but somwhat differing in forme, figure, and color, surelie, such a peece of workemanship compared with the Paterne it selfe, would better please the ease of honest, wise, and learned myndes, thã two of the fairest Venusses, that euer Apelles made.

And thus moch, for all kinde of *Paraphrasis*, fitte or vnfit, for Scholers or other, as I am led to thinke, not onelie, by mine owne experience, but chiefly by the authoritie & iudgement of those, whom I my selfe would gladliest folow, and do counsell all myne to do the same : not contendyng with any other, that will otherwise either thinke or do.

Metaphrasis.

This kinde of exercise is all one with *Paraphrasis*, saue it is out of verse, either into prose, or into some other kinde of meter : or els, out of prose into verse, which was *Socrates* exercise and pastime (as *Plato* reporteth) when he was in prison, to translate *Æsopes Fabules* into verse. *Quintilian* doth greatlie praise also this exercise : but bicause *Tullie* doth disalow it in yong men, by myne opinion, it were not well to vse it in Grammer Scholes, euen

Plato in Phædone.

for the selfe same causes, that be recited against *Paraphrasis*. And therfore, for the vse, or misuse of it, the same is to be thought, that is spoken of *Paraphrasis* before. This was *Sulpitius* exercise: and he gathering vp therby, a Poeticall kinde of talke, is iustlie named of *Cicero, grandis et Tragicus Orator*: which I think is spoken, not for his praise, but for other mens warning, to exchew the like faulte. Yet neuertheles, if our Scholemaster for his owne instruction, is desirous, to see a perfite example hereof, I will recite one, which I thinke, no man is so bold, will say, that he can amend it: & that is

Hom. I. *Il.*
Pla. 3. *Rep.*

Chrises the Priestes Oration to the *Grekes*, in the beginnyng of *Homers Ilias*, turned excellentlie into prose by *Socrates* him selfe, and that aduisedlie and purposelie for other to folow: and therfore he calleth this exercise, in the same place, μίμησις, that is, *Imitatio*, which is most trew: but, in this booke, for teachyng sake, I will name it *Metaphrasis*, reteinyng the word, that all teachers, in this case, do vse.

Homerus. I. 'Iλιάδ.

ὁ γὰρ ἦλθε θοὰς ἐπὶ νῆας 'Αχαιῶν,
λυσόμενός τε θύγατρα, φέρων τ' ἀπερείσι' ἄποινα,
στέμματ' ἔχων ἐν χερσὶν ἑκηβόλου 'Απόλλωνος,
χρυσέῳ ἀνὰ σκήπτρῳ· καὶ ἐλίσσετο πάντας 'Αχαιούς,
'Ατρείδα δὲ μάλιστα δύω, κοσμήτορε λαῶν.
  'Ατρείδαί τε, καὶ ἄλλοι ἐϋκνήμιδες 'Αχαιοί,
ὑμῖν μὲν θεοὶ δοῖεν, 'Ολύμπια δώματ' ἔχοντες,
ἐκπέρσαι Πριάμοιο πόλιν, εὖ δ' οἴκαδ' ἱκέσθαι·
παῖδα δ' ἐμοὶ λῦσαί τε φίλην, τά τ' ἄποινα δέχεσθαι,
ἁζόμενοι Διὸς υἱὸν ἑκηβόλον 'Απόλλωνα.
  ἔνθ' ἄλλοι μὲν πάντες ἐπευφήμησαν 'Αχαιοί
αἰδεῖσθαί θ' ἱερῆα, καὶ ἀγλαὰ δέχθαι ἄποινα·
ἀλλ' οὐκ 'Ατρείδῃ 'Αγαμέμνονι ἥνδανε θυμῷ,
ἀλλὰ κακῶς ἀφίει, κρατερὸν δ' ἐπὶ μῦθον ἔτελλεν.
  μή σε, γέρον, κοίλῃσιν ἐγὼ παρὰ νηυσὶ κιχείω,
ἢ νῦν δηθύνοντ', ἢ ὕστερον αὖτις ἰόντα,
μή νύ τοι οὐ χραίσμῃ σκῆπτρον, καὶ στέμμα θεοῖο.
τὴν δ' ἐγὼ οὐ λύσω, πρίν μιν καὶ γῆρας ἔπεισιν,
ἡμετέρῳ ἐνὶ οἴκῳ, ἐν "Αργεϊ τηλόθι πάτρης

ἱστὸν ἐποιχομένην, καὶ ἐμὸν λέχος ἀντιόωσαν.
ἀλλ' ἴθι, μή μ' ἐρέθιζε· σαώτερος ὥς κε νέηαι.

ὣς ἔφατ'· ἔδδεισεν δ' ὁ γέρων, καὶ ἐπείθετο μύθῳ·
βῆ δ' ἀκέων παρὰ θῖνα πολυφλοίσβοιο θαλάσσης,
πολλὰ δ' ἔπειτ' ἀπάνευθε κιὼν ἠρᾶθ' ὁ γεραιός
Ἀπόλλωνι ἄνακτι, τὸν ἠΰκομος τέκε Λητώ·
κλῦθί μευ, ἀργυρότοξ', ὃς Χρύσην ἀμφιβέβηκας,
κίλλαν τε ζαθέην, Τενέδοιό τε ἶφι ἀνάσσεις,
σμινθεῦ, εἴ ποτέ τοι χαρίεντ' ἐπὶ νηὸν ἔρεψα,
ἢ εἰ δή ποτέ τοι κατὰ πίονα μηρί' ἔκηα
ταύρων, ἠδ' αἰγῶν, τόδε μοι κρήηνον ἐέλδωρ·
τίσειαν Δαναοὶ ἐμὰ δάκρυα σοῖσι βέλεσσιν.

Socrates in 3. *de Rep.* saith thus,

Φράσω γὰρ ἄνευ μέτρου,
οὐ γάρ εἰμι ποιητικός.

ἦλθεν ὁ Χρύσης τῆς τε θυγατρὸς λύτρα φέρων, καὶ ἱκέτης
τῶν Ἀχαιῶν, μάλιστα δὲ τῶν βασιλέων: καὶ εὔχετο, ἐκείνοις
μὲν τοὺς θεοὺς δοῦναι ἑλόντας τὴν Τροίαν, αὐτοὺς δὲ σωθῆναι,
τὴν δὲ θυγατέρα οἱ αὐτῷ λῦσαι, δεξαμένους ἄποινα, καὶ τὸν
θεὸν αἰδεσθέντας. Τοιαῦτα δὲ εἰπόντος αὐτοῦ, οἱ μὲν ἄλλοι
ἐσέβοντο καὶ συνῄνουν, ὁ δὲ Ἀγαμέμνων ἠγρίαινεν, ἐντελ-
λόμενος νῦν τε ἀπιέναι, καὶ αὖθις μὴ ἐλθεῖν, μὴ αὐτῷ τό τε
σκῆπτρον, καὶ τὰ τοῦ θεοῦ στέμματα οὐκ ἐπαρκέσοι. πρὶν
δὲ λυθῆναι αὐτοῦ θυγατέρα, ἐν Ἄργει ἔφη γηράσειν μετὰ οὔ.
ἀπιέναι δὲ ἐκέλευε, καὶ μὴ ἐρεθίζειν, ἵνα σῶς οἴκαδε ἔλθοι.
ὁ δὲ πρεσβύτης ἀκούσας ἔδεισέ τε καὶ ἀπῄει σιγῇ, ἀποχω-
ρήσας δ' ἐκ τοῦ στρατοπέδου πολλὰ τῷ Ἀπόλλωνι εὔχετο,
τάς τε ἐπωνυμίας τοῦ θεοῦ ἀνακαλῶν καὶ ὑπομιμνήσκων καὶ
ἀπαιτῶν, εἴ τι πώποτε ἢ ἐν ναῶν οἰκοδομήσεσιν, ἢ ἐν ἱερῶν
θυσίαις κεχαρισμένον δωρήσαιτο. ὧν δὴ χάριν κατεύχετο
τῖσαι τοὺς Ἀχαιοὺς τὰ ἃ δάκρυα τοῖς ἐκείνου βέλεσιν.

To compare *Homer* and *Plato* together, two wonders of
nature and arte for witte and eloquence, is most pleasant and
profitable, for a man of ripe iudgement. *Platos* turning of
Homer in this place, doth not ride a loft in Poeticall termes,
but goeth low and soft on foote, as prose and *Pedestris oratio*
should do. If *Sulpitius* had had *Platos* consideration, in right

vsing this exercise, he had not deserued the name of *Tragicus Orator*, who should rather haue studied to expresse *vim Demosthenis*, than *furorem Pœtæ*, how good so euer he was, whom he did folow.

And therfore would I haue our Scholemaster wey well together *Homer* and *Plato*, and marke diligentlie these foure pointes, what is kept : what is added : what is left out : what is changed, either, in choise of wordes, or forme of sentences : which foure pointes, be the right tooles, to handle like a workeman, this kinde of worke : as our Scholer shall better vnderstand, when he hath bene a good while in the Vniuersitie : to which tyme and place, I chiefly remitte this kinde of exercise.

And bicause I euer thought examples to be the best kinde of teaching, I will recite a golden sentēce out of that Poete, which is next vnto *Homer*, not onelie in tyme, but also in worthines : which hath bene a paterne for many worthie wittes to follow, by this kind of *Metaphrasis*, but I will content my selfe, with foure workemen, two in *Greke*, and two in *Latin*, soch, as in both the tonges, wiser & worthier, can not be looked for. Surelie, no stone set in gold by most cunning workemē, is in deed, if right counte be made, more worthie the looking on, than this golden sentence, diuerslie wrought vpon, by soch foure excellent Masters.

Hesiodus.   2.

1. οὗτος μὲν πανάριστος, ὃς αὐτῷ πάντα νοήσῃ,
   φρασσάμενος τά κ᾽ ἔπειτα καὶ ἐς τέλος ἦσιν ἀμείνω:
2. ἐσθλὸς δ᾽ αὖ κἀκεῖνος, ὃς εὖ εἰπόντι πίθηται,
3. ὃς δέ κε μήτ᾽ αὐτὸς νοέῃ, μήτ᾽ ἄλλου ἀκούων
   ἐν θυμῷ βάλληται, ὁ δ᾽ αὖτ᾽ ἀχρήϊος ἀνήρ.

¶ Thus rudelie turned into
base English.

1. *That man in wisedome passeth all,*
   to know the best who hath a head :
2. *And meetlie wise eeke counted shall,*
   who yeildes him selfe to wise mens read :
3. *Who hath no witte, nor none will heare,*
   amongest all fooles the bell may beare.

Sophocles in Antigone.

1. Φήμ᾽ ἔγωγε πρεσβεύειν πολύ,
Φῦναι τὸν ἄνδρα πάντ᾽ ἐπιστήμης πλέων·
2. Εἰ δ᾽ οὖν (φιλεῖ γὰρ τοῦτο μὴ ταύτῃ ῥέπειν),
Καὶ τῶν λεγόντων εὖ καλὸν τὸ μανθάνειν.

Marke the wisedome of *Sophocles,* in leauyng out the last
sentence, because it was not cumlie for the sonne to vse it to
his father.

❡ *D. Basileus in his Exhortation to youth.*

Μέμνησθε τοῦ Ἡσιόδου, ὅς φησι, ἄριστον μὲν εἶναι
τὸν παρ᾽ ἑαυτοῦ τὰ δέοντα ξυνορῶντα. 2. Ἐσθλὸν δὲ κἀκεῖ-
νον, τὸν τοῖς, παρ᾽ ἑτέρων ὑποδειχθεῖσιν ἑπόμενον. 3. τὸν
δὲ πρὸς οὐδέτερον ἐπιτήδειον ἀχρεῖον εἶναι πρὸς ἅπαντα.

❡ M. Cic. Pro A. Cluentio.

1. *Sapientissimum esse dicunt eum, cui, quod opus sit, ipsi veniat in
mentē : 2. Proxime accedere illum, qui alterius bene inuentis
obtemperet. 3. In stulticia contra est : minus enim stultus est
is, cui nihil in mentem venit, quam ille, qui, quod stultè alteri venit
in mentem comprobat.*

Cicero doth not plainlie expresse the last sentence, but doth
inuent it fitlie for his purpose, to taunt the folie and simplicitie
in his aduersarie *Actius,* not weying wiselie, the sutle doynges
of *Chrysogonus* and *Staienus.*

❡ Tit. Liuius in Orat. Minutij. Lib. 22.

1. *Sæpe ego audiui milites ; eum primum esse virum, qui ipse
consulat, quid in rem sit : 2. Secundum eum, qui bene monenti
obediat : 3. Qui, nec ipse consulere, nec alteri parere scit, eum
extremi esse ingenij.*

Now, which of all these foure, *Sophocles, S. Basil, Cicero,* or
Liuie, hath expressed *Hesiodus* best, the iudgement is as hard, as
the workemanship of euerie one is most excellent in deede. An
other example out of the *Latin* tong also I will recite, for the
worthines of the workeman therof, and that is *Horace,* who hath

so turned the begynning of *Terence Eunuchus*, as doth worke in me, a pleasant admiration, as oft so euer, as I compare those two places togither. And though euerie Master, and euerie good Scholer to, do know the places, both in *Terence* and *Horace*, yet I will set them heare, in one place togither, that with more pleasure, they may be compared together.

¶ Terentius in Eunucho.

Quid igitur faciam? non eam? ne nunc quidem cum accersor vltrò? an potius ita me comparem, non perpeti meretricum contumelias? exclusit: reuocat, redeam? non, si me obsecret. PAR-MENO *a little after.* Here, *quæ res in se neǥ consilium neǥ modum habet vllum, eam consilio regere non potes. In Amore hæc omnia insunt vitia, iniuriæ, suspiciones, inimicitiæ, induciæ, bellum, pax rursum. Incerta hæc si tu postules ratione certa facere, nihilo plus agas, ǥ si des operam, vt cum ratione insanias.*

¶ Horatius, lib. Ser. 2. Saty. 3.

Nec nunc cum me vocet vltro,
Accedam? an potius mediter finire dolores?
Exclusit: reuocat, redeam? non si obsecret. Ecce
Seruus non Paulo sapientior: ô Here, quæ res
Nec modum habet, neǥ consilium, ratione modòǥ
Tractari non vult. In amore, hæc sunt mala, bellum,
Pax rursum: hæc si quis tempestatis propè ritu
Mobilia, et cæca fluitantia sorte, laboret
Reddere certa, sibi nihilò plus explicet, ac si
Insanire paret certa ratione, modòǥ.

This exercise may bring moch profite to ripe heads, and stayd iudgementes: bicause, in traueling in it, the mynde must nedes be verie attentiue, and busilie occupide, in turning and tossing it selfe many wayes: and conferryng with great pleasure, the varietie of worthie wittes and iudgementes togither: But this harme may sone cum therby, and namelie to yong Scholers, lesse, in seeking other wordes, and new forme of sentences, they chance vpon the worse: for the which onelie cause, *Cicero* thinketh this exercise not to be fit for yong men.

Epitome.

This is a way of studie, belonging, rather to matter, than to wordes : to memorie, than to vtterance : to those that be learned alreadie, and hath small place at all amonges yong scholers in Grammer scholes. It may proffet priuately some learned men, but it hath hurt generallie learning it selfe, very moch. For by it haue we lost whole *Trogus*, the best part of *T. Liuius*, the goodlie Dictionarie of *Pompeius festus*, a great deale of the Ciuill lawe, and other many notable bookes, for the which cause, I do the more mislike this exercise, both in old and yong.

Epitome, is good priuatelie for himselfe that doth worke it, but ill commonlie for all other that vse other mens labor therein: a silie poore kinde of studie, not vnlike to the doing of those poore folke, which neyther till, nor sowe, nor reape themselues, but gleane by stelth, vpon other mens growndes. Soch, haue emptie barnes, for deare yeares.

Grammer scholes haue fewe *Epitomes* to hurt them, except *Epitheta Textoris*, and such beggarlie gatheringes, as *Horman*, *whittington*, and other like vulgares for making of latines : yea I do wishe, that all rules for yong scholers, were shorter than they be. For without doute, *Grammatica* it selfe, is sooner and surer learned by examples of good authors, than by the naked rewles of *Grammarians*. *Epitome* hurteth more, in the vni-uersities and studie of Philosophie : but most of all, in diuinitie it selfe.

In deede bookes of common places be verie necessarie, to induce a man, into an orderlie generall knowledge, how to referre orderlie all that he readeth, *ad certa rerum Capita*, and not wander in studie. And to that end did *P. Lombardus* the master of sentences and *Ph. Melancthon* in our daies, write two notable bookes of common places.

But to dwell in *Epitomes* and bookes of common places, and not to binde himselfe dailie by orderlie studie, to reade with all diligence, principallie the holyest scripture and withall, the best Doctors, and so to learne to make trewe difference betwixt, the authoritie of the one, and the Counsell of the other, maketh so many seeming, and sonburnt ministers as we haue, whose learning is gotten in a sommer heat, and washed away, with a Christmas snow againe : who neuerthelesse, are lesse to be blamed, than those blind bussardes, who in late yeares, of wilfull maliciousnes, would neyther learne themselues, nor could teach others, any thing at all.

Paraphrasis hath done lesse hurt to learning, than *Epitome* : for no *Paraphrasis*, though there be many, shall neuer take away *Dauids* Psalter. *Erasmus Paraphrasis* being neuer so good, shall neuer banishe the new Testament. And in an other schole, the *Paraphrasis* of *Brocardus*, or *Sambucus*, shal neuer take *Aristotles* Rhetoricke, nor *Horace de Arte Poetica*, out of learned mens handes.

But, as concerning a schole *Epitome*, he that wold haue an example of it, let him read *Lucian* περὶ κάλλους which is the verie *Epitome* of *Isocrates* oration *de laudibus Helenæ*, whereby he may learne, at the least, this wise lesson, that a man ought to beware, to be ouer bold, in altering an excellent mans worke.

Neuertheles, some kinde of *Epitome* may be vsed, by men of skilful iudgement, to the great proffet also of others. As if a wise man would take · *Halles* Cronicle, where moch good matter is quite marde with Indenture Englishe, and first change, strange and inkhorne tearmes into proper, and commonlie vsed wordes : next, specially to wede out that, that is superfluous and idle, not onelie where wordes be vainlie heaped one vpon an other, but also where many sentences, of one meaning, be so clowted vp together as though *M. Hall* had bene, not writing the storie of England, but varying a sentence in Hitching schole : surelie a wise learned man, by this way of *Epitome*, in cutting away wordes and sentences, and diminishing nothing at all of the matter, shold leaue to mens vse, a storie, halfe as moch as it was in quantitie, but twise as good as it was, both for pleasure and also commoditie.

An other kinde of *Epitome* may be vsed likewise very well, to moch proffet. Som man either by lustines of nature, or brought by ill teaching, to a wrong iudgement, is ouer full of words, sētences, & matter, & yet all his words be proper, apt & well chosen : all his sētences be rownd and trimlie framed : his whole matter grownded vpon good reason, & stuffed with full argumēts, for his intent & purpose. Yet whē his talke shalbe heard, or his writing be red, of soch one, as is, either of my two dearest frendes, *M. Haddon* at home, or *Iohn Sturmius* in Germanie, that *Nimium* in him, which fooles and vnlearned will most commend, shall eyther of thies two, bite his lippe, or shake his heade at it.

This fulnes as it is not to be misliked in a yong man, so in farder aige, in greater skill, and weightier affaires, it is to be temperated, or else discretion and iudgement shall seeme to be wanting in him. But if his stile be still ouer rancke and lustie, as some men being neuer so old and spent by yeares, will still be full of youthfull conditions as was Syr *F. Bryan*, and euermore wold haue bene : soch a rancke and full writer, must vse, if he will do wiselie the exercise of a verie good kinde of *Epitome*, and do, as certaine wise men do, that be ouer fat and fleshie : who leauing their owne full and plentifull table, go to soiorne abrode from home for a while, at the temperate diet of some sober man : and so by litle and litle, cut away the grosnesse that is in them. As for an example : If *Osorius* would leaue of his lustines in striuing against *S. Austen*, and his ouer rancke rayling against poore *Luther*, and the troth of Gods doctrine, and giue his whole studie, not to write any thing of his owne for a while, but to trāslate *Demosthenes*, with so straite, fast, & temperate a style in latine, as he is in Greeke, he would becume so perfit & pure a writer, I beleue, as hath bene fewe or none sence *Ciceroes* dayes : And so, by doing himself and all learned moch good, do others lesse harme, & Christes doctrine lesse iniury, thā he doth : & with all, wyn vnto himselfe many worthy frends, who agreing with him gladly, in yᵉ loue & liking of excellent learning, are sorie to see so worthie a witte, so rare eloquence, wholie spent and consumed, in striuing with God and good men.

Emonges the rest, no man doth lament him more than I, not onelie for the excellent learning that I see in him, but also bicause there hath passed priuatelie betwixt him and me, sure tokens of moch good will, and frendlie opinion, the one toward the other. And surelie the distance betwixt London and Lysbon, should not stoppe, any kinde of frendlie dewtie, that I could, eyther shew to him, or do to his, if the greatest matter of all did not in certeyne pointes, separate our myndes.

And yet for my parte, both toward him, and diuerse others

here at home, for like cause of excellent learning, great wisdome, and gentle humanitie, which I haue seene in them, and felt at their handes my selfe, where the matter of difference is mere conscience in a quiet minde inwardlie, and not contentious malice with spitefull rayling openlie, I can be content to followe this rewle, in misliking some one thing, not to hate for anie thing els.

But as for all the bloodie beastes, as that fat Boore of the wood : or those brauling Bulles of Basan : or any lurking *Dormus*, blinde, not by nature, but by malice, & as may be gathered of their owne testimonie, giuen ouer to blindnes, for giuing ouer God & his word ; or soch as be so lustie runnegates, as first, runne from God & his trew doctrine, than, from their Lordes, Masters, & all dewtie, next, frō them selues & out of their wittes, lastly from their Prince, contrey, & all dew allegeāce, whether they ought rather to be pitied of good men, for their miserie, or contemned of wise men, for their malicious folie, let good and wise men determine.

Psal. 80.

And to returne to *Epitome* agayne, some will iudge moch boldnes in me, thus to iudge of *Osorius* style : but wise men do know, that meane lookers on, may trewelie say, for a well made Picture : This face had bene more cumlie, if that hie redde in the cheeke, were somwhat more pure sanguin than it is : and yet the stander by, can not amend it himselfe by any way.

And this is not written to the dispraise but to the great commendation of *Osorius*, because *Tullie* himselfe had the same fulnes in him : and therefore went to *Rodes* to cut it away : and saith himselfe, *recepi me domum prope mutatus, nam quasi referuerat iam oratio*. Which was brought to passe I beleue, not onelie by the teaching of *Molo Appollonius* but also by a good way of *Epitome*, in binding him selfe to translate *meros Atticos Oratores*, and so to bring his style, from all lowse grosnesse, to soch firme fastnes in latin, as is in *Demosthenes* in Greeke. And this to be most trew, may easelie be gathered, not onelie of *L. Crassus* talke in 1. *de Or.* but speciallie of *Ciceroes* owne deede in translating *Demosthenes* and *Æschines* orations περὶ στεφ. to that verie ende and purpose.

And although a man growndlie learned all readie, may take moch proffet him selfe in vsing, by *Epitome*, to draw other mens

workes for his owne memorie sake, into shorter rowme, as
Conterus hath done verie well the whole *Metamorphosis* of *Ouid*,
& *Dauid Cythræus* a great deale better, the ix. Muses of *Herodotus*, and *Melanchthon* in myne opinion, far best of all, the whole
storie of Time, not onelie to his own vse, but to other mens
proffet and hys great prayse, yet, *Epitome* is most necessarie of
all in a mans owne writing, as we learne of that noble Poet
Virgill, who, if *Donatus* say trewe, in writing that perfite worke
of the *Georgickes*, vsed dailie, when he had written 40. or 50.
verses, not to cease cutting, paring, and pollishing of them, till
he had brought them to the nomber of x. or xij.

And this exercise, is not more nedefullie done in a great
worke, than wiselie done, in your common dailie writing, either
of letter, or other thing else, that is to say, to peruse diligentlie,
and see and spie wiselie, what is alwaies more than nedeth :
For, twenty to one, offend more, in writing to moch, than to
litle : euen as twentie to one, fall into sicknesse, rather by ouer
moch fulnes, than by anie lacke or emptinesse. And therefore
is he alwaies the best English Physition, that best can geue
a purgation, that is, by way of *Epitome*, to cut all ouer much
away. And surelie mens bodies, be not more full of ill humors,
than commonlie mens myndes (if they be yong, lustie, proude,
like and loue them selues well, as most men do) be full of fansies,
opinions, errors, and faultes, not onelie in inward inuention, but
also in all their vtterance, either by pen or taulke.

And of all other men, euen those that haue yᵉ inuentiuest
heades, for all purposes, and roundest tonges in all matters and
places (except they learne and vse this good lesson of *Epitome*)
commit commonlie greater faultes, than dull, staying silent men
do. For, quicke inuentors, and faire readie speakers, being
boldned with their present habilitie to say more, and perchance
better to, at the soden for that present, than any other can do,
vse lesse helpe of diligence and studie than they ought to do :
and so haue in them commonlie, lesse learning, and weaker
iudgement, for all deepe considerations, than some duller heades,
and slower tonges haue.

And therefore, readie speakers, generallie be not the best,
playnest, and wisest writers, nor yet the deepest iudgers in
weightie affaires, bicause they do not tarry to weye and iudge
all thinges, as they should : but hauing their heades ouer full of

matter, be like pennes ouer full of incke, which will soner blotte, than make any faire letter at all. Tyme was, whan I had experience of two Ambassadors in one place, the one of a hote head to inuent, and of a hastie hand to write, the other, colde and stayd in both: but what difference of their doinges was made by wise men, is not vnknowne to some persons. The Bishop of Winchester *Steph*: *Gardiner* had a quicke head, and a readie tong, and yet was not the best writer in England. *Cicero* in *Brutus* doth wiselie note the same in *Serg: Galbo*, and *Q. Hortentius*, who were both, hote, lustie, and plaine speakers, but colde, lowse, and rough writers: And *Tullie* telleth the cause why, saying, whā they spake, their tong was naturally caried with full tyde & wynde of their witte: whan they wrote their head was solitarie, dull, and caulme, and so their style was blonte, and their writing colde: *Quod vitium*, sayth *Cicero*, *peringeniosis hominibus neq̃ satis doctis plerumq̃ accidit.*

And therfore all quick inuentors, & readie faire speakers, must be carefull, that, to their goodnes of nature, they adde also in any wise, studie, labor, leasure, learning, and iudgement, and than they shall in deede, passe all other, as I know some do, in whome all those qualities are fullie planted, or else if they giue ouer moch to their witte, and ouer litle to their labor and learning, they will sonest ouer reach in taulke, and fardest cum behinde in writing whatsoeuer they take in hand. The methode of *Epitome* is most necessarie for soch kinde of men. And thus much concerning the vse or misuse of all kinde of *Epitomes* in matters of learning.

✠ *Imitatio.*

Imitation, is a facultie to expresse liuelie and perfitelie that example: which ye go about to folow. And of it selfe, it is large and wide: for all the workes of nature, in a maner be examples for arte to folow.

But to our purpose, all languages, both learned and mother tonges, be gotten, and gotten onelie by *Imitation*. For as ye vse to heare, so ye learne to speake: if ye heare no other, ye speake not your selfe: and whome ye onelie heare, of them ye onelie learne.

And therefore, if ye would speake as the best and wisest do, ye must be conuersant, where the best and wisest are : but if yow be borne or brought vp in a rude contrie, ye shall not chose but speake rudelie : the rudest man of all knoweth this to be trewe.

Yet neuerthelesse, the rudenes of common and mother tonges, is no bar for wise speaking. For in the rudest contrie, and most barbarous mother language, many be found can speake verie wiselie : but in the Greeke and latin tong, the two onelie learned tonges, which be kept, not in common taulke, but in priuate bookes, we finde alwayes, wisdome and eloquence, good matter and good vtterance, neuer or seldom a sonder. For all soch Authors, as be fullest of good matter and right iudgement in doctrine, be likewise alwayes, most proper in wordes, most apte in sentence, most plaine and pure in vttering the same.

And contrariwise, in those two tonges, all writers, either in Religion, or any sect of Philosophie, who so euer be founde fonde in iudgement of matter, be commonlie found as rude in vttering their mynde. For Stoickes, Anabaptistes, and Friers : with Epicures, Libertines and Monkes, being most like in learning and life, are no fonder and pernicious in their opinions, than they be rude and barbarous in their writinges. They be not wise, therefore that say, what care I for a mans wordes and vtterance, if his matter and reasons be good. Soch men, say so, not so moch of ignorance, as eyther of some singular pride in themselues, or some speciall malice or other, or for some priuate & perciall matter, either in Religion or other kinde of learning. For good and choice meates, be no more requisite for helthie bodies, than proper and apte wordes be for good matters, and also plaine and sensible vtterance for the best and depest reasons : in which two pointes standeth perfite eloquence, one of the fairest and rarest giftes that God doth geue to man.

Ye know not, what hurt ye do to learning, that care not for wordes, but for matter, and so make a deuorse betwixt the tong and the hart. For marke all aiges : looke vpon the whole course of both the Greeke and Latin tonge, and ye shall surelie finde, that, whan apte and good wordes began to be neglected, and properties of those two tonges to be confounded, than also began, ill deedes to spring : strange maners to oppresse good orders, newe and fond opinions to striue with olde and trewe doctrine, first in Philosophie : and after in Religion : right iudgement of all thinges to be peruerted, and so vertue with learning is contemned, and studie left of: of ill thoughtes cummeth peruerse iudgement: of ill deedes springeth lewde taulke. Which fower misorders, as they mar mans life, so destroy they good learning withall.

But behold the goodnesse of Gods prouidence for learning: all olde authors and sectes of Philosophy, which were fondest in opinion, and rudest in vtterance, as Stoickes and Epicures, first contemned of wise men, and after forgotten of all men, be so consumed by tymes, as they be now, not onelie out of vse, but also out of memorie of man: which thing, I surelie thinke, will shortlie chance, to the whole doctrine and all the bookes of phantasticall Anabaptistes and Friers, and of the beastlie Libertines and Monkes.

Againe behold on the other side, how Gods wisdome hath wrought, that of *Academici* and *Peripatetici*, those that were wisest in iudgement of matters, and purest in vttering their myndes, the first and chiefest, that wrote most and best, in either tong, as *Plato* and *Aristotle* in Greeke, *Tullie* in Latin, be so either wholie, or sufficiently left vnto vs, as I neuer knew yet scholer, that gaue himselfe to like, and loue, and folow chieflie those three Authors but he proued, both learned, wise, and also an honest man, if he ioyned with all the trewe doctrine of Gods holie Bible, without the which, the other three, be but fine edge tooles in a fole or mad mans hand.

But to returne to *Imitation* agayne: There be three kindes of it in matters of learning.

The whole doctrine of Comedies and Tragedies, is a perfite *imitation*, or faire liuelie painted picture of the life of euerie degree of man. Of this *Imitation* writeth *Plato* at large in 3. *de Rep.* but it doth not moch belong at this time to our purpose.

The second kind of *Imitation*, is to folow for learning of tonges and sciences, the best authors. Here riseth, emonges proude and enuious wittes, a great controuersie, whether, one or many are to be folowed: and if one, who is that one: *Seneca*, or *Cicero*: *Salust* or *Cæsar*, and so forth in Greeke and Latin.

The third kinde of *Imitation*, belongeth to the second: as when you be determined, whether ye will folow one or mo, to know perfitlie, and which way to folow that one: in what

place : by what meane and order : by what tooles and instrumentes ye shall do it, by what skill and iudgement, ye shall
trewelie discerne, whether ye folow rightlie or no.

This *Imitatio*, is *dissimilis materiei similis traEtatio* : and also,
similis materiei dissimilis traEtatio, as *Virgill* folowed *Homer* : but
the Argument to the one was *Vlysses*, to the other *Æneas*.
Tullie persecuted *Antonie* with the same wepons of eloquence,
that *Demosthenes* vsed before against *Philippe*.

Horace foloweth *Pindar*, but either of them his owne
Argument and Person : as the one, *Hiero* king of *Sicilie*, the
other *Augustus* the Emperor : and yet both for like respectes,
that is, for their coragious stoutnes in warre, and iust gouernment in peace.

One of the best examples, for right *Imitation* we lacke, and
that is *Menander*, whom our *Terence*, (as the matter required) in
like argument, in the same Persons, with equall eloquence, foote
by foote did folow.

Som peeces remaine, like broken Iewelles, whereby men
may rightlie esteme, and iustlie lament, the losse of the
whole.

Erasmus, the ornament of learning, in our tyme, doth wish
that som man of learning and diligence, would take the like
paines in *Demosthenes* and *Tullie*, that *Macrobius* hath done in
Homer and *Virgill*, that is, to write out and ioyne together,
where the one doth imitate the other. *Erasmus* wishe is good,
but surelie, it is not good enough : for *Macrobius* gatherings for
the *Æneidos* out of *Homer*, and *Eobanus Hessus* more diligent
gatherings for the *Bucolikes* out of *Theocritus*, as they be not
fullie taken out of the whole heape, as they should be, but euen
as though they had not sought for them of purpose, but fownd
them scatered here and there by chance in their way, euen so,
onelie to point out, and nakedlie to ioyne togither their
sentences, with no farder declaring the maner and way, how
the one doth folow the other, were but a colde helpe, to the
encrease of learning.

But if a man would take this paine also, whan he hath layd
two places, of *Homer* and *Virgill*, or of *Demosthenes* and *Tullie*
togither, to teach plainlie withall, after this sort.

   1. *Tullie* reteyneth thus moch of the matter, thies
sentences, thies wordes :

2. This and that he leaueth out, which he doth wittelie to this end and purpose.

3. This he addeth here.

4. This he diminisheth there.

5. This he ordereth thus, with placing that here, not there.

6. This he altereth and changeth, either, in propertie of wordes, in forme of sentence, in substance of the matter, or in one, or other conuenient circumstance of the authors present purpose. In thies fewe rude English wordes, are wrapt vp all the necessarie tooles and instrumentes, wherewith trewe *Imitation* is rightlie wrought withall in any tonge. Which tooles, I openlie confesse, be not of myne owne forging, but partlie left vnto me by the cunningest Master, and one of the worthiest Ientlemen that euer England bred, Syr *Iohn Cheke*: partelie borowed by me out of the shoppe of the dearest frende I haue out of England, *Io. St.* And therefore I am the bolder to borow of him, and here to leaue them to other, and namelie to my Children: which tooles, if it please God, that an other day, they may be able to vse rightlie, as I do wish and daylie pray, they may do, I shal be more glad, than if I were able to leaue them a great quantitie of land.

This foresaide order and doctrine of *Imitation*, would bring forth more learning, and breed vp trewer iudgement, than any other exercise that can be vsed, but not for yong beginners, bicause they shall not be able to consider dulie therof. And trewelie, it may be a shame to good studentes who hauing so faire examples to follow, as *Plato* and *Tullie*, do not vse so wise wayes in folowing them for the obteyning of wisdome and learning, as rude ignorant Artificers do, for gayning a small commoditie. For surelie the meanest painter vseth more witte, better arte, greater diligence, in hys shoppe, in folowing the Picture of any meane mans face, than commonlie the best studentes do, euen in the vniuersitie, for the atteining of learning it selfe.

Some ignorant, vnlearned, and idle student: or some busie looker vpon this litle poore booke, that hath neither will to do good him selfe, nor skill to iudge right of others, but can lustelie contemne, by pride and ignorance, all painfull diligence and right order in study, will perchance say, that I am to precise, to curious, in marking and piteling thus about the imitation of others : and that the olde worthie Authors did neuer busie their heades and wittes, in folowyng so preciselie, either the matter what other men wrote, or els the maner how other men wrote. They will say, it were a plaine slauerie, & iniurie to, to shakkle and tye a good witte, and hinder the course of a mãs good nature with such bondes of seruitude, in folowyng other.

Except soch men thinke them selues wiser then *Cicero* for teaching of eloquence, they must be content to turne a new leafe.

The best booke that euer *Tullie* wrote, by all mens iudgement, and by his owne testimonie to, in writyng wherof, he employed most care, studie, learnyng and iudgement, is his booke *de Orat. ad Q. F.* Now let vs see, what he did for the matter, and also for the maner of writing therof. For the whole booke consisteth in these two pointes onelie : In good matter, and good handling of the matter. And first, for the matter, it is whole *Aristotles,* what so euer *Antonie* in the second, and *Crassus* in the third doth teach. Trust not me, but beleue *Tullie* him selfe, who writeth so, first, in that goodlie long Epistle *ad P. Lentulum,* and after in diuerse places *ad Atticum.* And in the verie booke it selfe, Tullie will not haue it hidden, but both *Catulus* and *Crassus* do oft and pleasantly lay that stelth to *Antonius* charge. Now, for the handling of the matter, was *Tullie* so precise and curious rather to follow an other mans Paterne, than to inuent some newe shape him selfe, namelie in that booke, wherin he purposed, to leaue to posteritie, the glorie of his witte? yea forsoth, that he did. And this is not my gessing and gathering, nor onelie performed by *Tullie* in verie deed, but vttered also by *Tullie* in plaine wordes : to teach other men thereby, what they should do, in taking like matter in hand.

And that which is specially to be marked, *Tullie* doth vtter plainlie his conceit and purpose therein, by the mouth of the wisest man in all that companie : for sayth *Scæuola* him selfe, *Cur non imitamur, Crasse, Socratem illum, qui est in Phædro Platonis &c.*

And furder to vnderstand, that *Tullie* did not *obiter* and bichance, but purposelie and mindfullie bend him selfe to a precise and curious Imitation of *Plato,* concernyng the shape aŋd forme of those bookes, marke I pray you, how curious *Tullie* is to vtter his purpose and doyng therein, writing thus to *Atticus*.

Quod in his Oratorijs libris, quos tantopere laudas, personam desideras Scæuolæ, non eam temerè dimoui : Sed feci idem, quod in πολιτεία *Deus ille noster Plato, cum in Piræeum Socrates venisset ad Cephalum locupletem & festiuum Senem, quoad primus ille sermo haberetur, adest in disputando senex : Deinde, cum ipse quoĝ commodissimè locutus esset, ad rem diuinā dicit se velle discedere, neĝ postea reuertitur. Credo Platonem vix putasse satis consonum fore, si hominem id ætatis in tam longo sermone diutius retinuisset : Multo ego satius hoc mihi cauendum putaui in Scæuola, qui & ætate et valetudine erat ea qua meministi, & his honoribus, vt vix satis decorum videretur eum plures dies esse in Crassi Tusculano. Et erat primi libri sermo non alienus à Scæuolæ studijs : reliqui libri* τεχνολογίαν *habent, vt scis. Huic ioculatoriæ disputationi senem illum vt noras, interesse sanè nolui.*

If *Cicero* had not opened him selfe, and declared hys owne thought and doynges herein, men that be idle, and ignorant, and enuious of other mens diligence and well doinges, would haue sworne that *Tullie* had neuer mynded any soch thing, but that of a precise curiositie, we fayne and forge and father soch thinges of *Tullie*, as he neuer ment in deed. I write this, not for nought : for I haue heard some both well learned, and otherwayes verie wise, that by their lustie misliking of soch diligence, haue drawen back the forwardnes of verie good wittes. But euen as such men them selues, do sometymes stumble vpon doyng well by chance and benefite of good witte, so would I haue our scholer alwayes able to do well by order of learnyng and right skill of iudgement.

Concernyng Imitation, many learned men haue written, with moch diuersitie for the matter, and therfore with great contrarietie and some stomacke amongest them selues. I haue read as many as I could get diligentlie, and what I thinke of euerie one of them, I will freelie say my mynde. With which freedome I trust good men will beare, bicause it shall tend to neither spitefull nor harmefull controuersie.

In *Tullie*, it is well touched, shortlie taught, not fullie
Cicero.   declared by *Ant. in* 2. *de Orat* : and afterward
in *Orat. ad Brutum*, for the liking and misliking

of *Isocrates*: and the contrarie iudgement of *Tullie* against *Caluus*, *Brutus*, and *Calidius*, *de genere dicendi Attico & Asiatico*. *Dionis. Halic.* περὶ μιμήσεως. I feare is lost : which Author, next *Aristotle*, *Plato*, and *Tullie*, of all other, that write of eloquence, by the iudgement of them that be best learned, deserueth the next prayse and place.

Dio. Halicar.

Quintilian writeth of it, shortly and coldlie for the matter, yet hotelie and spitefullie enough, agaynst the Imitation of *Tullie*.

Quintil.

Erasmus, beyng more occupied in spying other mens faultes, than declaryng his owne aduise, is mistaken of many, to the great hurt of studie, for his authoritie sake.   For he writeth rightlie, rightlie vnderstanded : he and *Longolius* onelie differing in this, that the one seemeth to giue ouermoch, the other ouer litle, to him, whom they both, best loued, and chiefly allowed of all other.

Erasmus.

Budæus in his Commentaries roughlie and obscurelie, after his kinde of writyng : and for the matter, caryed somwhat out of the way in ouermuch misliking the Imitation of *Tullie*.

Budæus.

Phil. Melancthon, learnedlie and trewlie.

Ph. Melanch.

Camerarius largely with a learned iudgement, but somewhat confusedly, and with ouer rough a stile.

Ioa. Cāmer.

Sambucus, largely, with a right iudgement but somewhat a crooked stile.

Sābucus.

Other haue written also, as *Cortesius* to *Politian*, and that verie well : *Bembus ad Picum* a great deale better, but *Ioan. Sturmius de Nobilitate literata, & de Amissa dicendi ratione*, farre best of all, in myne opinion, that euer tooke this matter in hand.   For all the rest, declare chiefly this point, whether one, or many, or all, are to be followed : but *Sturmius* onelie hath most learnedlie declared, who is to be followed, what is to be followed, and the best point of all, by what way & order, trew Imitatiō is rightlie to be exercised.   And although *Sturmius* herein doth farre passe all other, yet hath he not so fullie and perfitelie done it, as I do wishe he had, and as I know he could. For though he hath done it perfitelie for precept, yet hath he

Cortesius.
P. Bembus.
Ioan. Sturmius.

not done it perfitelie enough for example : which he did, neither for lacke of skill, nor by negligence, but of purpose, contēted with one or two examples, bicause he was mynded in those two bookes, to write of it both shortlie, and also had to touch other matters.

Barthol. Riccius Ferrariensis also hath written learnedlie, diligentlie and verie largelie of this matter euen as hee did before verie well *de Apparatu linguæ Lat.* He writeth the better in myne opinion, bicause his whole doctrine, iudgement, and order, semeth to be borowed out of *Io. Stur.* bookes. He addeth also examples, the best kinde of teaching : wherein he doth well, but not well enough : in deede, he committeth no faulte, but yet, deserueth small praise. He is content with the meane, and followeth not the best : as a man, that would feede vpon Acornes, whan he may eate, as good cheape, the finest wheat bread. He teacheth for example, where and how, two or three late *Italian* Poetes do follow *Virgil*: and how *Virgil* him selfe in the storie of *Dido*, doth wholie Imitate *Catullus* in the like matter of *Ariadna* : Wherein I like better his diligence and order of teaching, than his iudgemēt in choice of examples for *Imitation*. But, if he had done thus : if he had declared where and how, how oft and how many wayes *Virgil* doth folow *Homer*, as for example the cōming of *Vlysses* to *Alcynous* and *Calypso*, with the comming of *Æneas* to *Cartage* and *Dido* : Likewise the games running, wrestling, and shoting, that *Achilles* maketh in *Homer*, with the selfe same games, that *Æneas* maketh in *Virgil* : The harnesse of *Achilles*, with the harnesse of *Æneas*, and the maner of making of them both by *Vulcane* : The notable combate betwixt *Achilles* and *Hector*, with as notable a combate betwixt *Æneas* and *Turnus*. The going downe to hell of *Vlysses* in *Homer*, with the going downe to hell of *Æneas* in *Virgil* : and other places infinite mo, as similitudes, narrations, messages, discriptions of persones, places, battels, tempestes, shipwrackes, and common places for diuerse purposes, which be as precisely taken out of *Homer*, as euer did Painter in London follow the picture of any faire personage. And whē thies places had bene gathered together by this way of diligence than to haue conferred them together by this order of teaching as, diligently to marke what is kept and vsed in either author, in wordes, in sentences, in matter : what is added : what is left

out: what ordered otherwise, either *præponendo*, *interponendo*, or
postponendo : And what is altered for any respect, in word,
phrase, sentence, figure, reason, argument, or by any way of
circumstance : If *Riccius* had done this, he had not onely bene
well liked, for his diligence in teaching, but also iustlie commended for his right iudgement in right choice of examples for
the best *Imitation*.

Riccius also for *Imitation* of prose declareth where and how
Longolius doth folow *Tullie*, but as for *Longolius*, I would not
haue him the patern of our *Imitation*. In deede : in *Longolius*
shoppe, be proper and faire shewing colers, but as for shape,
figure, and naturall cumlines, by the iudgement of best iudging
artificers, he is rather allowed as one to be borne withall, than
especially commēded, as one chieflie to be folowed.

If *Riccius* had taken for his exāples, where *Tullie* him selfe
foloweth either *Plato* or *Demosthenes*, he had shot than at the
right marke. But to excuse *Riccius*, somwhat, though I can
not fullie defend him, it may be sayd, his purpose was, to teach
onelie the Latin tong, when thys way that I do wish, to ioyne
Virgil with *Homer*, to read *Tullie* with *Demosthenes* and *Plato*,
requireth a cunning and perfite Master in both the tonges. It
is my wish in deede, and that by good reason : For who so euer
will write well of any matter, must labor to expresse that, that
is perfite, and not to stay and content himselfe with the meane:
yea, I say farder, though it be not vnposible, yet it is verie rare,
and meruelous hard, to proue excellent in the Latin tong, for
him that is not also well seene in the Greeke tong. *Tullie* him
selfe, most excellent of nature, most diligent in labor, brought
vp from his cradle, in that place, and in that tyme, where and
whan the Latin tong most florished naturallie in euery mans
mouth, yet was not his owne tong able it selfe to make him so
cunning in his owne tong, as he was in deede : but the
knowledge and *Imitation* of the Greeke tong withall.

This he confesseth himselfe: this he vttereth in many places,
as those can tell best, that vse to read him most.

Therefore thou, that shotest at perfection in the Latin tong,
thinke not thy selfe wiser than *Tullie* was, in choice of the way,
that leadeth rightlie to the same: thinke not thy witte better
than *Tullies* was, as though that may serue thee that was not
sufficient for him. For euen as a hauke flieth not hie with one

wing: euen so a man reacheth not to excellency with one tong.

I haue bene a looker on in the Cokpit of learning thies many yeares: And one Cock onelie haue I knowne, which with one wing, euen at this day, doth passe all other, in myne opinion, that euer I saw in any pitte in England, though they had two winges. Yet neuerthelesse, to flie well with one wing, to runne fast with one leg, be rather, rare Maistreis moch to be merueled at, than sure examples safelie to be folowed. A Bushop that now liueth, a good man, whose iudgement in Religion I better like, than his opinion in perfitnes in other learning, said once vnto me: we haue no nede now of the Greeke tong, when all thinges be translated into Latin. But the good mā vnderstood not, that euen the best translation, is, for mere necessitie, but an euill imped wing to flie withall, or a heuie stompe leg of wood to go withall: soch, the hier they flie, the sooner they falter and faill: the faster they runne, the ofter they stumble, and sorer they fall. Soch as will nedes so flie, may flie at a Pye, and catch a Dawe: And soch runners, as commonlie, they shoue and sholder to stand formost, yet in the end they cum behind others & deserue but the hopshakles, if the Masters of the game be right iudgers.

Therefore in perusing thus, so many diuerse bookes for *Imitation*, it came into my head that a verie profitable booke might be made *de Imitatione*, after an other sort, than euer yet was attempted of that matter, conteyning a certaine fewe fitte preceptes, vnto the which should be gathered and applied plentie of examples, out of the choisest authors of both the tonges. This worke would stand, rather in good diligence, for the gathering, and right iudgement for the apte applying of those examples: than any great learning or vtterance at all.

Optima ratio Imitationis.

The doing thereof, would be more pleasant, than painfull, & would bring also moch proffet to all that should read it, and great praise to him would take it in hand, with iust desert of thankes.

Erasmus, giuyng him selfe to read ouer all Authors *Greke* and *Latin*, seemeth to haue prescribed to him selfe this order of readyng: that is, to note out by the way, three speciall pointes: All Adagies,

Erasmus order in his studie.

all similitudes, and all wittie sayinges of most notable personages: And so, by one labour, he left to posteritie, three notable
bookes, & namelie two his *Chiliades, Apophthegmata* and *Similia.*
Likewise, if a good student would bend him selfe to read
diligently ouer Tullie, and with him also at
the same tyme, as diligētly *Plato,* & *Xenophō,*
with his bookes of Philosophie, *Isocrates,* &   Cicero.
Demosthenes with his orations, & *Aristotle* with
his Rhetorickes: which fiue of all other, be

> *Plato.*
> *Xenophon.*
> *Isocrates.*
> *Demosth.*
> *Aristotles.*

those, whom *Tullie* best loued, & specially followed: & would
marke diligētly in *Tullie,* where he doth *exprimere* or *effingere*
(which be the verie propre wordes of Imitation) either, *Copiam
Platonis* or *venustatē Xenophontis, suauitatem Isocratis,* or *vim
Demosthenis, propriam & puram subtilitatem Aristotelis,* and not
onelie write out the places diligentlie, and lay them together
orderlie, but also to conferre them with skilfull iudgement by
those few rules, which I haue expressed now twise before: if
that diligence were taken, if that order were vsed, what perfite
knowledge of both the tonges, what readie and pithie vtterance
in all matters, what right and deepe iudgement in all kinde of
learnyng would follow, is scarse credible to be beleued.

These bookes, be not many, nor long, nor rude in speach,
nor meane in matter, but next the Maiestie of Gods holie word,
most worthie for a man, the louer of learning and honestie, to
spend his life in. Yea, I haue heard worthie *M. Cheke* many
tymes say: I would haue a good student passe and iorney
through all Authors both *Greke* and *Latin*: but he that will
dwell in these few bookes onelie: first, in Gods holie Bible, and
than ioyne with it, *Tullie* in *Latin, Plato, Aristotle*: *Xenophon*:
Isocrates: and *Demosthenes* in *Greke*: must nedes proue an excellent man.

Some men alreadie in our dayes, haue put to their helping
handes, to this worke of Imitation.   As *Peri-*
onius, Hēr. Stephanus in dictionario Ciceroniano,
and *P. Victorius* most praiseworthelie of all, in
that his learned worke conteyning xxv. bookes *de*
varia lectione: in which bookes be ioyned diligentlie together the
best Authors of both the tonges where one doth seeme to
imitate an other.

> *Perionius.*
> *H. Steph.*
> *P. Victor-*
> *ius.*

But all these, with *Macrobius, Hessus,* and other, be no

more but common porters, caryers, and bringers of matter and stuffe togither. They order nothing: They lay before you, what is done: they do not teach you, how it is done: They busie not them selues with forme of buildyng: They do not declare, this stuffe is thus framed by *Demosthenes*, and thus and thus by *Tullie*, and so likewise in *Xenophon*, *Plato* and *Isocrates* and *Aristotle*. For ioyning *Virgil* with *Homer* I haue sufficientlie declared before.

The like diligence I would wish to be taken in *Pindar* and *Horace* an equall match for all respectes.

Pindarus.
Horatius.

In Tragedies, (the goodliest Argument of all, and for the vse, either of a learned preacher, or a Ciuill Ientleman, more profitable than *Homer*, *Pindar*, *Virgill*, and *Horace*: yea comparable in myne opinion, with the doctrine of *Aristotle*, *Plato*, and *Xenophon*,) the *Grecians*, *Sophocles* and *Euripides* far ouer match our *Seneca*, in *Latin*, namely in οἰκονομία *et Decoro*, although *Senacaes* elocutiō and verse be verie commendable for his tyme. And for the matters of *Hercules*, *Thebes*, *Hippolytus*, and *Troie*, his Imitation is to be gathered into the same booke, and to be tryed by the same touchstone, as is spoken before.

Sophocles.
Euripides.
Seneca.

In histories, and namelie in *Liuie*, the like diligence of Imitation, could bring excellent learning, and breede stayde iudgement, in taking any like matter in hand.

Onely *Liuie* were a sufficient taske for one mans studie, to compare him, first with his fellow for all respectes, *Dion. Halicarnassæus*: who both, liued in one tyme: tooke both one historie in hande to write: deserued both like prayse of learnyng and eloquence. Than with *Polybius* that wise writer, whom *Liuie* professeth to follow: & if he would denie it, yet it is plaine, that the best part of the thyrd *Decade* in *Liuie*, is in a maner translated out of the thyrd and rest of *Polibius*: Lastlie with *Thucydides*, to whose Imitation *Liuie* is curiouslie bent, as may well appeare by that one Oration of those of *Campania*, asking aide of the *Romanes* agaynst the *Samnites*, which is wholie taken, Sentence, Reason, Argument, and order, out of the Oration of *Corcyra*, asking like aide of the *Athenienses* against them of *Corinth*. If some

Tit. Liuius.
Dion. Halicarn.
Polibius.
Thucidides.
1 Decad. Lib. 7.
Thucid. 1.

diligent student would take paynes to compare them togither, he should easelie perceiue, that I do say trew. A booke, thus wholie filled with examples of Imitatiō, first out of *Tullie*, compared with *Plato*, *Xenophon*, *Isocrates*, *Demosthenes* and *Aristotle*: than out of *Virgil* and *Horace*, with *Homer* and *Pindar*: next out of *Seneca* with *Sophocles* and *Euripides*: Lastlie out of *Liuie*, with *Thucydides*, *Polibius* and *Halicarnassæus*, gathered with good diligence, and compared with right order, as I haue expressed before, were an other maner of worke for all kinde of learning, & namely for eloquence, than be those cold gatheringes of *Macrobius*, *Hessus*, *Perionius*, *Stephanus*, and *Victorius*, which may be vsed, as I sayd before, in this case, as porters and caryers, deseruing like prayse, as soch men do wages ; but onely *Sturmius* is he, out of whō, the trew suruey and whole workemanship is speciallie to be learned.

I trust, this my writyng shall giue some good student occasion, to take some peece in hand of this worke of Imitation. And as I had rather haue any do it, than my selfe, yet surelie my selfe rather thā none at all. And by Gods grace, if God do lend me life, with health, free laysure and libertie, with good likyng Opus de recta imitandi ratione.

and a merie heart, I will turne the best part of my studie and tyme, to toyle in one or other peece of this worke of Imitation.

This diligence to gather examples, to giue light and vnderstandyng to good preceptes, is no new inuention, but speciallie vsed of the best Authors and oldest writers. For *Aristotle* him selfe, (as *Diog. Laertius* declareth) when he *Aristoteles.*
had written that goodlie booke of the *Topickes*, did gather out of stories and Orators, so many examples as filled xv. bookes, onelie to expresse the rules of his *Topickes*. These were the Commentaries, that *Aristotle* thought fit for hys *Topickes*: And therfore to speake as I thinke, I neuer saw yet any Commentarie vpon *Aristotles* Logicke, either in *Greke* or *Latin*, that euer I lyked, bicause they be rather spent in declaryng scholepoynt rules, than in gathering fit examples Commentarij Græci et Latini in Dialect. Aristotelis.

for vse and vtterance, either by pen or talke. For preceptes in all Authors, and namelie in *Aristotle*, without applying vnto them, the Imitation of examples, be hard, drie, and cold, and therfore barrayn, vnfruitfull and vnpleasant. But *Aristotle*, namelie in his *Topickes* and *Elenches*, should be, not onelie fruitfull, but also pleasant to, if examples out of *Plato*, and other good Authors, were diligentlie gathered, and aptlie applied vnto his most perfit preceptes there.

Precepta
in Aristot.

And it is notable, that my frende *Sturmius* writeth herein, that there is no precept in *Aristotles Topickes*, wherof plentie of examples be not manifest in *Platos* workes.

Exempla
in *Platone*.

And I heare say, that an excellent learned man, *Tomitanus* in *Italie*, hath expressed euerie fallacion in *Aristotle*, with diuerse examples out of *Plato*. Would to God, I might once see, some worthie student of *Aristotle* and *Plato* in Cambrige, that would ioyne in one booke the preceptes of the one, with the examples of the other. For such a labor, were one speciall peece of that worke of Imitation, which I do wishe were gathered together in one Volume.

Cambrige, at my first comming thither, but not at my going away, committed this fault in reading the preceptes of *Aristotle* without the examples of other Authors: But herein, in my time thies men of worthie memorie, *M. Redman*, *M. Cheke*, *M. Smith*, *M. Haddon*, *M. Watson*, put so to their helping handes, as that vniuersitie, and all studentes there, as long as learning shall last, shall be bounde vnto them, if that trade in studie be trewlie folowed, which those men left behinde them there.

By this small mention of Cambridge, I am caryed into three imaginations: first, into a sweete remembrance of my tyme spent there: than, into som carefull thoughts, for the greuous alteration that folowed sone after: lastlie, into much ioy to heare tell, of the good recouerie and earnest forwardnes in all good learning there agayne.

To vtter theis my thoughts somwhat more largelie, were somwhat beside my matter, yet not very farre out of the way, bycause it shall wholy tend to the good encoragement and right consideration of learning, which is my full purpose in writing this litle booke: whereby also shall well appeare this sentence to be most trewe, that onely good men, by their gouernment & example, make happie times, in euery degree and state.

Doctor *Nico. Medcalfe*, that honorable father, was Master of *S. Iohnes* Colledge, when I came thether: A man meanelie learned himselfe, but not meanely

D. Nic.
Medcalf.

affectioned to set forward learning in others. He found that Colledge spending scarse two hundred markes by yeare : he left it spending a thousand markes and more. Which he procured, not with his mony, but by his wisdome ; not chargeablie bought by him, but liberallie geuen by others by his meane, for the zeale & honor they bare to learning. And that which is worthy of memorie, all thies giuers were almost Northenmen: who being liberallie rewarded in the seruice of their Prince, bestowed it as liberallie for the good of their Contrie. Som men thought therefore, that *D. Medcalfe* was parciall to Northrenmen, but sure I am of this, that North-renmē were parciall, in doing more good, and geuing more lādes to yᵉ forderance of learning, than any other contrie mē, in those dayes, did : which deede should haue bene, rather an example of goodnes, for other to folowe, than matter of malice, for any to enuie, as some there were that did. Trewly, *D. Medcalfe* was parciall to none: but indifferent

The parci-
alitie of
Northren
men in
S. Iohnes
College.

to all : a master for the whole, a father to euery one, in that Colledge. There was none so poore, if he had, either wil to goodnes, or wit to learning, that could lacke being there, or should depart from thence for any need. I am witnes my selfe, that mony many times was brought into yong mens studies by strangers whom they knew not. In which doing, this worthy *Nicolaus* folowed the steppes of good olde *S. Nicolaus*, that learned Bishop. He was a Papist in deede, but would to God, amonges all vs Protestāts I might once see but one, that would winne like praise, in doing like good, for the aduauncement of learning and vertue. And yet, though he were a Papist, if any yong man, geuen to new learning (as they termed it) went beyond his fellowes, in witte, labor, and towardnes, euen the same, neyther lacked, open praise to encorage him, nor priuate exhibition to mainteyne hym, as worthy Syr *I. Cheke*, if he were aliue would beare good witnes and so can many mo. I my selfe one of the meanest of a great number, in that Colledge, because there appeared in me som small shew of towardnes and diligence, lacked not his fauor to forder me in learning.

And being a boy, new Bacheler of arte, I chanced amonges my companions to speake against the Pope : which matter was

than in euery mans mouth, bycause *D. Haines* and *D. Skippe*
were cum from the Court, to debate the same matter, by
preaching and disputation in the vniuersitie. This hapned the
same tyme, when I stoode to be felow there: my taulke came
to *D. Medcalfes* eare: I was called before him and the Seniores:
and after greuous rebuke, and some punishment, open warning
was geuen to all the felowes, none to be so hardie to geue me
his voice at that election. And yet for all those open threates,
the good father himselfe priuilie procured, that I should euen
than be chosen felow. But, the election being done, he made
countinance of great discontentation thereat. This good mans
goodnes, and fatherlie discretion, vsed towardes me that one
day, shall neuer out of my remembrance all the dayes of my
life. And for the same cause, haue I put it here, in this small
record of learning. For next Gods prouidence, surely that day,
was by that good fathers meanes, *Dies natalis*, to me, for the
whole foundation of the poore learning I haue, and of all the
furderance, that hetherto else where I haue obteyned.

This his goodnes stood not still in one or two, but flowed
aboundantlie ouer all that Colledge, and brake out also to
norishe good wittes in euery part of that vniuersitie: whereby,
at this departing thence, he left soch a companie of fellowes and
scholers in *S. Iohnes* Colledge, as can scarse be found now in
some whole vniuersitie: which, either for diuinitie, on the one
side or other, or for Ciuill seruice to their Prince and contrie,
haue bene, and are yet to this day, notable ornaments to this
whole Realme: Yea *S. Iohnes* did thē so florish, as Trinitie
college, that Princely house now, at the first erectiō, was but
Colonia deduɛta out of *S. Ihones*, not onelie for their Master,
fellowes, and scholers, but also, which is more, for their whole,
both order of learning, and discipline of maners: & yet to this
day, it neuer tooke Master but such as was bred vp before in
S. Iohnes: doing the dewtie of a good *Colonia* to her *Metropolis*,
as the auncient Cities in Greice and some yet in Italie, at this
day, are accustomed to do.

S. Iohnes stoode in this state, vntill those heuie tymes, and
that greuous change that chanced. An. 1553. whan mo perfite
scholers were dispersed from thence in one moneth, than many
yeares can reare vp againe. For, whan *Aper de
Sylua* had passed the seas, and fastned his foote

Psal. 80.

againe in England, not onely the two faire groues of learning
in England were eyther cut vp, by the roote, or troden downe
to the ground and wholie went to wracke, but the yong spring
there, and euerie where else, was pitifullie nipt and ouertroden
by very beastes, and also the fairest standers of all, were rooted
vp, and cast into the fire, to the great weakning euen at this
day of Christes Chirch in England, both for Religion and
learning.

And what good could chance than to the vniuersities, whan
som of the greatest, though not of the wisest nor best learned,
nor best men neither of that side, did labor to perswade, that
ignorance was better than knowledge, which they ment, not for
the laitie onelie, but also for the greatest rable of their spiritu-
altie, what other pretense openlie so euer they made : and
therefore did som of them at Cambrige (whom I will not name
openlie,) cause hedge priestes fette oute of the contrie, to be
made fellowes in the vniuersitie : saying, in their talke priuilie,
and declaring by their deedes openlie, that he was, felow good
enough for their tyme, if he could were a gowne and a tipet
cumlie, and haue hys crowne shorne faire and roundlie, and
could turne his Portesse and pie readilie : whiche I speake not
to reproue any order either of apparell, or other dewtie, that
may be well and indifferentlie vsed, but to note the miserie of
that time, whan the benefites prouided for learning were so
fowlie misused. And what was the frute of this seade ?
Verely, iudgement in doctrine was wholy altered : order in
discipline very sore changed : the loue of good learning, began
sodenly to wax cold : the knowledge of the tonges (in spite of
some that therein had florished) was manifestly contemned :
and so, ye way of right studie purposely peruerted : the choice
of good authors of mallice confownded. Olde sophistrie (I say
not well) not olde, but that new rotten sophistrie began to
beard and sholder logicke in her owne tong : yea, I know, that
heades were cast together, and counsell deuised, that *Duns*, with
all the rable of barbarous questionistes, should haue dispossessed
of their place and rowmes, *Aristotle, Plato, Tullie,*   *Aristoteles.*
and *Demosthenes*, when good *M. Redman*, and   *Plato.*
those two worthy starres of that vniuersitie,   *Cicero.*
M. Cheke, and *M. Smith*, with their scholers, had   *Demost.*
brought to florishe as notable in Cambrige, as

euer they did in Grece and in Italie : and for the doctrine of those fowre, the fowre pillers of learning, Cambrige than geuing place to no vniuersitie, neither in France, Spaine, Germanie, nor Italie.   Also in outward behauiour, than began simplicitie in apparell, to be layd aside : Courtlie galantnes to be taken vp : frugalitie in diet was priuately misliked : Towne going to good

Shoting.

cheare openly vsed : honest pastimes, ioyned with labor, left of in the fieldes : vnthrifty and idle games, haunted corners, and occupied the nightes : contention in youth, no where for learning : factions in the elders euery where for trifles.   All which miseries at length, by Gods prouidence, had their end 16. *Nouemb.* 1558.   Since which tyme, the yong spring hath shot vp so faire, as now there be in Cambrige againe, many goodly plantes (as did well appeare at the Queenes Maiesties late being there) which are like to grow to mightie great timber, to the honor of learning, and great good of their contrie, if they may stand their tyme, as the best plantes there were wont to do : and if som old dotterell trees, with standing ouer nie them, and dropping vpon them, do not either hinder, or crooke their growing, wherein my feare is ye lesse, seing so worthie a Iustice of an Oyre hath the present ouersight of that whole chace, who was himselfe somtym, in the fairest spring that euer was there of learning, one of the forwardest yong plantes, in all that worthy College of *S. Ihones* : who now by grace is growne to soch greatnesse, as, in the temperate and quiet shade of his wisdome, next the prouidēce of God, and goodnes of one, in theis our daies, *Religio* for sinceritie, *literæ* for order and aduauncement, *Respub.* for happie and quiet gouernment, haue to great rejoysing of all good men, speciallie reposed them selues.

Now to returne to that Question, whether one, a few, many or all, are to be folowed, my aunswere shalbe short : All, for him that is desirous to know all : yea, the worst of all, as Questionistes, and all the barbarous nation of scholemen, helpe for one or other consideration : But in euerie separate kinde of learning and studie, by it selfe, ye must follow, choiselie a few, and chieflie some one, and that namelie in our schole of eloquence, either for penne or talke.   And as in portraicture and paintyng wise men chose not that workman, that can onelie make a faire hand, or a well facioned legge but soch one, as can

furnish vp fullie, all the fetures of the whole body, of a man,
woman and child : and with all is able to, by good skill, to giue
to euerie one of these three, in their proper kinde, the right
forme, the trew figure, the naturall color, that is fit and dew,
to the dignitie of a man, to the bewtie of a woman, to the
sweetnes of a yong babe : euen likewise, do we seeke soch one
in our schole to folow, who is able alwayes, in all matters, to
teach plainlie, to delite pleasantlie, and to cary away by force of
wise talke, all that shall heare or read him : and is so excellent
in deed, as witte is able, or wishe can hope, to attaine vnto :
And this not onelie to serue in the *Latin* or *Greke* tong, but
also in our own English language.   But yet, bicause the prouidence of God hath left vnto vs in no other tong, saue onelie in
the *Greke* and *Latin* tong, the trew preceptes, and perfite
examples of eloquence, therefore must we seeke in the Authors
onelie of those two tonges, the trewe Paterne of Eloquence, if
in any other mother tongue we looke to attaine, either to perfit
vtterance of it our selues, or skilfull iudgement of it in others.

And now to know, what Author doth medle onelie with
some one peece and member of eloquence, and who doth
perfitelie make vp the whole bodie, I will declare, as I can call
to remembrance the goodlie talke, that I haue had oftentymes,
of the trew difference of Authors, with that Ientleman of
worthie memorie, my dearest frend, and teacher of all the litle
poore learning I haue, Syr *Iohn Cheke.*

The trew difference of Authors is best knowne, *per diuersa
genera dicendi*, that euerie one vsed.   And therfore here I will
deuide *genus dicendi*, not into these three, *Tenuè, mediocrè, &
grande*, but as the matter of euerie Author requireth, as

in Genus $\left\{ \begin{array}{l} \textit{Poeticum.} \\ \textit{Historicum.} \\ \textit{Philosophicum.} \\ \textit{Oratorium.} \end{array} \right.$

These differre one from an other, in choice of wordes, in
framyng of Sentences, in handling of Argumentes, and vse of
right forme, figure, and number, proper and fitte for euerie
matter, and euerie one of these is diuerse also in it selfe, as the
first.

$$Poeticum,\ in\ \begin{cases} Comicum. \\ Tragicum. \\ Epicum. \\ Melicum. \end{cases}$$

And here, who soeuer hath bene diligent to read aduisedlie ouer, *Terence, Seneca, Virgil, Horace,* or els *Aristophanes, Sophocles, Homer,* and *Pindar,* and shall diligētly marke the difference they vse, in proprietie of wordes, in forme of sentence, in handlyng of their matter, he shall easelie perceiue, what is fitte and *decorum* in euerie one, to the trew vse of perfite Imitation. Whan *M. Watson* in S. Iohns College at Cambrige wrote his excellent Tragedie of *Absalon, M. Cheke,* he and I, for that part of trew Imitation, had many pleasant talkes togither, in comparing the preceptes of *Aristotle* and *Horace de Arte Poetica,* with the examples of *Euripides, Sophocles,* and *Seneca.* Few men, in writyng of Tragedies in our dayes, haue shot at this marke. Some in *England,* moe in *France, Germanie,* and *Italie,* also haue written Tragedies in our tyme: of the which, not one I am sure is able to abyde the trew touch of *Aristotles* preceptes, and *Euripides* examples, saue onely two, that euer I saw, *M. Watsons Absalon,* and *Georgius Buckananus Iephthe.* One man in Cambrige, well liked of many, but best liked of him selfe, was many tymes bold and busie, to bryng matters vpon stages, which he called Tragedies. In one, wherby he looked to wynne his spurres, and whereat many ignorant felowes fast clapped their handes, he began the *Protasis* with *Trochæijs Octonarijs*: which kinde of verse, as it is but seldome and rare in Tragedies, so is it neuer vsed, saue onelie in *Epitasi*: whan the Tragedie is hiest and hotest, and full of greatest troubles. I remember ful well what *M. Watson* merelie sayd vnto me of his blindnesse and boldnes in that behalfe although otherwise, there passed much frendship betwene thē. *M. Watson* had an other maner care of perfection, with a feare and reuerence of the iudgement of the best learned: Who to this day would neuer suffer, yet his *Absalon* to go abroad, and that onelie, bicause, in *locis paribus, Anapestus* is twise or thrise vsed in stede of *Iambus.* A smal faulte, and such one, as perchance would neuer be marked, no neither in *Italie* nor *France.* This I write, not so much, to note the first, or praise the last, as to leaue in memorie of writing, for good example to posteritie, what perfection, in any tyme, was, most diligentlie sought for in like maner, in all kinde of learnyng, in that most worthie College of S. Iohns in Cambrige.

$$
Historicum\ in\ \begin{cases} Diaria. \\ Annales. \\ Commentarios. \\ Iustam\ Historiam. \end{cases}
$$

For what proprietie in wordes, simplicitie in sentences, plainnesse and light, is cumelie for these kindes, *Cæsar* and *Liuie*, for the two last, are perfite examples of Imitation : And for the two first, the old paternes be lost, and as for some that be present and of late tyme, they be fitter to be read once for some pleasure, than oft to be perused, for any good Imitation of them.

$$
Philosophicum\ in\ \begin{cases} Sermonem,\ \text{as}\ officia\ Cic.\ et\ Eth.\ Arist. \\ Contentionem. \end{cases}
$$

As, the Dialoges of *Plato*, *Xenophon*, and *Cicero*: of which kinde of learnyng, and right Imitation therof, *Carolus Sigonius* hath written of late, both learnedlie and eloquentlie : but best of all my frende *Ioan.* Sturmius in hys Commentaries vpon *Gorgias Platonis*, which booke I haue in writyng, and is not yet set out in Print.

$$
Oratorium\ in\ \begin{cases} Humile. \\ Mediocre. \\ Sublime. \end{cases}
$$

Examples of these three, in the *Greke* tong, be plentifull & perfite, as *Lycias*, *Isocrates*, and *Demosthenes*: and all three, in onelie *Demosthenes*, in diuerse orations as *contra Olimpiodorum*, *in leptinem*, & *pro Ctesiphonte*.   And trew it is, that *Hermogines* writeth of *Demosthenes*, that all formes of Eloquence be perfite in him. In *Ciceroes* Orations, *Medium* & *sublime* be most excellentlie handled, but *Humile* in his Orations, is seldome sene : yet neuerthelesse in other bookes, as in some part of his offices, & specially *in Partitionibus*, he is comparable *in hoc humili* & *disciplinabili genere*, euen with the best that euer

Lisias.
Isocrates.
Demost.

Cicero.

wrote in *Greke*. But of *Cicero* more fullie in fitter place.   And thus, the trew difference of stiles, in euerie Author, and euerie kinde of learnyng may easelie be knowne by this diuision.

in Genus $\begin{cases} Poeticum. \\ Historicum. \\ Philosophicum. \\ Oratorium. \end{cases}$

Which I thought in this place to touch onelie, not to prosecute at large, bicause, God willyng, in the *Latin* tong, I will fullie handle it, in my booke *de Imitatione*.

Now, to touch more particularlie, which of those Authors, that be now most commonlie in mens handes, will sone affourd you some peece of Eloquence, and what maner a peece of eloquence, and what is to be liked and folowed, and what to be misliked and eschewed in them: and how some agayne will furnish you fully withall, rightly, and wisely considered, somwhat I will write as I haue heard Syr *Ihon Cheke* many tymes say.

The Latin tong, concerning any part of purenesse of it, from the spring, to the decay of the same, did not endure moch longer, than is the life of a well aged man, scarse one hundred yeares from the tyme of the last *Scipio Africanus* and *Lælius*, to the Empire of *Augustus*.   And it is notable, that *Velleius Paterculus* writeth of *Tullie*, how that the perfection of eloquence did so remayne onelie in him and in his time, as before him, were few, which might moch delight a man, or after him any, worthy admiration, but soch as *Tullie* might haue seene, and such as might haue seene *Tullie*.   And good cause why: for no perfection is durable.   Encrease hath a time, & decay likewise, but all perfit ripenesse remaineth but a momēt: as is plainly seen in fruits, plummes and cherries : but more sensibly in flowers, as Roses & such like, and yet as trewlie in all greater matters. For what naturallie, can go no hier, must naturallie yeld & stoupe againe.

Of this short tyme of any purenesse of the Latin tong, for the first fortie yeare of it, and all the tyme before, we haue no peece of learning left, saue *Plautus* and *Terence*, with a litle rude vnperfit pamflet of the elder *Cato*.   And as for *Plautus*, except the scholemaster be able to make wise and ware choice, first in proprietie of wordes, than in framing of Phrases and sentences, and chieflie in choice of honestie of matter, your scholer were better to play, thē learne all that is in him.　But surelie, if iudgement for the tong, and direction for the maners, be wisely ioyned with the diligent reading of *Plautus*, than trewlie *Plautus*, for that purenesse of the Latin tong in Rome, whan Rome did most florish in wel doing, and so thereby, in well speaking also, is soch a plentifull storehouse, for common eloquence, in meane matters, and all priuate mens affaires, as the Latin tong, for that respect, hath not the like agayne. Whan I remember the worthy tyme of Rome, wherein *Plautus* did liue, I must nedes honor the talke of that tyme, which we see *Plautus* doth vse.

Terence is also a storehouse of the same tong, for an other tyme, following soone after, & although he be not so full & plentiful as *Plautus* is, for multitude of matters, & diuersitie of wordes, yet his wordes, be chosen so purelie, placed so orderly, and all his stuffe so neetlie packed vp, and wittely compassed in euerie place, as, by all wise mens iudgement, he is counted the cunninger workeman, and to haue his shop, for the rowme that is in it, more finely appointed, and trimlier ordered, than *Plautus* is.

Three thinges chiefly, both in *Plautus* and *Terence*, are to be specially considered.　The matter, the vtterance, the words, the meter.　The matter in both, is altogether within the compasse of the meanest mens maners, and doth not stretch to any thing of any great weight at all, but standeth chiefly in vtteryng the thoughtes and conditions of hard fathers, foolish mothers, vnthrifty yong men, craftie seruantes, sotle bawdes, and wilie harlots, and so, is moch spent, in finding out fine fetches, and packing vp pelting matters, soch as in London commonlie cum to the hearing of the Masters of Bridewell. Here is base stuffe for that scholer, that should becum hereafter, either a good minister in Religion, or a Ciuill Ientleman in seruice of his Prince and contrie : except the preacher do know soch matters to confute them, whan ignorance surelie in all soch thinges were better for a Ciuill Ientleman, than knowledge. And thus, for matter, both *Plautus* and *Terence*, be like meane painters, that worke by halfes, and be cunning onelie, in making the worst part of the picture, as if one were skilfull in painting the bodie of a naked person, from the nauell downward, but nothing else.

For word and speach, *Plautus* is more plentifull, and *Terence* more pure and proper: And for one respect, *Terence* is to be embraced aboue all that euer wrote in hys kinde of argument: Bicause it is well known, by good recorde of learning, and that by *Ciceroes* owne witnes that some Comedies bearyng *Terence* name, were written by worthy *Scipio,* and wise *Lælius,* and namely *Heauton :* and *Adelphi.* And therefore as oft as I reade those Comedies, so oft doth sound in myne eare, the pure fine talke of Rome, which was vsed by the floure of the worthiest nobilitie that euer Rome bred. Let the wisest man, and best learned that liueth, read aduisedlie ouer, the first scene of *Heauton,* and the first scene of *Adelphi,* and let him consideratlie iudge, whether it is the talke of a seruile stranger borne, or rather euen that milde eloquent wise speach, which *Cicero* in *Brutus* doth so liuely expresse in *Lælius.* And yet neuerthelesse, in all this good proprietie of wordes, and purenesse of phrases which be in *Terence,* ye must not follow him alwayes in placing of them, bicause for the meter sake, some wordes in him, somtyme, be driuen awrie, which require a straighter placing in plaine prose, if ye will forme, as I would ye should do, your speach and writing, to that excellent perfitnesse, which was onely in *Tullie,* or onelie in *Tullies* tyme.

The meter and verse of *Plautus* and *Terence* be verie meane, and not to be followed: which is not their reproch, *Meter in* but the fault of the tyme, wherein they wrote, whan *Plautus &* no kinde of Poetrie, in the Latin tong, was brought *Terence.* to perfection, as doth well appeare in the fragmentes of *Ennius, Cæcilius,* and others, and euidentlie in *Plautus* & *Terence,* if thies in Latin be compared with right skil, with *Homer, Euripides, Aristophanes,* and other in Greeke of like sort. *Cicero* him selfe doth complaine of this vnperfitnes, but more plainly *Quintilian,* saying, *in Comœdia maximè claudicamus, et vix leuem consequimur vmbram :* and most earnestly of all *Horace in Arte Poetica,* which he doth namely *propter carmen Iambicum,* and referreth all good studentes herein to the Imitation of the Greeke tong, saying.

Exemplaria Græca
noɕturna versate manu, versate diurna.

This matter maketh me gladly remember, my sweete tyme spent at Cambrige, and the pleasant talke which I had oft with *M. Cheke*, and *M. Watson*, of this fault, not onely in the olde Latin Poets, but also in our new English Rymers at this day. They wished as *Virgil* and *Horace* were not wedded to follow the faultes of former fathers (a shrewd mariage in greater matters) but by right *Imitation* of the perfit Greciãs, had brought Poetrie to perfitnesse also in the Latin tong, that we Englishmen likewise would acknowledge and vnderstand rightfully our rude beggerly ryming, brought first into Italie by *Gothes* and *Hunnes*, whan all good verses and all good learning to, were destroyd by them : and after caryed into France and Germanie : and at last receyued into England by men of excellent wit in deede, but of small learning, and lesse iudgement in that behalfe.

But now, when men know the difference, and haue the examples, both of the best, and of the worst, surelie, to follow rather the *Gothes* in Ryming, than the Greekes in trew versifiyng, were euen to eate ackornes with swyne, when we may freely eate wheate bread emonges men. In deede, *Chauser*, *Th. Norton*, of Bristow, my L. of Surrey, *M. Wiat*, *Th. Phaer*, and other Ientlemen, in translating *Ouide*, *Palingenius*, and *Seneca*, haue gonne as farre to their great praise, as the copie they followed could cary them, but, if soch good wittes, and forward diligence, had bene directed to follow the best examples, and not haue bene caryed by tyme and custome, to content themselues with that barbarous and rude Ryming, emonges their other worthy praises, which they haue iustly deserued, this had not bene the least, to be counted emonges men of learning and skill, more like vnto the Grecians, than vnto the Gothians, in handling of their verse.

In deed, our English tong, hauing in vse chiefly, wordes of one syllable which commonly be long, doth not well receiue the nature of *Carmen Heroicum*, bicause *dactylus*, the aptest foote for that verse, cõteining one long & two short, is seldom therefore found in English : and doth also rather stumble than stand vpon *Monosyllabis*. *Quintilian* in hys learned Chapiter *de Compositione*, geueth this lesson *de Monosyllabis*, before me : and in the same place doth iustlie inuey against all Ryming, that if there be any, who be angrie with me, for misliking of Ryming, may be angry for company to, with *Quintilian* also, for the same thing: And yet *Quintilian* had not so iust cause to mislike of it than, as mē haue at this day.

And although *Carmen Exametrum* doth rather trotte and hoble, than runne smothly in our English tong, yet I am sure, our English tong will receiue *carmen Iambicum* as naturallie, as either *Greke* or *Latin*. But for ignorance, men cā not like, & for idlenes, men will not labor, to cum to any perfitenes at all. For, as the worthie Poetes in *Athens* and *Rome*, were more carefull to satisfie the iudgement of one learned, than rashe in pleasing the humor of a rude multitude, euen so if men in England now, had the like reuerend regard to learning skill and iudgement, and durst not presume to write, except they came with the like learnyng, and also did vse like diligence, in searchyng out, not onelie iust measure in euerie meter, as euerie ignorant person may easely do, but also trew quantitie in euery foote and sillable, as onelie the learned shalbe able to do, and as the *Grekes* and *Romanes* were wont to do, surelie than rash ignorant heads, which now can easely recken vp fourten sillables, and easelie stumble on euery Ryme, either durst not, for lacke of such learnyng: or els would not, in auoyding such labor, be

☞ so busie, as euerie where they be: and shoppes in London should not be so full of lewd and rude rymes, as commonlie they are. But now, the ripest of tong, be readiest to write: And many dayly in setting out bookes and balettes make great shew of blossomes and buddes, in whom is neither, roote of learning, nor frute of wisedome at all. Some that make *Chaucer* in English and *Petrarch* in *Italian*, their Gods in verses, and yet be not able to make trew difference, what is a fault, and what is a iust prayse, in those two worthie wittes, will moch mislike this my writyng. But such men be euen like followers of *Chaucer* and *Petrarke*, as one here in England did folow Syr *Tho. More*: who, being most vnlike vnto him, in wit and learnyng, neuertheles in wearing his gowne awrye vpon the one shoulder, as Syr *Tho. More* was wont to do, would nedes be counted lyke vnto him.

This mislikyng of Ryming, beginneth not now of any newfangle singularitie, but hath bene long misliked of many, and that of men, of greatest learnyng, and deepest iudgemēt. And soch, that defend it, do so, either for lacke of knowledge

what is best, or els of verie enuie, that any should performe that
in learnyng, whereunto they, as I sayd before, either for
ignorance, can not, or for idlenes will not, labor to attaine vnto.

And you that prayse this Ryming, bicause ye neither haue
reason, why to like it, nor can shew learning to defend it, yet I
will helpe you, with the authoritie of the oldest and learnedst
tyme. In *Grece*, whan Poetrie was euen at the hiest pitch of perfitnes, one *Simmias Rhodius* of a certaine singularitie wrote a
booke in ryming *Greke* verses, naming it ὠὸν, conteyning the
fable, how *Iupiter* in likenes of a swan, gat that egge vpon *Leda*,
whereof came *Castor*, *Pollux* and faire *Elena*. This booke was
so liked, that it had few to read it, but none to folow it:
But was presentlie contemned : and sone after, both Author and
booke, so forgotten by men, and consumed by tyme, as scarse
the name of either is kept in memorie of learnyng: And the like
folie was neuer folowed of any, many hondred yeares after
vntill yᵉ *Hunnes* and *Gothians*, and other barbarous nations, of
ignorance and rude singularitie, did reuiue the same folie agayne.

The noble Lord *Th*. Earle of Surrey, first of all English
men, in trāslating the fourth booke of *Virgill*:   The Earle of
and *Gonsaluo Periz* that excellent learned man,   Surrey.
and Secretarie to kyng *Philip* of *Spaine*, in   *Gonsaluo*
translating the *Vlisses* of *Homer* out of *Greke* into   *Periz.*
Spanish, haue both, by good iudgement, auoyded the fault of
Ryming, yet neither of them hath fullie hite perfite and trew
versifiyng. In deede, they obserue iust number, and euen feete :
but here is the fault, that their feete : be feete without ioyntes,
that is to say, not distinct by trew quantitie of sillables: And so,
soch feete, be but numme feete : and be, euē as vnfitte for
a verse to turne and runne roundly withall, as feete of brasse or
wood be vnweeldie to go well withall. And as a foote of wood,
is a plaine shew of a manifest maime, euen so feete, in our
English versifiing, without quātitie and ioyntes, be sure signes,
that the verse is either, borne deformed, vnnaturall and lame,
and so verie vnseemlie to looke vpon, except to men that be
gogle eyed thē selues.

The spying of this fault now is not the curiositie of English
eyes, but euen the good iudgement also of the best   *Senese*
that write in these dayes in *Italie*: and namelie of   *Felice*
that worthie *Senese Felice Figliucci*, who, writyng   *Figliucci.*

vpon *Aristotles Ethickes* so excellentlie in *Italian*, as neuer did yet any one in myne opinion either in *Greke* or *Latin*, amongest other thynges doth most earnestlie inuey agaynst the rude ryming of verses in that tong : And whan soeuer he expresseth *Aristotles* preceptes, with any example, out of *Homer* or *Euripides*, he translateth them, not after the Rymes of *Petrarke*, but into soch kinde of perfite verse, with like feete and quantitie of sillables, as he found them before in the *Greke* tonge : exhortyng earnestlie all the *Italian* nation, to leaue of their rude barbariousnesse in ryming, and folow diligently the excellent *Greke* and *Latin* examples, in trew versifiyng.

And you, that be able to vnderstand no more, then ye finde in the *Italian* tong : and neuer went farder than the schole of *Petrarke* and *Ariostus* abroad, or els of *Chaucer* at home though you haue pleasure to wander blindlie still in your foule wrong way, enuie not others, that seeke, as wise men haue done before them, the fairest and rightest way : or els, beside the iust reproch of malice, wisemen shall trewlie iudge, that you do so, as I haue sayd and say yet agayne vnto you, bicause, either, for idlenes ye will not, or for ignorance ye can not, cum by no better your selfe.

And therfore euen as *Virgill* and *Horace* deserue most worthie prayse, that they spying the vnperfitnes in *Ennius* and *Plautus*, by trew Imitation of *Homer* and *Euripides*, brought Poetrie to the same perfitnes in *Latin*, as it was in *Greke*, euen so those, that by the same way would benefite their tong and contrey, deserue rather thankes than disprayse in that behalfe.

And I reioyce, that euen poore England preuented *Italie*, first in spying out, than in seekyng to amend this fault in learnyng.

And here, for my pleasure I purpose a litle, by the way, to play and sporte with my Master *Tully* : from whom commonlie I am neuer wont to dissent. He him selfe, for this point of learnyng, in his verses doth halt a litle by his leaue. He could not denie it, if he were aliue, nor those defend hym now that loue him best. This fault I lay to his charge : bicause once it pleased him, though somwhat merelie, yet oueruncurteslie, to rayle vpon poore England, obiecting both, extreme beggerie, and

Tullies saying against England.

mere barbariousnes vnto it, writyng thus vnto his frend *Atticus*: There is not one scruple of siluer in that whole Isle, or any one that knoweth either learnyng or letter.

Ad Att. Lib. iv. Ep. 16.

But now master *Cicero*, blessed be God, and his sonne Iesu Christ, whom you neuer knew, except it were as it pleased him to lighten you by some shadow, as couertlie in one place ye cōfesse saying: *Veritatis tantum vmbrā consectamur*, as your Master *Plato* did before you: blessed be God, I say, that sixten hūdred yeare after you were dead and gone, it may trewly be sayd, that for siluer, there is more cumlie plate, in one Citie of England, than is in foure of the proudest Cities in all *Italie*, and take *Rome* for one of them. And for learnyng, beside the knowledge of all learned tongs and liberall sciences, euen your owne bookes *Cicero*, be as well read, and your excellent eloquence is as well liked and loued, and as trewlie folowed in England at this day, as it is now, or euer was, sence your owne tyme, in any place of *Italie*, either at *Arpinum*, where ye were borne, or els at *Rome* where ye were brought vp. And a litle to brag with you *Cicero*, where you your selfe, by your leaue, halted in some point of learnyng in your owne tong, many in England at this day go streight vp, both in trewe skill, and right doing therein.

Offic.

This I write, not to reprehend *Tullie*, whom, aboue all other, I like and loue best, but to excuse *Terence*, because in his tyme, and a good while after, Poetrie was neuer perfited in *Latin*, vntill by trew *Imitation* of the Grecians, it was at length brought to perfection : And also thereby to exhorte the goodlie wittes of England, which apte by nature, & willing by desire, geue thē selues to Poetrie, that they, rightly vnderstanding the barbarous bringing in of Rymes, would labor, as *Virgil* and *Horace* did in Latin, to make perfit also this point of learning, in our English tong.

And thus much for *Plautus* and *Terence*, for matter, tong, and meter, what is to be followed, and what to be exchewed in them.

After *Plautus* and *Terence*, no writing remayneth vntill *Tullies* tyme, except a fewe short fragmentes of *L. Crassus* excellent wit, here and there recited of *Cicero* for example sake, whereby the louers of learnyng may the more lament the losse of soch a worthie witte.

And although the Latin tong did faire blome and blossome in *L. Crassus*, and *M. Antonius*, yet in *Tullies* tyme onely, and in Tullie himselfe chieflie, was the Latin tong fullie ripe, and growne to the hiest pitch of all perfection.

And yet in the same tyme, it began to fade and stoupe, as *Tullie* him selfe, in *Brutus de Claris Oratoribus*, with weeping wordes doth witnesse.

And bicause, emongs them of that tyme, there was some difference, good reason is, that of them of that tyme, should be made right choice also. And yet let the best *Ciceronian* in Italie read *Tullies* familiar epistles aduisedly ouer, and I beleue he shall finde small difference, for the Latin tong, either in propriety of wordes or framing of the stile, betwixt *Tullie*, and those that write vnto him. As *ser. Sulpitius*, *A. Cecinna*, *M. Cælius*, *M. et D. Bruti*, *A. Pollio*, *L. Plancus*, and diuerse

Epi. Planci   other: read the epistles of *L. Plancus* in *x. Lib.*
x. lib. Epist.   and for an assay, that Epistle namely to the *Coss.*
8.   and whole *Senate*, the eight Epistle in number,
and what could be, eyther more eloquentlie, or more wiselie written, yea by *Tullie* himselfe, a man may iustly doubt. Thies men and *Tullie*, liued all in one tyme, were like in authoritie, not vnlike in learning and studie, which might be iust causes of this their equalitie in writing: And yet surely, they neyther were in deed, nor yet were counted in mens opinions, equall with *Tullie* in that facultie. And how is the difference hid in his Epistles? verelie, as the cunning of an expert Sea man, in a faire calme fresh Ryuer, doth litle differ from the doing of a meaner workman therein, euen so, in the short cut of a priuate letter, where, matter is common, wordes easie, and order not moch diuerse, small shew of difference can appeare. But where *Tullie* doth set vp his saile of eloquence, in some broad deep Argument, caried with full tyde and winde, of his witte and learnyng, all other may rather stand and looke after him, than hope to ouertake him, what course so euer he hold, either in faire or foule. Foure men onely whan the Latin tong was full ripe, be left vnto vs, who in that tyme did florish, and did leaue to posteritie, the fruite of their witte and learning: *Varro*, *Salust*, *Cæsar*, and *Cicero*. Whan I say, these foure onely, I am not ignorant, that euen in the same tyme, most excellent Poetes, deseruing well of the Latin tong, as *Lucretius*,

Cattullus, *Virgill* and *Horace*, did write: But, bicause, in this litle booke, I purpose to teach a yong scholer, to go, not to daunce: to speake, not to sing, whan Poetes in deed, namelie *Epici* and *Lyrici*, as these be, are fine dauncers, and trime singers, but *Oratores* and *Historici* be those cumlie goers, and faire and wise speakers, of whom I wishe my scholer to wayte vpon first, and after in good order, & dew tyme, to be brought forth, to the singing and dauncing schole: And for this consideration, do I name these foure, to be the onelie writers of that tyme.

¶ *Varro.*

Varro, in his bookes *de lingua Latina*, *et Analogia* as these be left mangled and patched vnto vs, doth not enter there in to any great depth of eloquence, but as one caried in a small low vessell him selfe verie nie the common shore, not much vnlike the fisher mē of Rye, and Hering men of Yarmouth. Who deserue by common mens opinion, small commendacion, for any cunning saling at all, yet neuertheles in those bookes of *Varro* good and necessarie stuffe, for that meane kinde of Argument, be verie well and learnedlie gathered togither.

Varro.

His bookes of Husbandrie, are moch to be regarded, and diligentlie to be read, not onelie for the proprietie, but also for the plentie of good wordes, in all contrey and husbandmens affaires: which can not be had, by so good authoritie, out of any other Author, either of so good a tyme, or of so great learnyng, as out of *Varro*. And yet bicause, he was fourescore yeare old, whan he wrote those bookes, the forme of his style there compared with *Tullies* writyng, is but euen the talke of a spent old man: whose wordes commonlie fall out of his mouth, though verie wiselie, yet hardly and coldie, and more heauelie also, than some eares can well beare, except onelie for age, and authorities sake. And perchance, in a rude contrey argument, of purpose and iudgement, he rather vsed, the speach of the contrey, than talke of the Citie.

De Rep. Rustica.

And so, for matter sake, his wordes sometyme, be somewhat rude: and by the imitation of the elder *Cato*, old and out of vse:

And beyng depe stept in age, by negligence some wordes do so
scape & fall from him in those bookes, as be not worth the
taking vp, by him, that is carefull to speake or
write trew Latin, as that sentence in him, *Romani*,
in pace à rusticis alebantur, et in bello ab his tuebantur.
A good student must be therfore carefull and diligent, to read
with iudgement ouer euen those Authors, which did write in the
most perfite tyme: and let him not be affrayd to trie them,
both in proprietie of wordes, and forme of style, by the touch
stone of *Cæsar* and *Cicero*, whose puritie was neuer soiled, no
not by the sentence of those, that loued them worst.

In the left margin: Lib. 3. Cap. 1.

All louers of learnyng may sore lament the losse of those
bookes of *Varro*, which he wrote in his yong and
lustie yeares, with good leysure, and great learnyng
of all partes of Philosophie: of the goodliest argumentes, perteyning both to the common wealth,
and priuate life of man, as, *de Ratione studij, et educandis liberis*,
which booke, is oft recited, and moch praysed, in the fragmentes
of *Nonius*, euen for authoritie sake.   He wrote most diligentlie
and largelie, also the whole historie of the state of *Rome*: the
mysteries of their whole Religion: their lawes, customes, and
gouernement in peace: their maners, and whole discipline in
warre: And this is not my gessing, as one in deed that neuer
saw those bookes, but euen, the verie iudgement, & playne
testimonie of *Tullie* him selfe, who knew & read those bookes,
in these wordes: *Tu ætatem Patriæ: Tu descriptiones temporum:
Tu sacrorum, tu sacerdotum Iura: Tu domesticam,
tu bellicam disciplinam: Tu sedem Regionum, locorum,
tu omnium diuinarum humanarumq̃ rerū nomina,
genera, officia, causas aperuisti. &c.*

In the left margin: The loue of Var-roes bookes.

In the left margin: In Acad. Quest.

But this great losse of *Varro*, is a litle recompensed by the
happy comming of *Dionysius Halicarnassæus* to *Rome* in
Augustus dayes: who getting the possession of *Varros* librarie,
out of that treasure house of learning, did leaue vnto vs some
frute of *Varros* witte and diligence, I meane, his goodlie bookes
de Antiquitatibus Romanorum. *Varro* was so estemed for his
excellent learnyng, as *Tullie* him selfe had a reuerence to his
iudgement in all doutes of learnyng.   And
Antonius Triumuir, his enemie, and of a contrarie
faction, who had power to kill and bannish whom

In the left margin: Cic. ad Att.

he listed, whan *Varros* name amongest others was brought in a schedule vnto him, to be noted to death, he tooke his penne and wrote his warrant of sauegard with these most goodlie wordes, *Viuat Varro vir doctissimus*. In later tyme, no man knew better, nor liked and loued more *Varros* learnyng, than did *S. Augustine*, as they do well vnderstand, that haue diligentlie read ouer his learned bookes *de Ciuitate Dei*: Where he hath this most notable sentēce: Whan I see, how much *Varro* wrote, I meruell much, that euer he had any leasure to read: and whan I perceiue how many thinges he read, I meruell more, that euer he had any leasure to write. &c.

And surelie, if *Varros* bookes had remained to posteritie, as by Gods prouidence, the most part of *Tullies* did, than trewlie the *Latin* tong might haue made good comparison with the *Greke*.

Saluste.

Salust, is a wise and worthy writer: but he requireth a learned Reader, and a right considerer of him. My dearest frend, and best master that euer I had or heard in learning, Syr *I. Cheke*, soch a man, as if I should liue to see England breed the like againe, I feare, I should liue ouer long, did once giue me a lesson for *Salust*, which, as I shall neuer forget my selfe, so is it worthy to be remembred of all those, that would cum to perfite iudgement of the Latin tong. He said, that *Salust* was not verie fitte for yong men, to learne out of him, the puritie of the Latin tong: because, he was not the purest in proprietie of wordes, nor choisest in aptnes of phrases, nor the best in framing of sentences: and therefore is his writing, sayd he neyther plaine for the matter, nor sensible for mens vnderstanding. And what is the cause thereof, Syr, quoth I. Verilie said he, bicause in *Salust* writing, is more Arte than nature, and more labor than Arte: and in his labor also, to moch toyle, as it were, with an vncontented care to write better than he could, a fault common to very many men. And therefore he doth not expresse the matter liuely and naturally with common speach as ye see *Xenophon* doth in Greeke, but it is caried and driuen forth

Salust.

Syr Iohn Chekes iudgement and counsell for readyng of *Saluste*.

artificiallie, after to learned a sorte, as *Thucydides* doth in his orations. And how cummeth it to passe, sayd I, that *Cæsar* and *Ciceroes* talke, is so naturall & plaine, and *Salust* writing so artificiall and darke, whan all they three liued in one tyme? I will freelie tell you my fansie herein, said he: surely, *Cæsar* and *Cicero*, beside a singular prerogatiue of naturall eloquence geuen vnto them by God, both two, by vse of life, were daylie orators emonges the common people, and greatest councellers in the Senate house: and therefore gaue themselues to vse soch speach as the meanest should well vnderstand, and the wisest best allow: folowing carefullie that good councell of *Aristotle*, *loquendum vt multi, sapiendum vt pauci*. *Salust* was no soch man, neyther for will to goodnes, nor skill by learning: but ill geuen by nature, and made worse by bringing vp, spent the most part of his yougth very misorderly in ryot and lechery. In the company of soch, who, neuer geuing theyr mynde to honest doyng, could neuer inure their tong to wise speaking. But at last cummyng to better yeares, and bying witte at the dearest hand, that is, by long experience of the hurt and shame that commeth of mischeif, moued, by the councell of them that were wise, and caried by the example of soch as were good, first fell to honestie of life, and after to the loue of studie and learning: and so became so new a man, that *Cæsar* being dictator, made him Pretor in *Numidia* where he absent from his contrie, and not inured with the common talke of Rome, but shut vp in his studie, and bent wholy to reading, did write the storie of the Romanes. And for the better accomplishing of the same, he red *Cato* and *Piso* in Latin for gathering of matter and troth: and *Thucydides* in Greeke for the order of his storie, and furnishing of his style. *Cato* (as his tyme required) had more troth for the matter, than eloquence for the style. And so *Salust*, by gathering troth out of *Cato*, smelleth moch of the roughnes of his style: euen as a man that eateth garlike for helth, shall cary away with him the sauor of it also, whether he will or not. And yet the vse of old wordes is not the greatest cause of *Salustes* roughnes and darknesse: There be in *Salust*

Lib. 8. some old wordes in deed as *patrare bellum, duɛtare*
Cap. 3. *exercitum*, well noted by *Quintilian*, and verie
De Orna- much misliked of him: and *supplicium* for *suppli-*
tu. *catio*, a word smellyng of an older store, than the

other two so misliked by *Quint* : And yet is that word also in
Varro, speaking of Oxen thus, *boues ad victimas faciunt, atᵹ ad
Deorum supplicia* : and a few old wordes mo.   Read *Saluste* and
Tullie aduisedly together : and in wordes ye shall finde small
difference : yea *Salust* is more geuen to new wordes, than to
olde, though som olde writers say the contrarie : as *Claritudo*
for *Gloria* : *exactè* for *perfectè* : *Facundia* for *eloquentia.*   Thies
two last wordes *exactè* and *facundia* now in euery mans mouth,
be neuer (as I do remember) vsed of *Tullie,* and therefore
I thinke they be not good : For surely *Tullie* speaking euery
where so moch of the matter of eloquence, would not so
precisely haue absteyned from the word *Facundia,* if it had
bene good : that is proper for the tong, & common for mens
vse.   I could be long, in reciting many soch like, both olde &
new wordes in *Salust* : but in very dede neyther oldnes nor
newnesse of wordes maketh the greatest difference   The cause why
betwixt *Salust* and *Tullie,* but first strange phrases   Salust is not
made of good Latin wordes, but framed after the   like Tully.
Greeke tonge, which be neyther choisly borowed of them, nor
properly vsed by him : than, a hard composition and crooked
framing of his wordes and sentences, as a man would say,
English talke placed and framed outlandish like.   As for
example first in phrases, *nimius et animus* be two vsed wordes,
yet *homo nimius animi,* is an vnused phrase.   *Vulgus, et amat, et
fieri,* be as common and well known wordes as may be in the
Latin tong, yet *id quod vulgò amat fieri,* for *solet fieri,* is but
a strange and grekish kind of writing.   *Ingens et vires* be
proper wordes, yet *vir ingens virium* is an vnproper kinde of
speaking and so be likewise,

> *æger consilij.*
> *promptissimus belli.*
> *territus animi.*

and many soch like phrases in *Salust,* borowed as I sayd not
choisly out of Greeke, and vsed therefore vnproperlie in Latin.
Againe, in whole sentences, where the matter is good, the
wordes proper and plaine, yet the sense is hard and darke, and
namely in his prefaces and orations, wherein he vsed most
labor, which fault is likewise in *Thucydides* in Greeke, of whom
Salust hath taken the greatest part of his darkenesse.   For

Thucydides likewise wrote his storie, not at home in Grece, but abrode in Italie, and therefore smelleth of a certaine outlandish kinde of talke, strange to them of *Athens*, and diuerse from their writing, that liued in Athens and Grece, and wrote the same tyme that *Thucydides* did, as *Lysias*, *Xenophon*, *Plato*, and *Isocrates*, the purest and playnest writers, that euer wrote in any tong, and best examples for any man to follow whether he write, Latin, Italian, French, or English. *Thucydides* also semeth in his writing, not so much benefited by nature, as holpen by Arte, and caried forth by desire, studie, labor, toyle, and ouer great curiositie : who spent xxvii. yeares in writing his eight bookes of his history. *Salust* likewise wrote out of his

Dionys. Halycar. ad Q. Tub. de Hist. Thuc.

contrie, and followed the faultes of *Thuc.* to moch : and boroweth of him som kinde of writing, which the Latin tong can not well beare, as *Casus nominatiuus* in diuerse places *absolutè positus*, as in that place of *Iugurth*, speaking *de leptitanis*, *itaq̧ ab imperatore facilè quæ petebant adepti, missæ sunt eò cohortes ligurum quatuor.* This thing in participles, vsed so oft in *Thucyd.* and other Greeke authors to, may better be borne with all, but *Salust* vseth the same more strangelie and boldlie, as in thies wordes, *Multis sibi quisq̧ imperium petentibus.* I beleue, the best Grammarien in England can scarse giue a good reule, why *quisq̧* the nominatiue case, without any verbe, is so thrust vp amongest so many oblique cases. Some man perchance will smile, and laugh to scorne this my writyng, and call it idle curiositie, thus to busie my selfe in pickling about these small pointes of Grammer, not fitte for my age, place and calling, to trifle in : I trust that man, be he neuer so great in authoritie, neuer so wise and learned, either, by other mens iudgement, or his owne opinion, will yet thinke, that he is not greater in England, than *Tullie* was at *Rome*, not yet wiser, nor better learned than *Tullie* was him selfe, who, at the pitch of three score yeares, in the middes of the broyle betwixt *Cæsar* and *Pompeie*, whan he knew not, whether to send wife & children, which way to go, where to hide him selfe, yet, in an earnest letter, amongest his earnest

Ad Att. Lib. 7. Epi- stola. 3.

councelles for those heuie tymes concerning both the common state of his contrey, and his owne priuate great affaires he was neither vnmyndfull nor ashamed to reason at large, and learne gladlie of *Atticus*, a lesse point of Grammer than these be, noted of me in *Salust*, as, whether he should write, *ad Piræa*, *in Piræa*, or *in Piræeum*, or *Piræeum sine præpositione* : And in those heuie tymes, he was so carefull to know this small point of Grammer, that he addeth these wordes *Si hoc mihi* ζήτημα *persolueris, magna me molestia liberaris.* If *Tullie*, at that age, in that authoritie, in that care for his contrey, in that ieoperdie for him selfe, and extreme necessitie of hys dearest frendes, beyng also the Prince of Eloquence hym selfe, was not ashamed to descend to these low pointes of Grammer, in his owne naturall tong, what should scholers do, yea what should any man do, if he do thinke well doyng, better than ill doyng : And had rather be, perfite than meane, sure than doutefull, to be what he should be, in deed, not seeme what he is not, in opinion. He that maketh perfitnes in the *Latin* tong his marke, must cume to it by choice & certaine knowledge, not stumble vpon it by chance and doubtfull ignorance : And the right steppes to reach vnto it, be these, linked thus orderlie together, aptnes of nature, loue of learnyng, diligence in right order, constancie with pleasant moderation, and alwayes to learne of them that be best, and so shall you iudge as they that be wisest. And these be those reules, which worthie Master *Cheke* dyd impart vnto me concernyng *Salust*, and the right iudgement of the *Latin* tong.

¶ *Cæsar.*

Cæsar for that litle of him, that is left vnto vs, is like the halfe face of a *Venus*, the other part of the head beyng hidden, the bodie and the rest of the members vnbegon, yet so excellentlie done by *Apelles*, as all men may stand still to mase and muse vpon it, and no man step forth with any hope to performe the like.

His seuen bookes *de bello Gallico*, and three *de bello Ciuili*, be written, so wiselie for the matter, so eloquentlie for the tong, that neither his greatest enemies could euer finde the least note of parcialitie in him (a meruelous wisdome of a man, namely writyng of his owne doynges) nor yet the best iudegers of the *Latin* tong, nor the most enuious lookers vpon other mēs writynges, can say any other, but all things be most perfitelie done by him.

Brutus, *Caluus*, and *Calidius*, who found fault with *Tullies* fulnes in woordes and matter, and that rightlie, for *Tullie* did both, confesse it, and mend it, yet in *Cæsar*, they neither did, nor could finde the like, or any other fault.

And therfore thus iustlie I may conclude of *Cæsar*, that where, in all other, the best that euer wrote, in any tyme, or in any tong, in *Greke* or *Latin*, I except neither *Plato*, *Demosthenes*, nor *Tullie*, some fault is iustlie noted, in *Cæsar* onelie, could neuer yet fault be found.

Yet neuertheles, for all this perfite excellencie in
him, yet it is but in one member of eloquence, and
that but of one side neither, whan we must
looke for that example to folow, which hath
a perfite head, a whole bodie, forward
and backward, armes and
legges and all.

FINIS.

ERRATA OF THE ORIGINAL COPIES.

p. xix. l. 13. Herhen for Hethen.

p. 8 l. 13 up. thinges, onelie *for* thinges onelie,   p. 24 l. 16. some copies read, dealyng crafty *for* dealyng, crafty   p. 27 l. 12 up. stode, by *for* stode by,   do doynge *for* doynge   p. 30 l. 17. tymes: it *for* tymes it   p. 33 l. 14. (and if *for* and (if   p. 46 l. 2. some copies read, health *for* welth   p. 47 l. 10 up. some copies read, Pertians *for* Parthians   p. 48 l. 8 up. some copies read, ill wyll *for* euelwyll   l. 7 up. some copies read, open battayle *for* contention p. 56 l. 2 up. doch *for* doth   p. 57 last line. ye *for* yet (as in ed. 1571)   p. 61 l. 5 up. shouthfulnesse *for* slouthfulnesse   p. 72 l. 3 up. lesse *for* leste   p. 78 l. 16. that I *for* than I   p. 80 l. 3 up. peeces to farre *for* peeces, to farre   l. 2 up. drawynge, brake *for* drawynge brake   p. 81 l. 26. bowe *for* A bowe (the catch-word on the previous page is And)   p. 83 l. 16. yarde. *for* yarde, l. 9 up. woodes. as. *for* woodes, as,   p. 85 l. 21. studding *for* scudding l. 11 up. conclude that, *for* conclude, that   p. 86 l. 12 up. wyde some *for* wyde, some   p. 89 l. 4 up. gouse, *for* gouse.   last line. bēlonging *for* belonging   p. 91 l. 4 up. is, *for* is   p. 93 l. 2. Peno-lepe *for* Penelope   p. 96 l. 4 up. ought, to *for* ought to   p. 99 l. 29. hansomely, they *for* hansomely they   p. 100 ll. 13, 14. shootynge, is... shootynge but *for* shootynge is...shootynge, but   l. 27. man, woulde *for* man woulde   p. 105 l. 2. lefte *for* right   l. 12. οὐτιδανον *for* οὐτιδανόν   p. 113 l. 8 up. worst *for* worst.   p. 114 l. 9. braye *for* braye,   p. 115 l. 6 up. ieopardyt *for* ieopardye   p. 116 l. 10 up. waies. *for* waies,   p. 126 l. 4. First, point *for* First point   l. 15 up. of in *for* of   l. 3 up. or in *for* in   p. 128 last line. ceased, to *for* ceased to   p. 130 l. 15. meaner *for* meanes   p. 133 l. 7. *Fraunce.* as *for* *Fraunce,* as   p. 137 l. 12 up. *Gionan* for *Giouan*   p. 139 l. 11. it *for* it.   l. 15. yᵗ *for* yᵉ   p. 145 ll. 20, 21. reproch which *for* reproch. Which   l. 9 up. doyng. And *for* doyng, and   p. 146 marg. κυρπ. *for* κυρου.   p. 147 l. 8. Geeke *for* Greeke   p. 148 l. 6. prodest *for* poorest (?)   p. 152 l. 6 up. *Manrice* for *Maurice*   p. 153 l. 2 up. wife children *for* wife, children   p. 156 l. 5. dishinherite *for* disinherite l. 10 up. suspected. But *for* suspected, but   p. 161 ll. 23, 26. *emig* for *einig*   p. 165 l. 7 up. yᵗ *for* yᵉ   p. 167 l. 8 up. *Mauricus* for

Maurus   p. 168 l. 4. any *for* my   l. 17. lesse *for* leste   p. 178 l. 12. concerning, the *for* concerning the   l. 5 up. frend. *for* frend, p. 186 l. 8 up. *Exardescere* for *Exardescere*.   last line. *abijcerē* for *abjicere* p. 188 l. 4 up. youge *for* yonge.   p. 193 l. 5. I speaking *for* in speaking (?)   p. 195 l. 15. sadle *for* sadle.   l. 20. learning: *for* learning, p. 199 l. 10 up. werison *for* werisom   p. 200 l. 4 up. God, *for* God p. 202 l. 7 up. withall *for* with all   p. 204 l. 1. *Cræsus* for *Cræsus* p. 207 l. 18. greatie *for* greatlie   p. 213 l. 1. *Eph* : for *Ephorus* (as in ed. 1571)   l. 14 up. laie *for* saie   p. 215 l. 2.   Courte. *for* Courte, p. 224 l. 13 up. sillabes *for* sillables (as elsewhere)   l. 12 up. verifiyng *for* versifiyng   p. 228 l. 9 up. sutlie *for* suttle   p. 231 l. 7. aduoulteres *for* aduoulteries   pp. 236 l. 11 up and 239 l. 12 up. with in *for* within   p. 241 l. 7 up. *sowne.* for *sowne*,   l. 5 up. ill *for* will (as in ed. 1571)   p. 243 l. 2. all *for* also (as in ed. 1571)   l. 12 marg. de. Or. *for* de Or.   p. 244 marg. Epist. lib. 6, 7 li. Epist. *for* Epist. lib. 7, Epist. 9.   p. 247 l. 17. *Iliodos* for *Iliados*   marg. λ. *for* 'Ιλ.   l. 12 up. *Andration* for *Androtion*   p. 249 l. 5 up. liuyng *for* louyng   p. 251 l. 12 up. *meraui* for *meram*   l. 10 up. συντάξεος *for* συντάξεως l. 9 up. *Candaulus* for *Candaules*   p. 253 last line. it Grammer *for* it in Grammer (as in ed. 1571)   p. 255 l. 13. de Rep for *de Rep.*   p. 257 l. 11 up. *Stalenus* for *Staienus*   p. 264 l. 16. *plerunɡʒ* for *plerumɡʒ*   p. 267 ll. 4, 5. *materei* for *materiei* (as in ed. 1571)   l. 25. *Erasmus*, wishe *for Erasmus* wishe   l. 27. *Æneados* for *Æneidos*   p. 268 l. 14. cunnigest *for* cunningest (as in ed. 1571)   p. 272 l. 19. *Adriadna* for *Ariadna* l. 11 up. *Turmis* for *Turnus*   p. 273 l. 12 up. palce *for* place   p. 276 marg. *Thucid.* 10. *for Thucid.* 1.   p. 280 l. 2 up. *Apor* for *Aper* p. 282 l. 5 up. choselie *for* choiselie   l. 3 up. portiacture *for* portraic-ture   p. 283 l. 7 up. *Genus.* for *Genus*   p. 284 l. 6. *Aristophanus* for *Aristophanes*   p. 285 l. 16. *in Sermonem* for *Sermonem*   p. 286 l. 11. some *for* sone   p. 287 l. 8. storehose *for* storehouse   l. 8 up. be cum *for* becum   p. 288 l. 8. *Lilius* for *Lælius*   l. 11 up. *Cerilius* for *Cæcilius*   euidentie *for* euidentlie   p. 289 l. 7 up.   *dastylus* for *dactylus*   ll. 3 and 4 up. *Monasyllabis* for *Monosyllabis*   p. 290 l. 19. sillabes *for* sillables (pp. 291 l. 13 up, 292 l. 8)   l. 13 up. *Petrach* for *Petrarch*   p. 291 l. 7. as *for* at last line and marg. *Figlincci* for *Figliucci*   p. 292 marg. Enland *for* England   p. 294 l. 15. *Pollia* for *Pollio*   ll. 15, 16. *Plaucus* for *Plancus*   marg. Plauci *for* Planci   p. 295 l. 3. (whan *for* whan   p. 296 l. 10. foiled *for* soiled   p. 298 marg. ornata *for* ornatu   p. 299 l. 3 up. oration *for* orations   p. 301 l. 4 up. ludegers *for* iudegers